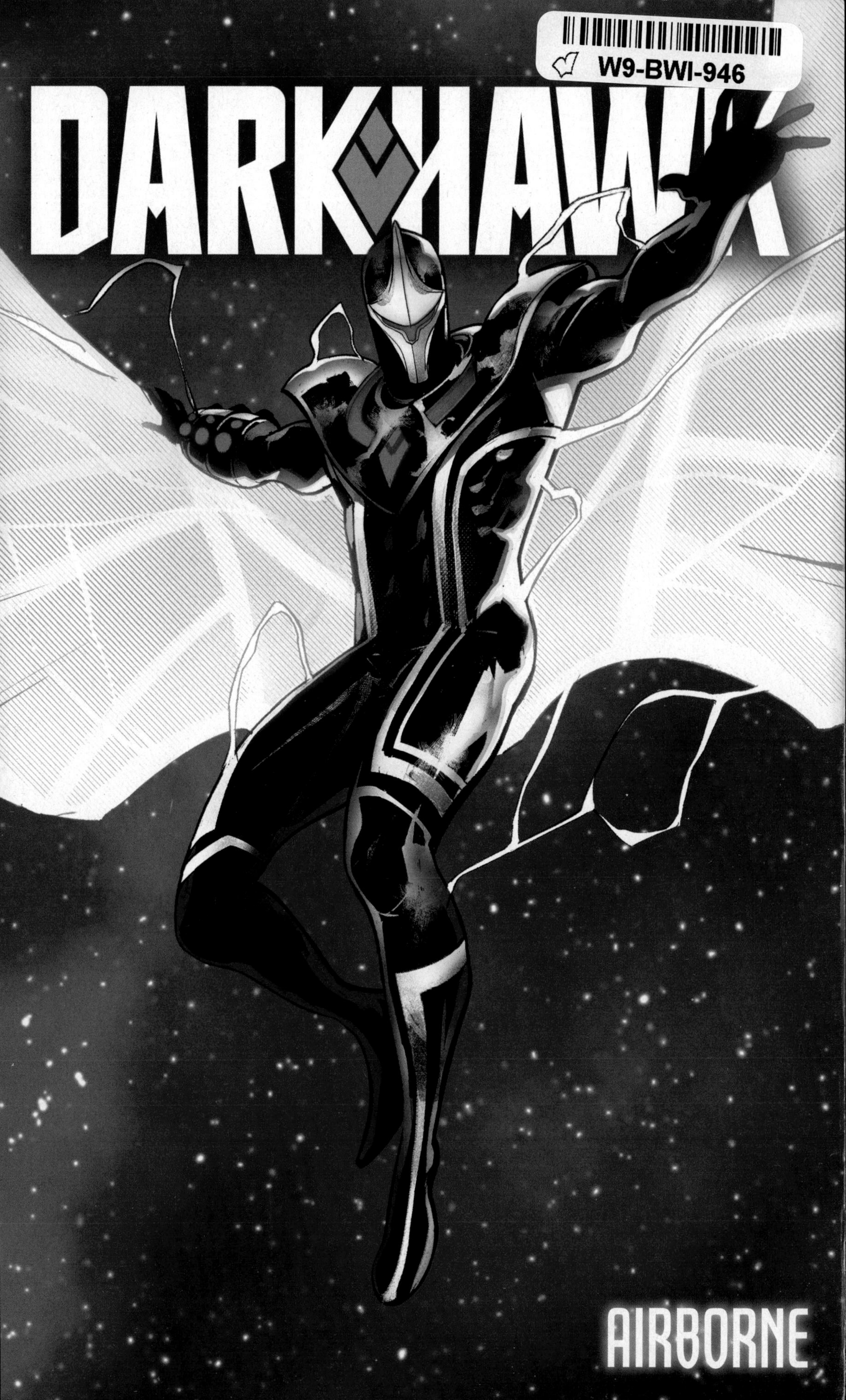
DARKHAWK
AIRBORNE

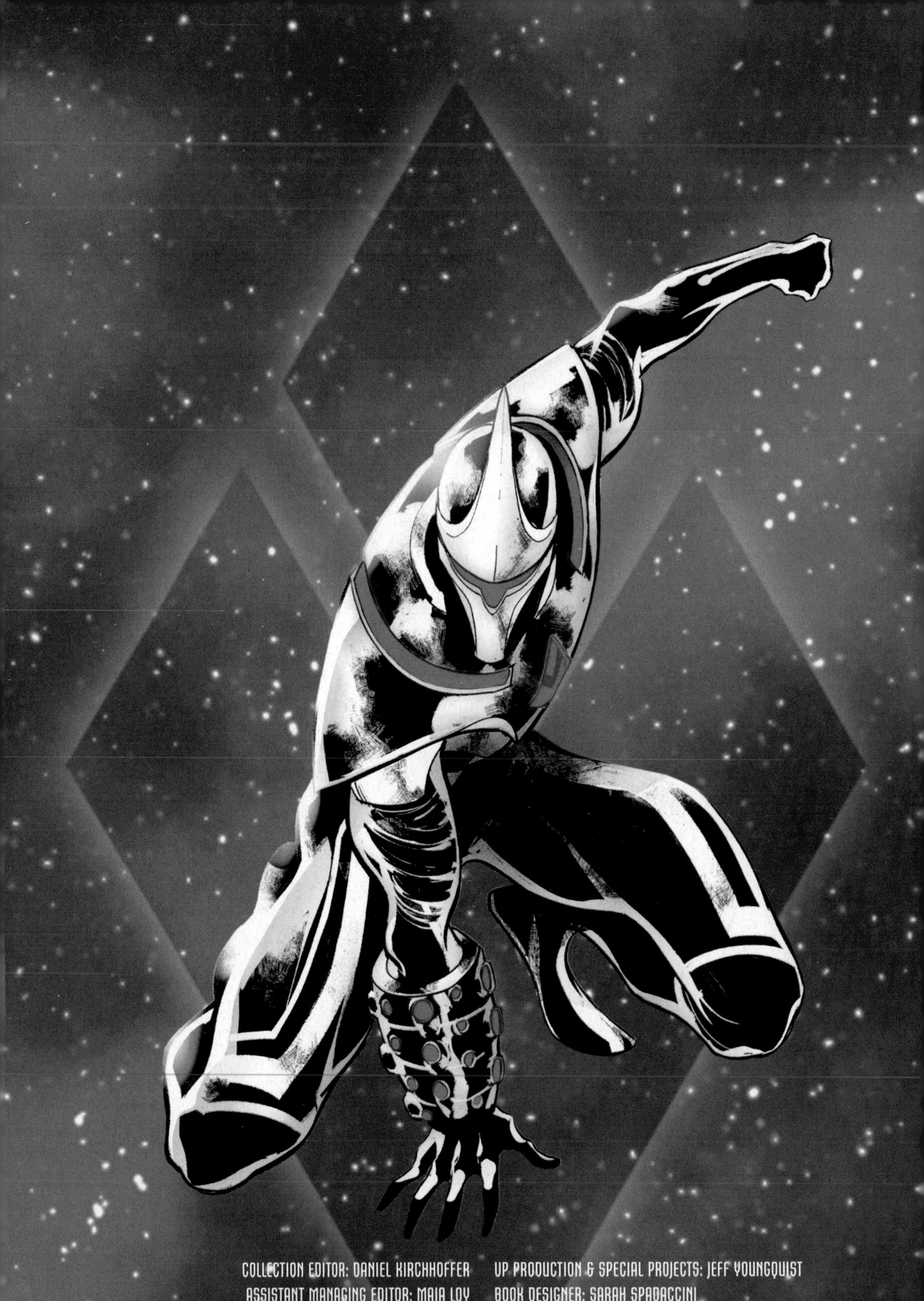

COLLECTION EDITOR: DANIEL KIRCHHOFFER
ASSISTANT MANAGING EDITOR: MAIA LOY
ASSOCIATE MANAGER, TALENT RELATIONS: LISA MONTALBANO
DIRECTOR, PRODUCTION & SPECIAL PROJECTS: JENNIFER GRÜNWALD
VP PRODUCTION & SPECIAL PROJECTS: JEFF YOUNGQUIST
BOOK DESIGNER: SARAH SPADACCINI
SVP PRINT, SALES & MARKETING: DAVID GABRIEL
EDITOR IN CHIEF: C.B. CEBULSKI

DARKHAWK: AIRBORNE. Contains material originally published in magazine form as DARKHAWK (2021) #1-5 and DARKHAWK: HEART OF THE HAWK (2021) #1. First printing 2021. ISBN 978-1-302-92906-0. Publishe by MARVEL WORLDWIDE, INC., a subsidiary of MARVEL ENTERTAINMENT, LLC. OFFICE OF PUBLICATION: 1290 Avenue of the Americas, New York, NY 10104. **Printed in Canada.** KEVIN FEIG Chief Creative Officer; DAN BUCKLEY, President, Marvel Entertainment; JOE QUESADA, EVP & Creative Director; DAVID BOGART, Associate Publisher & SVP of Talent Affairs; TOM BREVOORT, VP, Executive Editor; NIC LOWE, Executive Editor, VP of Content, Digital Publishing; DAVID GABRIEL, VP of Print & Digital Publishing; JEFF YOUNGQUIwST, VP of Production & Special Projects; ALEX MORALES, Director of Publishing Operation DAN EDINGTON, Managing Editor; RICKEY PURDIN, Director of Talent Relations; JENNIFER GRÜNWALD, Senior Editor, Special Projects; SUSAN CRESPI, Production Manager; STAN LEE, Chairman Emeritus. For informatic regarding advertising in Marvel Comics or on Marvel.com, please contact Vit DeBellis, Custom Solutions & Integrated Advertising Manager, at vdebellis@marvel.com. For Marvel subscription inquiries, please call 88

DARKHAWK

DARKHAWK: HEART OF THE HAWK

"CRY OF THE CITY"

DANNY FINGEROTH
WRITER

MIKE MANLEY
ARTIST

CHRIS SOTOMAYOR
COLOR ARTIST

"LONG WAY FROM HOME"

DAN ABNETT
WRITER

ANDREA DI VITO
PENCILER

LE BEAU UNDERWOOD
INKER

SEBASTIAN CHENG
COLOR ARTIST

"LAST FLIGHT"

KYLE HIGGINS
WRITER

JUANAN RAMÍREZ
ARTIST

ERICK ARCINIEGA
COLOR ARTIST

INHYUK LEE
COVER ART

VC's TRAVIS LANHAM
LETTERER

DARKHAWK #1-5

KYLE HIGGINS
WRITER

JUANAN RAMÍREZ
ARTIST

ERICK ARCINIEGA
COLOR ARTIST

**IBAN COELLO &
JESUS ABURTOV** [#1-3]
AND **JUANAN RAMÍREZ
& JESUS ABURTOV** [#4-5]
COVER ART

VC's TRAVIS LANHAM
LETTERER

ADAM DEL RE
LOGO DESIGN

PEPE LARRAZ
COSTUME DESIGN

KAT GREGOROWICZ
ASSISTANT EDITOR

DARREN SHAN
EDITOR

SPECIAL THANKS TO
BROOKE PELCZYNSKI & DR. LAUREN KRUPP

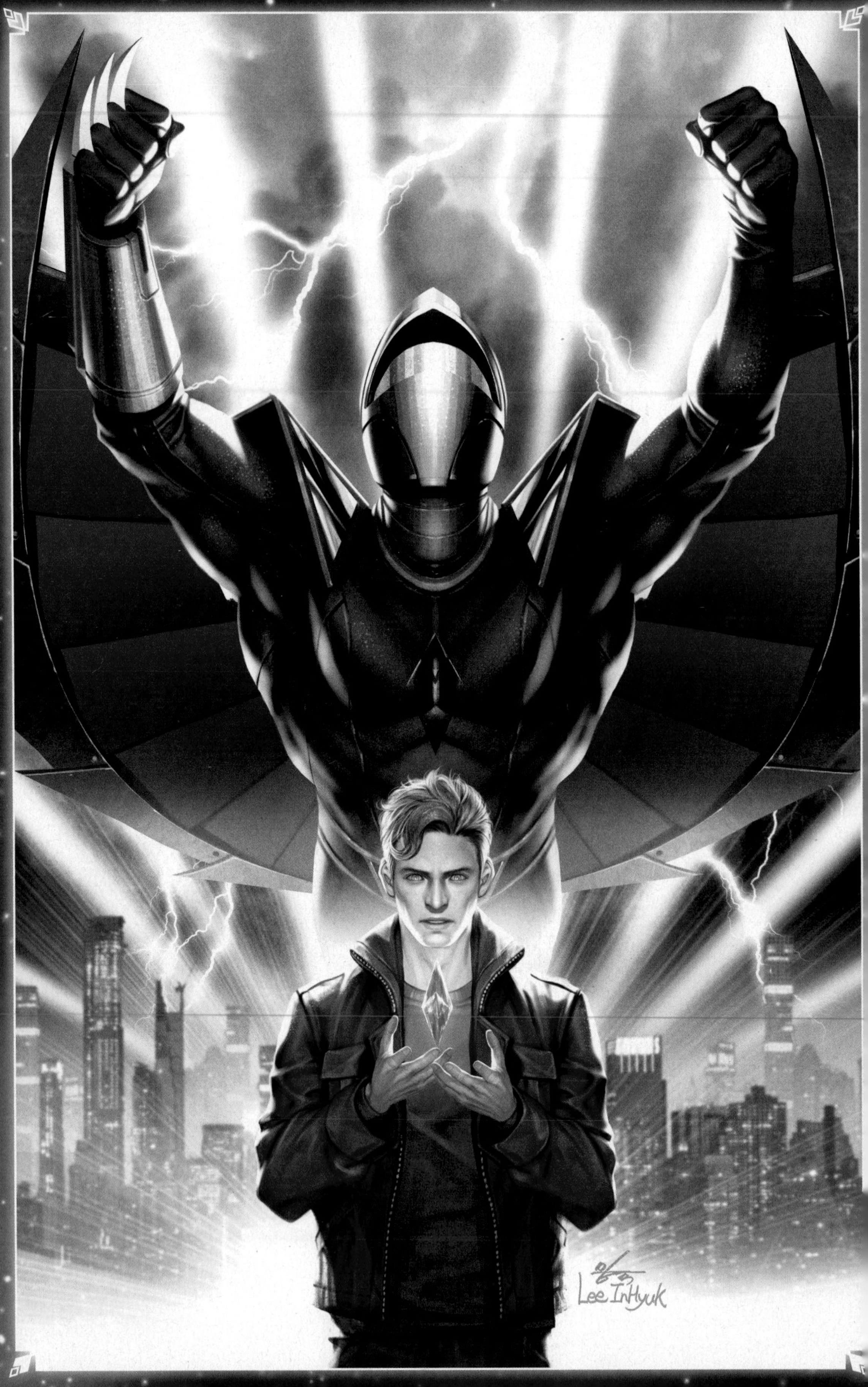
Lee InHyuk

NO ONE KNEW WHERE THE AMULET CAME FROM OR WHY IT APPEARED IN THE RUINS OF THE OLD AMUSEMENT PARK. ALL CHRIS POWELL KNEW WAS THAT WHEN HE GRASPED IT AND CONCENTRATED, HE WAS TRANSFORMED INTO A BEING OF GREAT POWER. AND HE SWORE TO USE THAT POWER AS THE EDGE AGAINST CRIME.

DARKHAWK

HEART OF THE HAWK

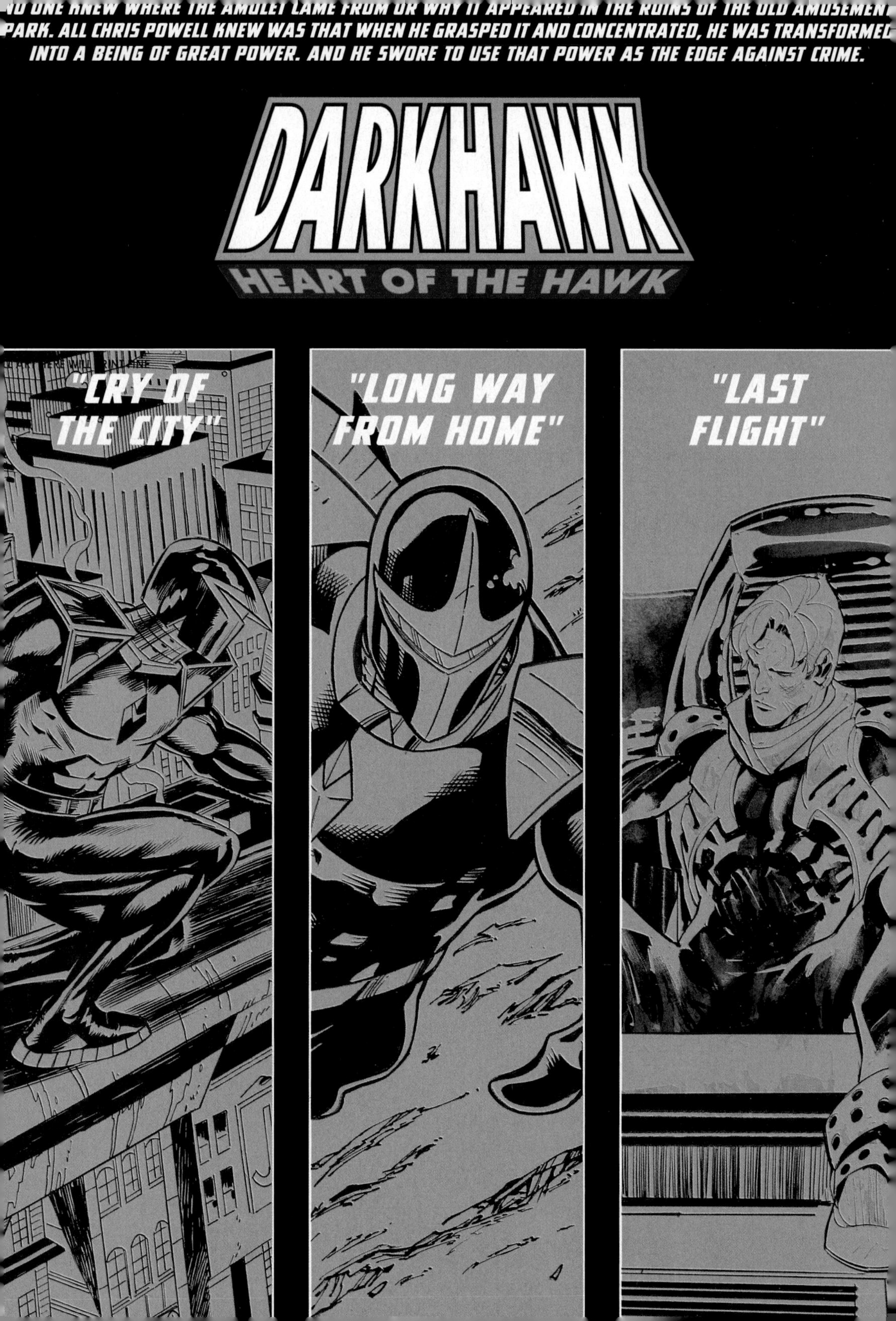
"CRY OF THE CITY"
"LONG WAY FROM HOME"
"LAST FLIGHT"

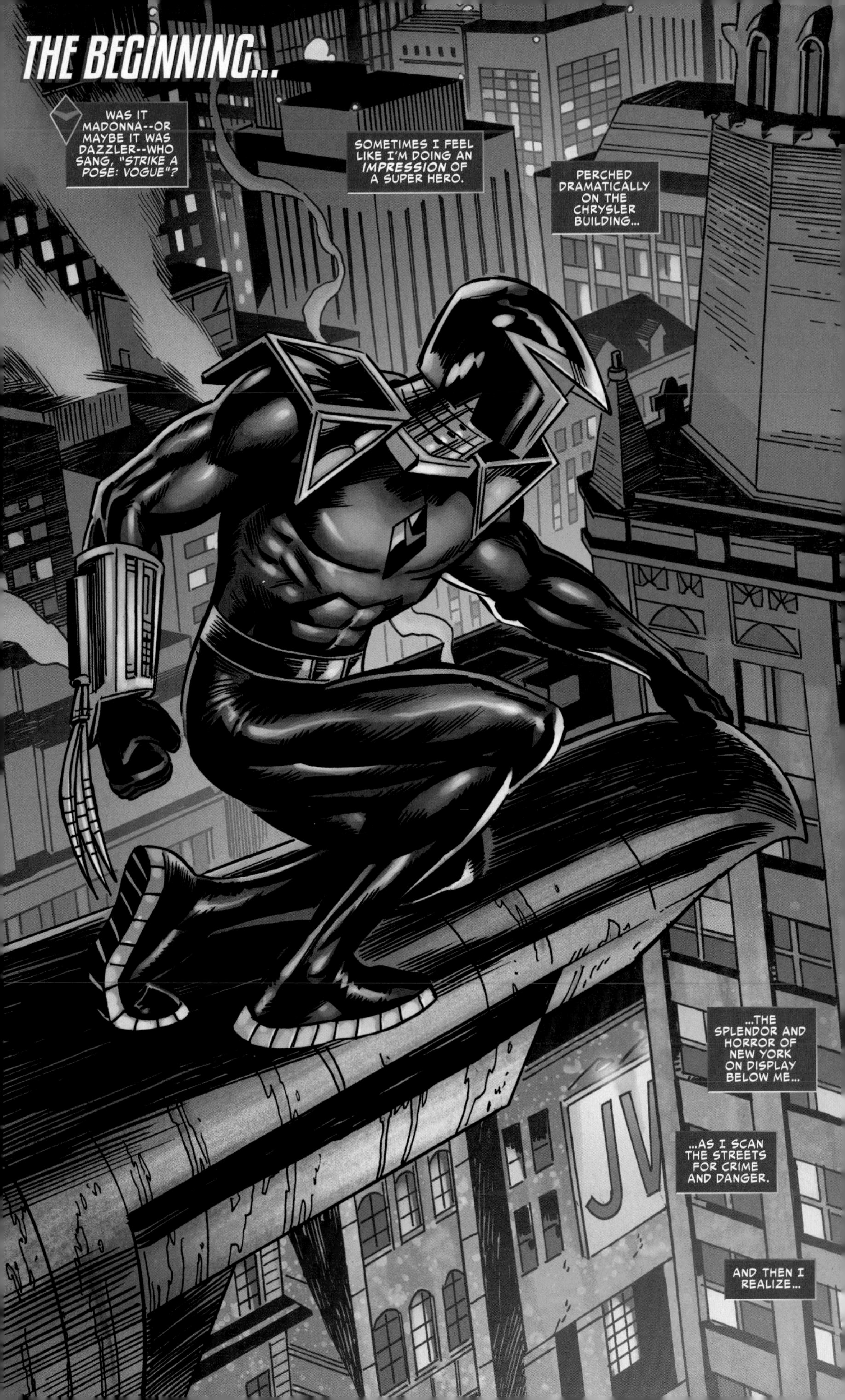
THE BEGINNING...
WAS IT MADONNA--OR MAYBE IT WAS DAZZLER--WHO SANG, "STRIKE A POSE: VOGUE"?
SOMETIMES I FEEL LIKE I'M DOING AN IMPRESSION OF A SUPER HERO.
PERCHED DRAMATICALLY ON THE CHRYSLER BUILDING...
...THE SPLENDOR AND HORROR OF NEW YORK ON DISPLAY BELOW ME...
...AS I SCAN THE STREETS FOR CRIME AND DANGER.
AND THEN I REALIZE...

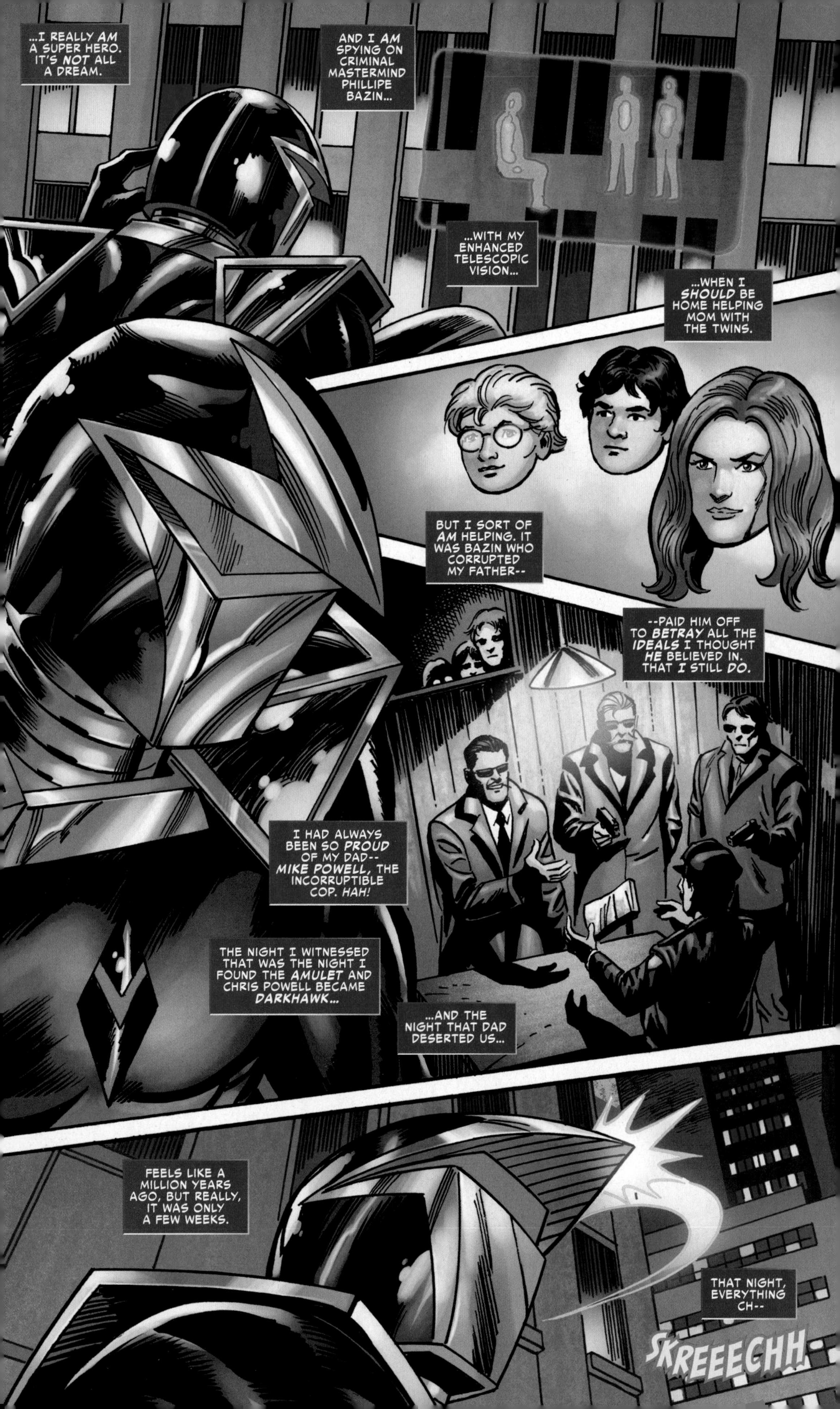
...I REALLY AM A SUPER HERO. IT'S NOT ALL A DREAM.
AND I AM SPYING ON CRIMINAL MASTERMIND PHILLIPE BAZIN...
...WITH MY ENHANCED TELESCOPIC VISION...
...WHEN I SHOULD BE HOME HELPING MOM WITH THE TWINS.
BUT I SORT OF AM HELPING. IT WAS BAZIN WHO CORRUPTED MY FATHER--
--PAID HIM OFF TO BETRAY ALL THE IDEALS I THOUGHT HE BELIEVED IN. THAT I STILL DO.
I HAD ALWAYS BEEN SO PROUD OF MY DAD-- MIKE POWELL, THE INCORRUPTIBLE COP. HAH!
THE NIGHT I WITNESSED THAT WAS THE NIGHT I FOUND THE AMULET AND CHRIS POWELL BECAME DARKHAWK...
...AND THE NIGHT THAT DAD DESERTED US...
FEELS LIKE A MILLION YEARS AGO, BUT REALLY, IT WAS ONLY A FEW WEEKS.
THAT NIGHT, EVERYTHING CH--
SKREEEECHH

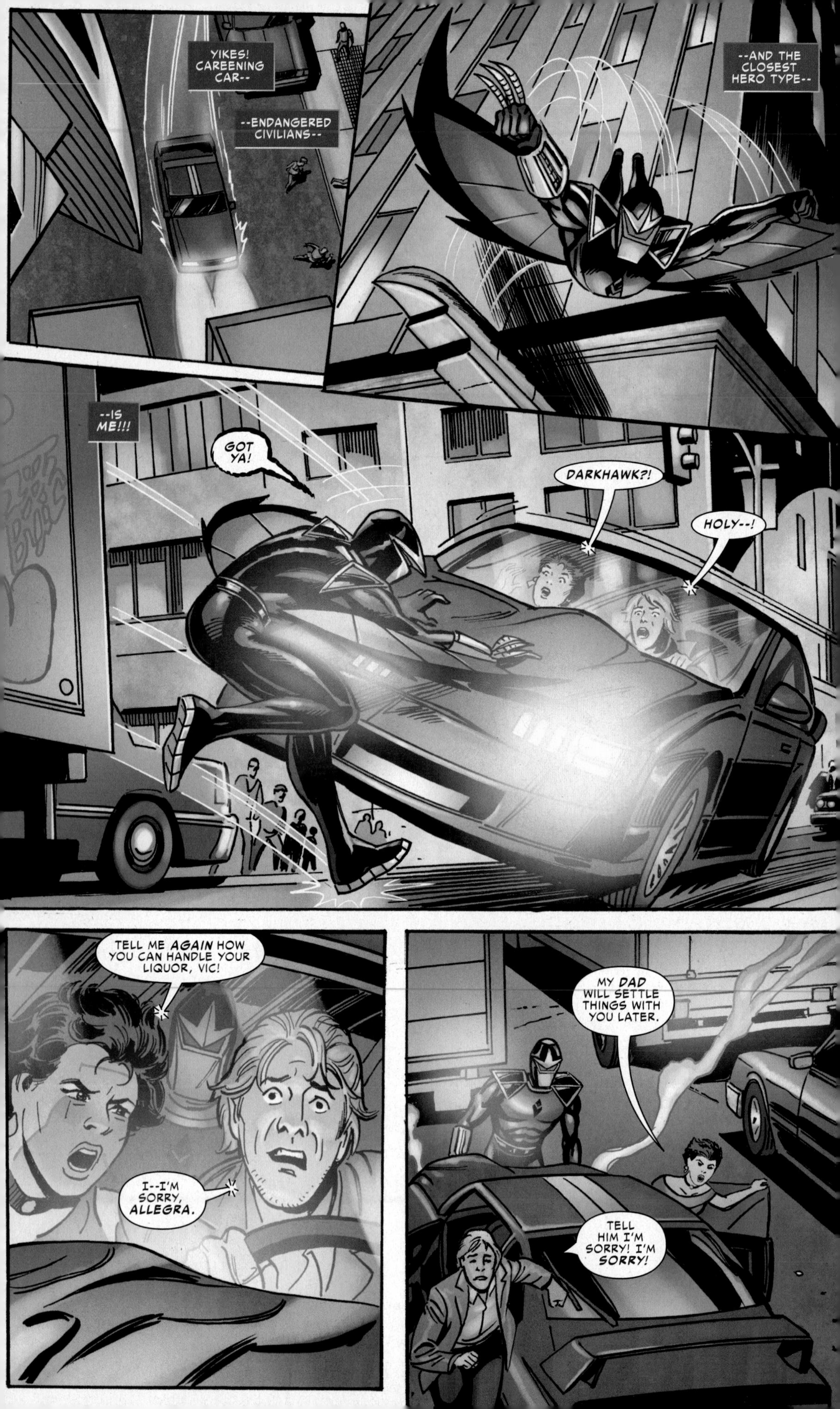
YIKES! CAREENING CAR--
--ENDANGERED CIVILIANS--
--AND THE CLOSEST HERO TYPE--
--IS ME!!!
GOT YA!
DARKHAWK?!
HOLY--!
TELL ME AGAIN HOW YOU CAN HANDLE YOUR LIQUOR, VIC!
I--I'M SORRY, ALLEGRA.
MY DAD WILL SETTLE THINGS WITH YOU LATER.
TELL HIM I'M SORRY! I'M SORRY!

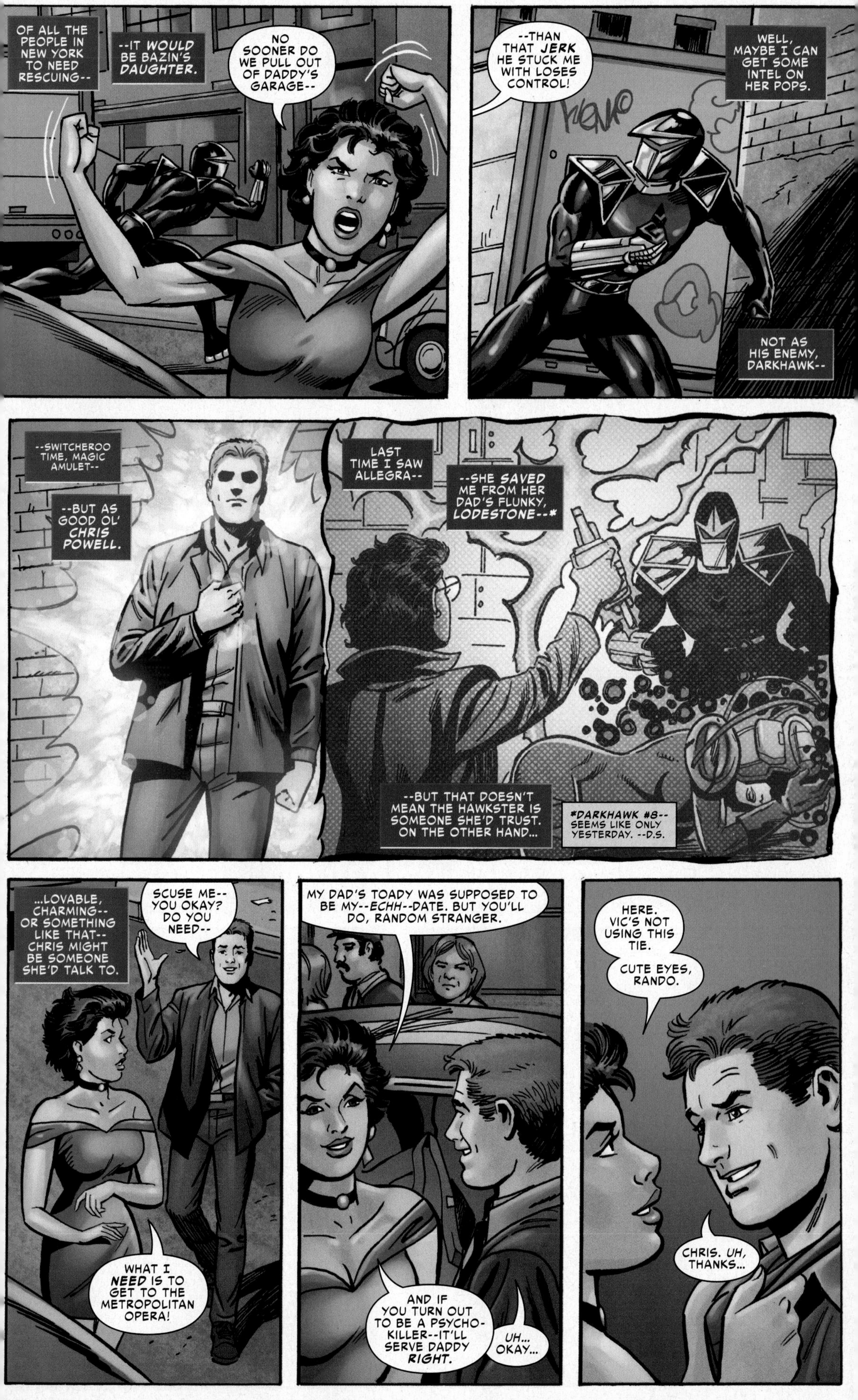
OF ALL THE PEOPLE IN NEW YORK TO NEED RESCUING--
--IT WOULD BE BAZIN'S DAUGHTER.
NO SOONER DO WE PULL OUT OF DADDY'S GARAGE--
--THAN THAT JERK HE STUCK ME WITH LOSES CONTROL!
WELL, MAYBE I CAN GET SOME INTEL ON HER POPS.
NOT AS HIS ENEMY, DARKHAWK--
--SWITCHEROO TIME, MAGIC AMULET--
--BUT AS GOOD OL' CHRIS POWELL.
LAST TIME I SAW ALLEGRA--
--SHE SAVED ME FROM HER DAD'S FLUNKY, LODESTONE--*
--BUT THAT DOESN'T MEAN THE HAWKSTER IS SOMEONE SHE'D TRUST. ON THE OTHER HAND...
*DARKHAWK #8--SEEMS LIKE ONLY YESTERDAY. --D.S.
...LOVABLE, CHARMING--OR SOMETHING LIKE THAT--CHRIS MIGHT BE SOMEONE SHE'D TALK TO.
SCUSE ME--YOU OKAY? DO YOU NEED--
WHAT I NEED IS TO GET TO THE METROPOLITAN OPERA!
MY DAD'S TOADY WAS SUPPOSED TO BE MY--ECHH--DATE. BUT YOU'LL DO, RANDOM STRANGER.
AND IF YOU TURN OUT TO BE A PSYCHO-KILLER--IT'LL SERVE DADDY RIGHT.
UH... OKAY...
HERE. VIC'S NOT USING THIS TIE.
CUTE EYES, RANDO.
CHRIS. UH, THANKS...

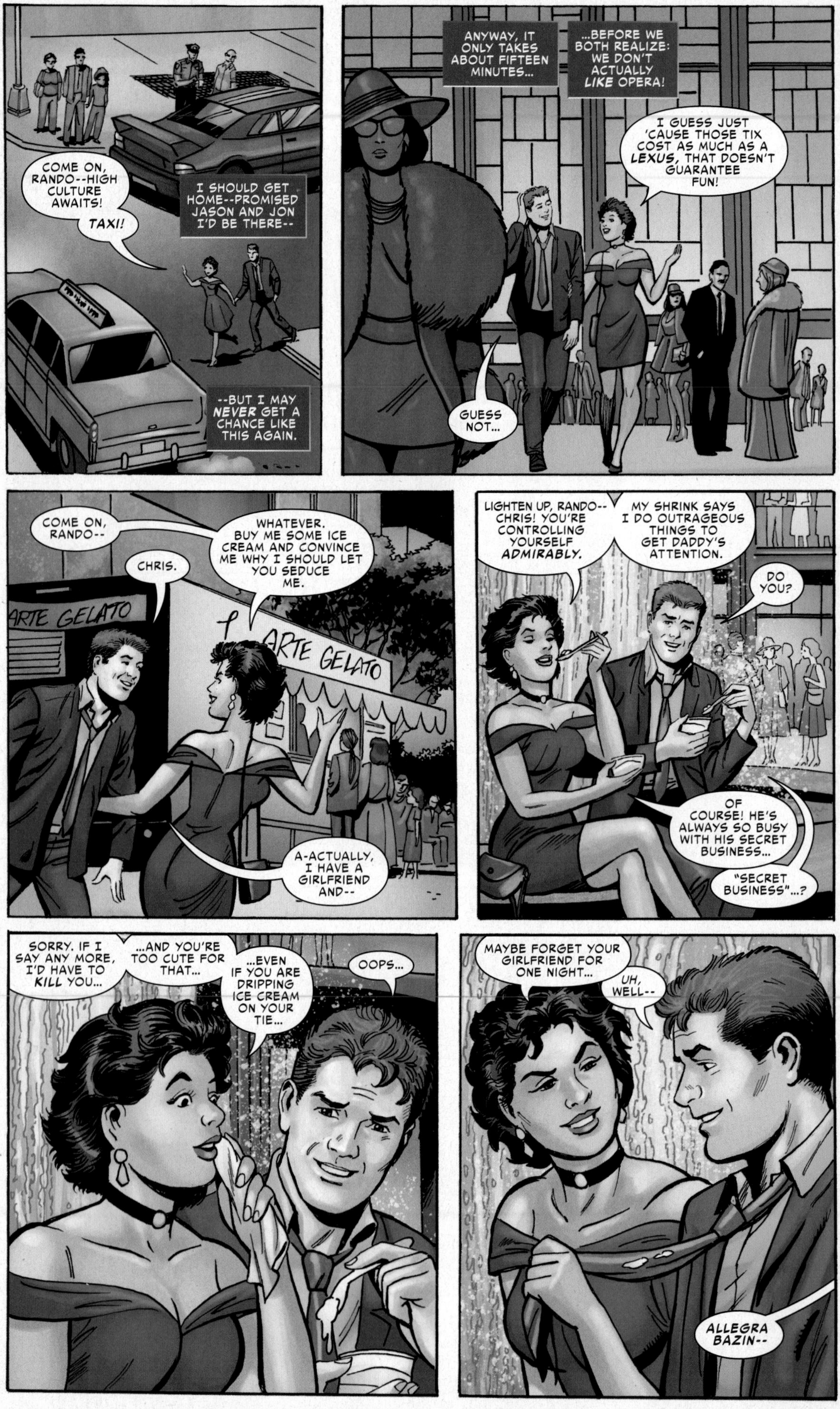
COME ON, RANDO--HIGH CULTURE AWAITS!
TAXI!
I SHOULD GET HOME--PROMISED JASON AND JON I'D BE THERE--
--BUT I MAY NEVER GET A CHANCE LIKE THIS AGAIN.
ANYWAY, IT ONLY TAKES ABOUT FIFTEEN MINUTES...
...BEFORE WE BOTH REALIZE: WE DON'T ACTUALLY LIKE OPERA!
I GUESS JUST 'CAUSE THOSE TIX COST AS MUCH AS A LEXUS, THAT DOESN'T GUARANTEE FUN!
GUESS NOT...
COME ON, RANDO--
WHATEVER. BUY ME SOME ICE CREAM AND CONVINCE ME WHY I SHOULD LET YOU SEDUCE ME.
CHRIS.
ARTE GELATO
ARTE GELATO
A-ACTUALLY, I HAVE A GIRLFRIEND AND--
LIGHTEN UP, RANDO--CHRIS! YOU'RE CONTROLLING YOURSELF ADMIRABLY.
MY SHRINK SAYS I DO OUTRAGEOUS THINGS TO GET DADDY'S ATTENTION.
DO YOU?
OF COURSE! HE'S ALWAYS SO BUSY WITH HIS SECRET BUSINESS...
"SECRET BUSINESS"...?
SORRY. IF I SAY ANY MORE, I'D HAVE TO KILL YOU...
...AND YOU'RE TOO CUTE FOR THAT...
...EVEN IF YOU ARE DRIPPING ICE CREAM ON YOUR TIE...
OOPS...
MAYBE FORGET YOUR GIRLFRIEND FOR ONE NIGHT...
UH, WELL--
ALLEGRA BAZIN--

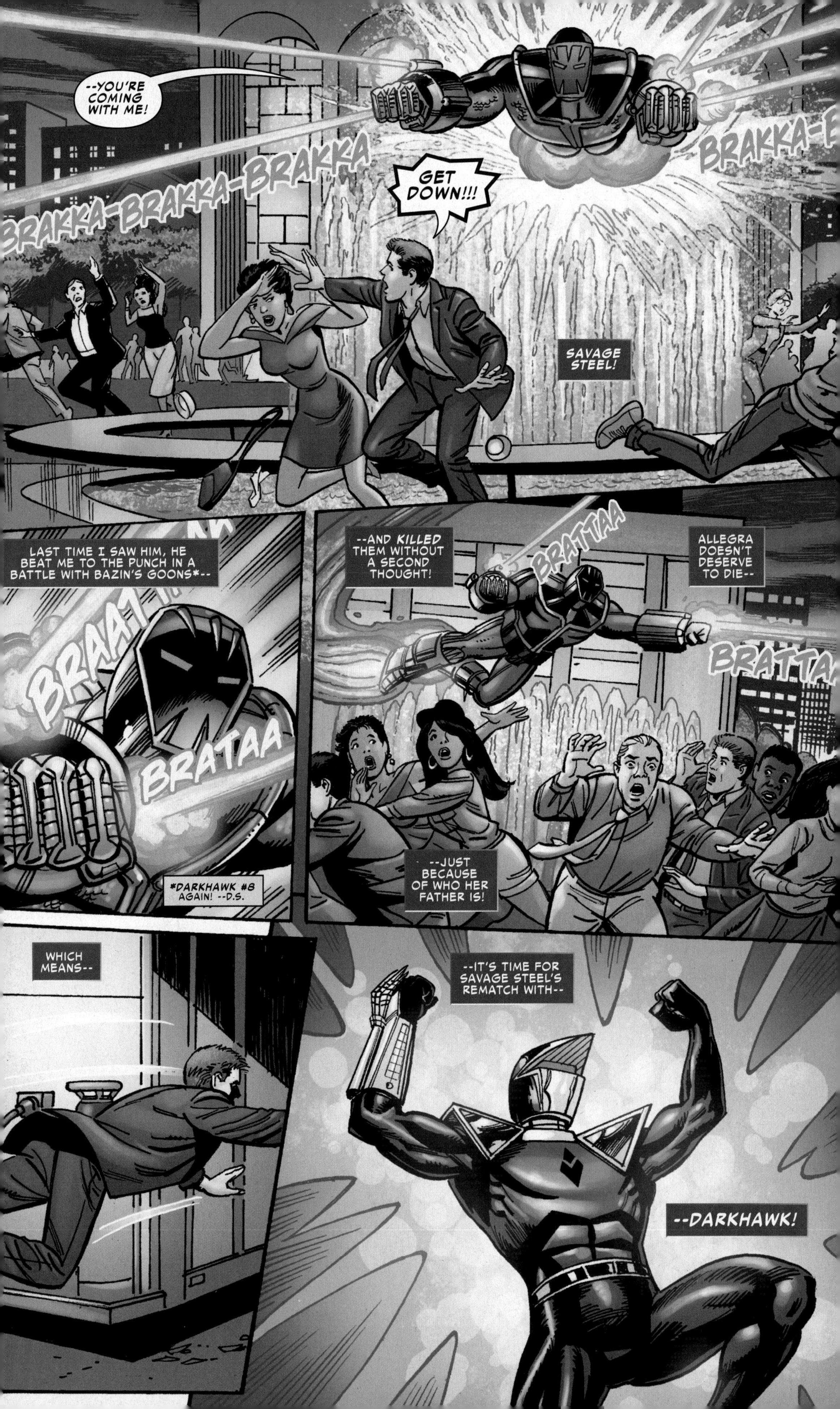
--YOU'RE COMING WITH ME!
BRAKKA-BRAKKA-BRAKKA
BRAKKA-B
GET DOWN!!!
SAVAGE STEEL!
LAST TIME I SAW HIM, HE BEAT ME TO THE PUNCH IN A BATTLE WITH BAZIN'S GOONS*--
BRATAA
*DARKHAWK #8 AGAIN! --D.S.
--AND KILLED THEM WITHOUT A SECOND THOUGHT!
BRATTAA
ALLEGRA DOESN'T DESERVE TO DIE--
BRATTA
--JUST BECAUSE OF WHO HER FATHER IS!
WHICH MEANS--
--IT'S TIME FOR SAVAGE STEEL'S REMATCH WITH--
--DARKHAWK!

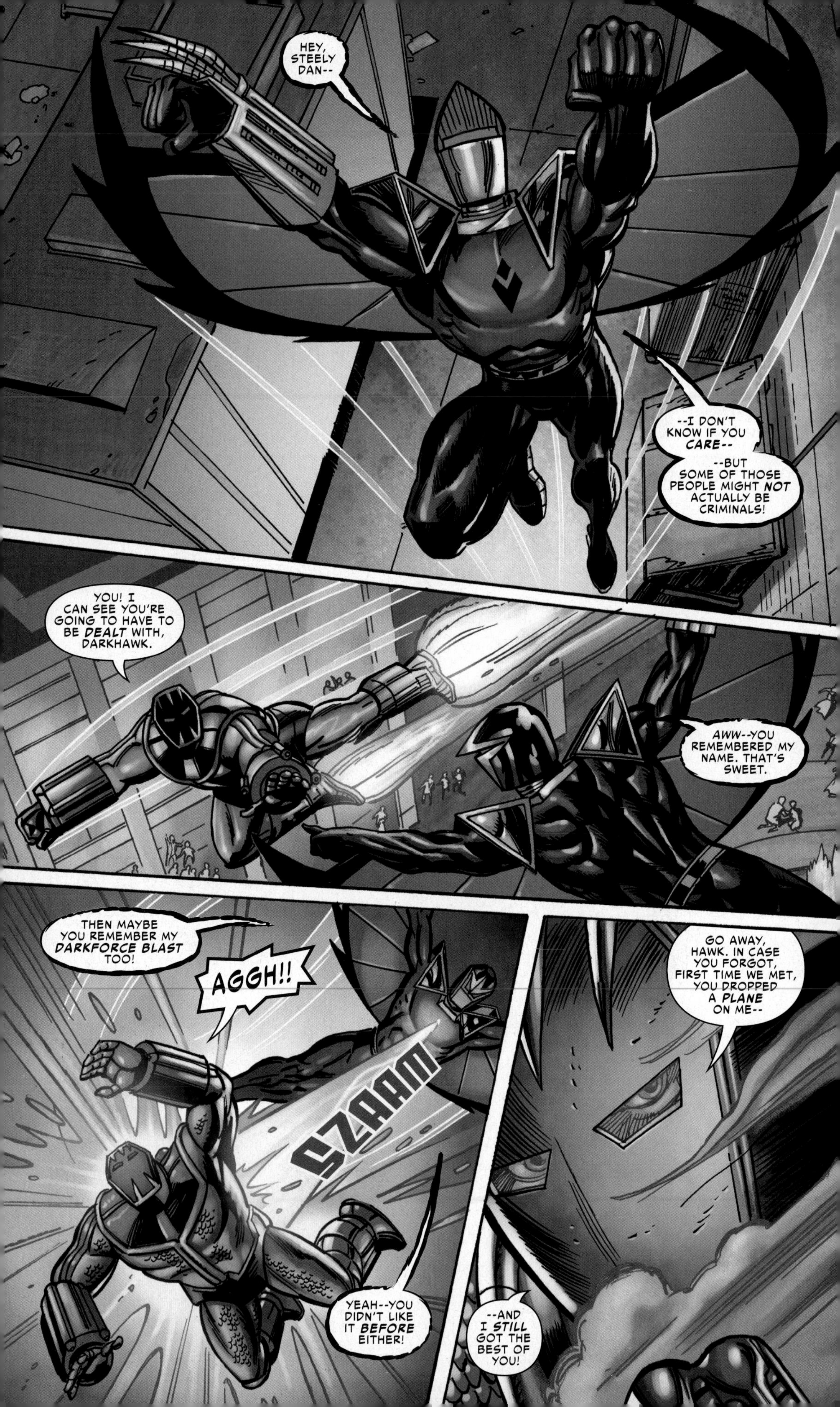
HEY, STEELY DAN--
--I DON'T KNOW IF YOU *CARE--*
--BUT SOME OF THOSE PEOPLE MIGHT *NOT* ACTUALLY BE CRIMINALS!
YOU! I CAN SEE YOU'RE GOING TO HAVE TO BE *DEALT* WITH, DARKHAWK.
*AWW--*YOU REMEMBERED MY NAME. THAT'S SWEET.
THEN MAYBE YOU REMEMBER MY *DARKFORCE BLAST* TOO!
AGGH!!
SZAAM
YEAH--YOU DIDN'T LIKE IT *BEFORE* EITHER!
GO AWAY, HAWK. IN CASE YOU FORGOT, FIRST TIME WE MET, YOU DROPPED A *PLANE* ON ME--
--AND I *STILL* GOT THE BEST OF YOU!

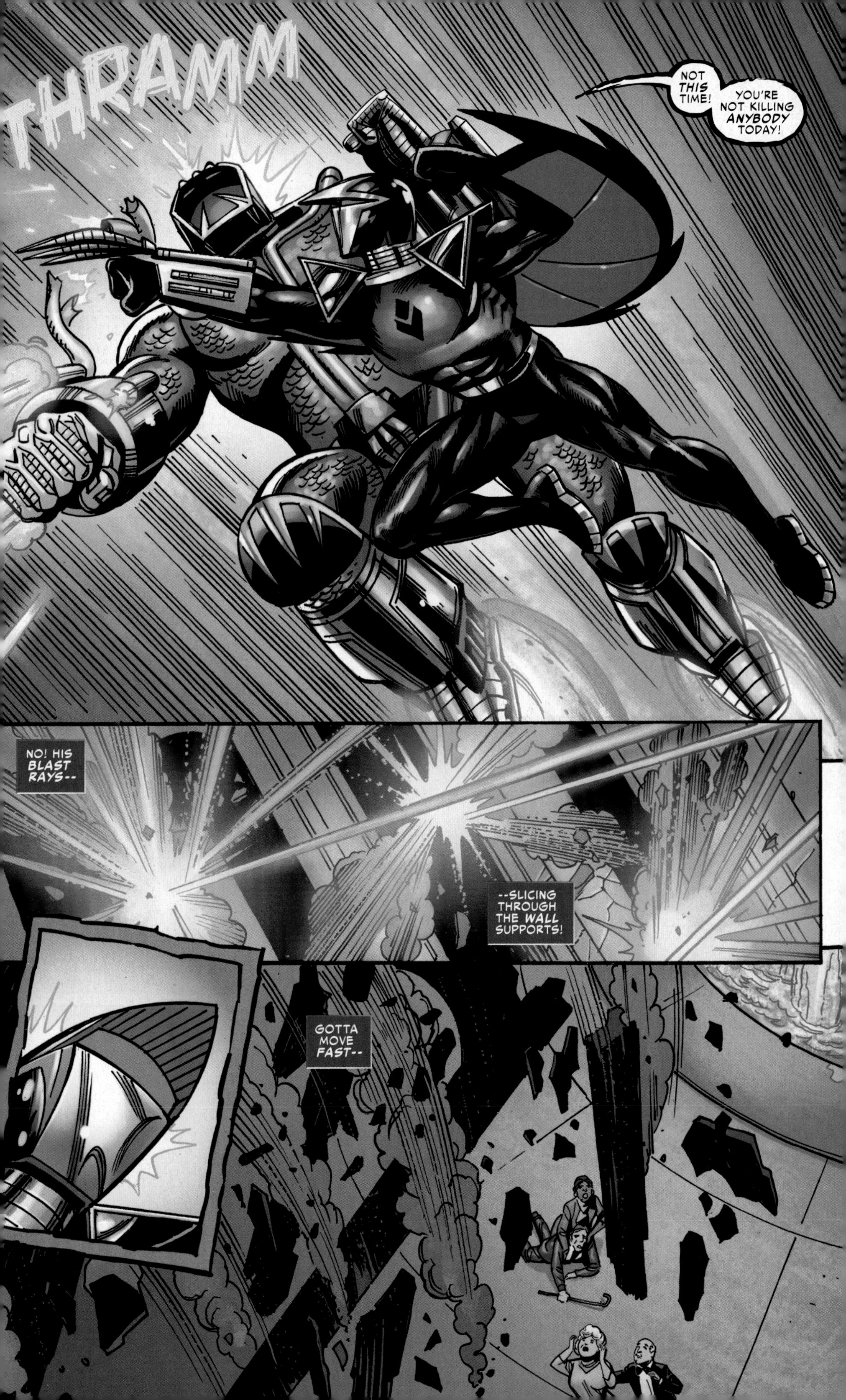
THRAMM
NOT THIS TIME!
YOU'RE NOT KILLING ANYBODY TODAY!
NO! HIS BLAST RAYS--
--SLICING THROUGH THE WALL SUPPORTS!
GOTTA MOVE FAST--

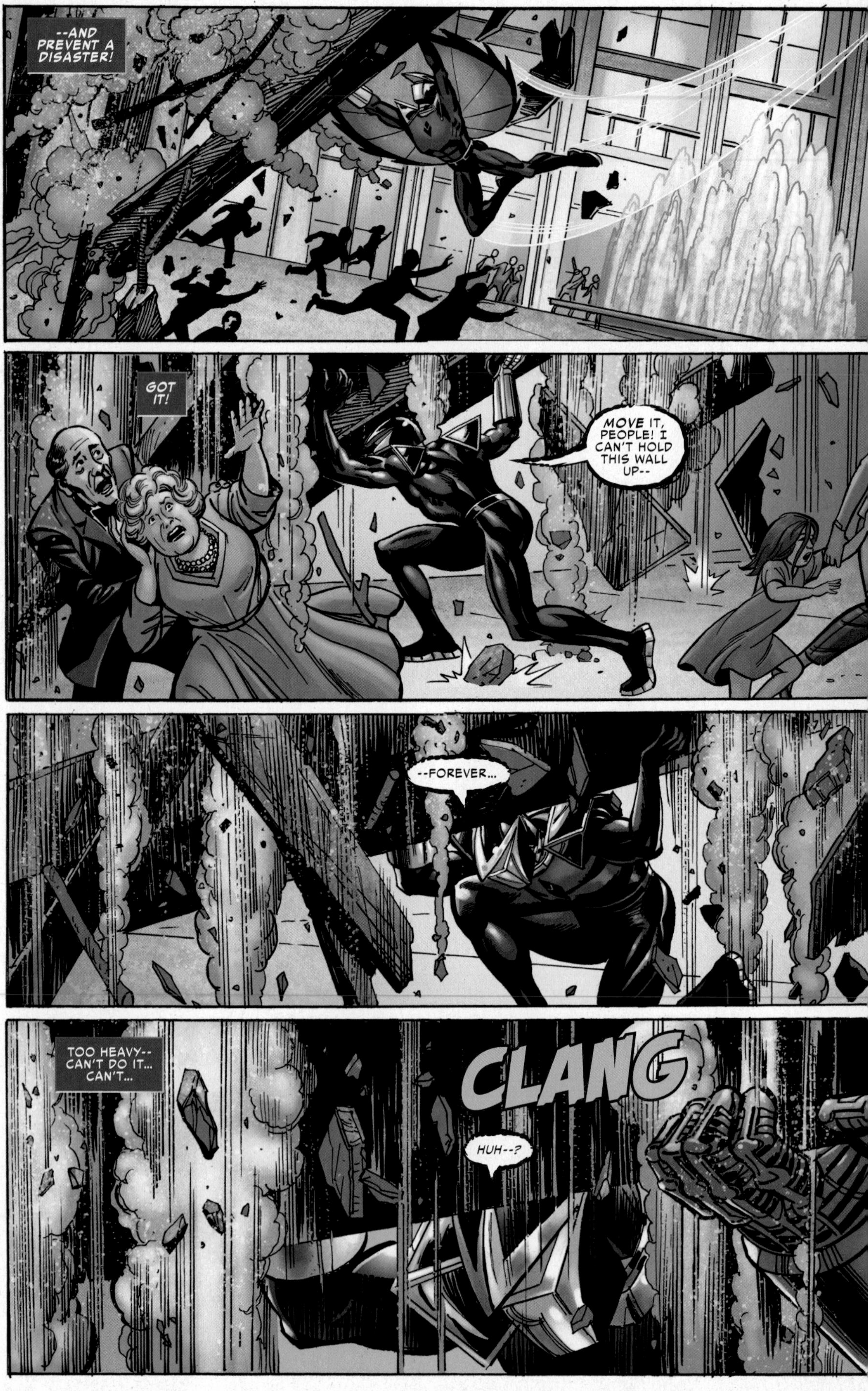
--AND PREVENT A DISASTER!
GOT IT!
MOVE IT, PEOPLE! I CAN'T HOLD THIS WALL UP--
--FOREVER...
TOO HEAVY--CAN'T DO IT... CAN'T...
CLANG
HUH--?

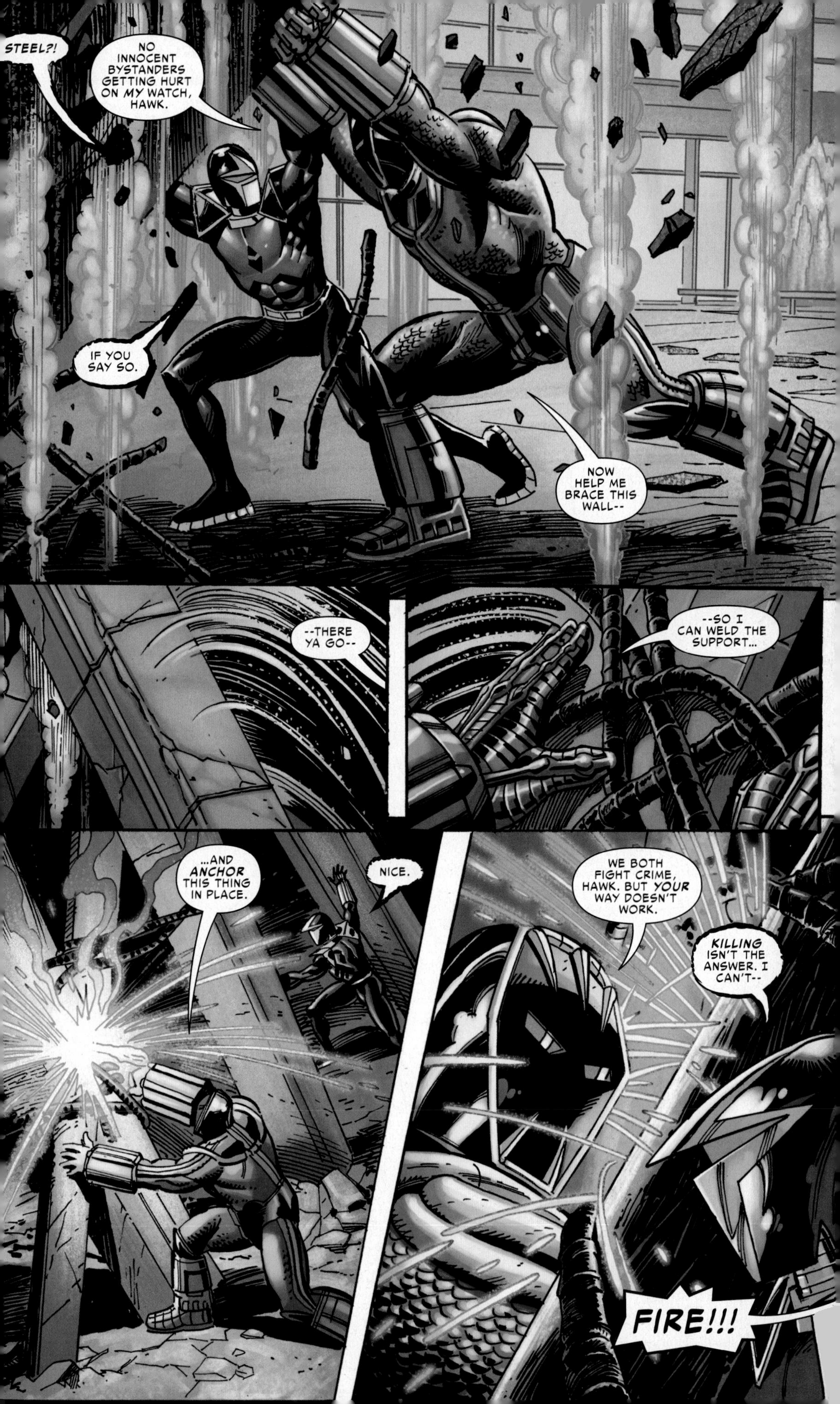
STEEL?!
NO INNOCENT BYSTANDERS GETTING HURT ON MY WATCH, HAWK.
IF YOU SAY SO.
NOW HELP ME BRACE THIS WALL--
--THERE YA GO--
--SO I CAN WELD THE SUPPORT...
...AND ANCHOR THIS THING IN PLACE.
NICE.
WE BOTH FIGHT CRIME, HAWK. BUT YOUR WAY DOESN'T WORK.
KILLING ISN'T THE ANSWER. I CAN'T--
FIRE!!!

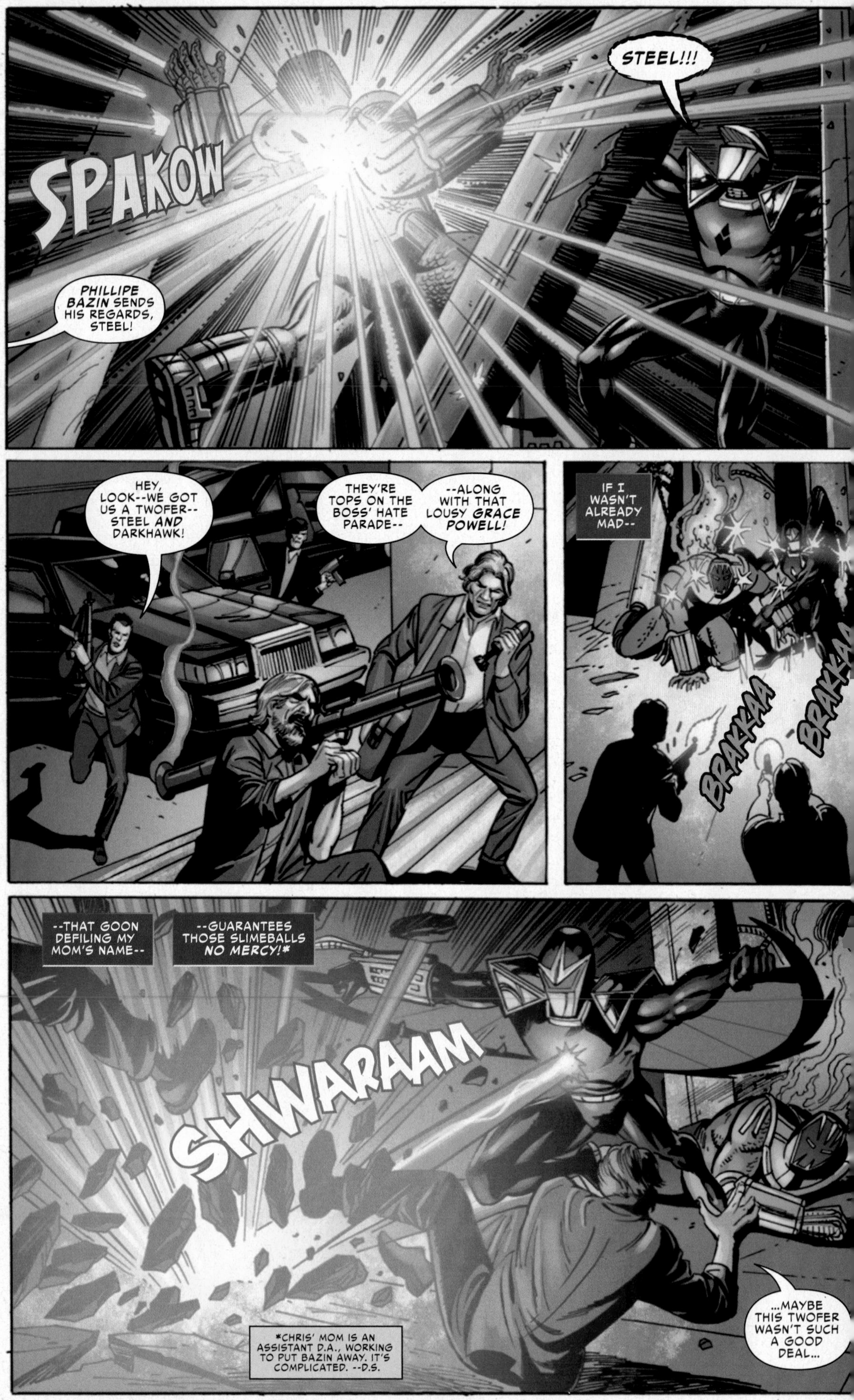
STEEL!!!
SPAKOW
PHILLIPE BAZIN SENDS HIS REGARDS, STEEL!
HEY, LOOK--WE GOT US A TWOFER--STEEL AND DARKHAWK!
THEY'RE TOPS ON THE BOSS' HATE PARADE--
--ALONG WITH THAT LOUSY GRACE POWELL!
IF I WASN'T ALREADY MAD--
BRAKKAA
BRAKKAA
--THAT GOON DEFILING MY MOM'S NAME--
--GUARANTEES THOSE SLIMEBALLS NO MERCY!*
SHWARAAM
*CHRIS' MOM IS AN ASSISTANT D.A., WORKING TO PUT BAZIN AWAY. IT'S COMPLICATED. --D.S.
...MAYBE THIS TWOFER WASN'T SUCH A GOOD DEAL...

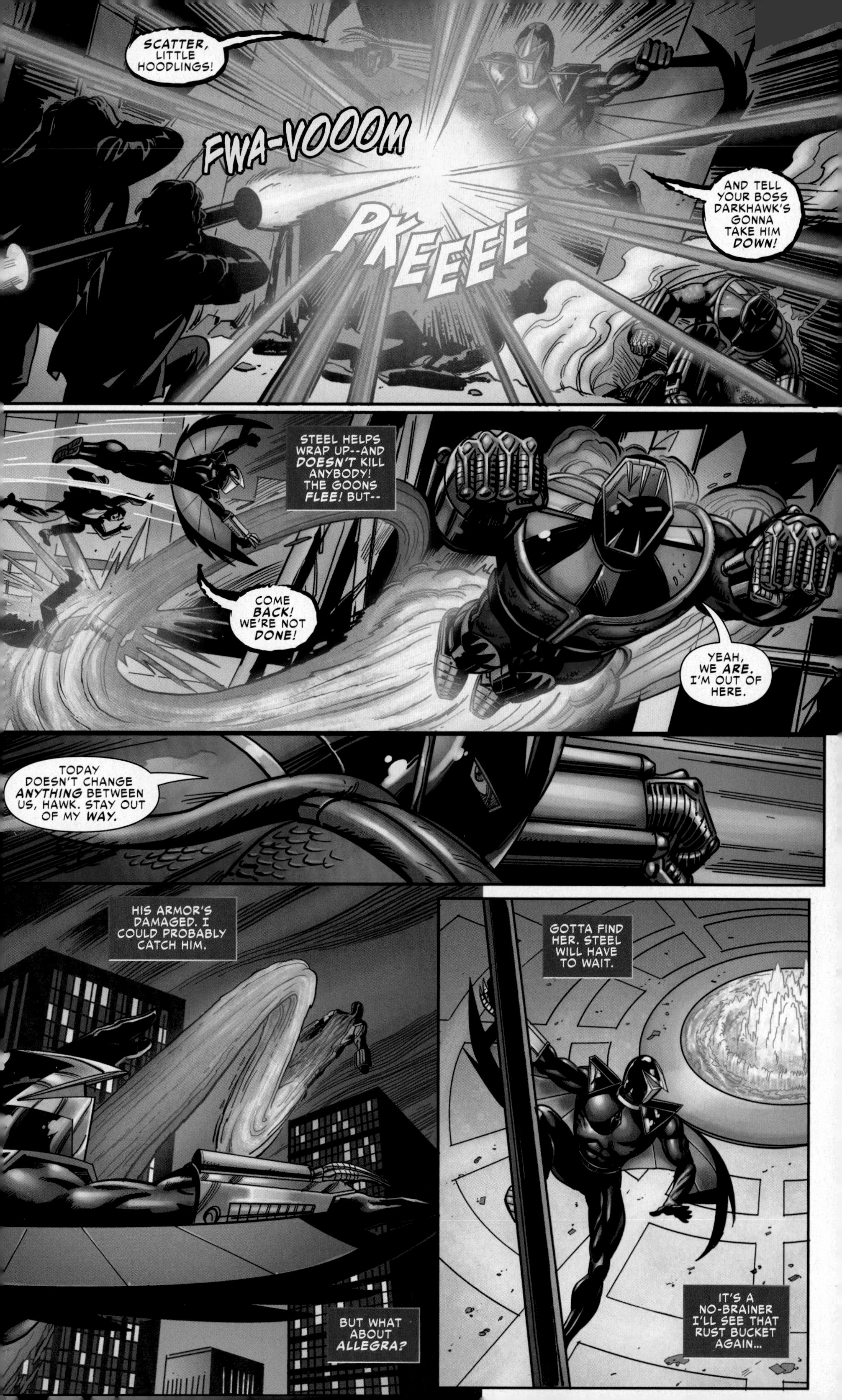
SCATTER, LITTLE HOODLINGS!
FWA-VOOOM
PKEEEE
AND TELL YOUR BOSS DARKHAWK'S GONNA TAKE HIM DOWN!
STEEL HELPS WRAP UP--AND DOESN'T KILL ANYBODY! THE GOONS FLEE! BUT--
COME BACK! WE'RE NOT DONE!
YEAH, WE ARE. I'M OUT OF HERE.
TODAY DOESN'T CHANGE ANYTHING BETWEEN US, HAWK. STAY OUT OF MY WAY.
HIS ARMOR'S DAMAGED. I COULD PROBABLY CATCH HIM.
BUT WHAT ABOUT ALLEGRA?
GOTTA FIND HER. STEEL WILL HAVE TO WAIT.
IT'S A NO-BRAINER I'LL SEE THAT RUST BUCKET AGAIN...

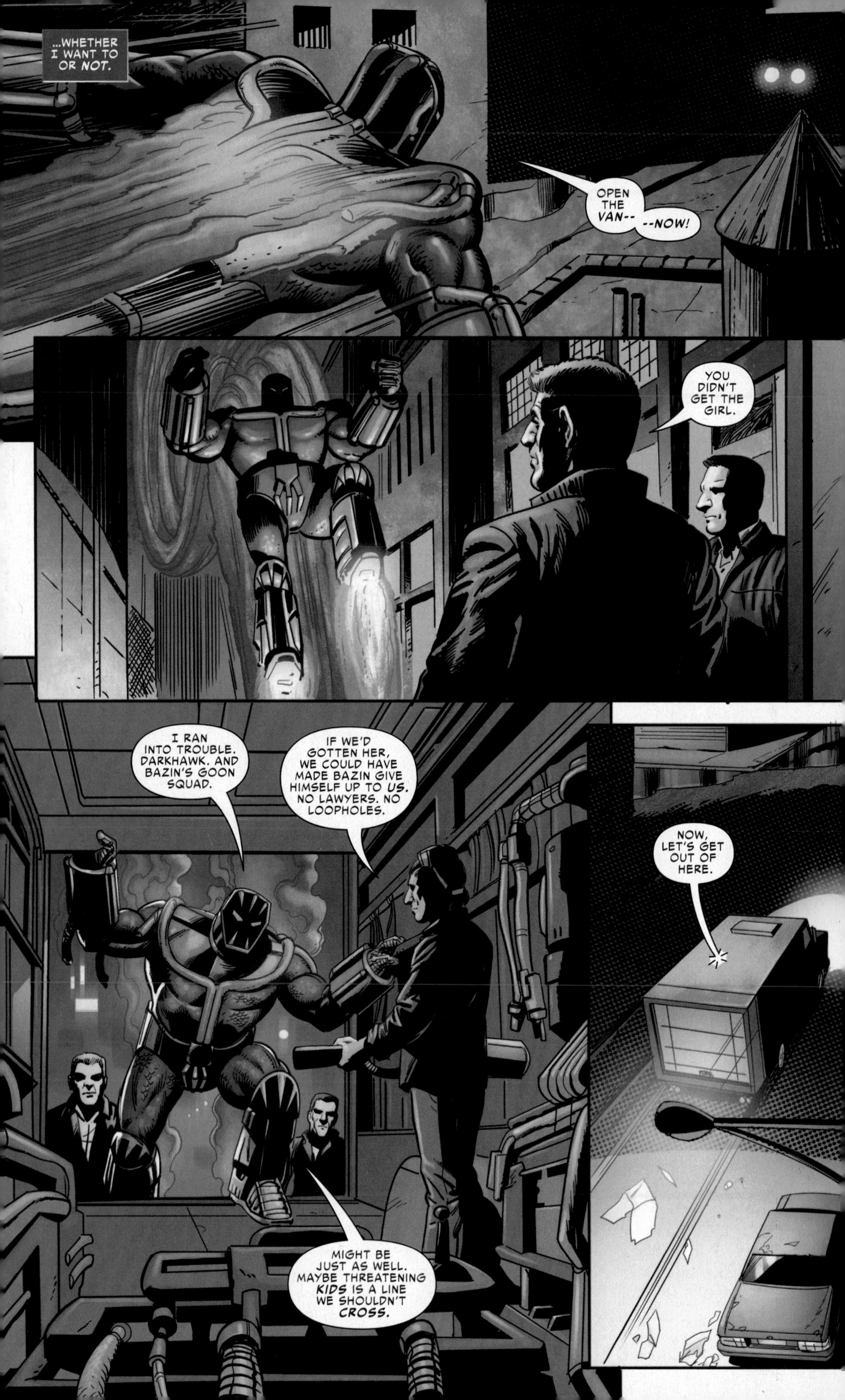
...WHETHER I WANT TO OR NOT.
OPEN THE VAN--
--NOW!
YOU DIDN'T GET THE GIRL.
I RAN INTO TROUBLE. DARKHAWK. AND BAZIN'S GOON SQUAD.
IF WE'D GOTTEN HER, WE COULD HAVE MADE BAZIN GIVE HIMSELF UP TO US. NO LAWYERS. NO LOOPHOLES.
MIGHT BE JUST AS WELL. MAYBE THREATENING KIDS IS A LINE WE SHOULDN'T CROSS.
NOW, LET'S GET OUT OF HERE.

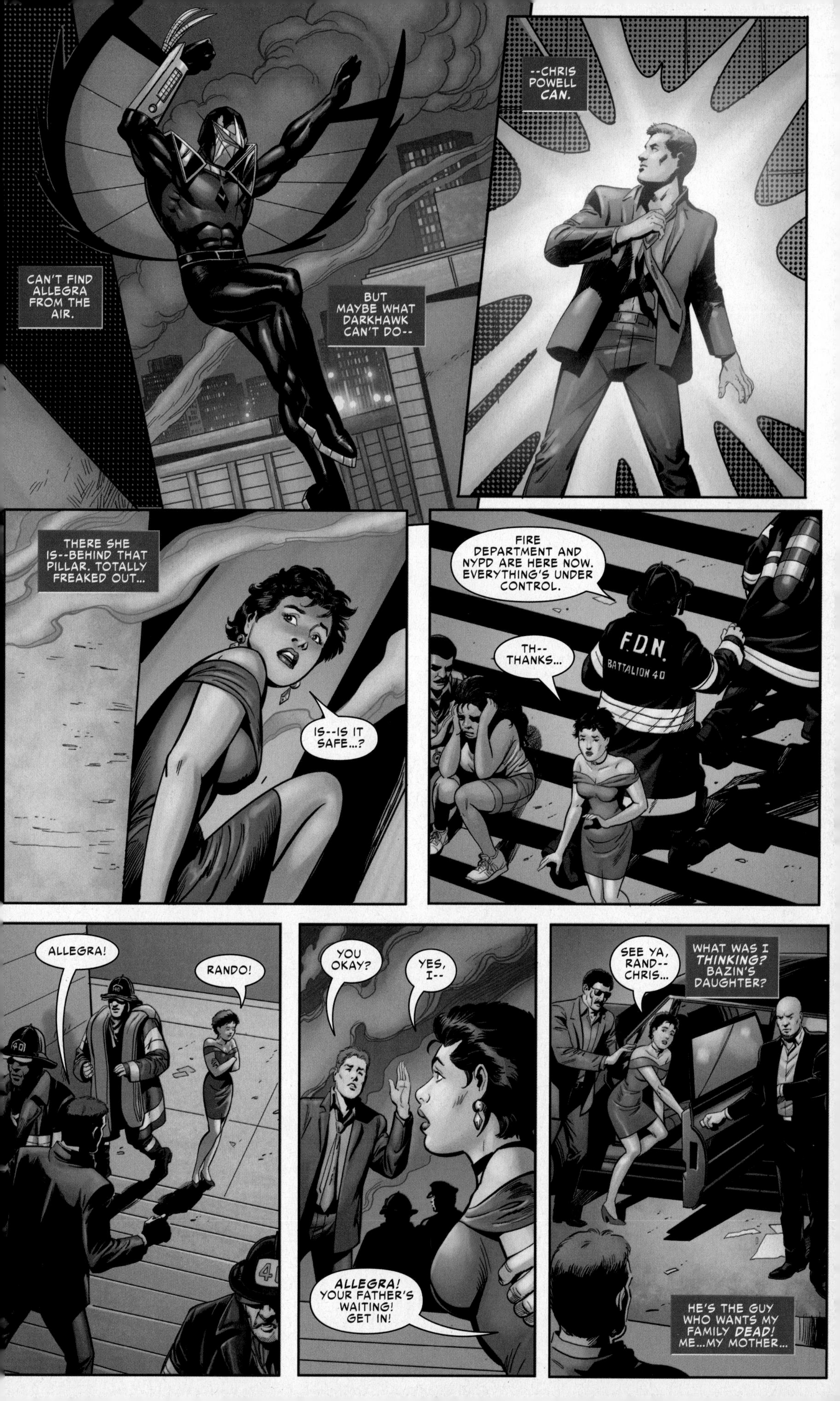
CAN'T FIND ALLEGRA FROM THE AIR.
BUT MAYBE WHAT DARKHAWK CAN'T DO--
--CHRIS POWELL CAN.
THERE SHE IS--BEHIND THAT PILLAR. TOTALLY FREAKED OUT...
IS--IS IT SAFE...?
FIRE DEPARTMENT AND NYPD ARE HERE NOW. EVERYTHING'S UNDER CONTROL.
TH-- THANKS...
F.D.N.
BATTALION 40
ALLEGRA!
RANDO!
YOU OKAY?
YES, I--
ALLEGRA! YOUR FATHER'S WAITING! GET IN!
SEE YA, RAND-- CHRIS...
WHAT WAS I THINKING? BAZIN'S DAUGHTER?
HE'S THE GUY WHO WANTS MY FAMILY DEAD! ME...MY MOTHER...

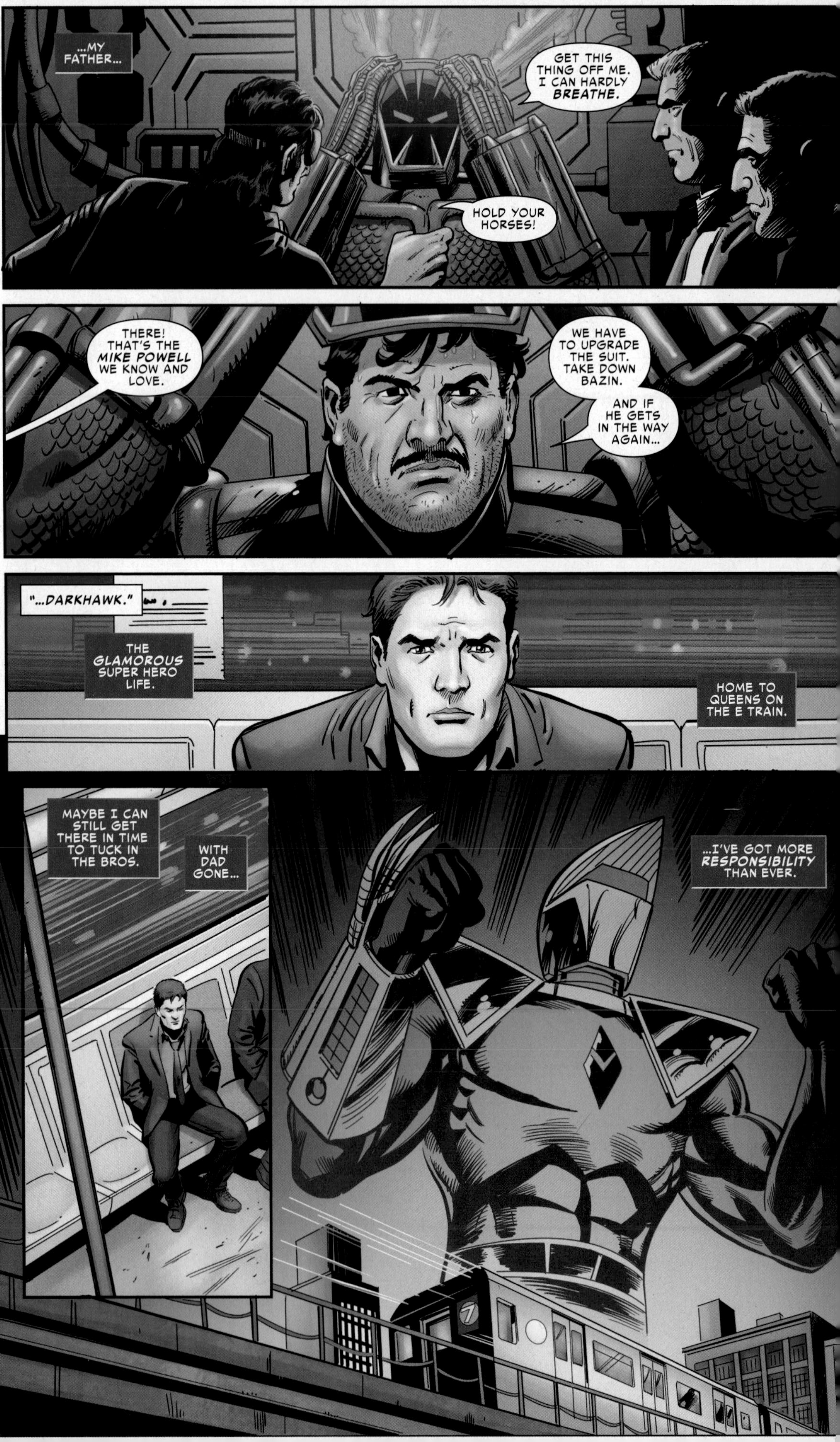
...MY FATHER...
GET THIS THING OFF ME. I CAN HARDLY BREATHE.
HOLD YOUR HORSES!
THERE! THAT'S THE MIKE POWELL WE KNOW AND LOVE.
WE HAVE TO UPGRADE THE SUIT. TAKE DOWN BAZIN.
AND IF HE GETS IN THE WAY AGAIN...
"...DARKHAWK."
THE GLAMOROUS SUPER HERO LIFE.
HOME TO QUEENS ON THE E TRAIN.
MAYBE I CAN STILL GET THERE IN TIME TO TUCK IN THE BROS.
WITH DAD GONE...
...I'VE GOT MORE RESPONSIBILITY THAN EVER.
7

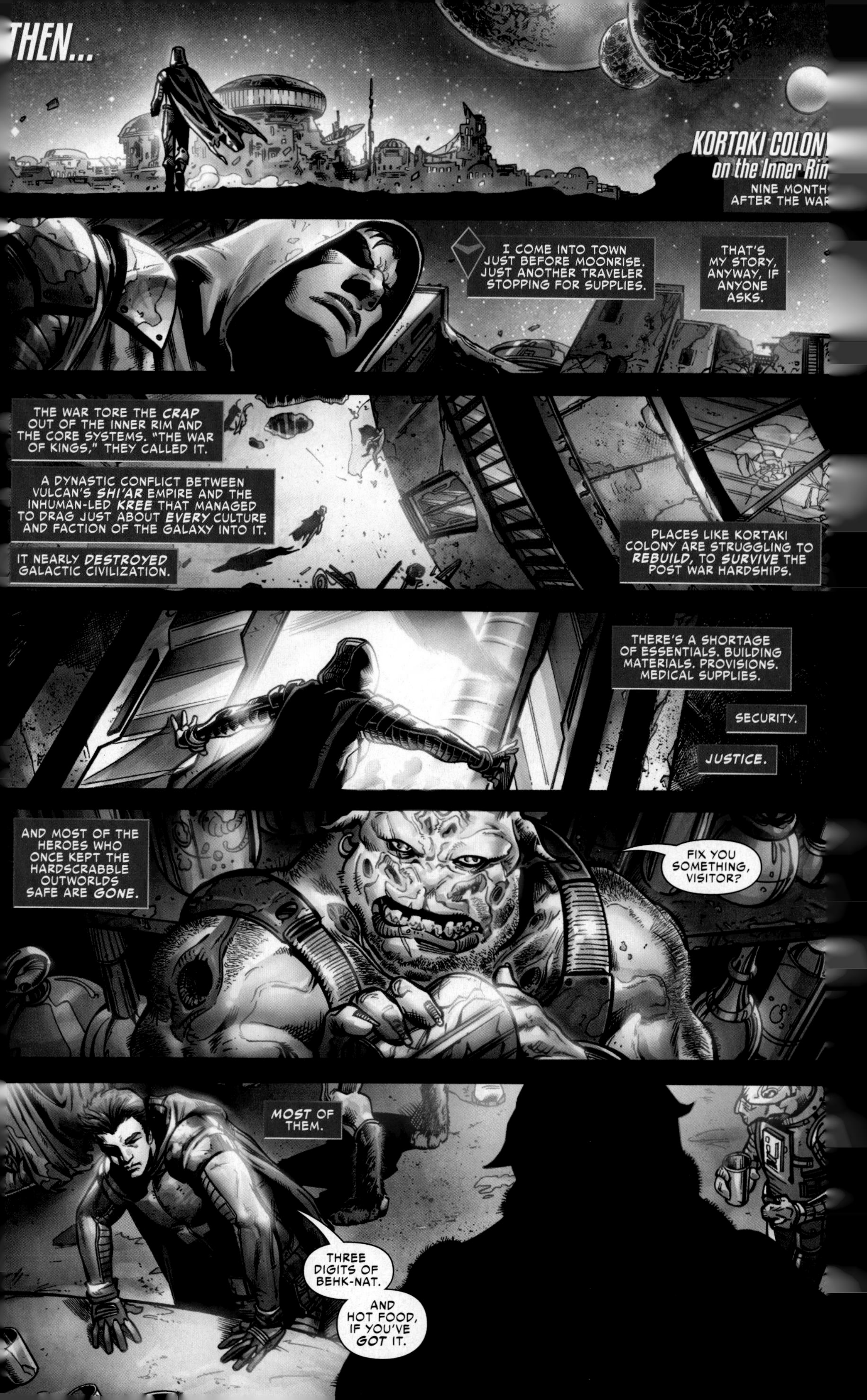
THEN...
KORTAKI COLONY on the Inner Rim
NINE MONTHS AFTER THE WAR
I COME INTO TOWN JUST BEFORE MOONRISE. JUST ANOTHER TRAVELER STOPPING FOR SUPPLIES.
THAT'S MY STORY, ANYWAY, IF ANYONE ASKS.
THE WAR TORE THE CRAP OUT OF THE INNER RIM AND THE CORE SYSTEMS. "THE WAR OF KINGS," THEY CALLED IT.
A DYNASTIC CONFLICT BETWEEN VULCAN'S SHI'AR EMPIRE AND THE INHUMAN-LED KREE THAT MANAGED TO DRAG JUST ABOUT EVERY CULTURE AND FACTION OF THE GALAXY INTO IT.
IT NEARLY DESTROYED GALACTIC CIVILIZATION.
PLACES LIKE KORTAKI COLONY ARE STRUGGLING TO REBUILD, TO SURVIVE THE POST WAR HARDSHIPS.
THERE'S A SHORTAGE OF ESSENTIALS. BUILDING MATERIALS. PROVISIONS. MEDICAL SUPPLIES.
SECURITY.
JUSTICE.
AND MOST OF THE HEROES WHO ONCE KEPT THE HARDSCRABBLE OUTWORLDS SAFE ARE GONE.
FIX YOU SOMETHING, VISITOR?
MOST OF THEM.
THREE DIGITS OF BEHK-NAT.
AND HOT FOOD, IF YOU'VE GOT IT.

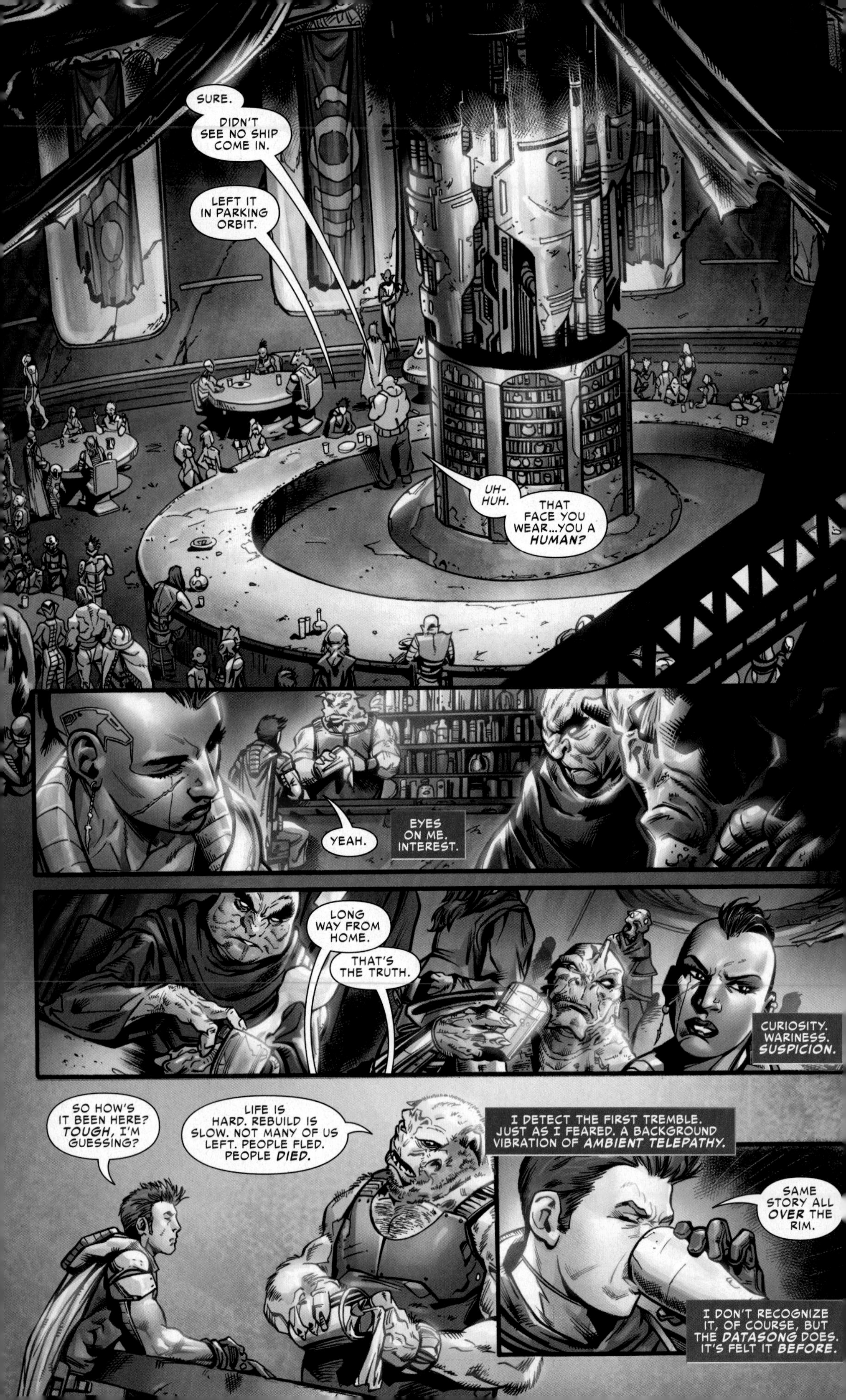
SURE.
DIDN'T SEE NO SHIP COME IN.
LEFT IT IN PARKING ORBIT.
UH-HUH.
THAT FACE YOU WEAR...YOU A HUMAN?
YEAH.
EYES ON ME. INTEREST.
LONG WAY FROM HOME.
THAT'S THE TRUTH.
CURIOSITY. WARINESS. SUSPICION.
SO HOW'S IT BEEN HERE? TOUGH, I'M GUESSING?
LIFE IS HARD. REBUILD IS SLOW. NOT MANY OF US LEFT. PEOPLE FLED. PEOPLE DIED.
I DETECT THE FIRST TREMBLE. JUST AS I FEARED. A BACKGROUND VIBRATION OF AMBIENT TELEPATHY.
SAME STORY ALL OVER THE RIM.
I DON'T RECOGNIZE IT, OF COURSE, BUT THE DATASONG DOES. IT'S FELT IT BEFORE.

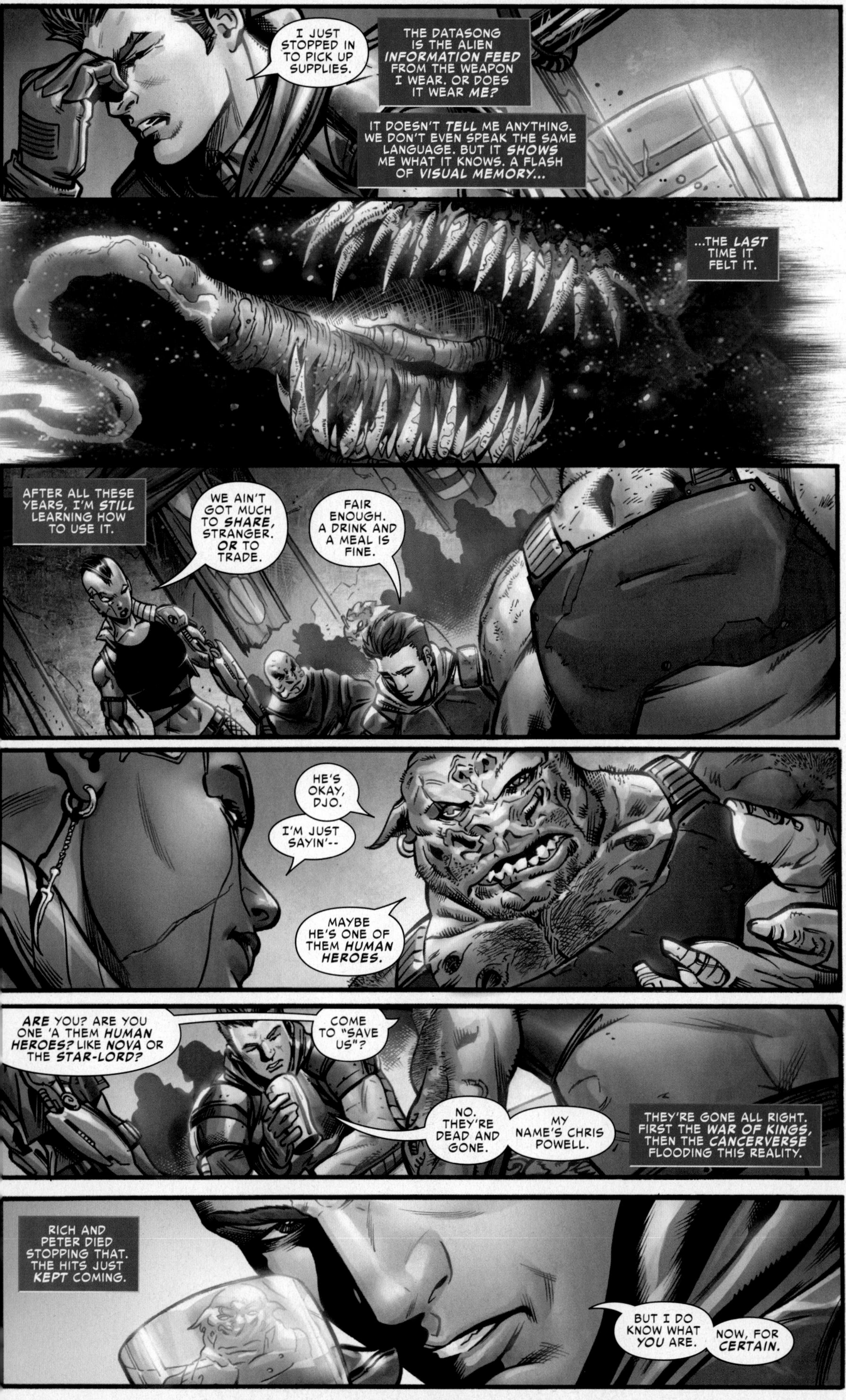

I JUST STOPPED IN TO PICK UP SUPPLIES.
THE DATASONG IS THE ALIEN INFORMATION FEED FROM THE WEAPON I WEAR. OR DOES IT WEAR ME?
IT DOESN'T TELL ME ANYTHING. WE DON'T EVEN SPEAK THE SAME LANGUAGE. BUT IT SHOWS ME WHAT IT KNOWS. A FLASH OF VISUAL MEMORY...
...THE LAST TIME IT FELT IT.
AFTER ALL THESE YEARS, I'M STILL LEARNING HOW TO USE IT.
WE AIN'T GOT MUCH TO SHARE, STRANGER. OR TO TRADE.
FAIR ENOUGH. A DRINK AND A MEAL IS FINE.
HE'S OKAY, DJO.
I'M JUST SAYIN'--
MAYBE HE'S ONE OF THEM HUMAN HEROES.
ARE YOU? ARE YOU ONE 'A THEM HUMAN HEROES? LIKE NOVA OR THE STAR-LORD?
COME TO "SAVE US"?
NO. THEY'RE DEAD AND GONE.
MY NAME'S CHRIS POWELL.
THEY'RE GONE ALL RIGHT. FIRST THE WAR OF KINGS, THEN THE CANCERVERSE FLOODING THIS REALITY.
RICH AND PETER DIED STOPPING THAT. THE HITS JUST KEPT COMING.
BUT I DO KNOW WHAT YOU ARE.
NOW, FOR CERTAIN.

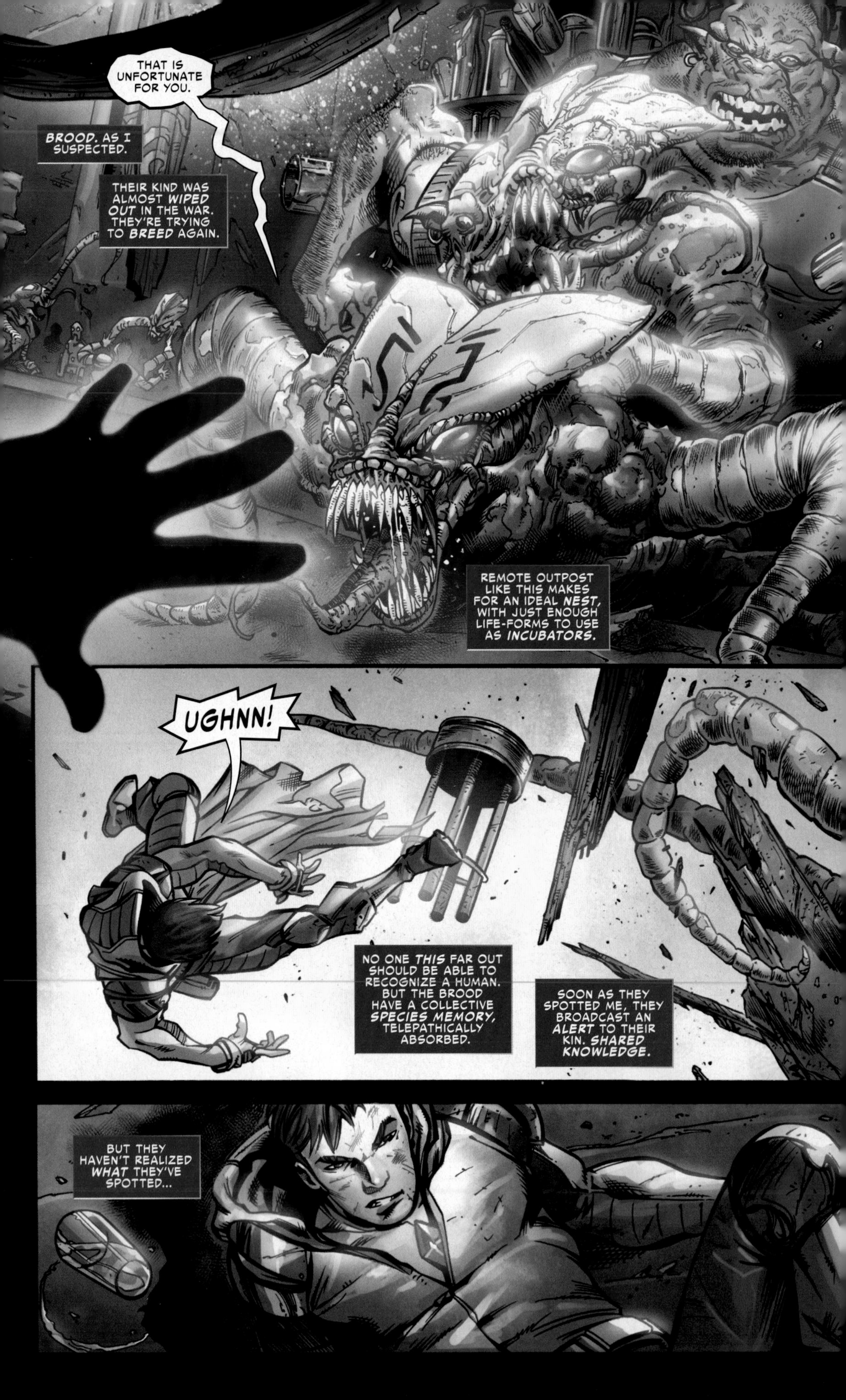
THAT IS UNFORTUNATE FOR YOU.
BROOD. AS I SUSPECTED.
THEIR KIND WAS ALMOST WIPED OUT IN THE WAR. THEY'RE TRYING TO BREED AGAIN.
REMOTE OUTPOST LIKE THIS MAKES FOR AN IDEAL NEST, WITH JUST ENOUGH LIFE-FORMS TO USE AS INCUBATORS.
UGHNN!
NO ONE THIS FAR OUT SHOULD BE ABLE TO RECOGNIZE A HUMAN. BUT THE BROOD HAVE A COLLECTIVE SPECIES MEMORY, TELEPATHICALLY ABSORBED.
SOON AS THEY SPOTTED ME, THEY BROADCAST AN ALERT TO THEIR KIN. SHARED KNOWLEDGE.
BUT THEY HAVEN'T REALIZED WHAT THEY'VE SPOTTED...

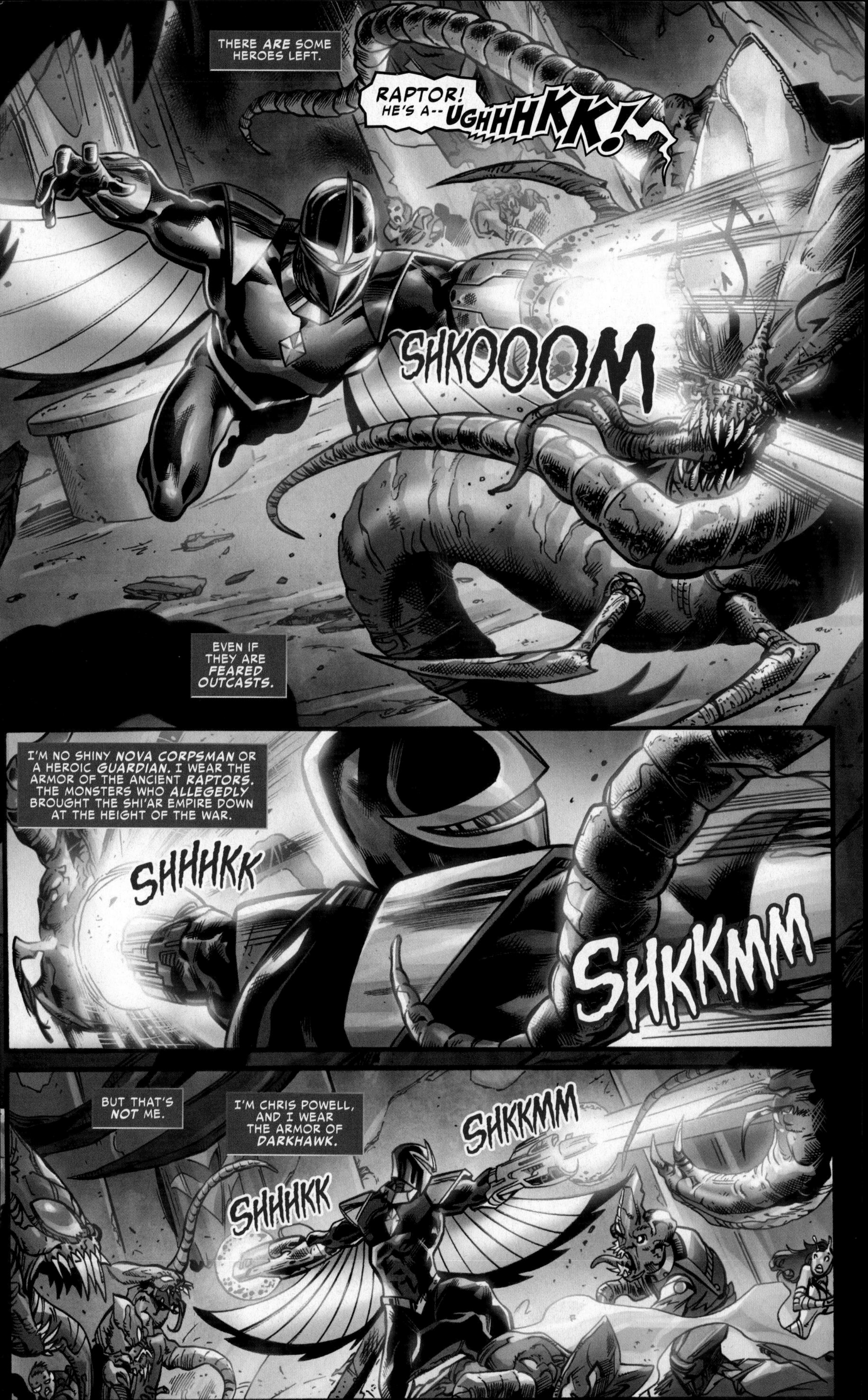
THERE ARE SOME HEROES LEFT.
RAPTOR! HE'S A-- UGHHHKK!
SHKOOOM
EVEN IF THEY ARE FEARED OUTCASTS.
I'M NO SHINY NOVA CORPSMAN OR A HEROIC GUARDIAN. I WEAR THE ARMOR OF THE ANCIENT RAPTORS. THE MONSTERS WHO ALLEGEDLY BROUGHT THE SHI'AR EMPIRE DOWN AT THE HEIGHT OF THE WAR.
SHHHKK
SHKMM
BUT THAT'S NOT ME.
I'M CHRIS POWELL, AND I WEAR THE ARMOR OF DARKHAWK.
SHKKMM
SHHHKK

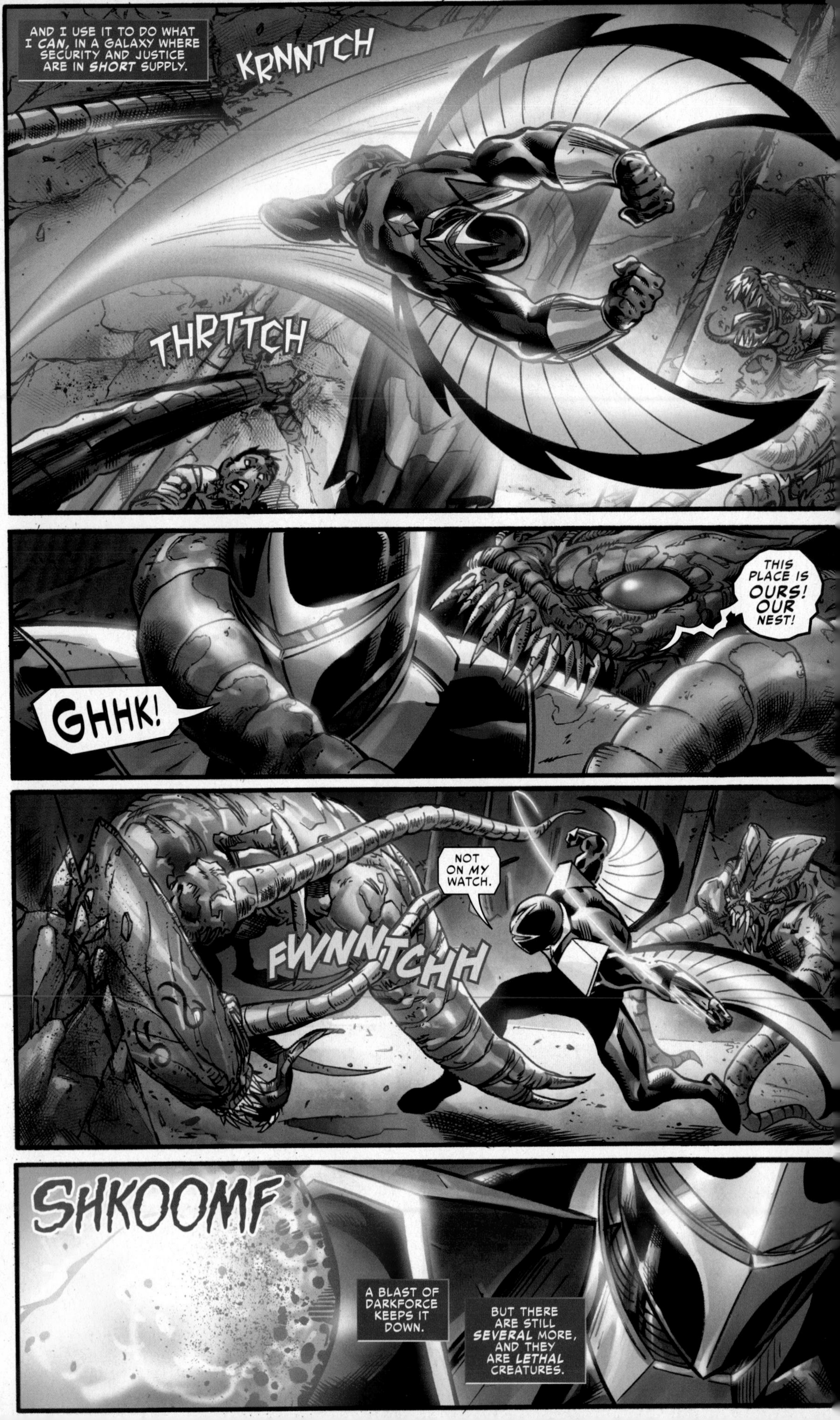

AND I USE IT TO DO WHAT I CAN, IN A GALAXY WHERE SECURITY AND JUSTICE ARE IN SHORT SUPPLY.
KRNNTCH
THRTTCH
THIS PLACE IS OURS! OUR NEST!
GHHK!
NOT ON MY WATCH.
FWNNTCHH
SHKOOMF
A BLAST OF DARKFORCE KEEPS IT DOWN.
BUT THERE ARE STILL SEVERAL MORE, AND THEY ARE LETHAL CREATURES.

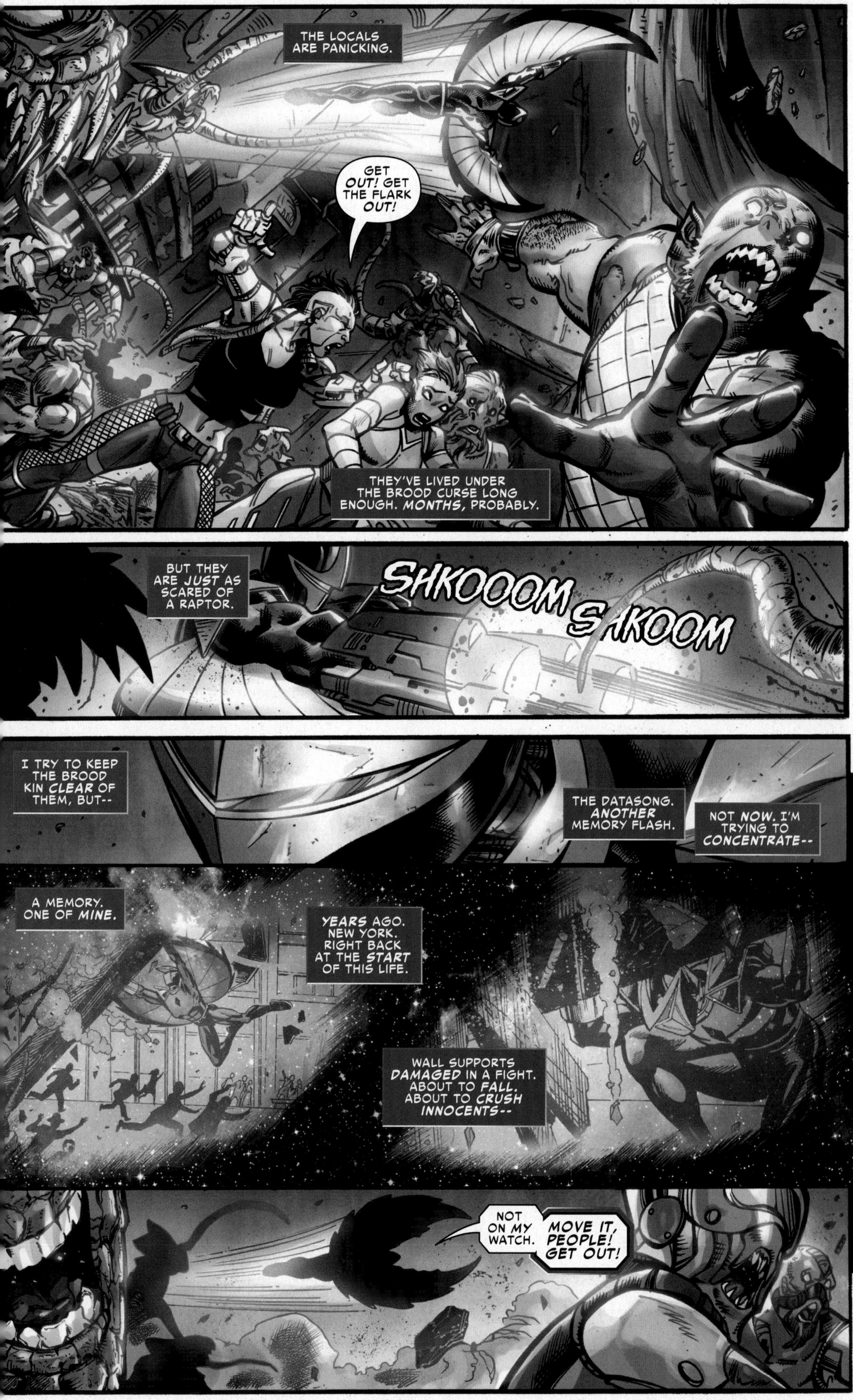
THE LOCALS ARE PANICKING.
GET OUT! GET THE FLARK OUT!
THEY'VE LIVED UNDER THE BROOD CURSE LONG ENOUGH. MONTHS, PROBABLY.
BUT THEY ARE JUST AS SCARED OF A RAPTOR.
SHKOOOM
SHKOOM
I TRY TO KEEP THE BROOD KIN CLEAR OF THEM, BUT--
THE DATASONG. ANOTHER MEMORY FLASH.
NOT NOW. I'M TRYING TO CONCENTRATE--
A MEMORY. ONE OF MINE.
YEARS AGO. NEW YORK. RIGHT BACK AT THE START OF THIS LIFE.
WALL SUPPORTS DAMAGED IN A FIGHT. ABOUT TO FALL, ABOUT TO CRUSH INNOCENTS--
NOT ON MY WATCH.
MOVE IT, PEOPLE! GET OUT!

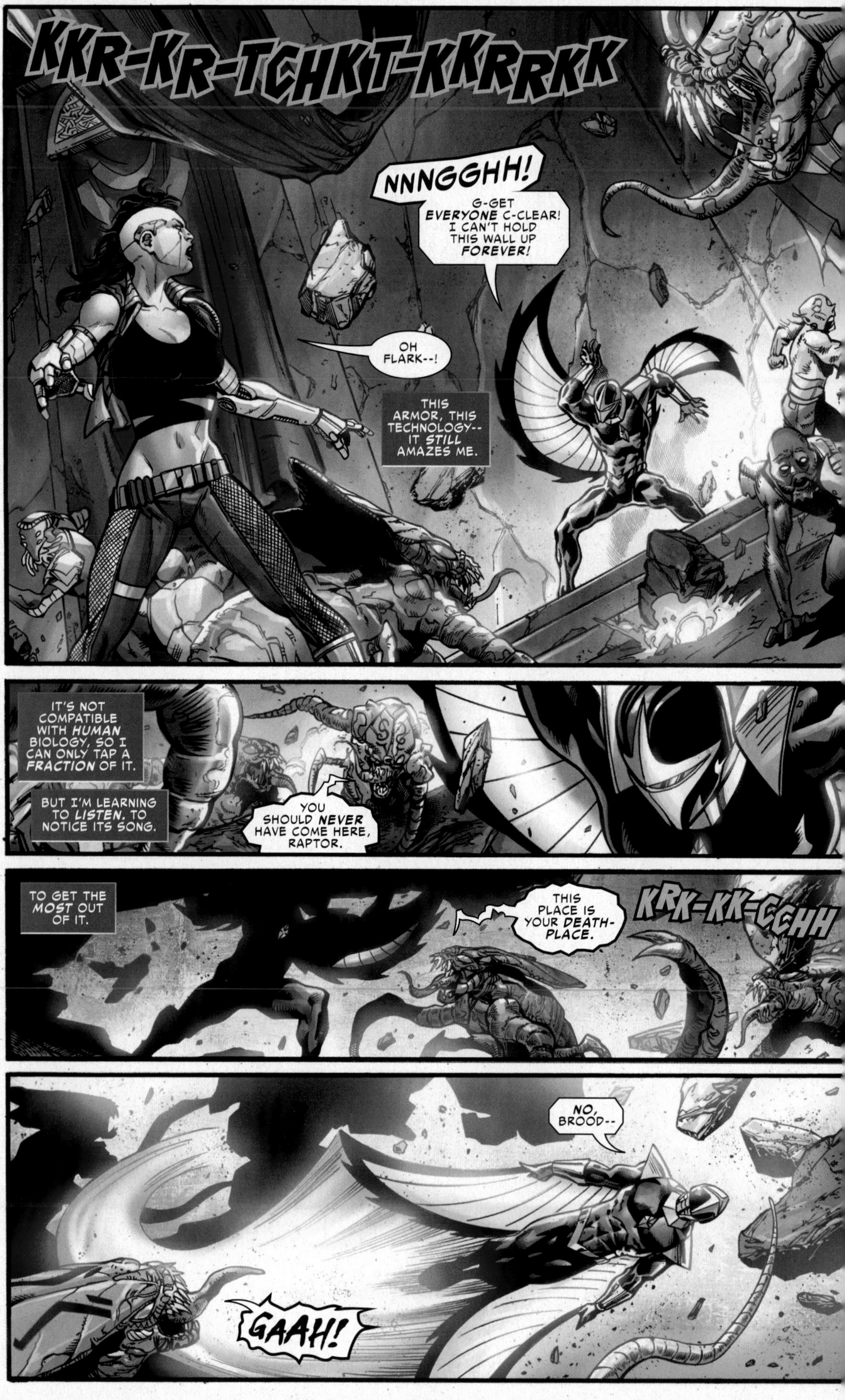
KKR-KR-TCHKT-KKRRKK
NNNGGHH!
G-GET EVERYONE C-CLEAR! I CAN'T HOLD THIS WALL UP FOREVER!
OH FLARK--!
THIS ARMOR, THIS TECHNOLOGY-- IT STILL AMAZES ME.
IT'S NOT COMPATIBLE WITH HUMAN BIOLOGY, SO I CAN ONLY TAP A FRACTION OF IT.
BUT I'M LEARNING TO LISTEN, TO NOTICE ITS SONG.
YOU SHOULD NEVER HAVE COME HERE, RAPTOR.
TO GET THE MOST OUT OF IT.
THIS PLACE IS YOUR DEATH-PLACE.
KRK-KK-CCHH
NO, BROOD--
GAAH!

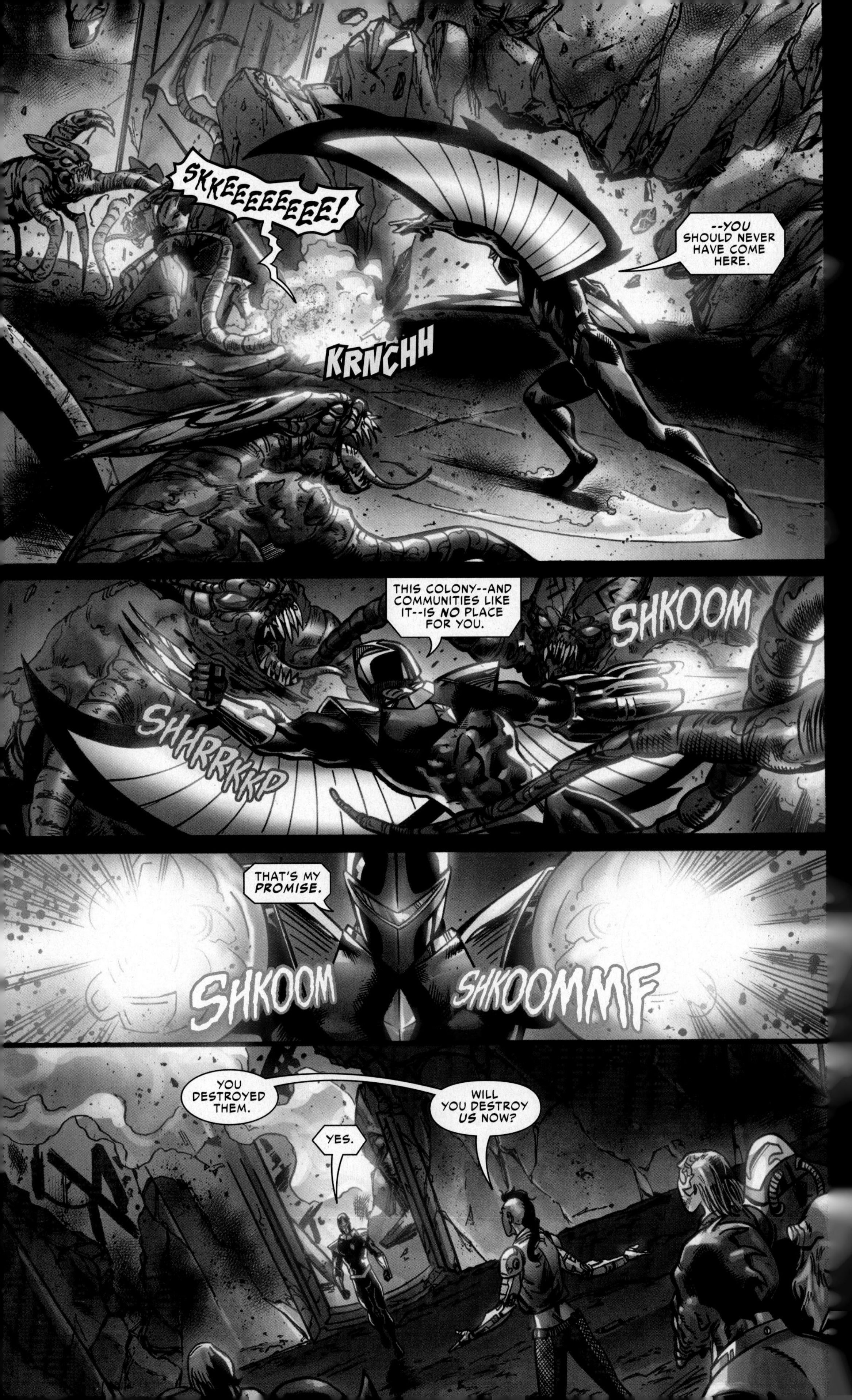
SKKEEEEEEEEE!
--YOU SHOULD NEVER HAVE COME HERE.
KRNCHH
THIS COLONY--AND COMMUNITIES LIKE IT--IS NO PLACE FOR YOU.
SHKOOM
SHHRRKKP
THAT'S MY PROMISE.
SHKOOM
SHKOOMMF
YOU DESTROYED THEM.
WILL YOU DESTROY US NOW?
YES.

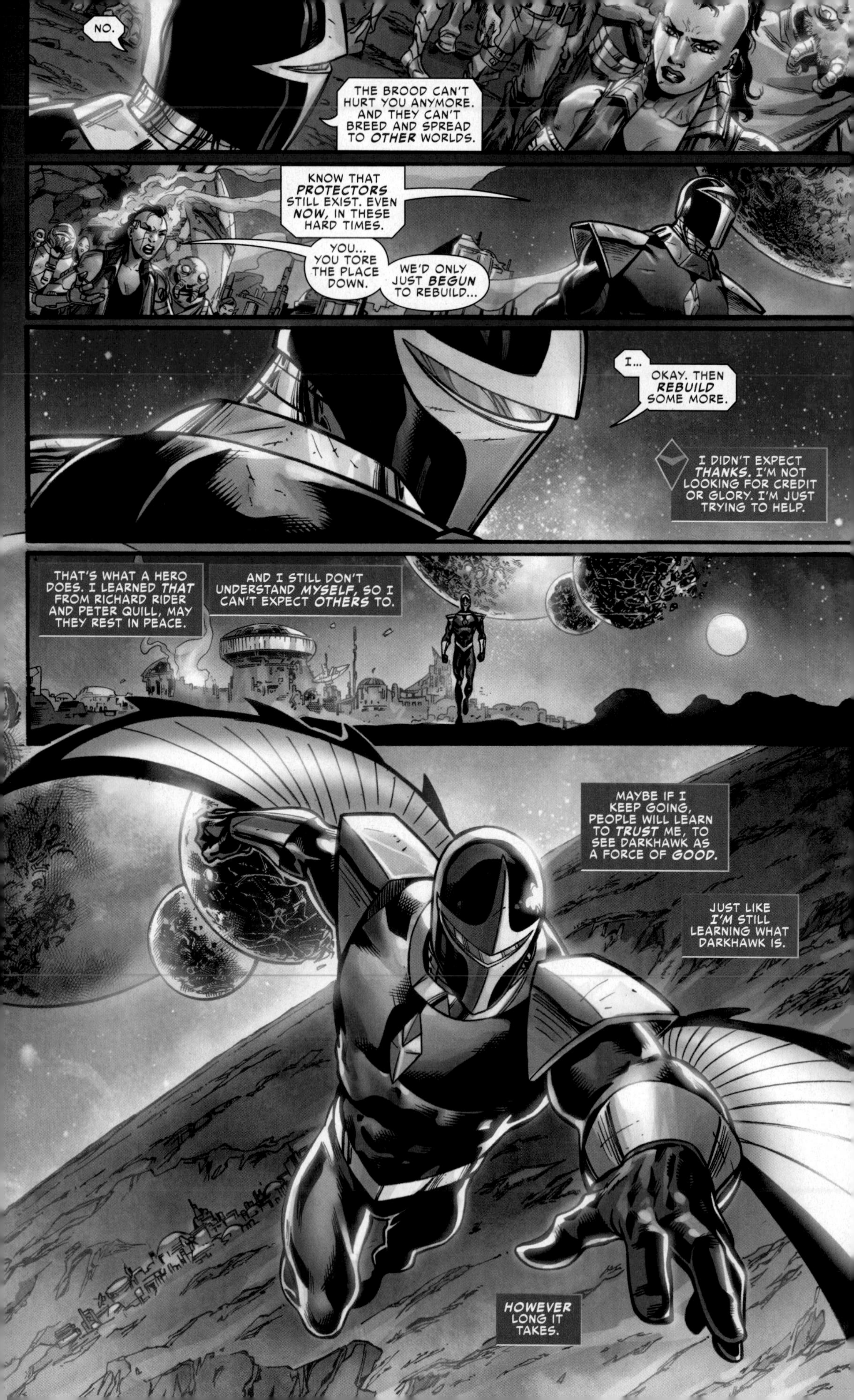
NO.
THE BROOD CAN'T HURT YOU ANYMORE. AND THEY CAN'T BREED AND SPREAD TO OTHER WORLDS.
KNOW THAT PROTECTORS STILL EXIST. EVEN NOW, IN THESE HARD TIMES.
YOU... YOU TORE THE PLACE DOWN.
WE'D ONLY JUST BEGUN TO REBUILD...
I... OKAY. THEN REBUILD SOME MORE.
I DIDN'T EXPECT THANKS. I'M NOT LOOKING FOR CREDIT OR GLORY. I'M JUST TRYING TO HELP.
THAT'S WHAT A HERO DOES. I LEARNED THAT FROM RICHARD RIDER AND PETER QUILL, MAY THEY REST IN PEACE.
AND I STILL DON'T UNDERSTAND MYSELF, SO I CAN'T EXPECT OTHERS TO.
MAYBE IF I KEEP GOING, PEOPLE WILL LEARN TO TRUST ME, TO SEE DARKHAWK AS A FORCE OF GOOD.
JUST LIKE I'M STILL LEARNING WHAT DARKHAWK IS.
HOWEVER LONG IT TAKES.

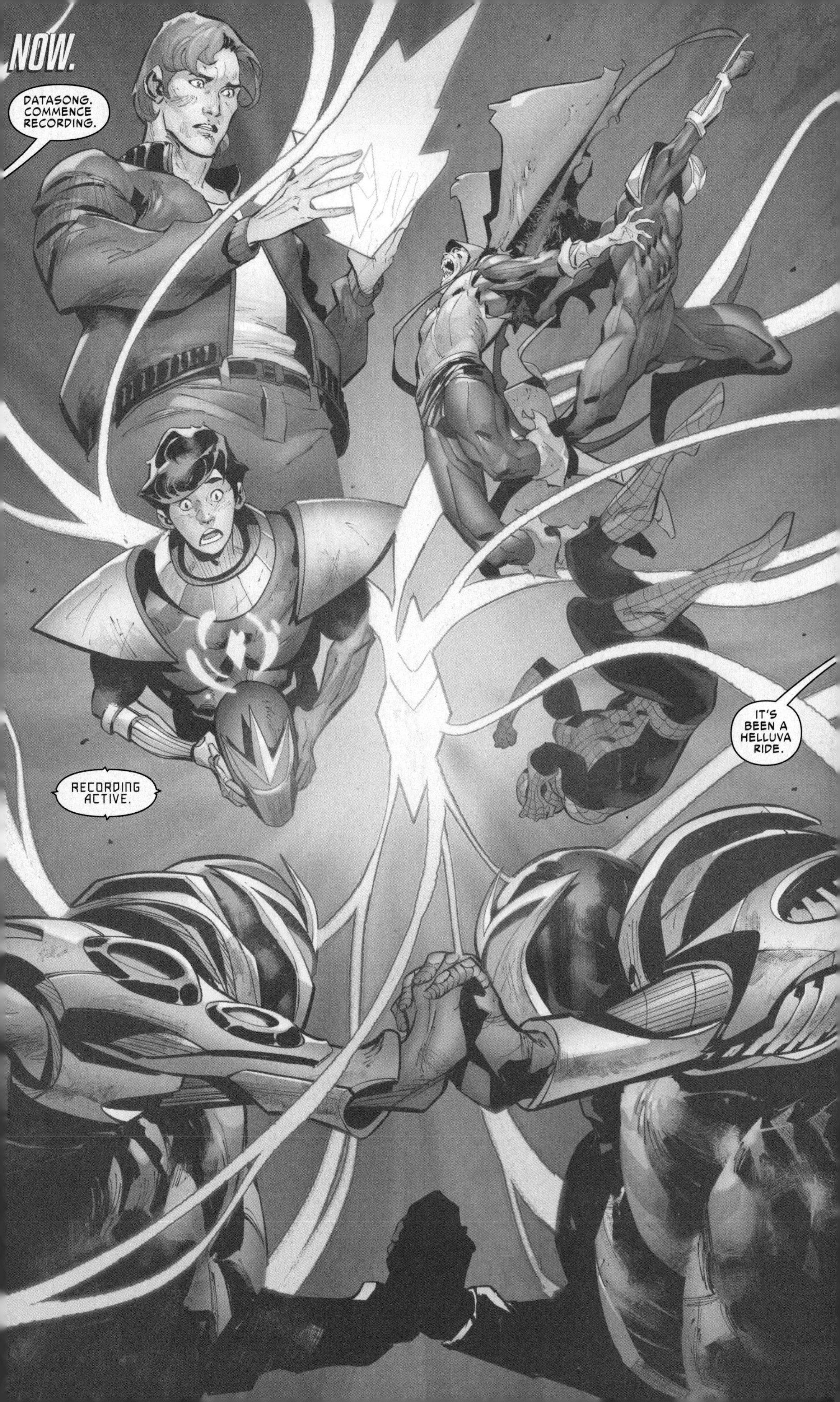
NOW.
DATASONG. COMMENCE RECORDING.
RECORDING ACTIVE.
IT'S BEEN A HELLUVA RIDE.

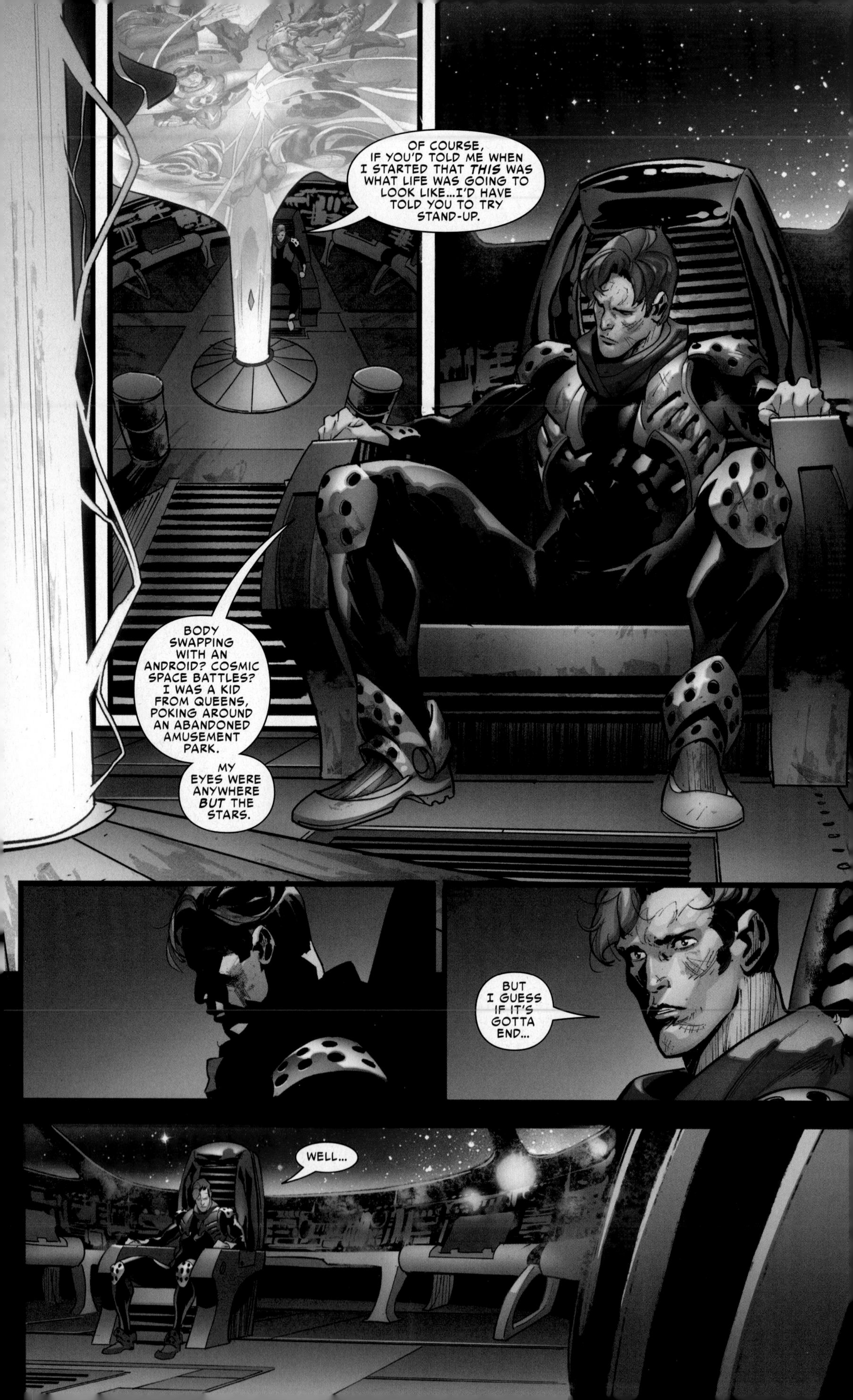
OF COURSE, IF YOU'D TOLD ME WHEN I STARTED THAT *THIS* WAS WHAT LIFE WAS GOING TO LOOK LIKE...I'D HAVE TOLD YOU TO TRY STAND-UP.
BODY SWAPPING WITH AN ANDROID? COSMIC SPACE BATTLES? I WAS A KID FROM QUEENS, POKING AROUND AN ABANDONED AMUSEMENT PARK.
MY EYES WERE ANYWHERE *BUT* THE STARS.
BUT I GUESS IF IT'S GOTTA END...
WELL...

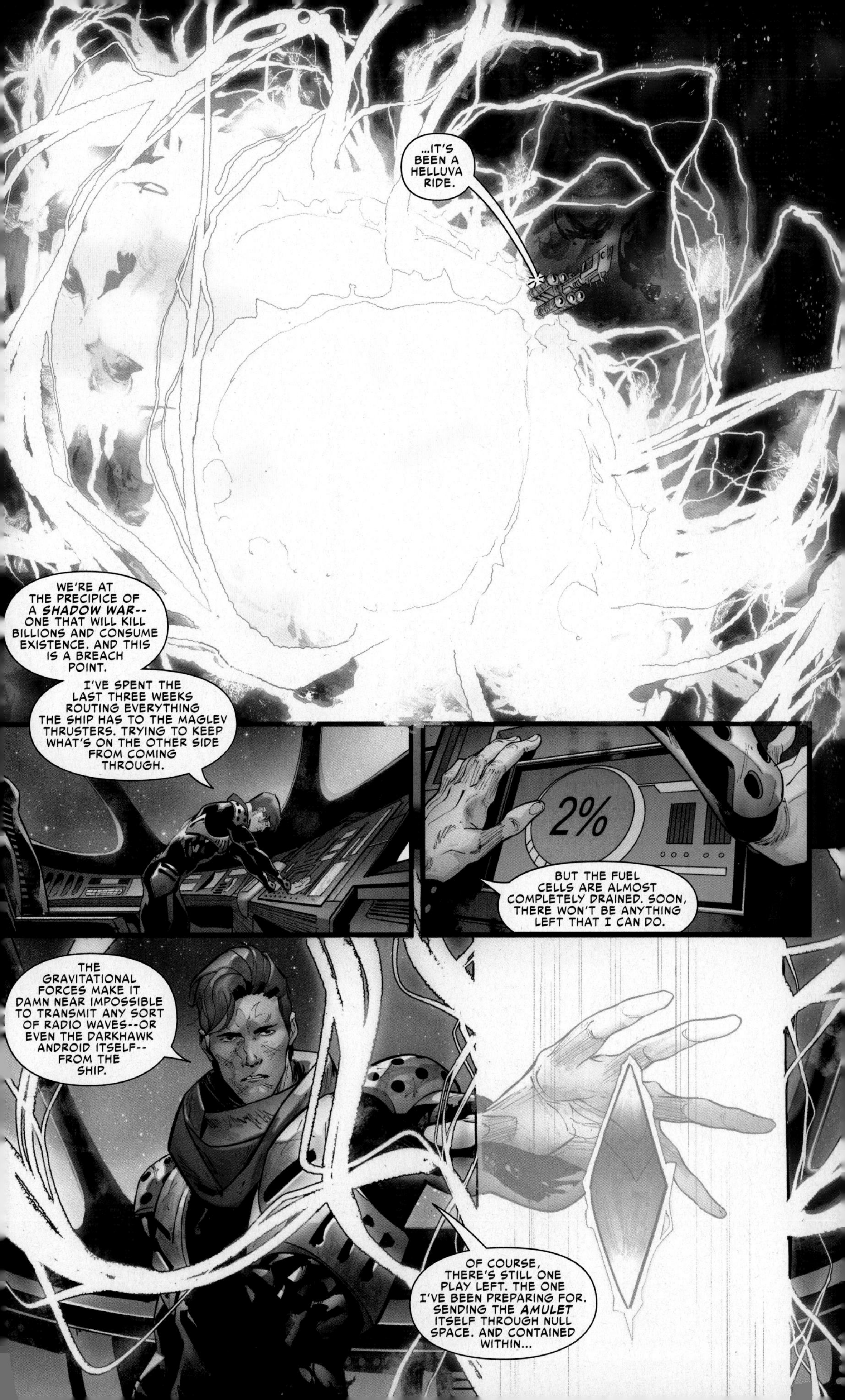
...IT'S BEEN A HELLUVA RIDE.
WE'RE AT THE PRECIPICE OF A *SHADOW WAR*-- ONE THAT WILL KILL BILLIONS AND CONSUME EXISTENCE. AND THIS IS A BREACH POINT.
I'VE SPENT THE LAST THREE WEEKS ROUTING EVERYTHING THE SHIP HAS TO THE MAGLEV THRUSTERS. TRYING TO KEEP WHAT'S ON THE OTHER SIDE FROM COMING THROUGH.
2%
BUT THE FUEL CELLS ARE ALMOST COMPLETELY DRAINED. SOON, THERE WON'T BE ANYTHING LEFT THAT I CAN DO.
THE GRAVITATIONAL FORCES MAKE IT DAMN NEAR IMPOSSIBLE TO TRANSMIT ANY SORT OF RADIO WAVES--OR EVEN THE DARKHAWK ANDROID ITSELF-- FROM THE SHIP.
OF COURSE, THERE'S STILL ONE PLAY LEFT. THE ONE I'VE BEEN PREPARING FOR. SENDING THE *AMULET* ITSELF THROUGH NULL SPACE. AND CONTAINED WITHIN...

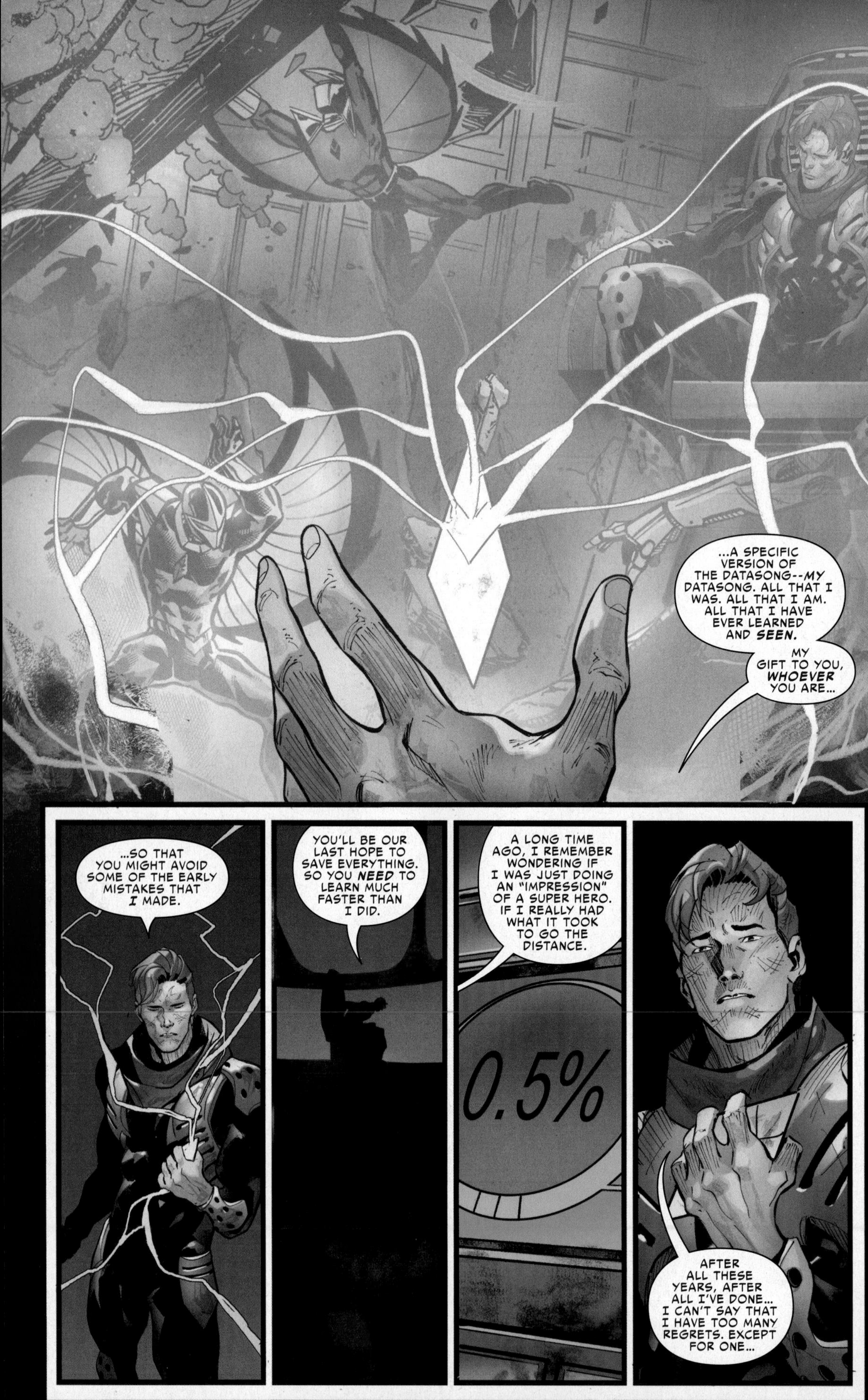

...A SPECIFIC VERSION OF THE DATASONG--MY DATASONG. ALL THAT I WAS. ALL THAT I AM. ALL THAT I HAVE EVER LEARNED AND SEEN.
MY GIFT TO YOU, WHOEVER YOU ARE...
...SO THAT YOU MIGHT AVOID SOME OF THE EARLY MISTAKES THAT I MADE.
YOU'LL BE OUR LAST HOPE TO SAVE EVERYTHING. SO YOU NEED TO LEARN MUCH FASTER THAN I DID.
A LONG TIME AGO, I REMEMBER WONDERING IF I WAS JUST DOING AN "IMPRESSION" OF A SUPER HERO. IF I REALLY HAD WHAT IT TOOK TO GO THE DISTANCE.
0.5%
AFTER ALL THESE YEARS, AFTER ALL I'VE DONE... I CAN'T SAY THAT I HAVE TOO MANY REGRETS. EXCEPT FOR ONE...

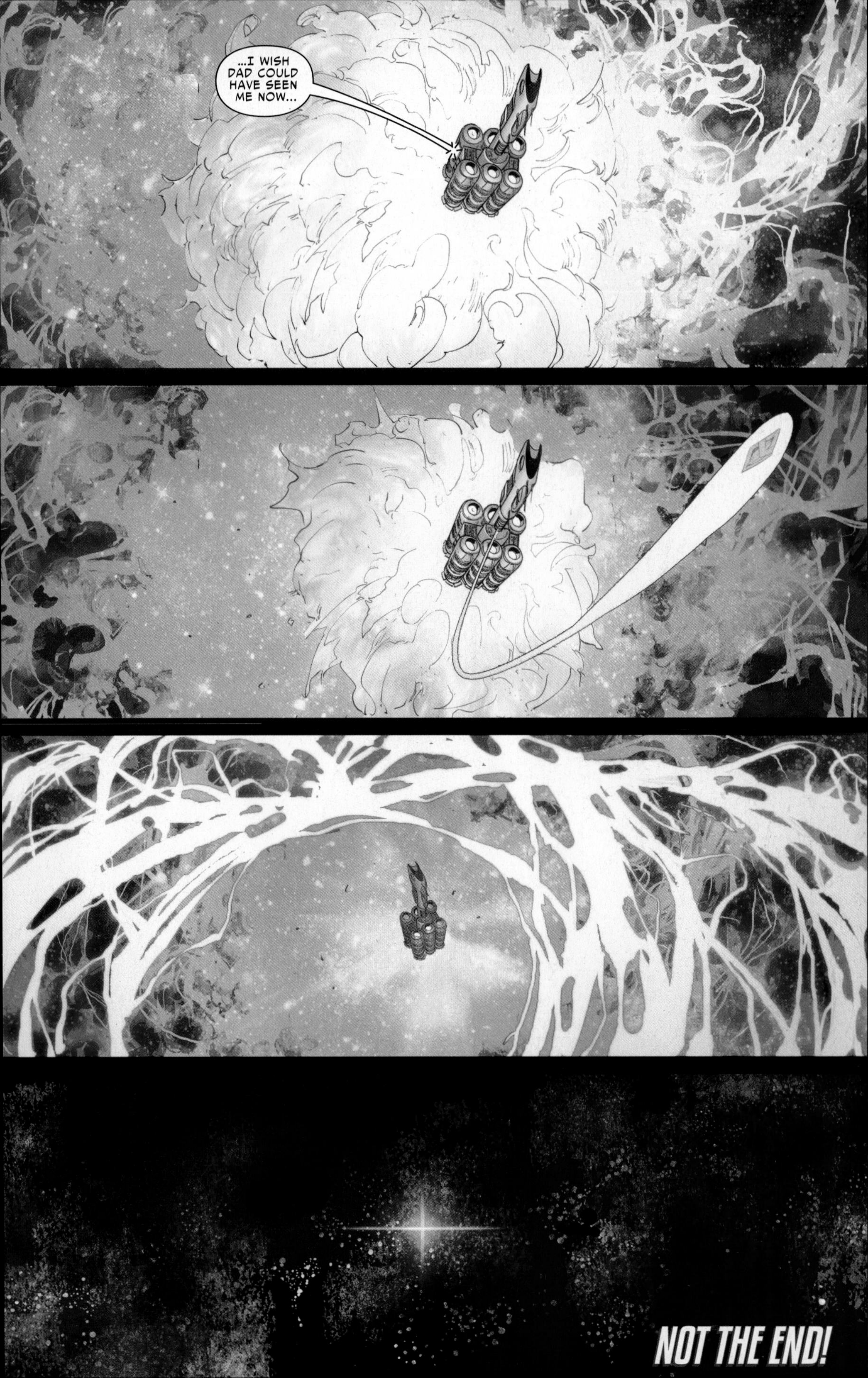
...I WISH DAD COULD HAVE SEEN ME NOW...
NOT THE END!

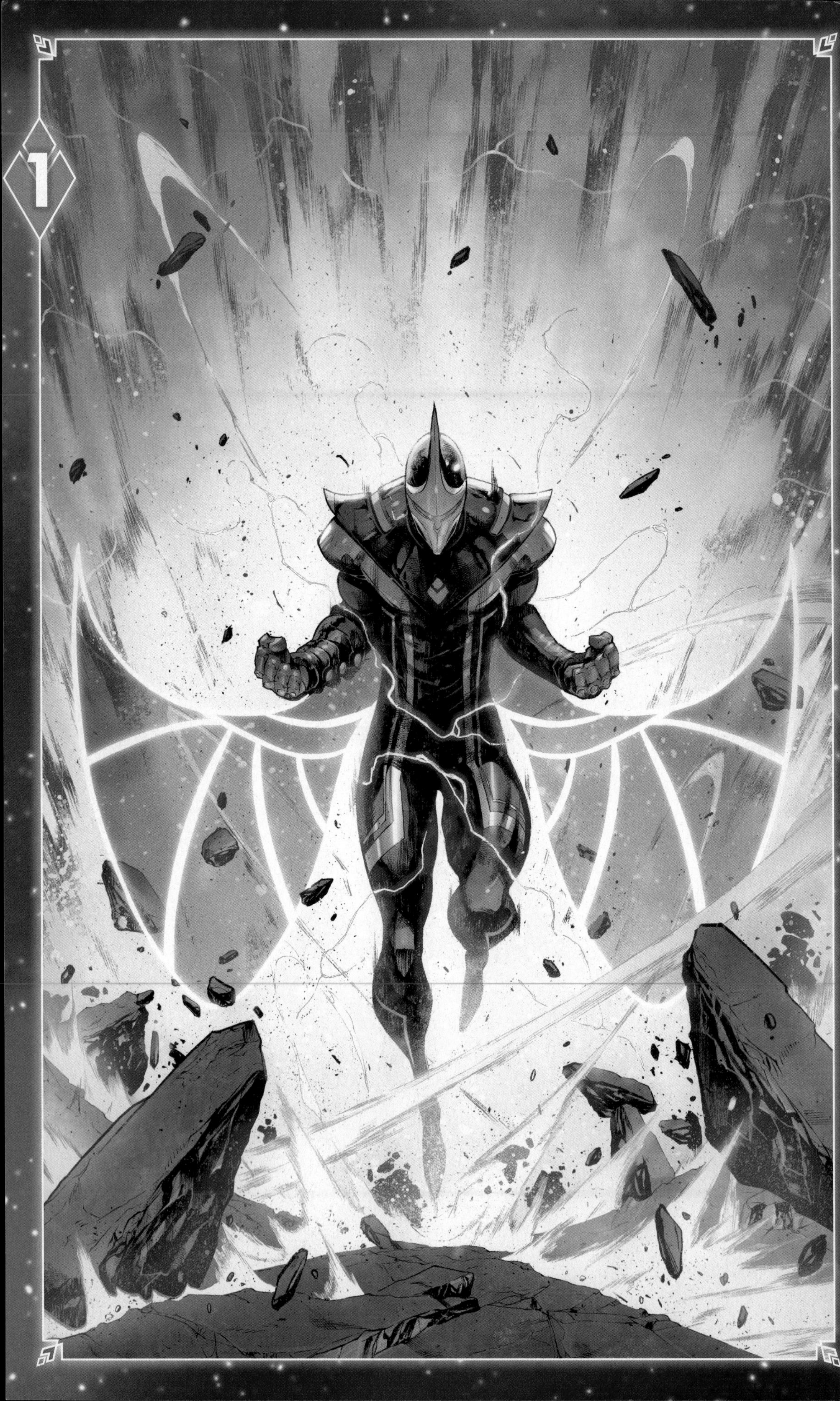
1

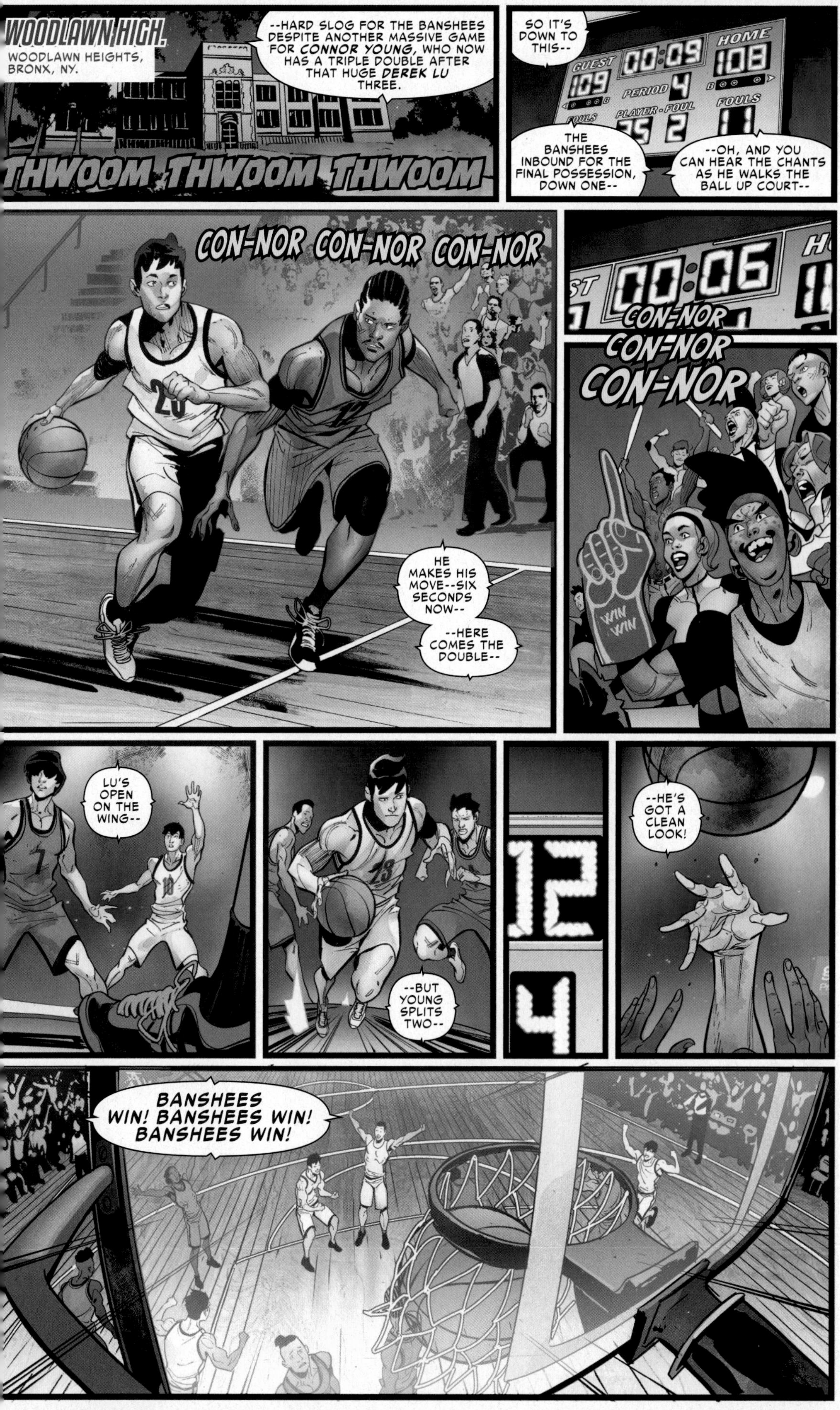
WOODLAWN HIGH.
WOODLAWN HEIGHTS, BRONX, NY.
--HARD SLOG FOR THE BANSHEES DESPITE ANOTHER MASSIVE GAME FOR CONNOR YOUNG, WHO NOW HAS A TRIPLE DOUBLE AFTER THAT HUGE DEREK LU THREE.
THWOOM THWOOM THWOOM
SO IT'S DOWN TO THIS--
GUEST 109 00:09 HOME 108
PERIOD 4
FOULS PLAYER-FOUL 25 2 FOULS 11
THE BANSHEES INBOUND FOR THE FINAL POSSESSION, DOWN ONE--
--OH, AND YOU CAN HEAR THE CHANTS AS HE WALKS THE BALL UP COURT--
CON-NOR CON-NOR CON-NOR
HE MAKES HIS MOVE--SIX SECONDS NOW--
--HERE COMES THE DOUBLE--
00:06
CON-NOR
CON-NOR
CON-NOR
WIN WIN
LU'S OPEN ON THE WING--
--BUT YOUNG SPLITS TWO--
12
4
--HE'S GOT A CLEAN LOOK!
BANSHEES WIN! BANSHEES WIN! BANSHEES WIN!

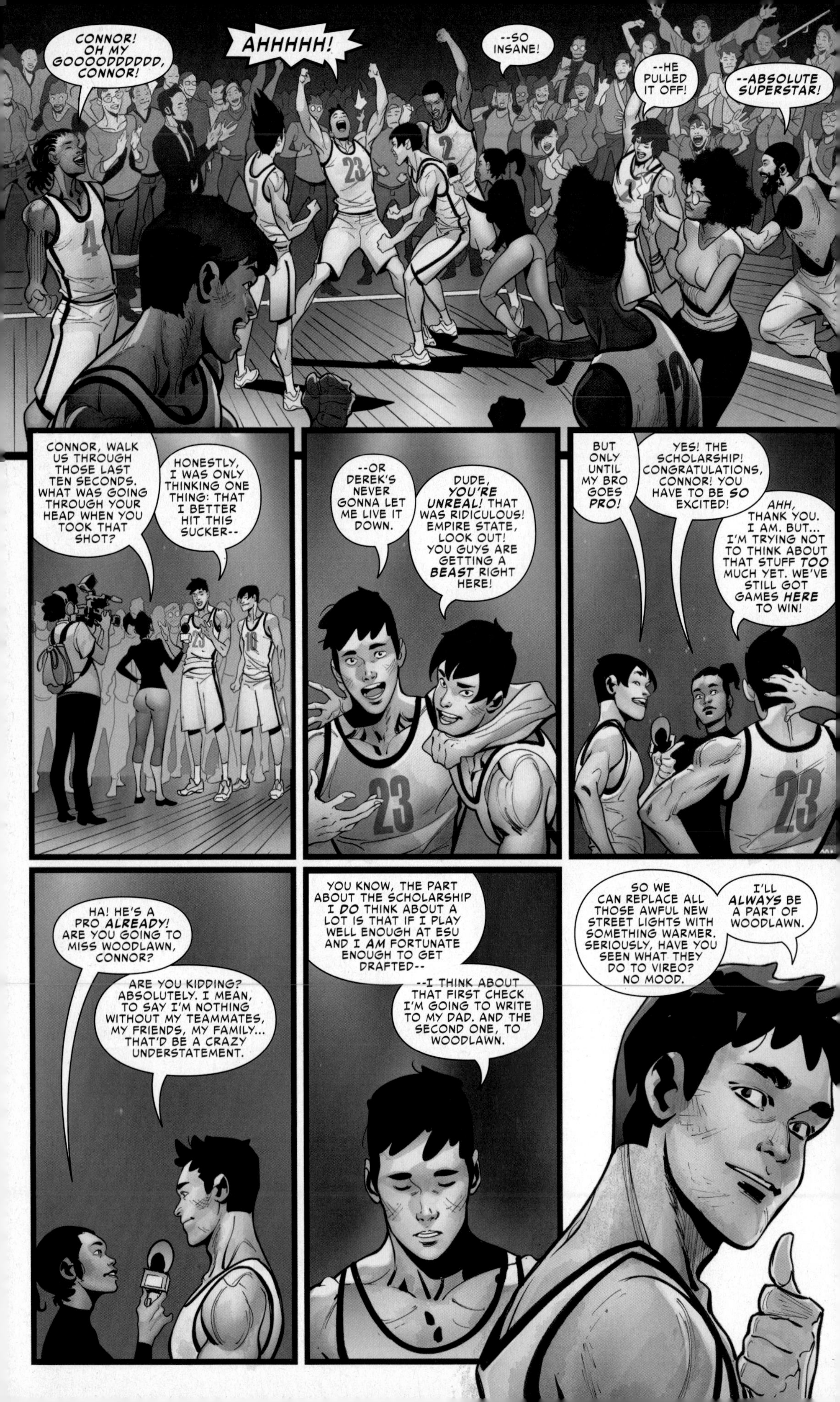

CONNOR! OH MY GOOOODDDDDD, CONNOR!
AHHHHH!
--SO INSANE!
--HE PULLED IT OFF!
--ABSOLUTE SUPERSTAR!
CONNOR, WALK US THROUGH THOSE LAST TEN SECONDS. WHAT WAS GOING THROUGH YOUR HEAD WHEN YOU TOOK THAT SHOT?
HONESTLY, I WAS ONLY THINKING ONE THING: THAT I BETTER HIT THIS SUCKER--
--OR DEREK'S NEVER GONNA LET ME LIVE IT DOWN.
DUDE, YOU'RE UNREAL! THAT WAS RIDICULOUS! EMPIRE STATE, LOOK OUT! YOU GUYS ARE GETTING A BEAST RIGHT HERE!
BUT ONLY UNTIL MY BRO GOES PRO!
YES! THE SCHOLARSHIP! CONGRATULATIONS, CONNOR! YOU HAVE TO BE SO EXCITED!
AHH, THANK YOU. I AM. BUT... I'M TRYING NOT TO THINK ABOUT THAT STUFF TOO MUCH YET. WE'VE STILL GOT GAMES HERE TO WIN!
HA! HE'S A PRO ALREADY! ARE YOU GOING TO MISS WOODLAWN, CONNOR?
ARE YOU KIDDING? ABSOLUTELY. I MEAN, TO SAY I'M NOTHING WITHOUT MY TEAMMATES, MY FRIENDS, MY FAMILY... THAT'D BE A CRAZY UNDERSTATEMENT.
YOU KNOW, THE PART ABOUT THE SCHOLARSHIP I DO THINK ABOUT A LOT IS THAT IF I PLAY WELL ENOUGH AT ESU AND I AM FORTUNATE ENOUGH TO GET DRAFTED--
--I THINK ABOUT THAT FIRST CHECK I'M GOING TO WRITE TO MY DAD. AND THE SECOND ONE, TO WOODLAWN.
SO WE CAN REPLACE ALL THOSE AWFUL NEW STREET LIGHTS WITH SOMETHING WARMER. SERIOUSLY, HAVE YOU SEEN WHAT THEY DO TO VIREO? NO MOOD.
I'LL ALWAYS BE A PART OF WOODLAWN.

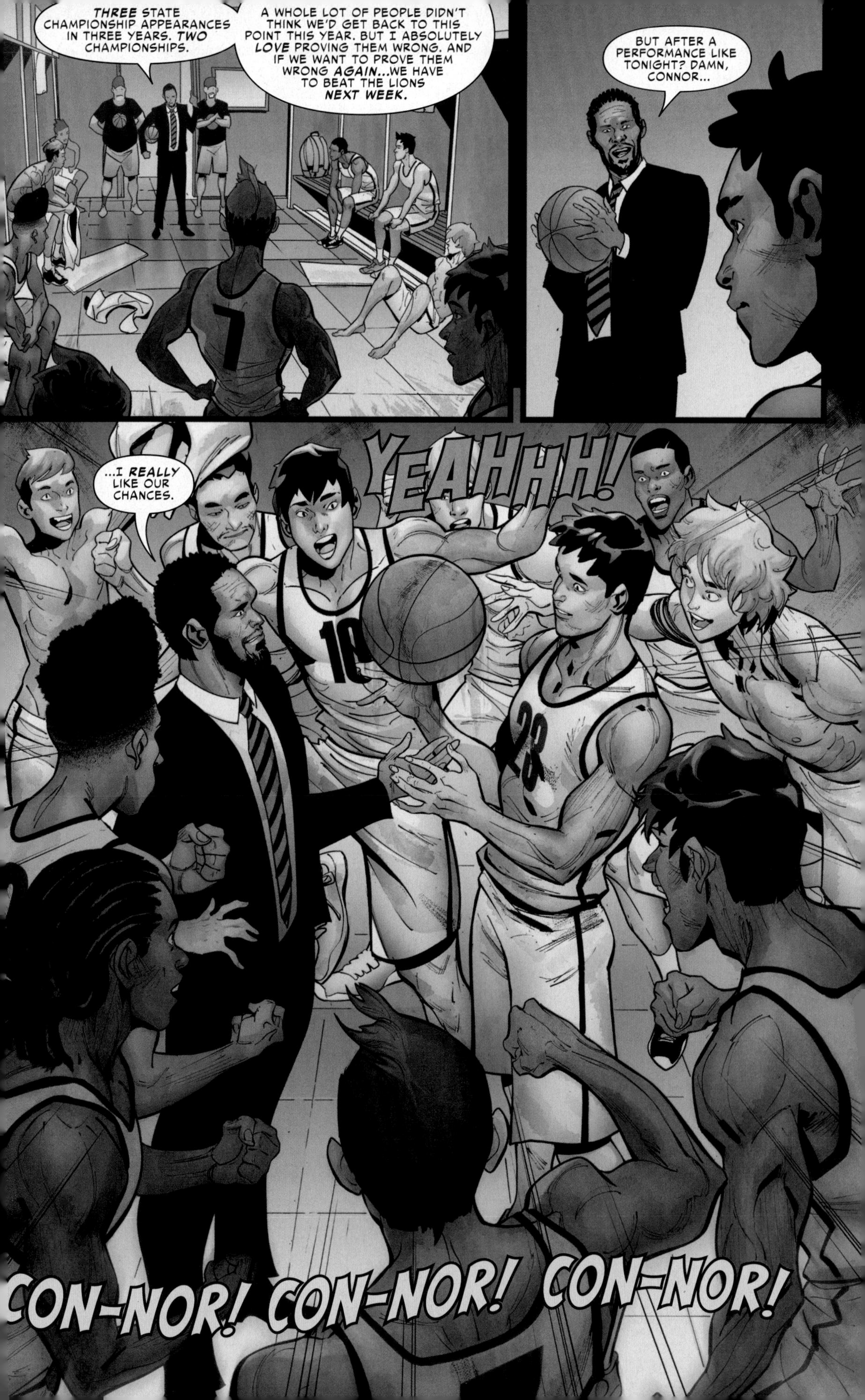
THREE STATE CHAMPIONSHIP APPEARANCES IN THREE YEARS. TWO CHAMPIONSHIPS.
A WHOLE LOT OF PEOPLE DIDN'T THINK WE'D GET BACK TO THIS POINT THIS YEAR. BUT I ABSOLUTELY LOVE PROVING THEM WRONG. AND IF WE WANT TO PROVE THEM WRONG AGAIN...WE HAVE TO BEAT THE LIONS NEXT WEEK.
BUT AFTER A PERFORMANCE LIKE TONIGHT? DAMN, CONNOR...
...I REALLY LIKE OUR CHANCES.
YEAHHH!
CON-NOR! CON-NOR! CON-NOR!

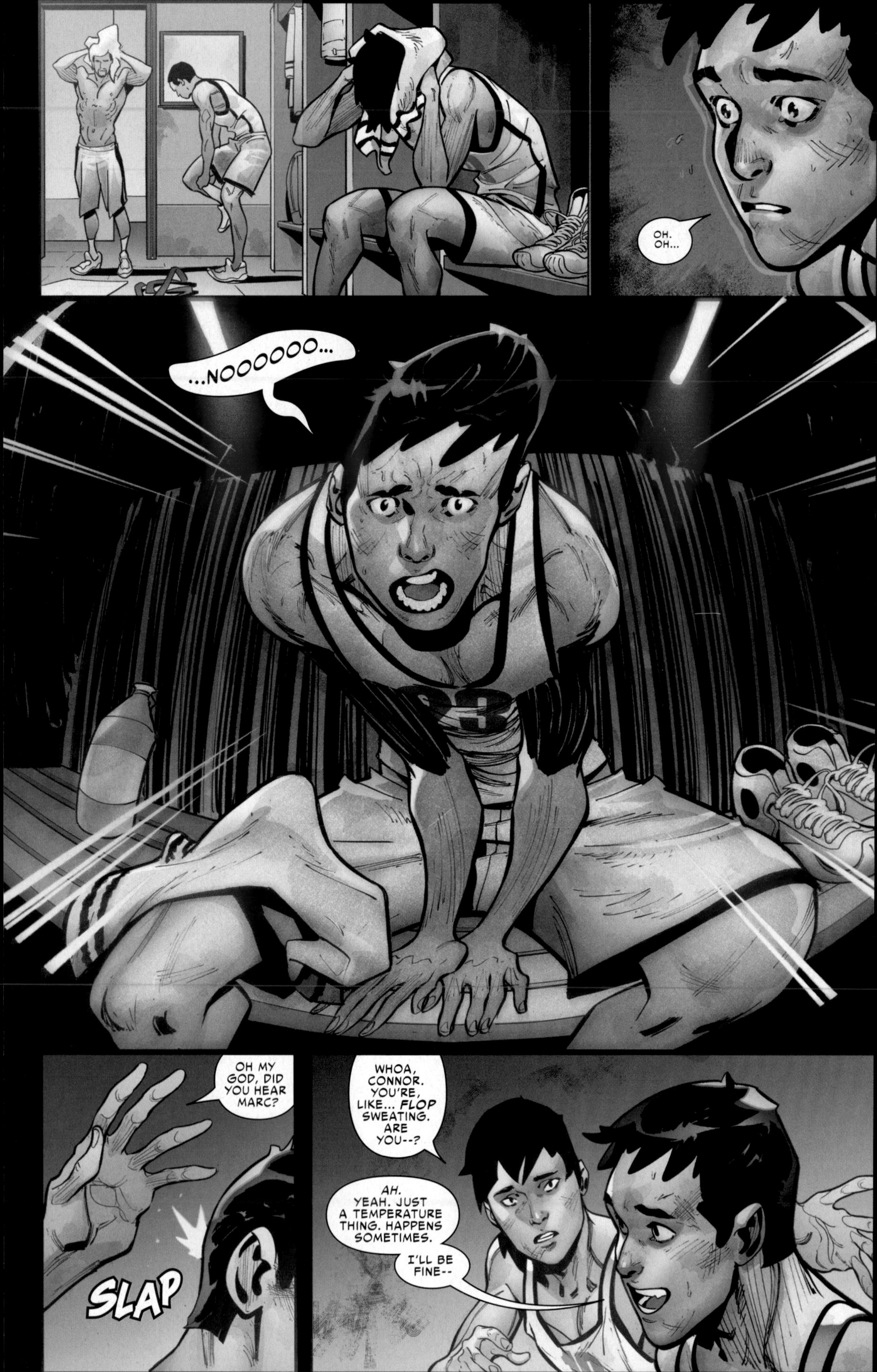
OH.
OH...
...NOOOOOO...
OH MY GOD, DID YOU HEAR MARC?
SLAP
WHOA, CONNOR. YOU'RE, LIKE... FLOP SWEATING. ARE YOU--?
AH. YEAH. JUST A TEMPERATURE THING. HAPPENS SOMETIMES.
I'LL BE FINE--

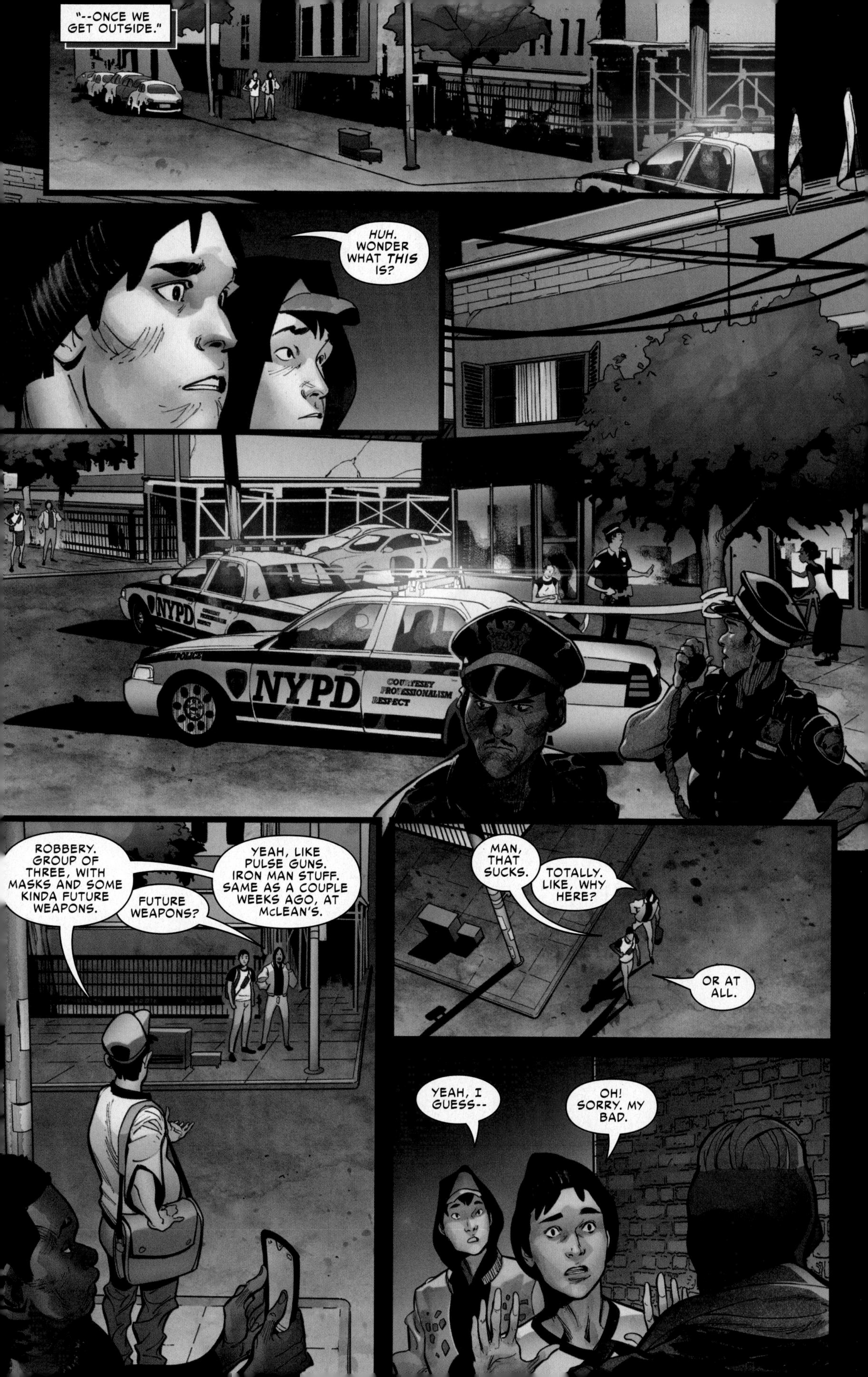
"--ONCE WE GET OUTSIDE."
HUH. WONDER WHAT THIS IS?
NYPD
COURTESY PROFESSIONALISM RESPECT
ROBBERY. GROUP OF THREE, WITH MASKS AND SOME KINDA FUTURE WEAPONS.
FUTURE WEAPONS?
YEAH, LIKE PULSE GUNS. IRON MAN STUFF. SAME AS A COUPLE WEEKS AGO, AT McLEAN'S.
MAN, THAT SUCKS.
TOTALLY. LIKE, WHY HERE?
OR AT ALL.
YEAH, I GUESS--
OH! SORRY. MY BAD.

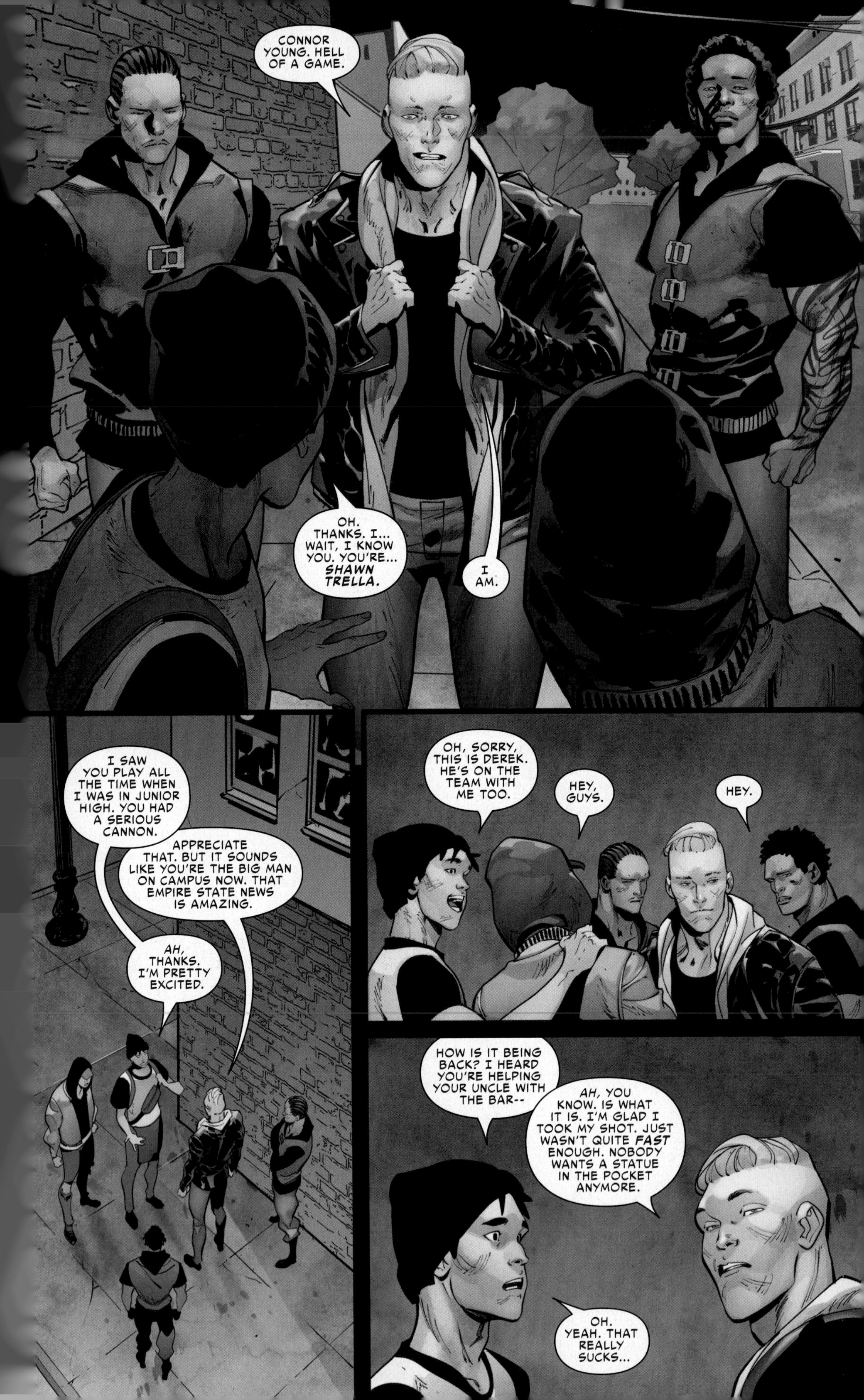

CONNOR YOUNG. HELL OF A GAME.
OH. THANKS. I... WAIT, I KNOW YOU. YOU'RE... **SHAWN TRELLA.**
I AM.
I SAW YOU PLAY ALL THE TIME WHEN I WAS IN JUNIOR HIGH. YOU HAD A SERIOUS CANNON.
APPRECIATE THAT. BUT IT SOUNDS LIKE YOU'RE THE BIG MAN ON CAMPUS NOW. THAT EMPIRE STATE NEWS IS AMAZING.
AH, THANKS. I'M PRETTY EXCITED.
OH, SORRY, THIS IS DEREK. HE'S ON THE TEAM WITH ME TOO.
HEY, GUYS.
HEY.
HOW IS IT BEING BACK? I HEARD YOU'RE HELPING YOUR UNCLE WITH THE BAR--
AH, YOU KNOW. IS WHAT IT IS. I'M GLAD I TOOK MY SHOT. JUST WASN'T QUITE ***FAST*** ENOUGH. NOBODY WANTS A STATUE IN THE POCKET ANYMORE.
OH. YEAH. THAT REALLY SUCKS...

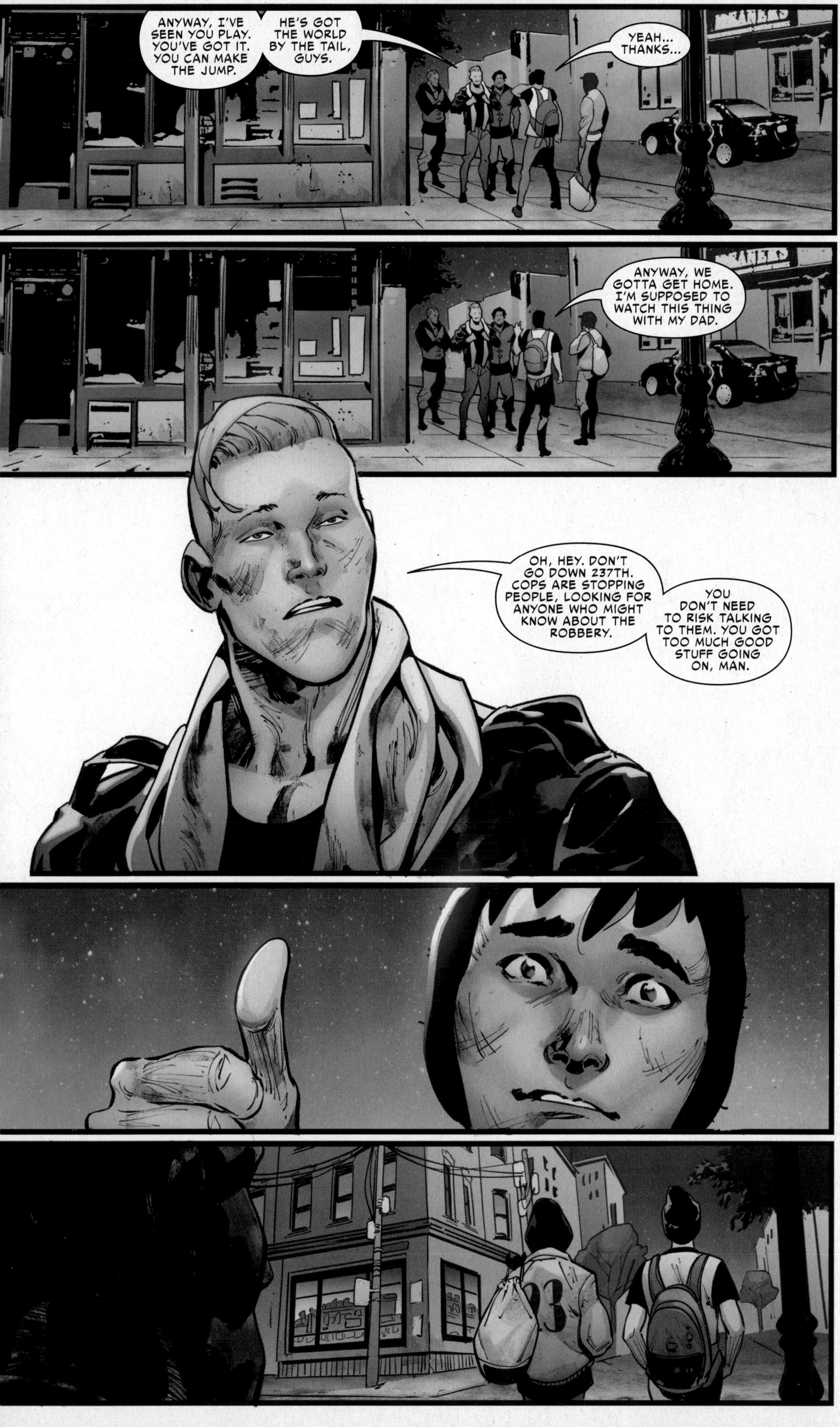

ANYWAY, I'VE SEEN YOU PLAY. YOU'VE GOT IT. YOU CAN MAKE THE JUMP.
HE'S GOT THE WORLD BY THE TAIL, GUYS.
YEAH... THANKS...
ANYWAY, WE GOTTA GET HOME. I'M SUPPOSED TO WATCH THIS THING WITH MY DAD.
OH, HEY. DON'T GO DOWN 237TH. COPS ARE STOPPING PEOPLE, LOOKING FOR ANYONE WHO MIGHT KNOW ABOUT THE ROBBERY.
YOU DON'T NEED TO RISK TALKING TO THEM. YOU GOT TOO MUCH GOOD STUFF GOING ON, MAN.

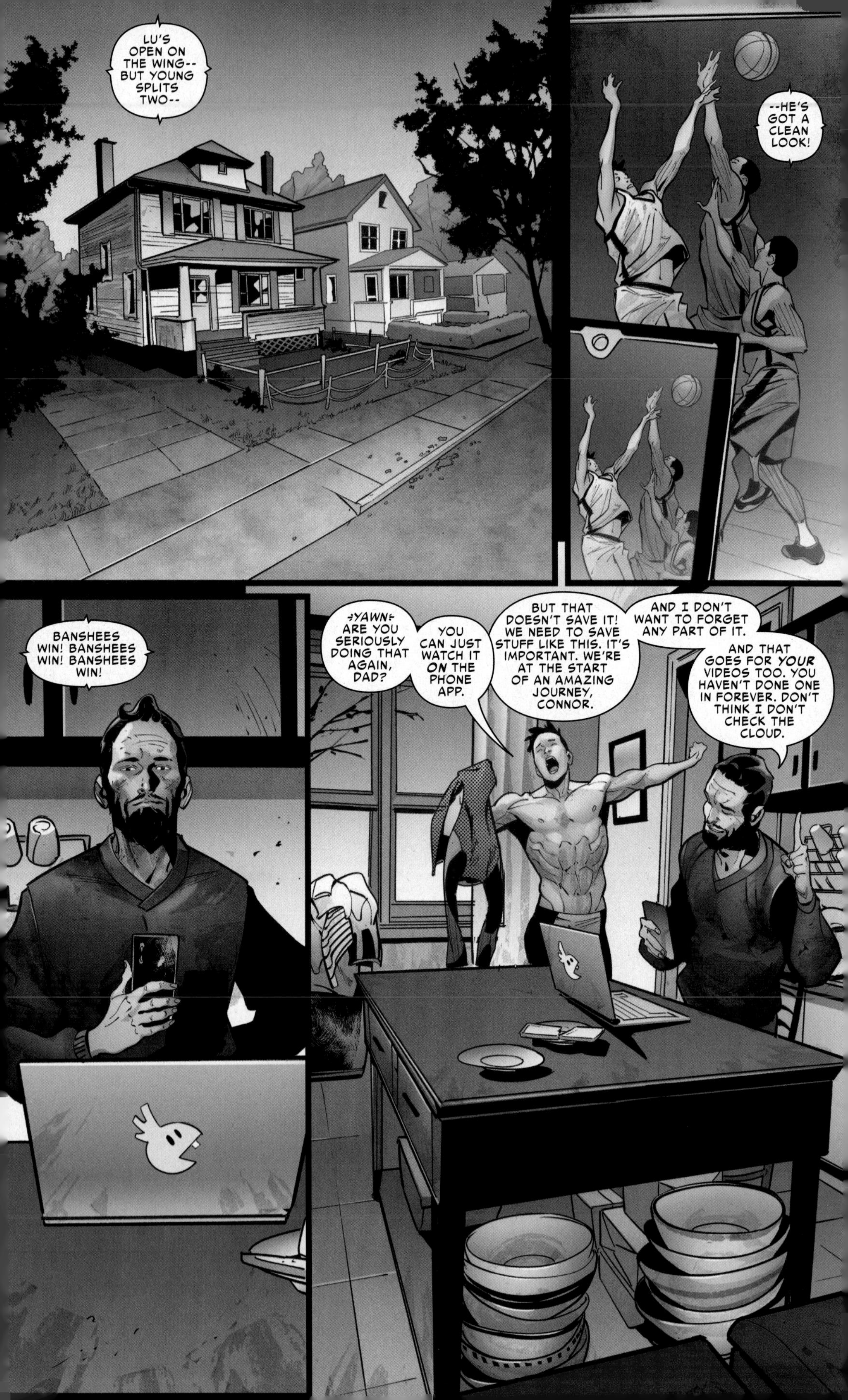

LU'S OPEN ON THE WING-- BUT YOUNG SPLITS TWO--
--HE'S GOT A CLEAN LOOK!
BANSHEES WIN! BANSHEES WIN! BANSHEES WIN!
YAWN ARE YOU SERIOUSLY DOING THAT AGAIN, DAD?
YOU CAN JUST WATCH IT ON THE PHONE APP.
BUT THAT DOESN'T SAVE IT! WE NEED TO SAVE STUFF LIKE THIS. IT'S IMPORTANT. WE'RE AT THE START OF AN AMAZING JOURNEY, CONNOR.
AND I DON'T WANT TO FORGET ANY PART OF IT.
AND THAT GOES FOR YOUR VIDEOS TOO. YOU HAVEN'T DONE ONE IN FOREVER. DON'T THINK I DON'T CHECK THE CLOUD.

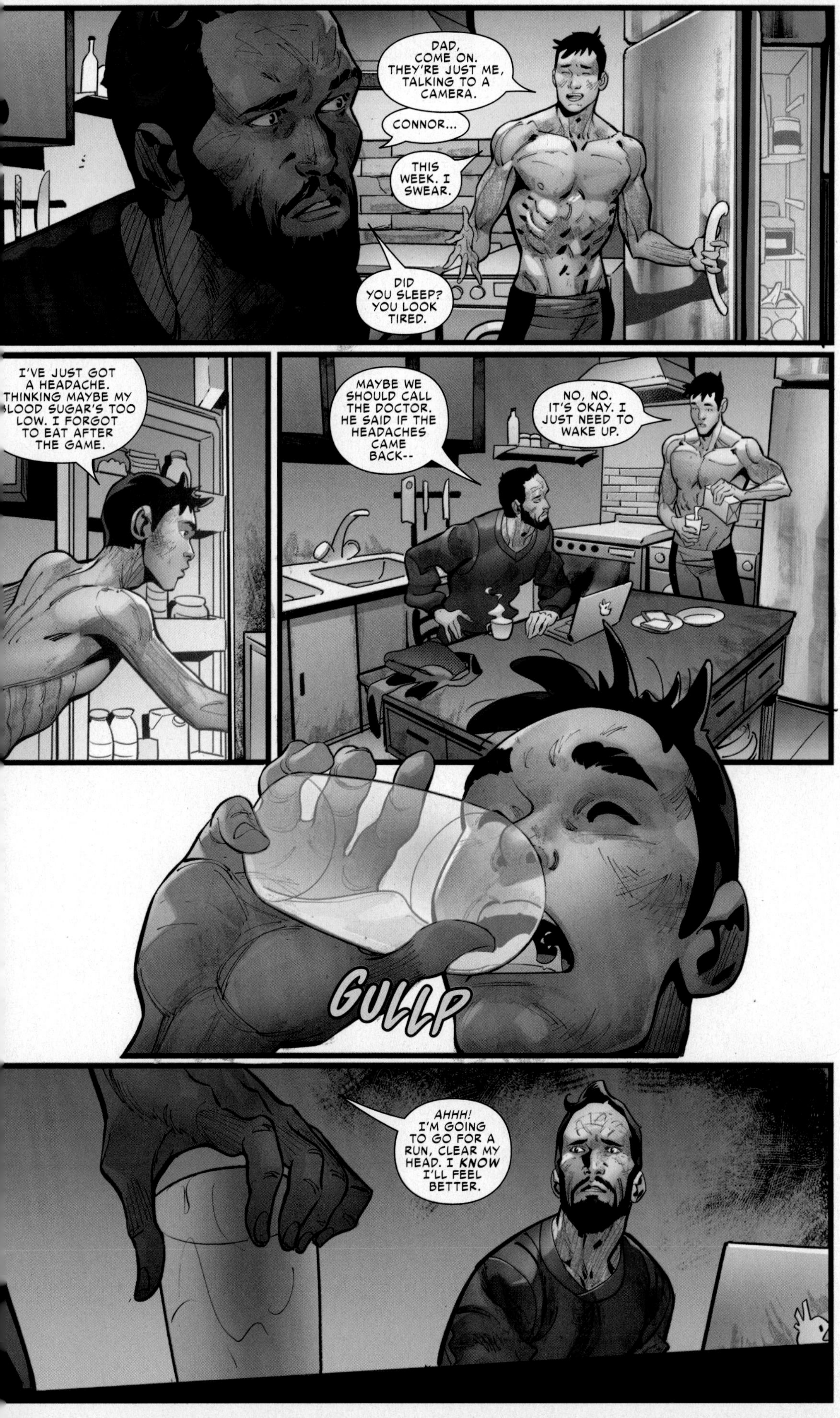
DAD, COME ON. THEY'RE JUST ME, TALKING TO A CAMERA.
CONNOR...
THIS WEEK. I SWEAR.
DID YOU SLEEP? YOU LOOK TIRED.
I'VE JUST GOT A HEADACHE. THINKING MAYBE MY BLOOD SUGAR'S TOO LOW. I FORGOT TO EAT AFTER THE GAME.
MAYBE WE SHOULD CALL THE DOCTOR. HE SAID IF THE HEADACHES CAME BACK--
NO, NO. IT'S OKAY. I JUST NEED TO WAKE UP.
GULLP
AHHH! I'M GOING TO GO FOR A RUN, CLEAR MY HEAD. I KNOW I'LL FEEL BETTER.

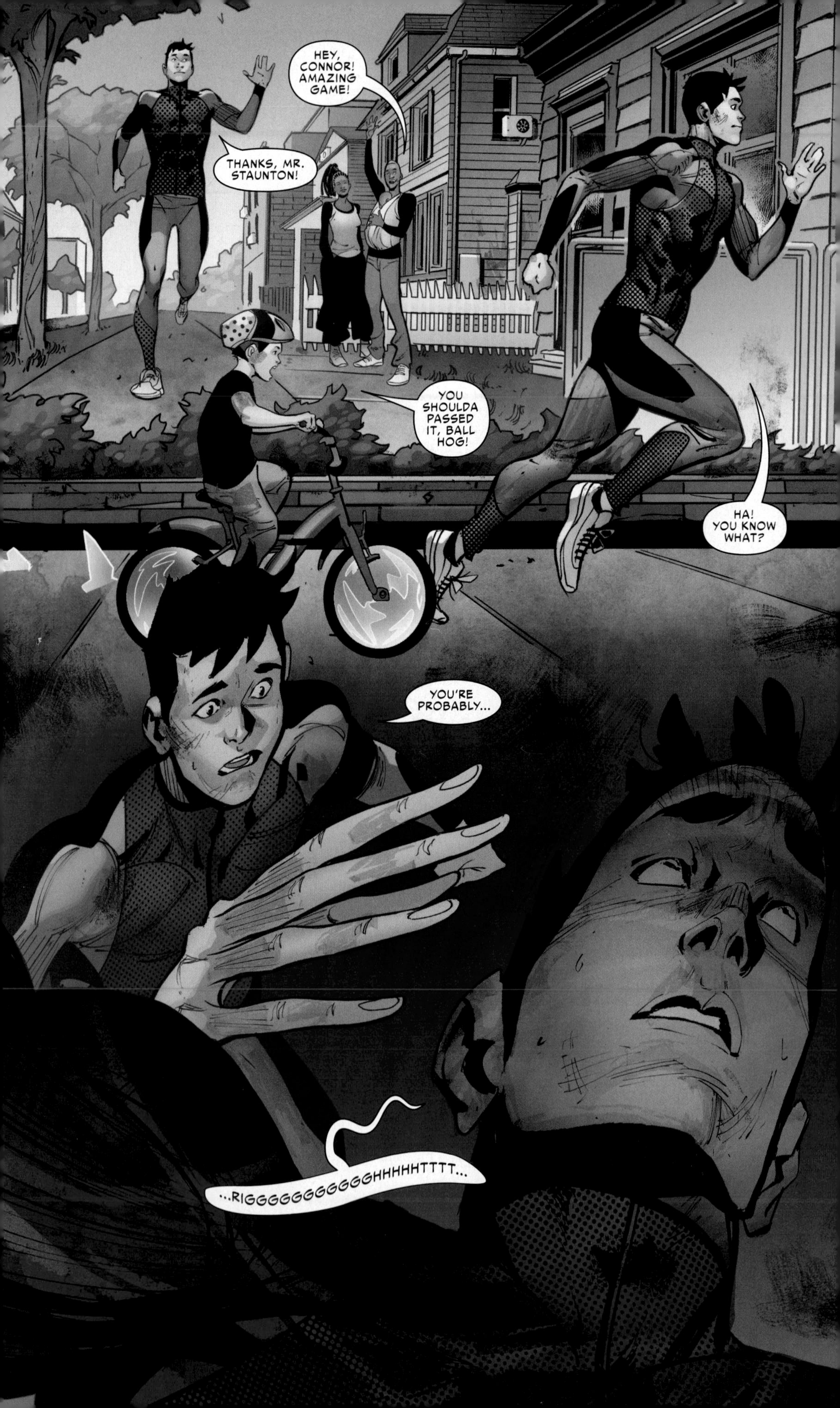
HEY, CONNOR! AMAZING GAME!
THANKS, MR. STAUNTON!
YOU SHOULDA PASSED IT, BALL HOG!
HA! YOU KNOW WHAT?
YOU'RE PROBABLY...
...RIGGGGGGGGGGGHHHHHTTTT...

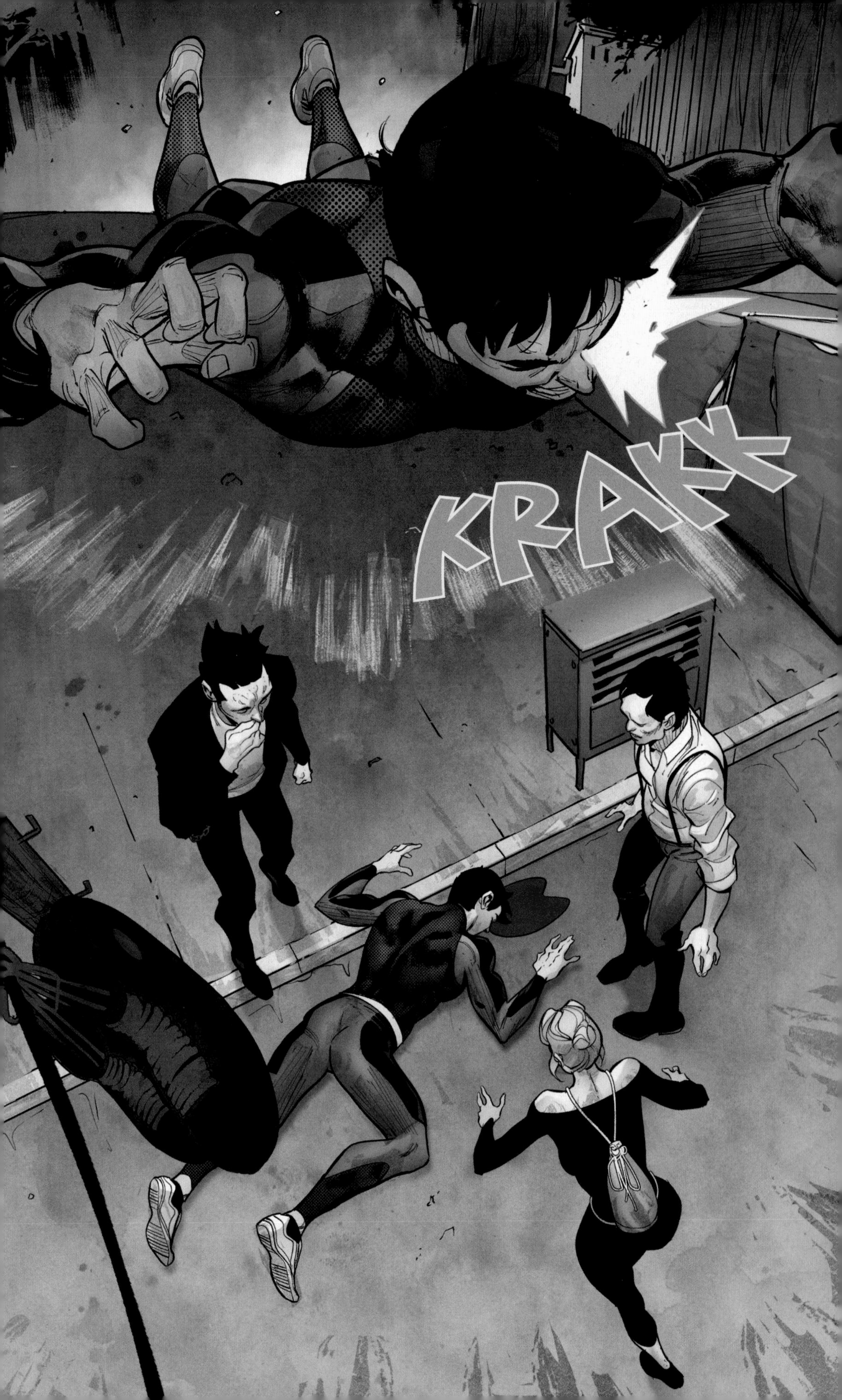
KRAKK

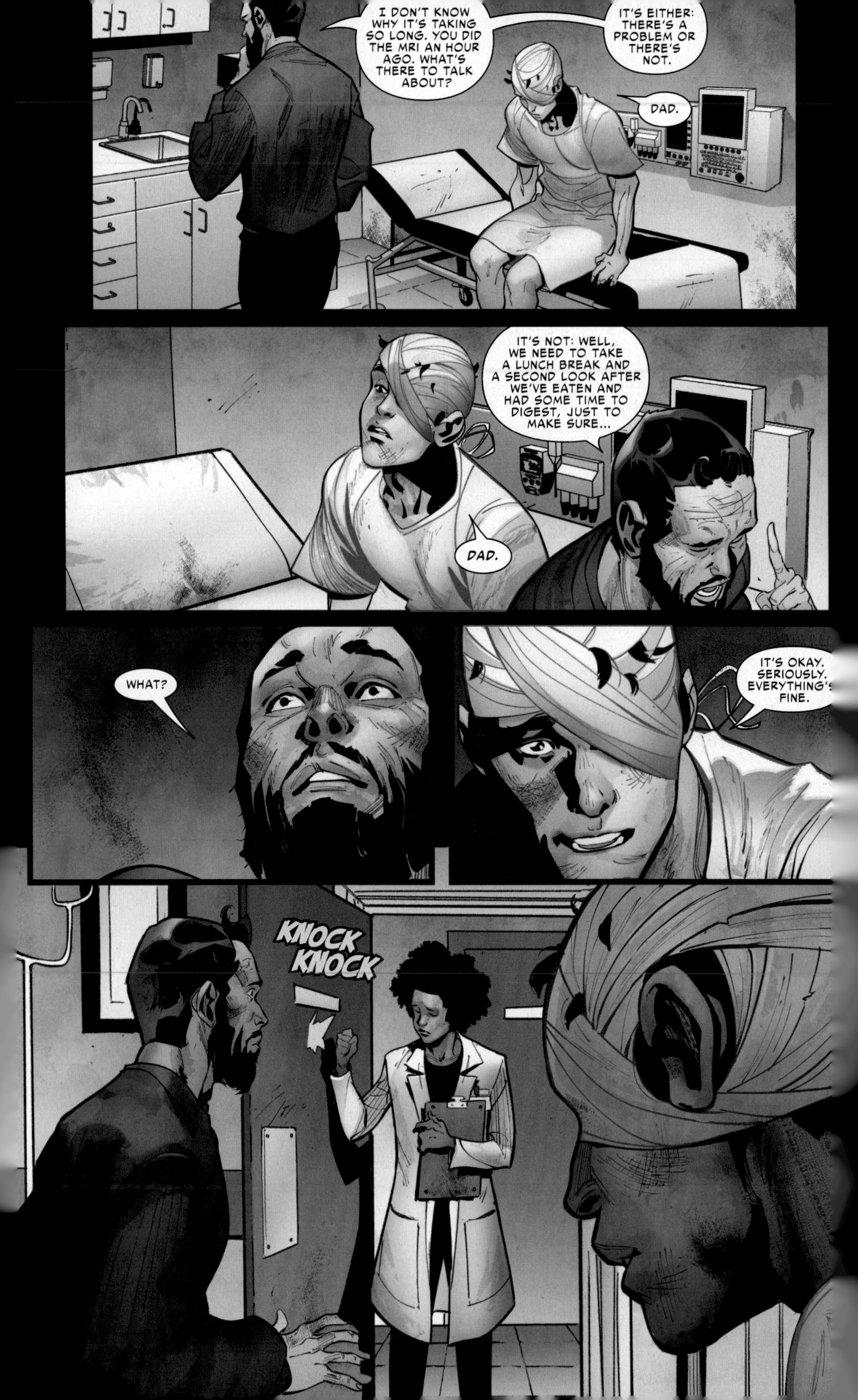
I DON'T KNOW WHY IT'S TAKING SO LONG. YOU DID THE MRI AN HOUR AGO. WHAT'S THERE TO TALK ABOUT?
IT'S EITHER: THERE'S A PROBLEM OR THERE'S NOT.
DAD.
IT'S NOT: WELL, WE NEED TO TAKE A LUNCH BREAK AND A SECOND LOOK AFTER WE'VE EATEN AND HAD SOME TIME TO DIGEST, JUST TO MAKE SURE...
DAD.
WHAT?
IT'S OKAY. SERIOUSLY. EVERYTHING'S FINE.
KNOCK KNOCK

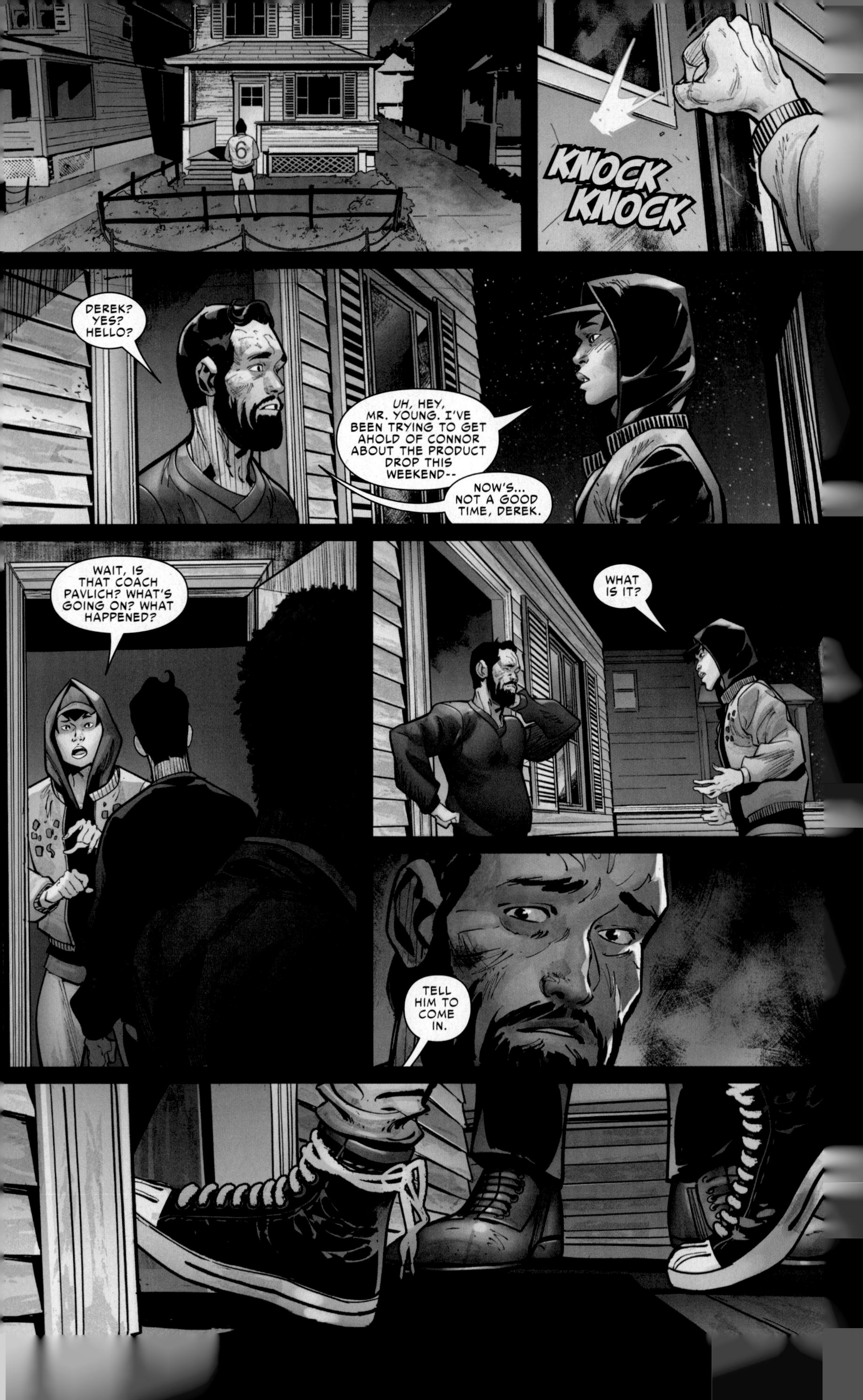
KNOCK KNOCK
DEREK? YES? HELLO?
UH, HEY, MR. YOUNG. I'VE BEEN TRYING TO GET AHOLD OF CONNOR ABOUT THE PRODUCT DROP THIS WEEKEND--
NOW'S... NOT A GOOD TIME, DEREK.
WAIT, IS THAT COACH PAVLICH? WHAT'S GOING ON? WHAT HAPPENED?
WHAT IS IT?
TELL HIM TO COME IN.

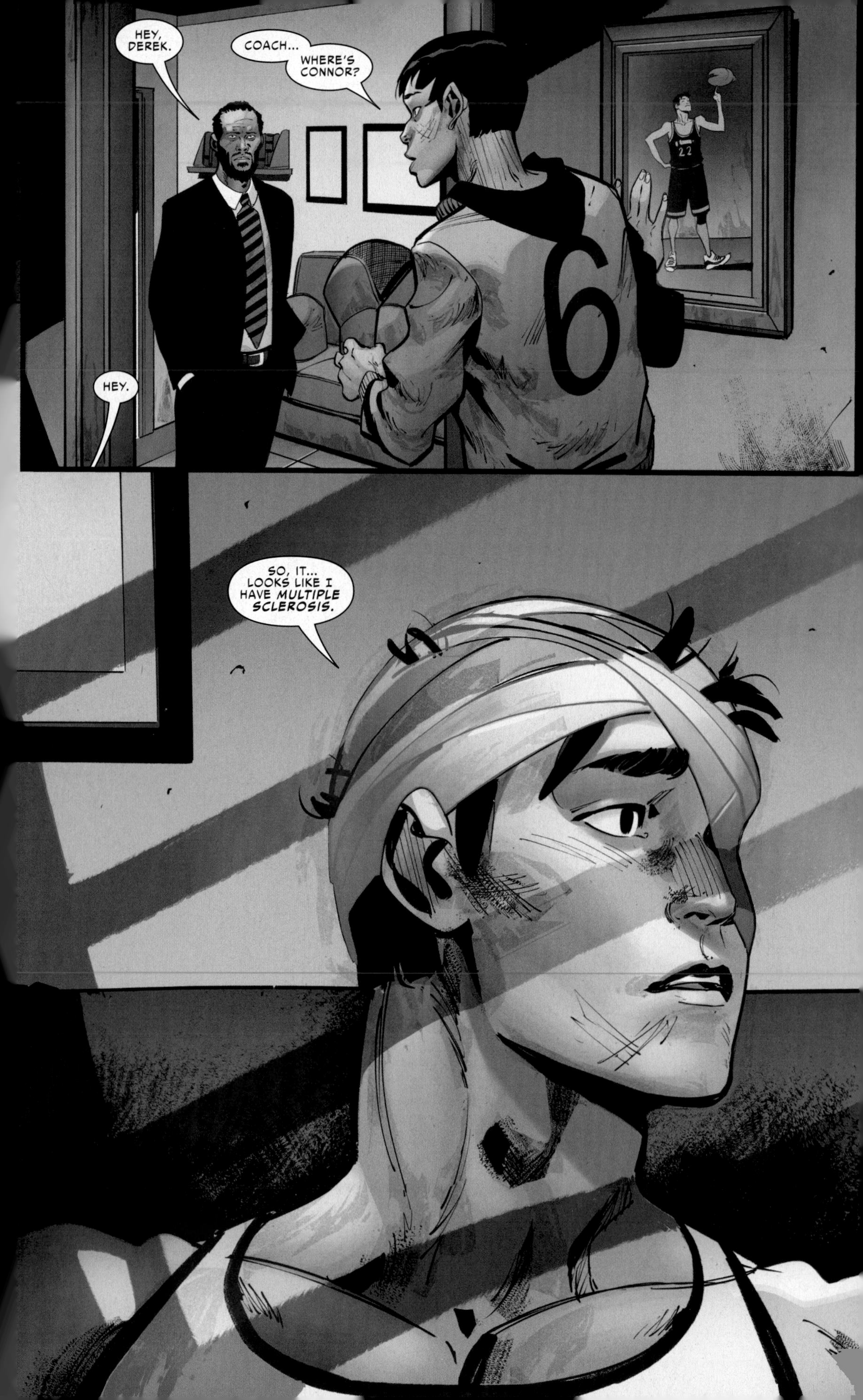
HEY, DEREK.
COACH... WHERE'S CONNOR?
HEY.
SO, IT... LOOKS LIKE I HAVE *MULTIPLE SCLEROSIS.*

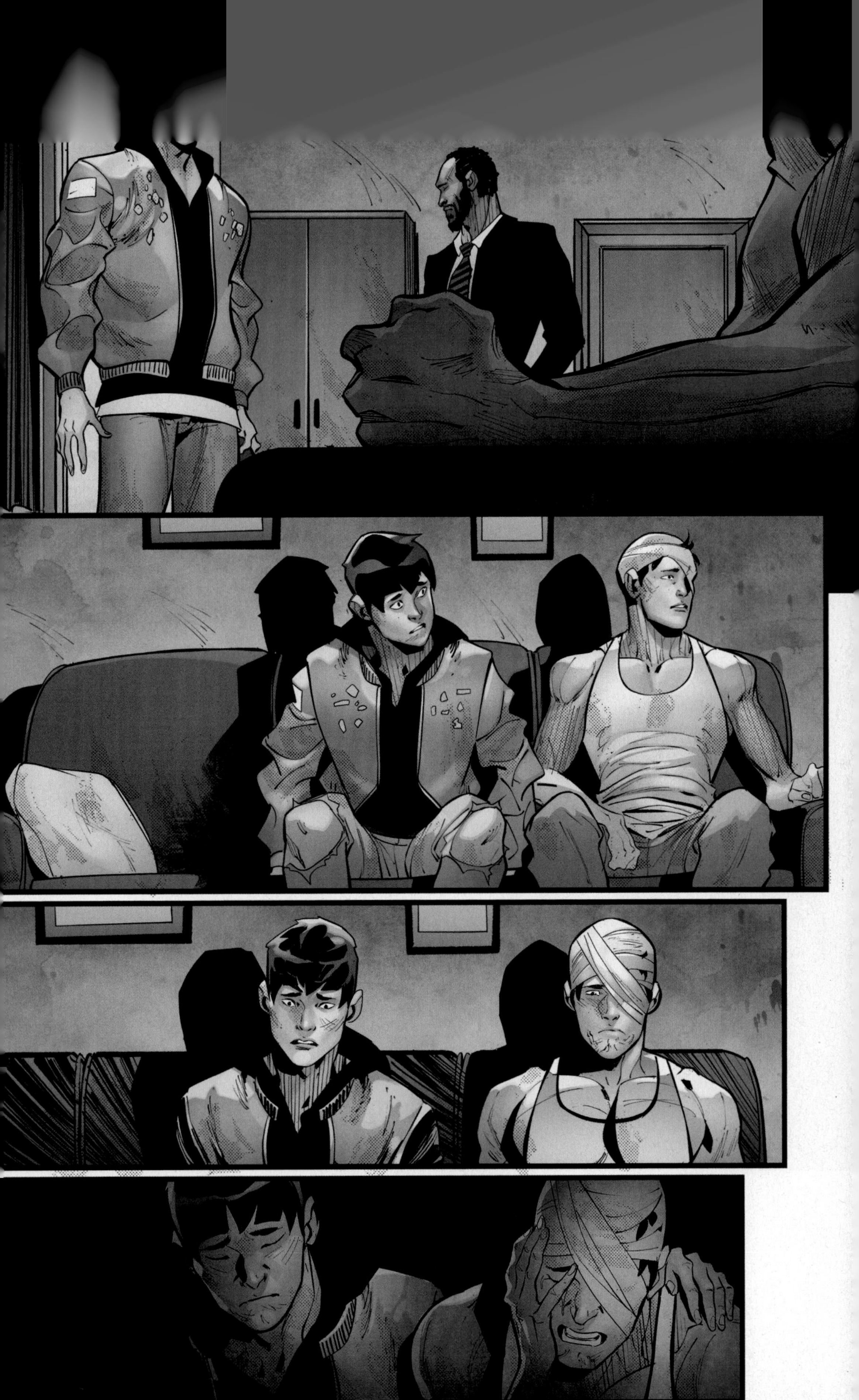

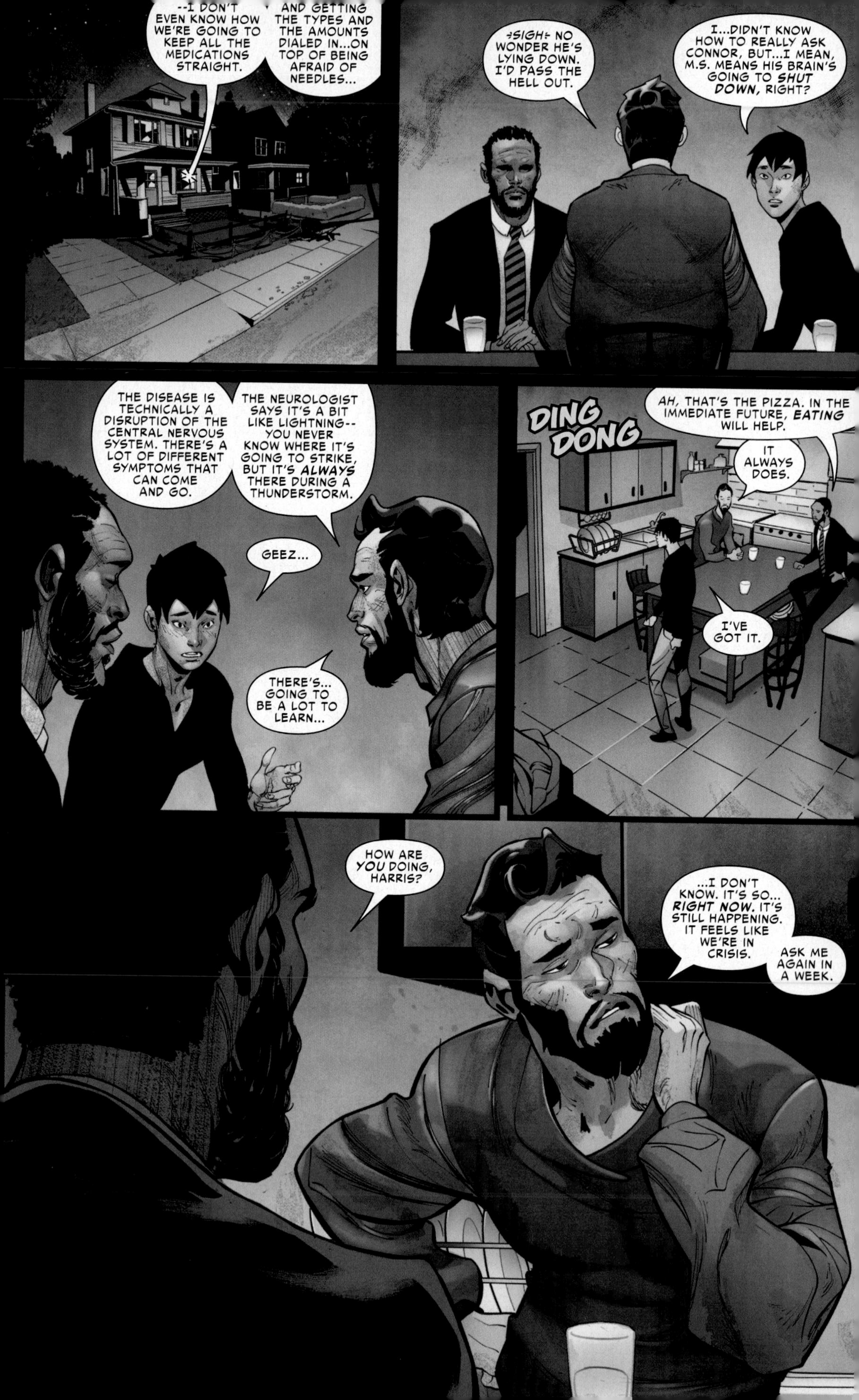
--I DON'T EVEN KNOW HOW WE'RE GOING TO KEEP ALL THE MEDICATIONS STRAIGHT.
AND GETTING THE TYPES AND THE AMOUNTS DIALED IN...ON TOP OF BEING AFRAID OF NEEDLES...
SIGH NO WONDER HE'S LYING DOWN. I'D PASS THE HELL OUT.
I...DIDN'T KNOW HOW TO REALLY ASK CONNOR, BUT...I MEAN, M.S. MEANS HIS BRAIN'S GOING TO SHUT DOWN, RIGHT?
THE DISEASE IS TECHNICALLY A DISRUPTION OF THE CENTRAL NERVOUS SYSTEM. THERE'S A LOT OF DIFFERENT SYMPTOMS THAT CAN COME AND GO.
THE NEUROLOGIST SAYS IT'S A BIT LIKE LIGHTNING--YOU NEVER KNOW WHERE IT'S GOING TO STRIKE, BUT IT'S ALWAYS THERE DURING A THUNDERSTORM.
GEEZ...
THERE'S... GOING TO BE A LOT TO LEARN...
DING DONG
AH, THAT'S THE PIZZA. IN THE IMMEDIATE FUTURE, EATING WILL HELP.
IT ALWAYS DOES.
I'VE GOT IT.
HOW ARE YOU DOING, HARRIS?
...I DON'T KNOW. IT'S SO... RIGHT NOW. IT'S STILL HAPPENING. IT FEELS LIKE WE'RE IN CRISIS.
ASK ME AGAIN IN A WEEK.

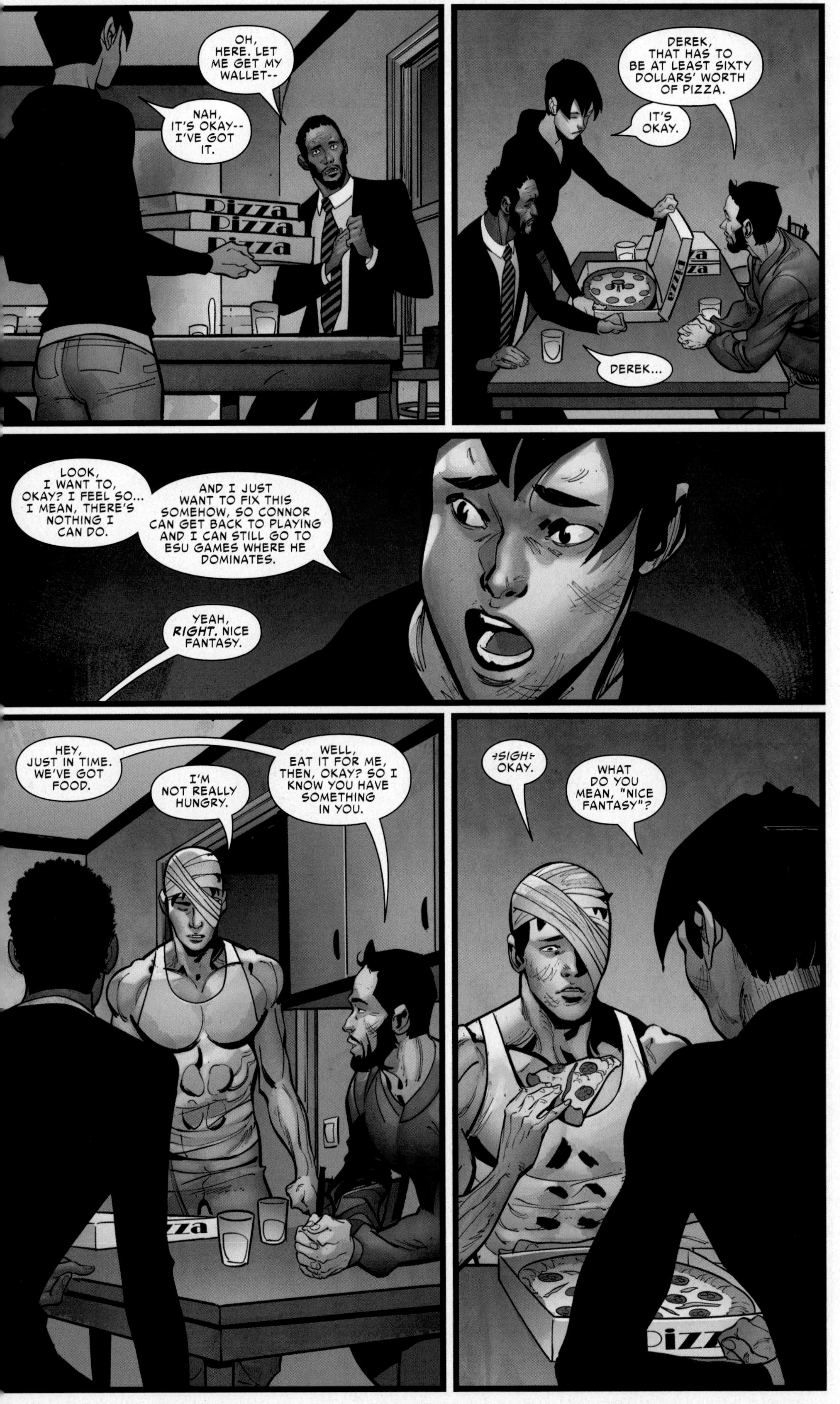
OH, HERE. LET ME GET MY WALLET--
NAH, IT'S OKAY-- I'VE GOT IT.
DEREK, THAT HAS TO BE AT LEAST SIXTY DOLLARS' WORTH OF PIZZA.
IT'S OKAY.
DEREK...
LOOK, I WANT TO, OKAY? I FEEL SO... I MEAN, THERE'S NOTHING I CAN DO.
AND I JUST WANT TO FIX THIS SOMEHOW, SO CONNOR CAN GET BACK TO PLAYING AND I CAN STILL GO TO ESU GAMES WHERE HE DOMINATES.
YEAH, RIGHT. NICE FANTASY.
HEY, JUST IN TIME. WE'VE GOT FOOD.
I'M NOT REALLY HUNGRY.
WELL, EAT IT FOR ME, THEN, OKAY? SO I KNOW YOU HAVE SOMETHING IN YOU.
=SIGH= OKAY.
WHAT DO YOU MEAN, "NICE FANTASY"?

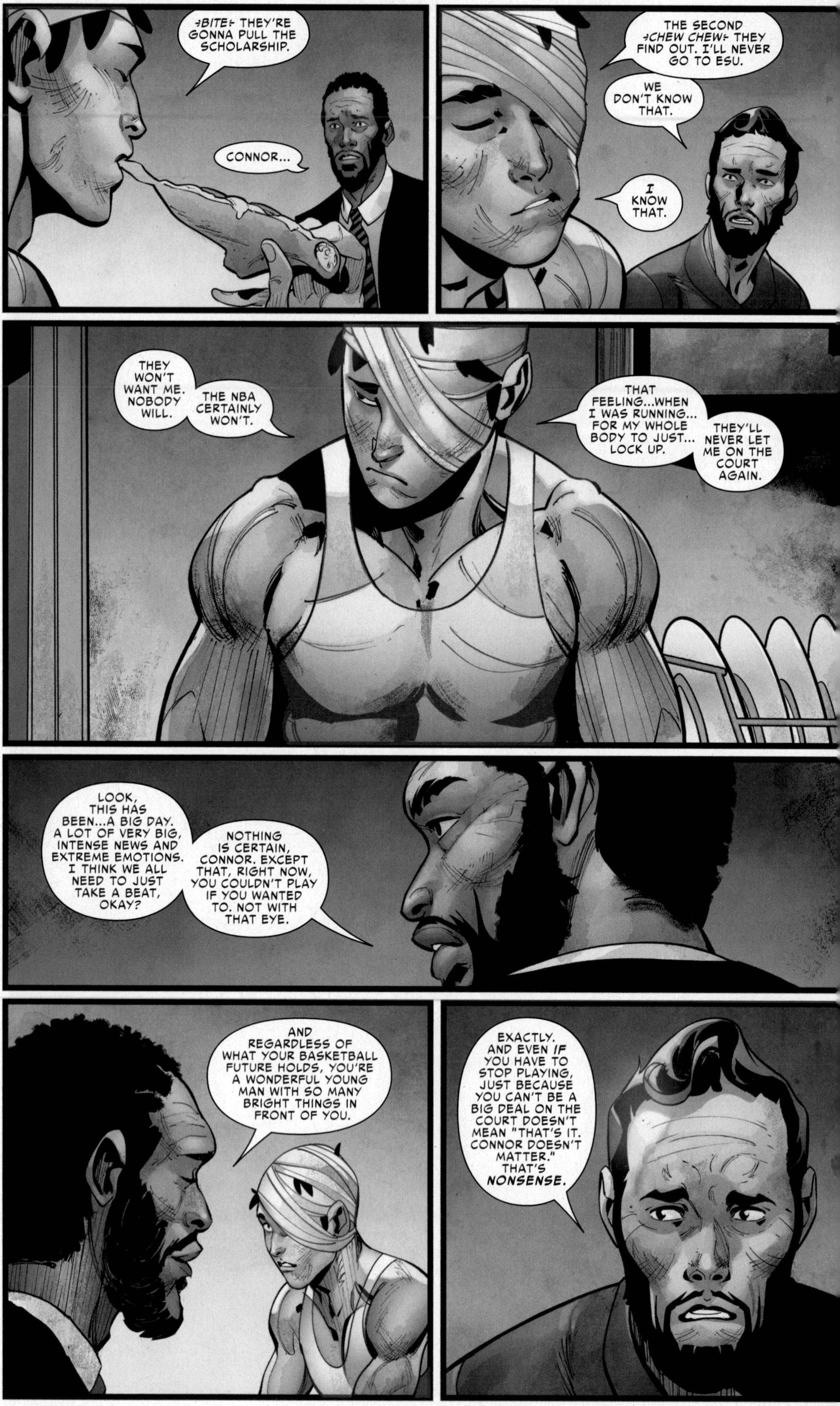

BITE THEY'RE GONNA PULL THE SCHOLARSHIP.
CONNOR...
THE SECOND *CHEW CHEW* THEY FIND OUT. I'LL NEVER GO TO ESU.
WE DON'T KNOW THAT.
I KNOW THAT.
THEY WON'T WANT ME. NOBODY WILL.
THE NBA CERTAINLY WON'T.
THAT FEELING...WHEN I WAS RUNNING... FOR MY WHOLE BODY TO JUST... LOCK UP.
THEY'LL NEVER LET ME ON THE COURT AGAIN.
LOOK, THIS HAS BEEN...A BIG DAY. A LOT OF VERY BIG, INTENSE NEWS AND EXTREME EMOTIONS. I THINK WE ALL NEED TO JUST TAKE A BEAT, OKAY?
NOTHING IS CERTAIN, CONNOR. EXCEPT THAT, RIGHT NOW, YOU COULDN'T PLAY IF YOU WANTED TO. NOT WITH THAT EYE.
AND REGARDLESS OF WHAT YOUR BASKETBALL FUTURE HOLDS, YOU'RE A WONDERFUL YOUNG MAN WITH SO MANY BRIGHT THINGS IN FRONT OF YOU.
EXACTLY. AND EVEN *IF* YOU HAVE TO STOP PLAYING, JUST BECAUSE YOU CAN'T BE A BIG DEAL ON THE COURT DOESN'T MEAN "THAT'S IT. CONNOR DOESN'T MATTER." THAT'S ***NONSENSE***.

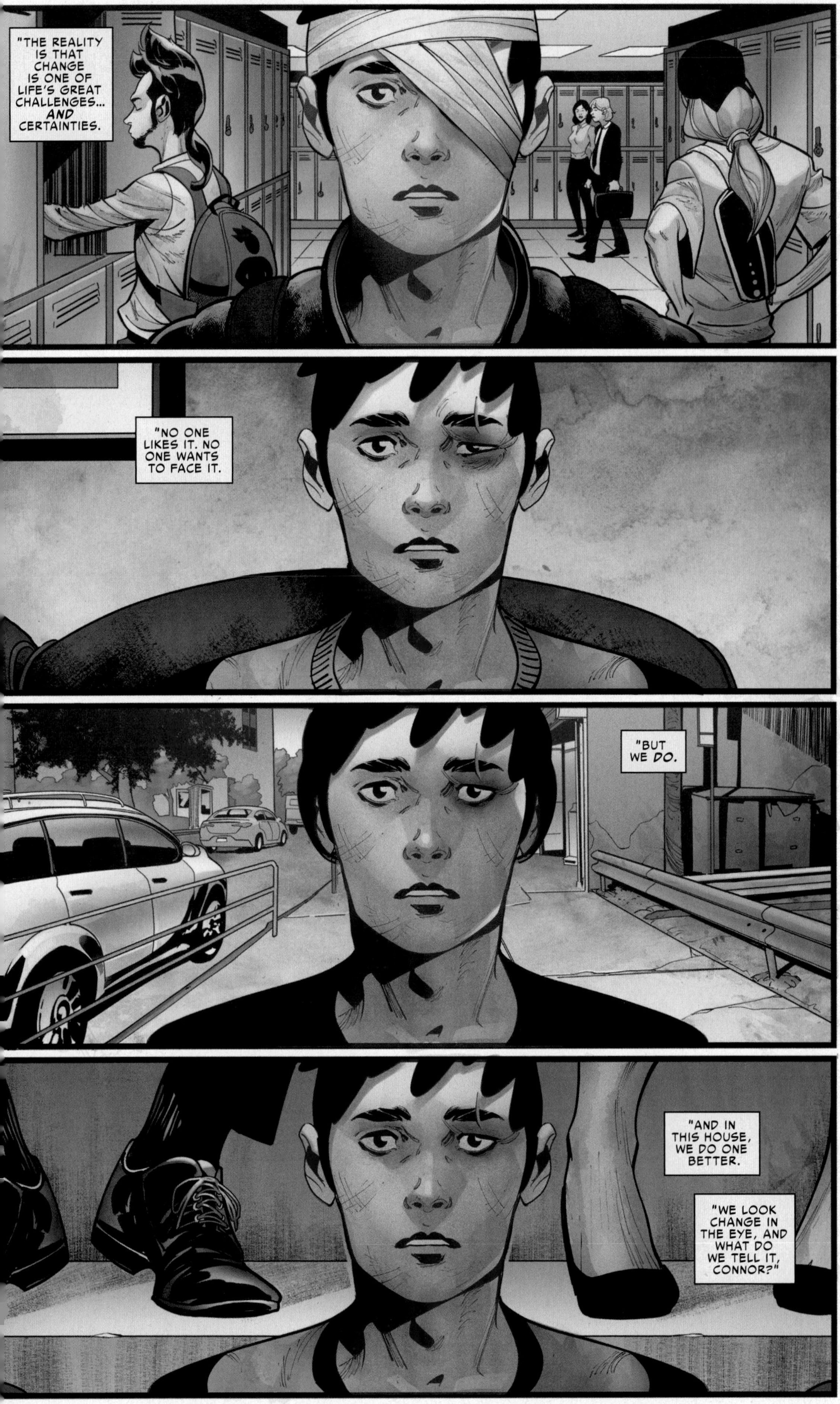
"THE REALITY IS THAT CHANGE IS ONE OF LIFE'S GREAT CHALLENGES... AND CERTAINTIES.
"NO ONE LIKES IT. NO ONE WANTS TO FACE IT.
"BUT WE DO.
"AND IN THIS HOUSE, WE DO ONE BETTER.
"WE LOOK CHANGE IN THE EYE, AND WHAT DO WE TELL IT, CONNOR?"

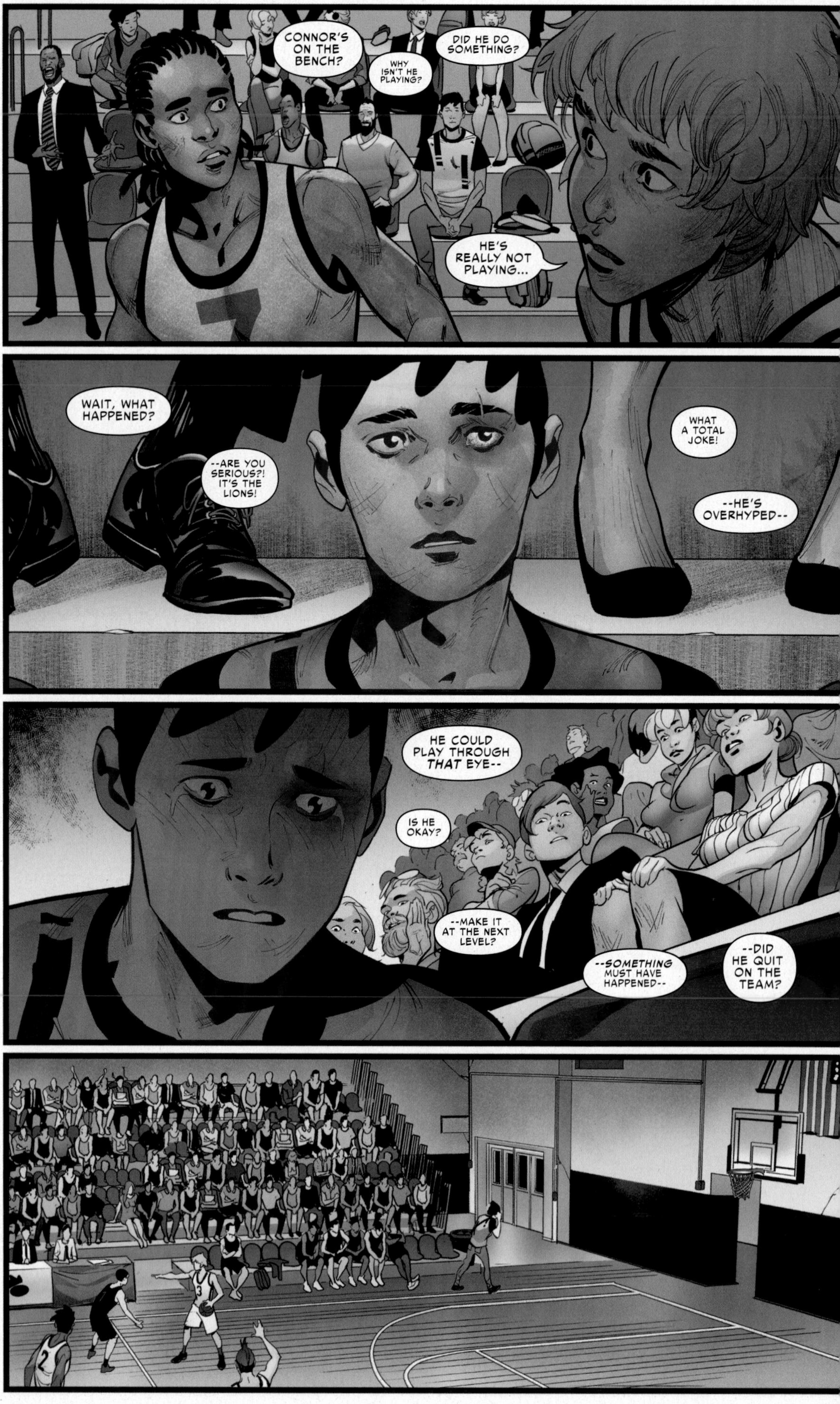
CONNOR'S ON THE BENCH?
WHY ISN'T HE PLAYING?
DID HE DO SOMETHING?
HE'S REALLY NOT PLAYING...
WAIT, WHAT HAPPENED?
--ARE YOU SERIOUS?! IT'S THE LIONS!
WHAT A TOTAL JOKE!
--HE'S OVERHYPED--
HE COULD PLAY THROUGH THAT EYE--
IS HE OKAY?
--MAKE IT AT THE NEXT LEVEL?
--SOMETHING MUST HAVE HAPPENED--
--DID HE QUIT ON THE TEAM?

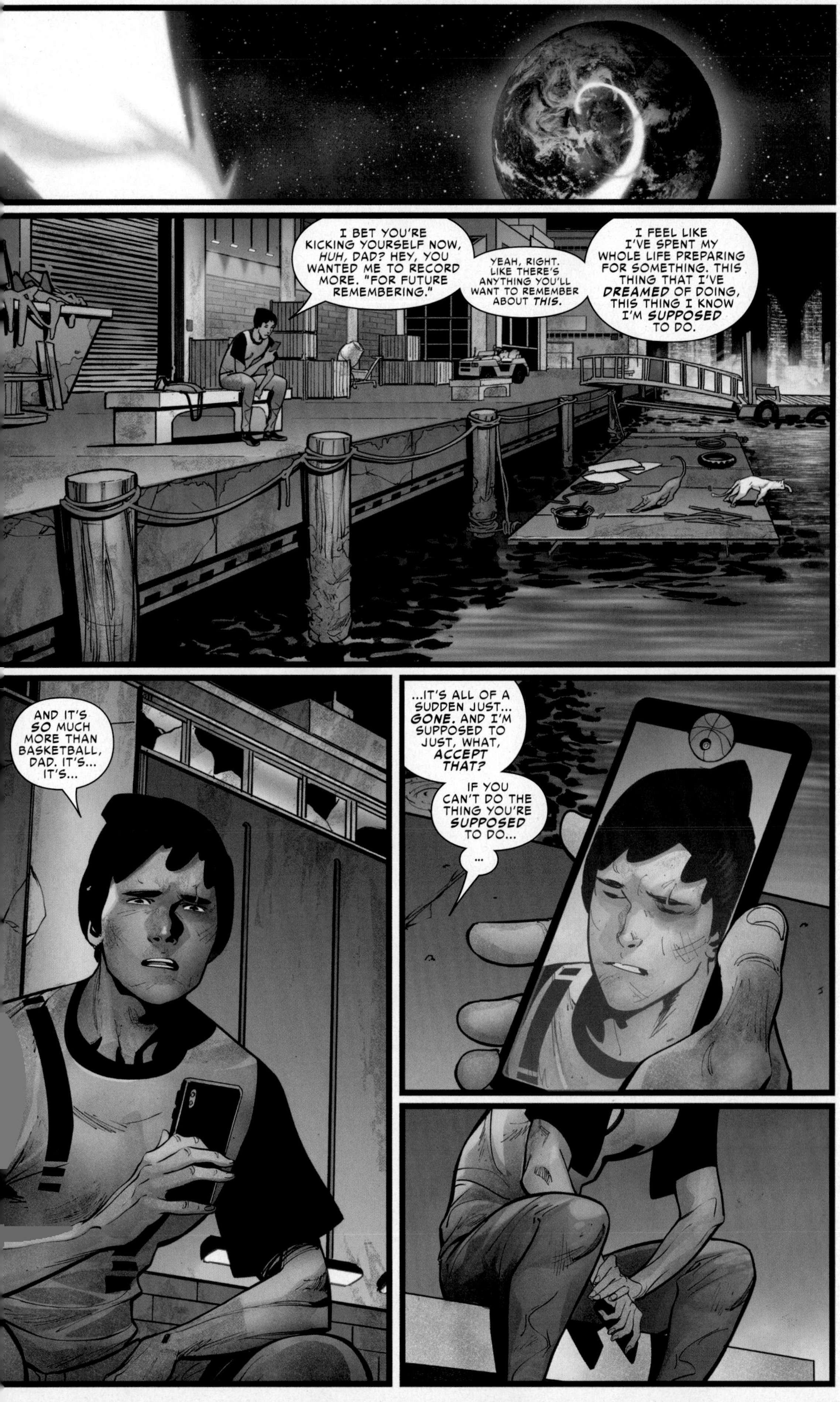
I BET YOU'RE KICKING YOURSELF NOW, HUH, DAD? HEY, YOU WANTED ME TO RECORD MORE. "FOR FUTURE REMEMBERING."
YEAH, RIGHT. LIKE THERE'S ANYTHING YOU'LL WANT TO REMEMBER ABOUT THIS.
I FEEL LIKE I'VE SPENT MY WHOLE LIFE PREPARING FOR SOMETHING. THIS THING THAT I'VE DREAMED OF DOING, THIS THING I KNOW I'M SUPPOSED TO DO.
AND IT'S SO MUCH MORE THAN BASKETBALL, DAD. IT'S... IT'S...
...IT'S ALL OF A SUDDEN JUST... GONE. AND I'M SUPPOSED TO JUST, WHAT, ACCEPT THAT?
IF YOU CAN'T DO THE THING YOU'RE SUPPOSED TO DO...
...

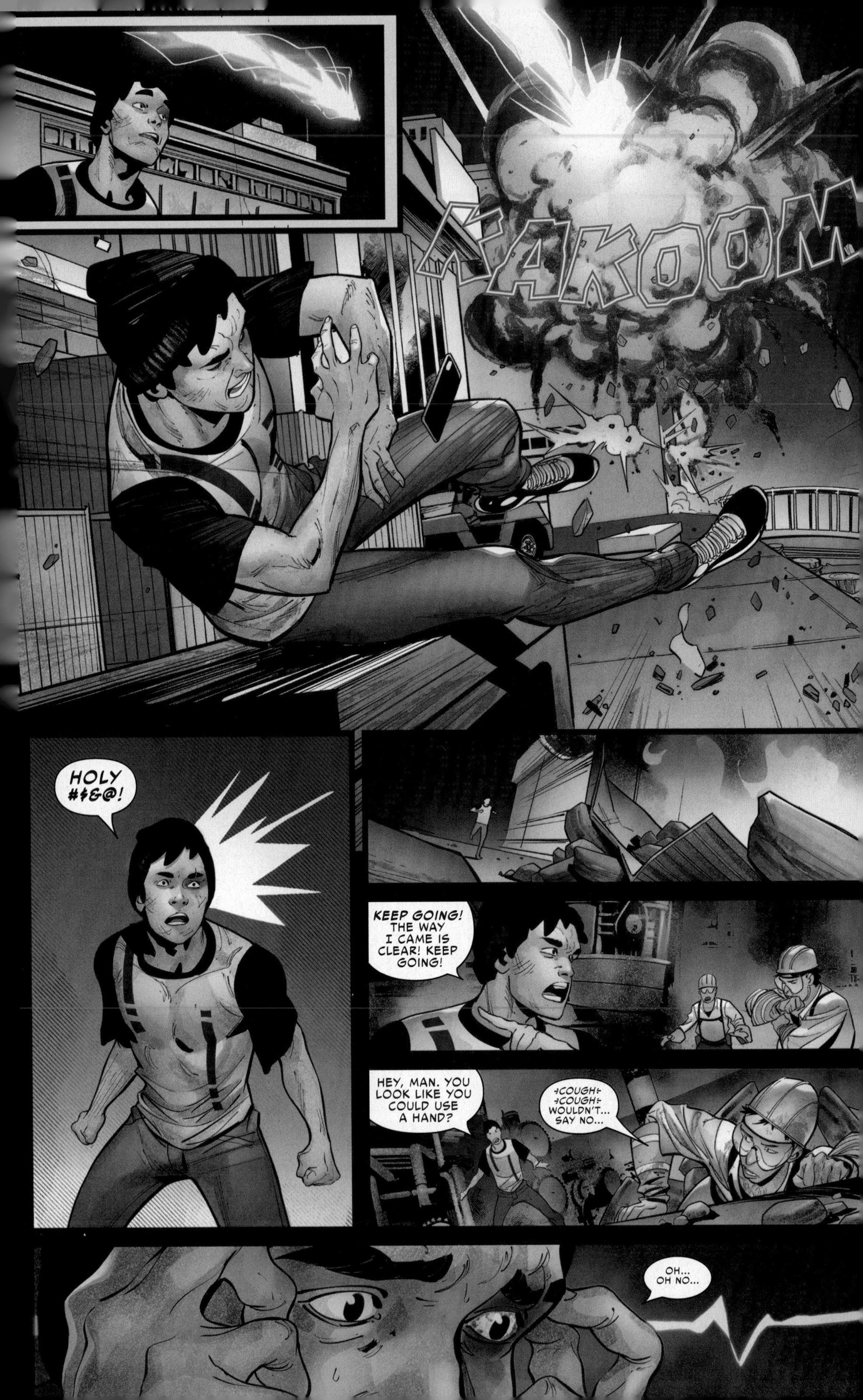
KAKOOM
HOLY #$&@!
KEEP GOING! THE WAY I CAME IS CLEAR! KEEP GOING!
HEY, MAN. YOU LOOK LIKE YOU COULD USE A HAND?
COUGH *COUGH* WOULDN'T... SAY NO...
OH... OH NO...

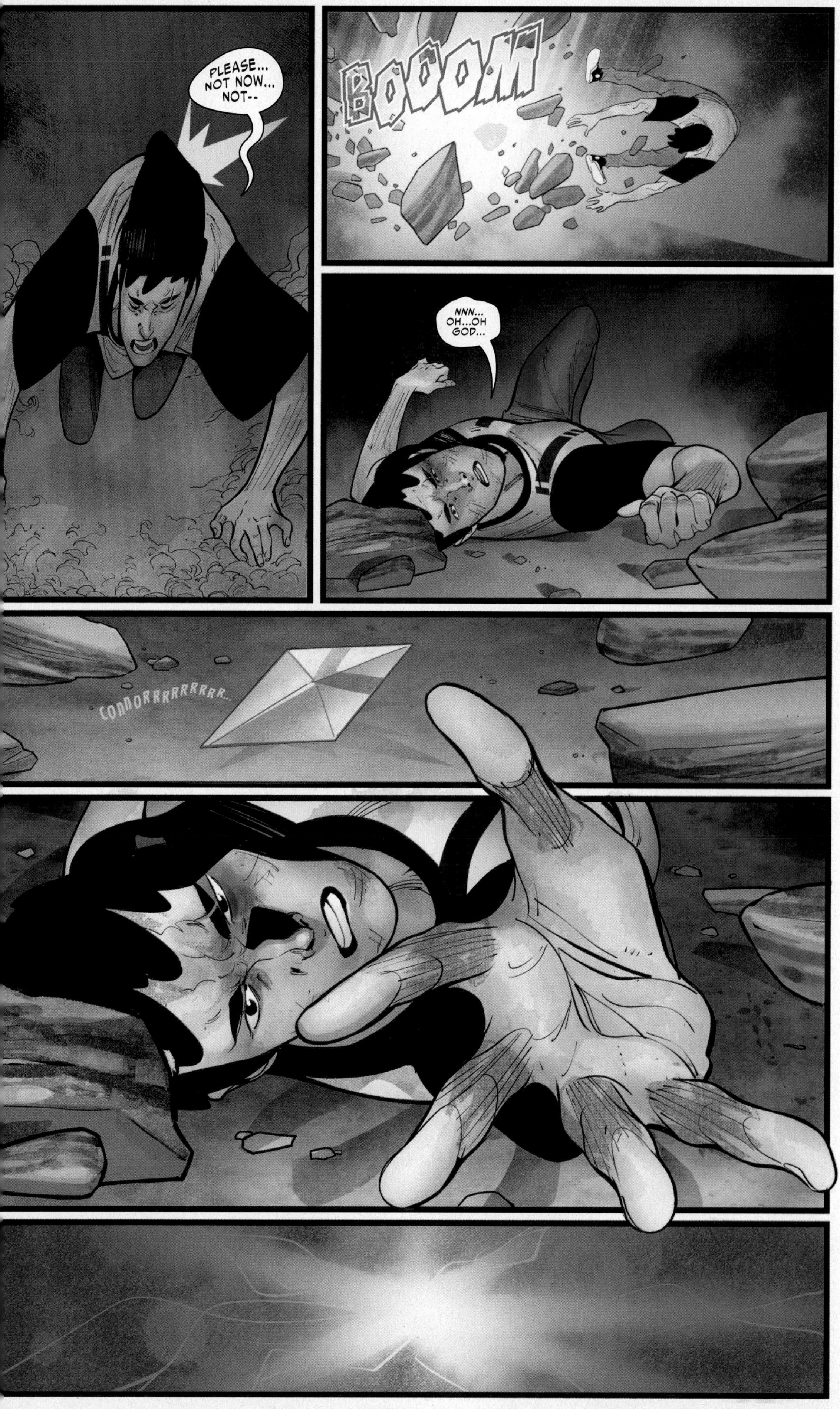
PLEASE... NOT NOW... NOT--
BOOOM
NNN... OH...OH GOD...
CONNORRRRRRRR...

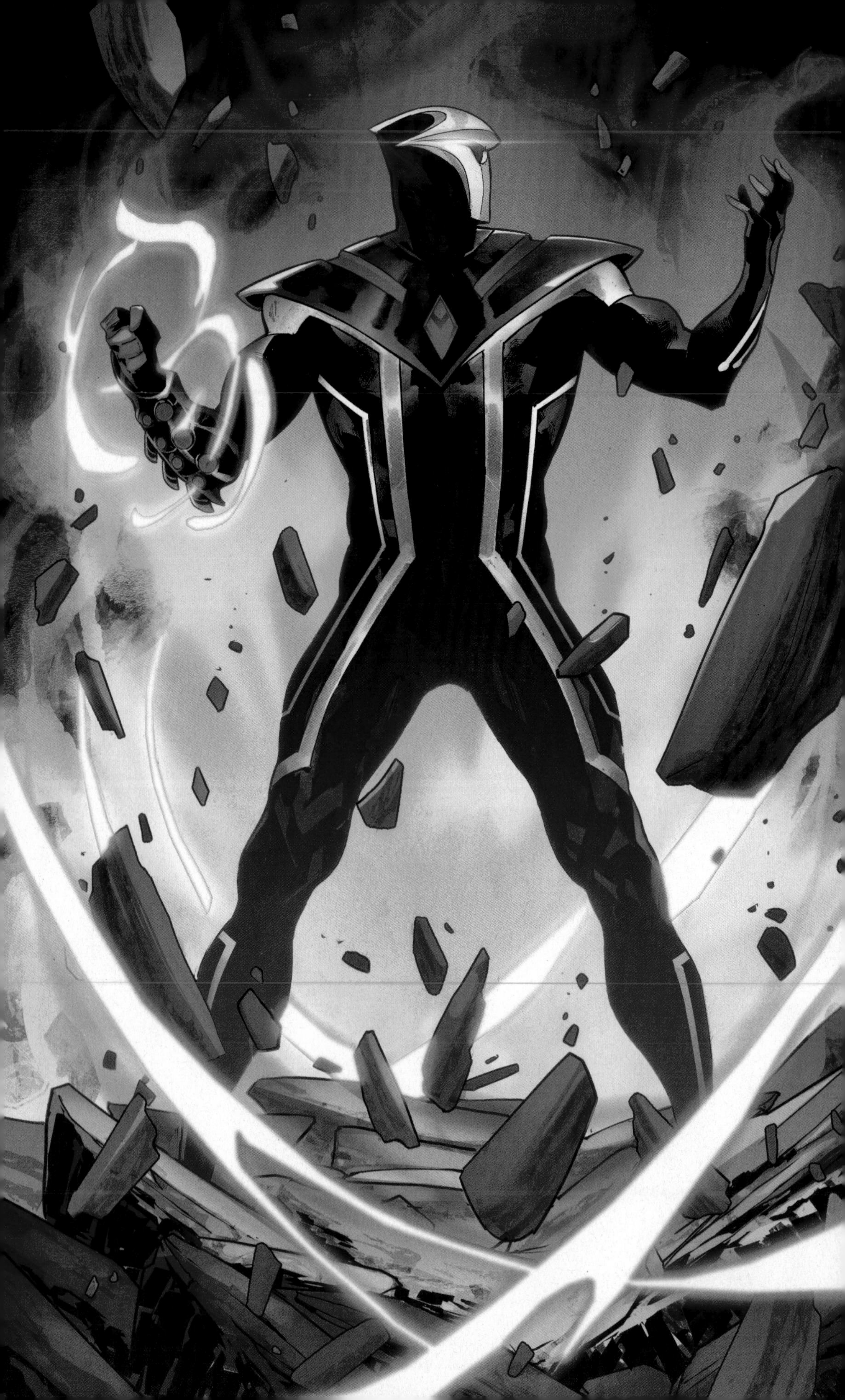

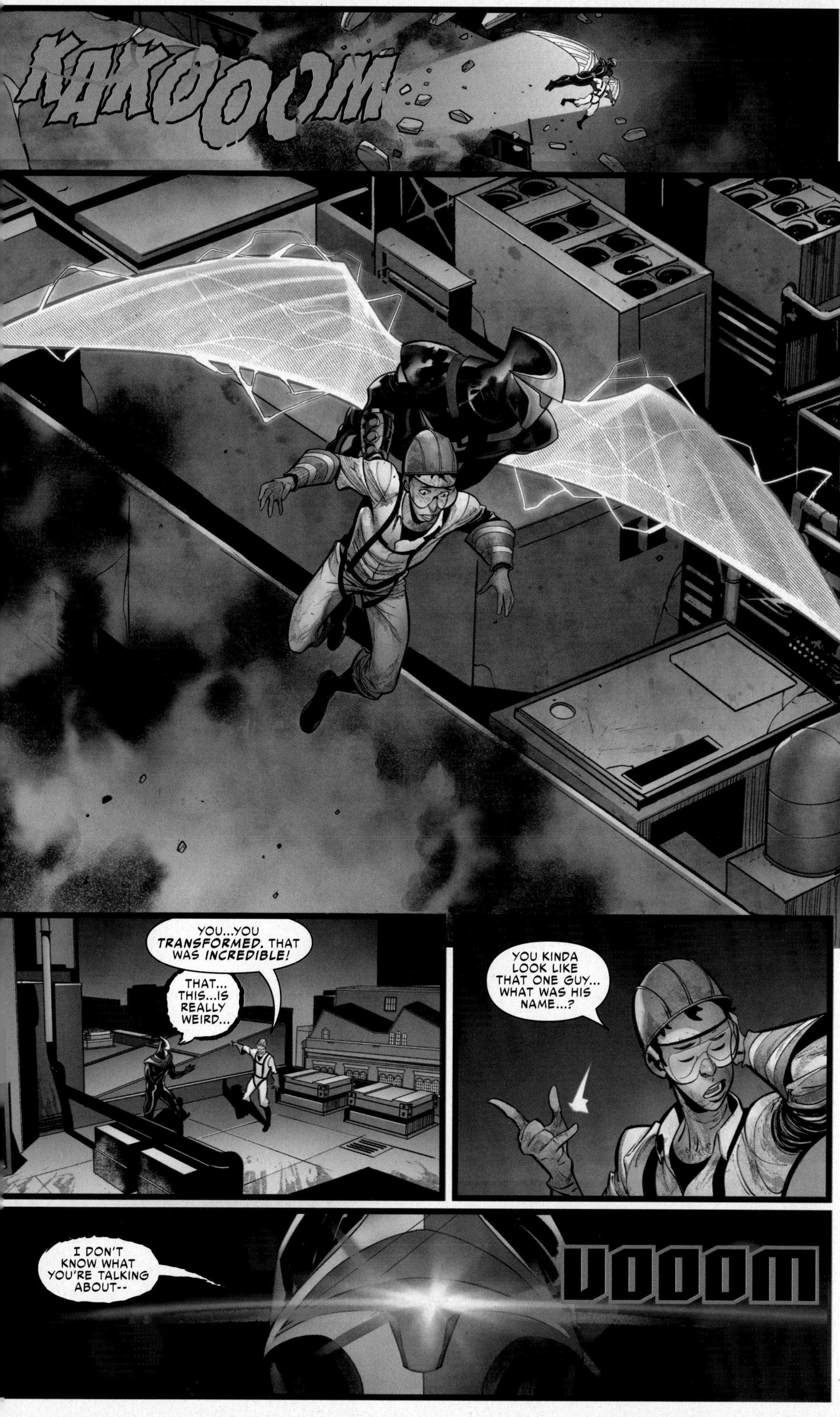
KAKOOOM
YOU...YOU TRANSFORMED. THAT WAS INCREDIBLE!
THAT... THIS...IS REALLY WEIRD...
YOU KINDA LOOK LIKE THAT ONE GUY... WHAT WAS HIS NAME...?
I DON'T KNOW WHAT YOU'RE TALKING ABOUT--
VOOOM

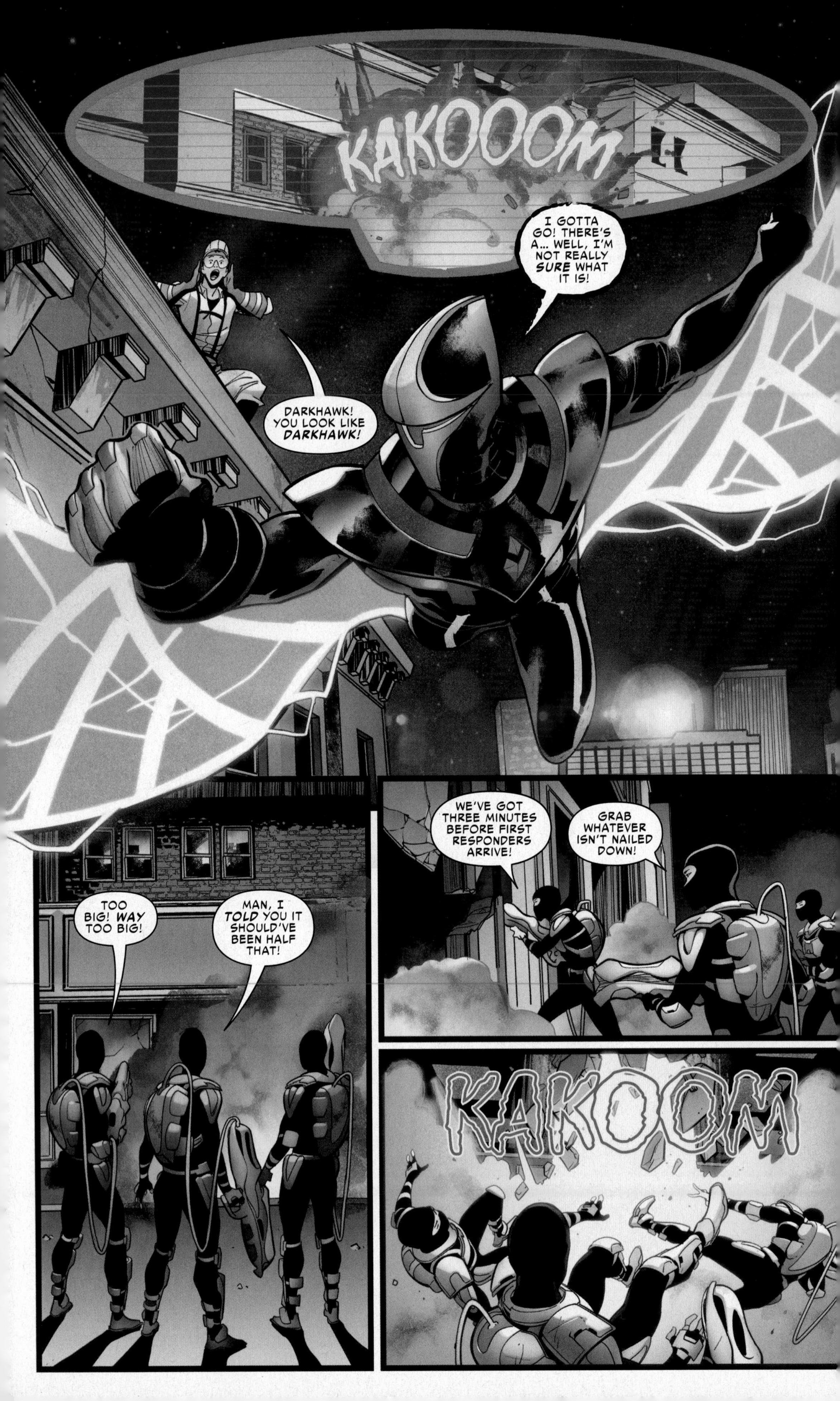
KAKOOOM
I GOTTA GO! THERE'S A... WELL, I'M NOT REALLY SURE WHAT IT IS!
DARKHAWK! YOU LOOK LIKE DARKHAWK!
TOO BIG! WAY TOO BIG!
MAN, I TOLD YOU IT SHOULD'VE BEEN HALF THAT!
WE'VE GOT THREE MINUTES BEFORE FIRST RESPONDERS ARRIVE!
GRAB WHATEVER ISN'T NAILED DOWN!
KAKOOM

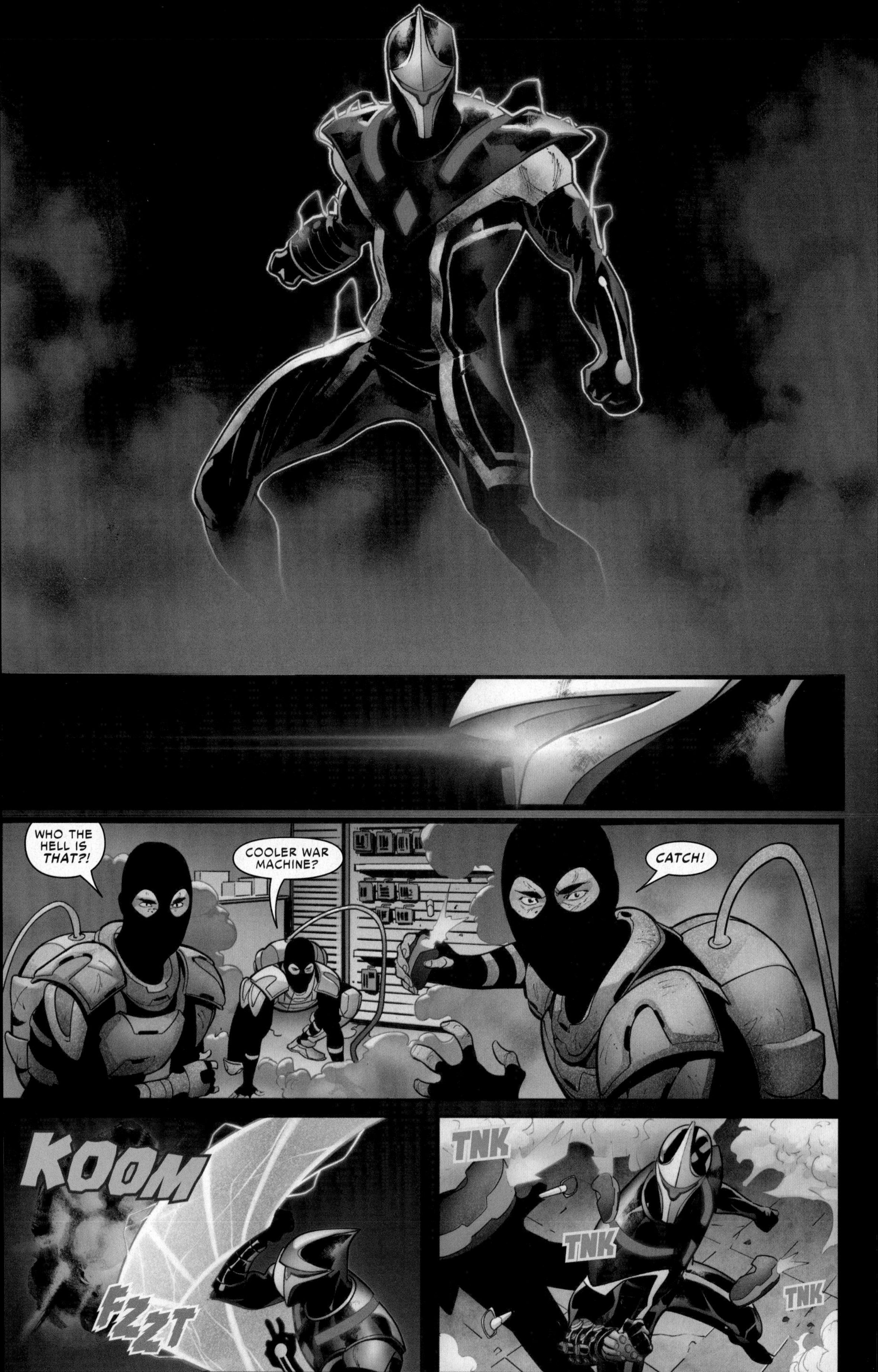
WHO THE HELL IS *THAT?!*
COOLER WAR MACHINE?
CATCH!
KOOM
FZZT
TNK
TNK
TNK

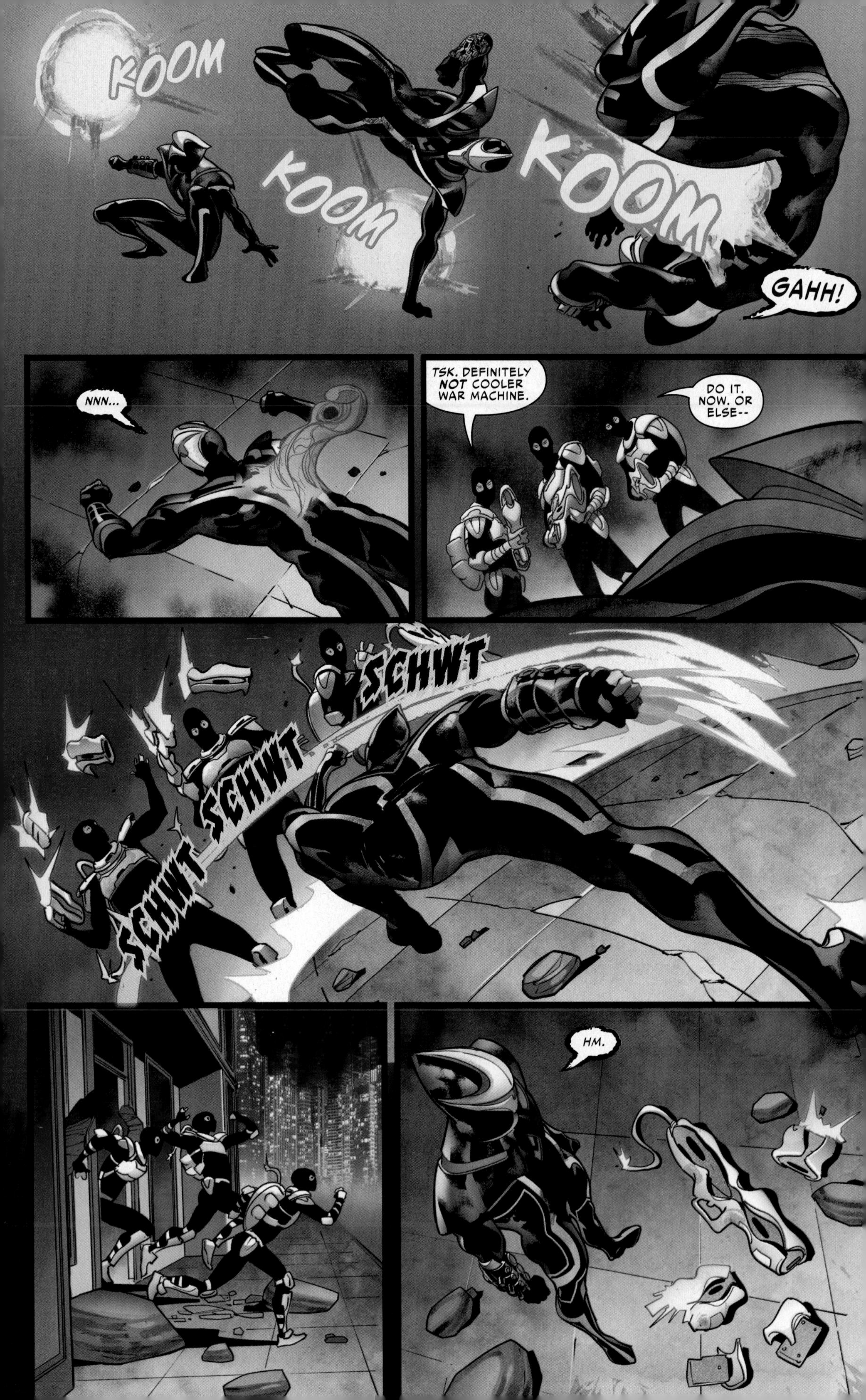
KOOM
KOOM
KOOM
GAHH!
NNN...
TSK. DEFINITELY NOT COOLER WAR MACHINE.
DO IT. NOW. OR ELSE--
SCHWT
SCHWT
SCHWT
HM.

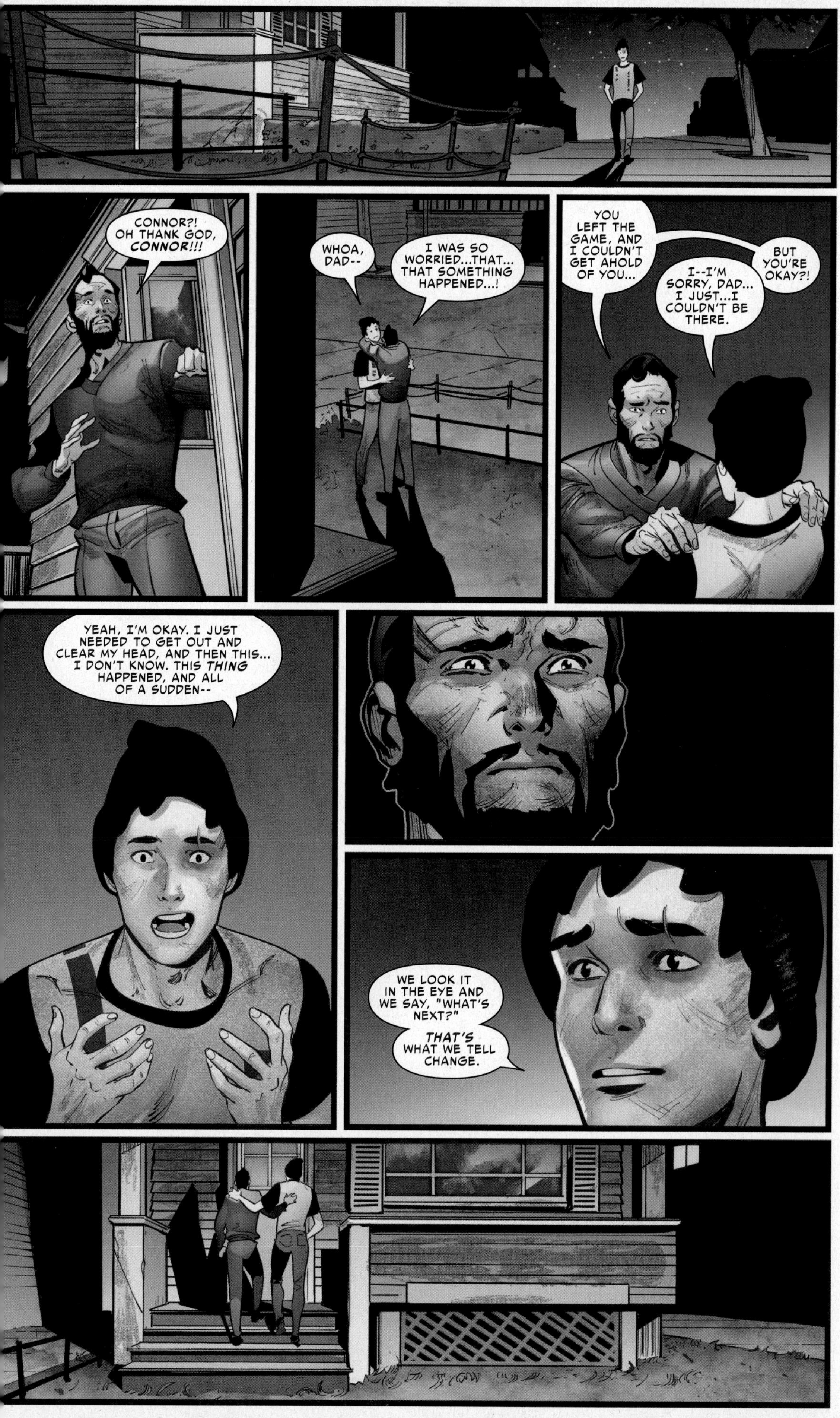
CONNOR?! OH THANK GOD, CONNOR!!!
WHOA, DAD--
I WAS SO WORRIED...THAT... THAT SOMETHING HAPPENED...!
YOU LEFT THE GAME, AND I COULDN'T GET AHOLD OF YOU...
BUT YOU'RE OKAY?!
I--I'M SORRY, DAD... I JUST...I COULDN'T BE THERE.
YEAH, I'M OKAY. I JUST NEEDED TO GET OUT AND CLEAR MY HEAD, AND THEN THIS... I DON'T KNOW. THIS THING HAPPENED, AND ALL OF A SUDDEN--
WE LOOK IT IN THE EYE AND WE SAY, "WHAT'S NEXT?"
THAT'S WHAT WE TELL CHANGE.

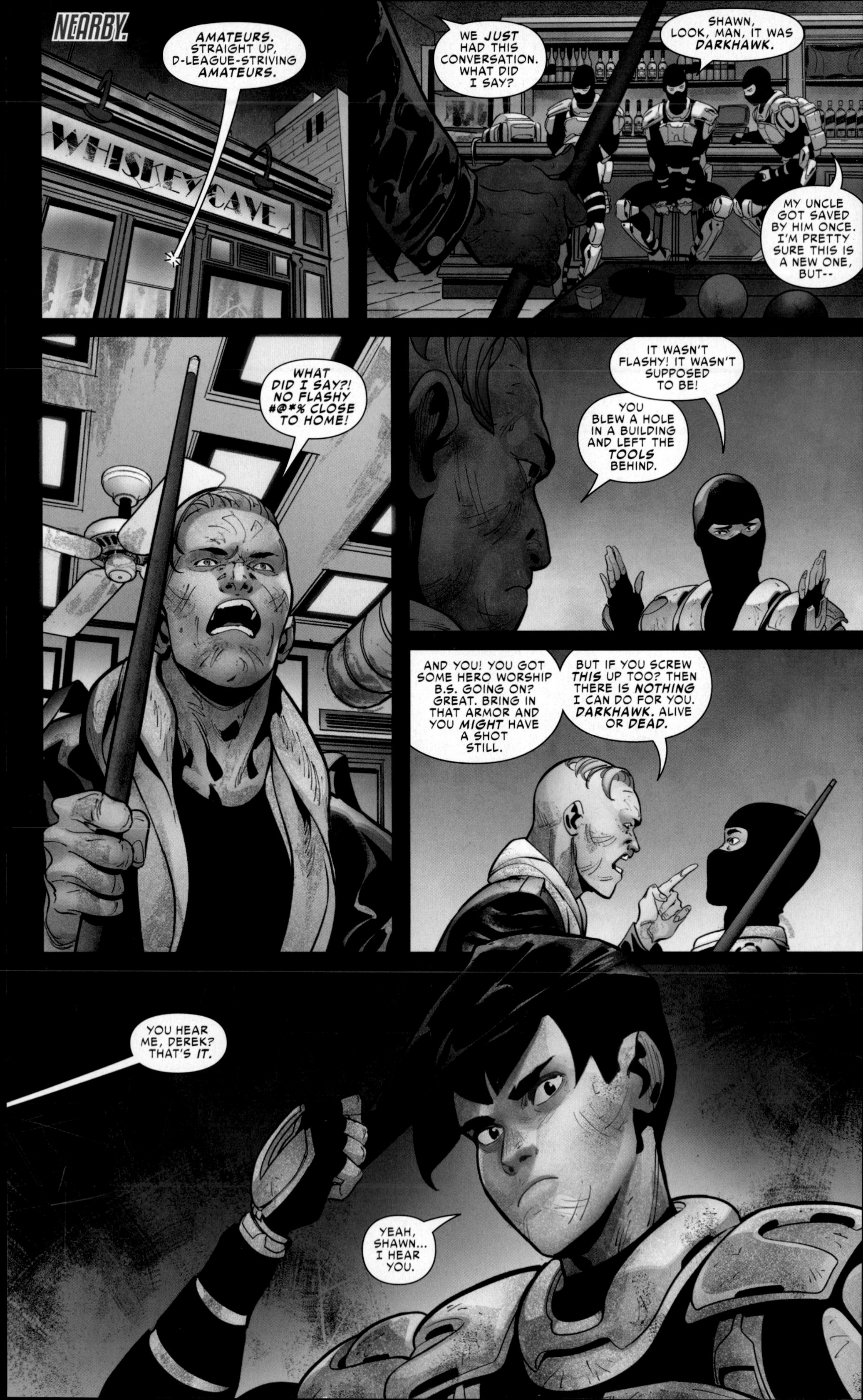
NEARBY.
AMATEURS. STRAIGHT UP, D-LEAGUE-STRIVING AMATEURS.
WHISKEY CAVE
WE JUST HAD THIS CONVERSATION. WHAT DID I SAY?
SHAWN, LOOK, MAN, IT WAS DARKHAWK.
MY UNCLE GOT SAVED BY HIM ONCE. I'M PRETTY SURE THIS IS A NEW ONE, BUT--
WHAT DID I SAY?! NO FLASHY #@*% CLOSE TO HOME!
IT WASN'T FLASHY! IT WASN'T SUPPOSED TO BE!
YOU BLEW A HOLE IN A BUILDING AND LEFT THE TOOLS BEHIND.
AND YOU! YOU GOT SOME HERO WORSHIP B.S. GOING ON? GREAT. BRING IN THAT ARMOR AND YOU MIGHT HAVE A SHOT STILL.
BUT IF YOU SCREW THIS UP TOO? THEN THERE IS NOTHING I CAN DO FOR YOU. DARKHAWK. ALIVE OR DEAD.
YOU HEAR ME, DEREK? THAT'S IT.
YEAH, SHAWN... I HEAR YOU.

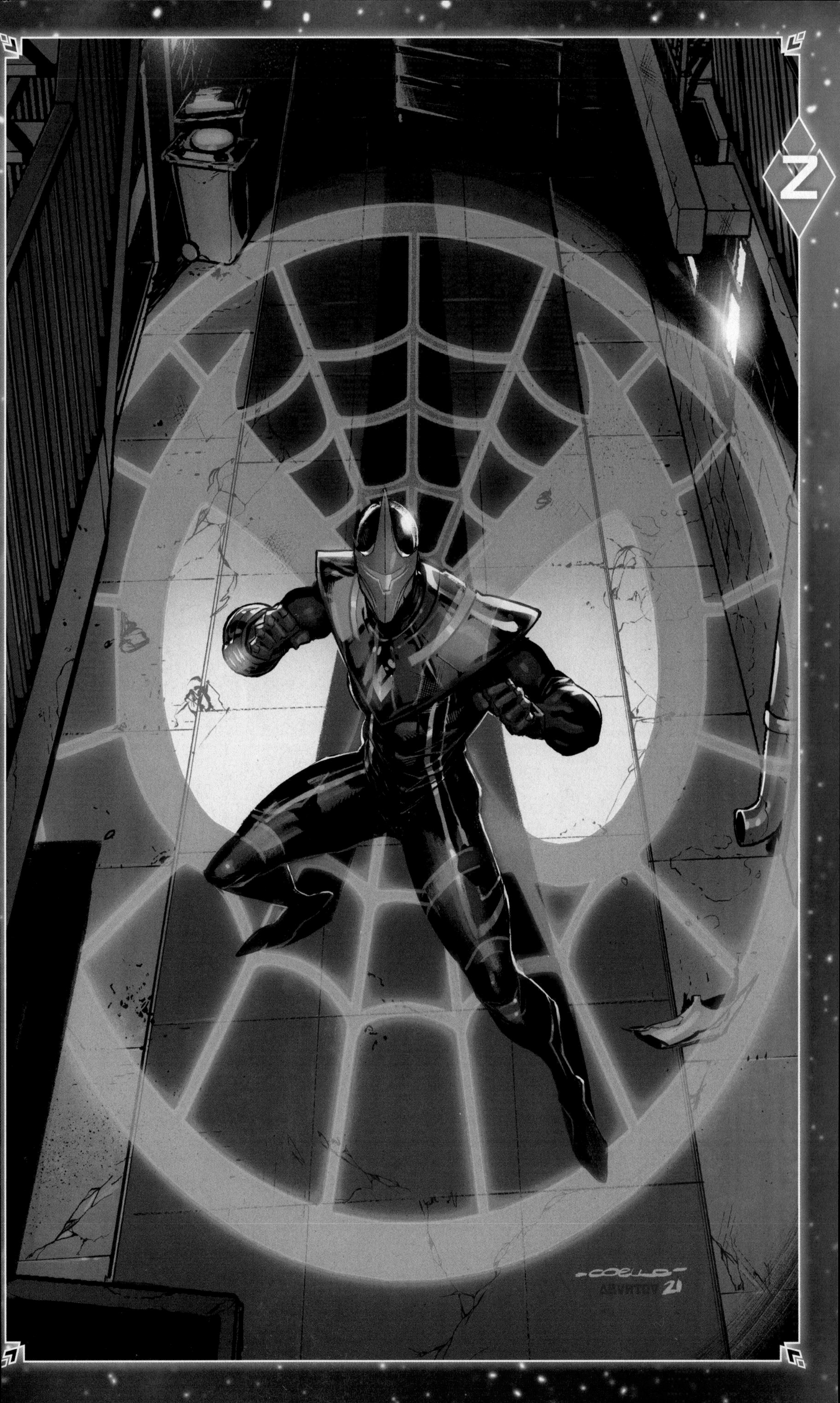

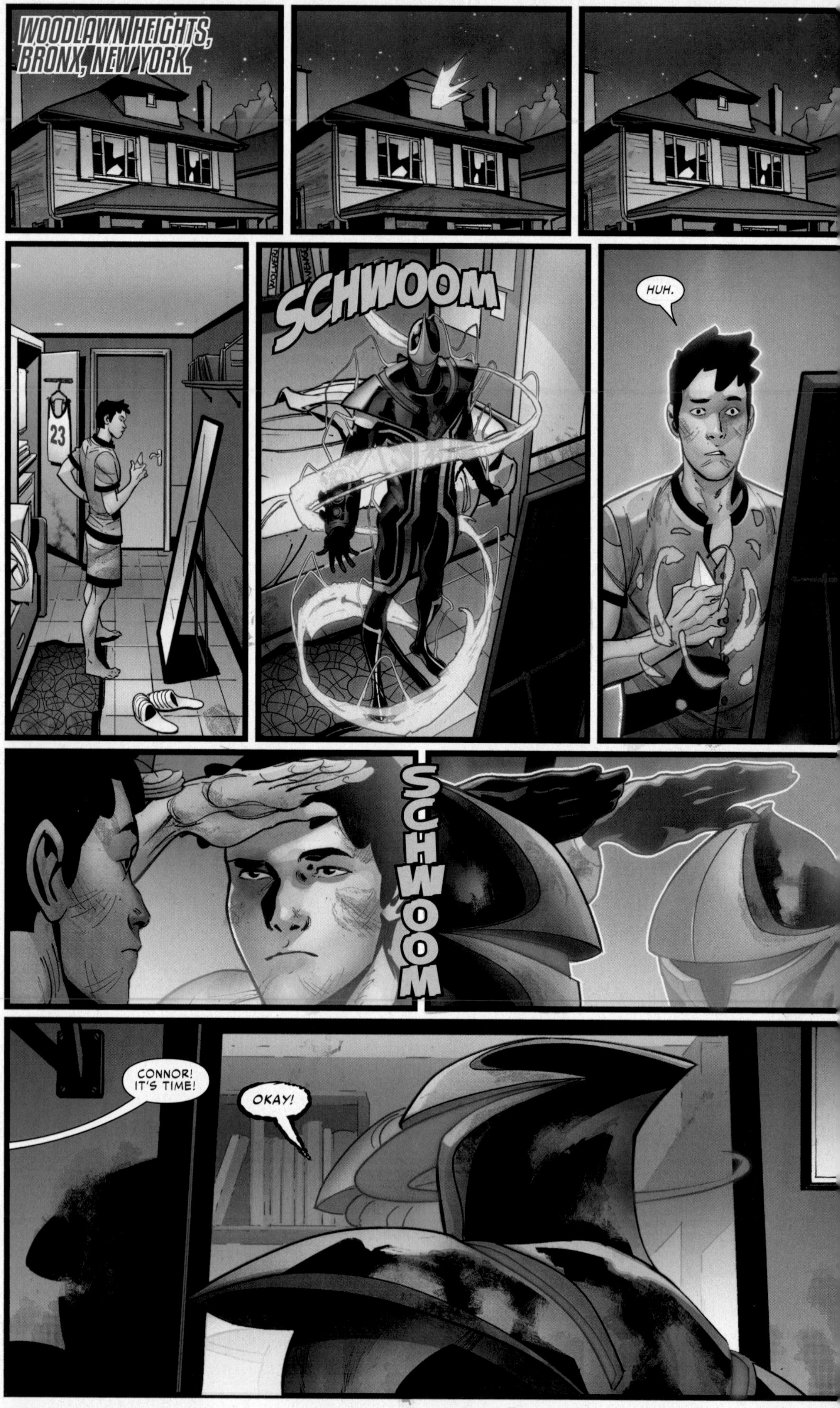
WOODLAWN HEIGHTS, BRONX, NEW YORK.
SCHWOOM
HUH.
SCHWOOM
CONNOR! IT'S TIME!
OKAY!

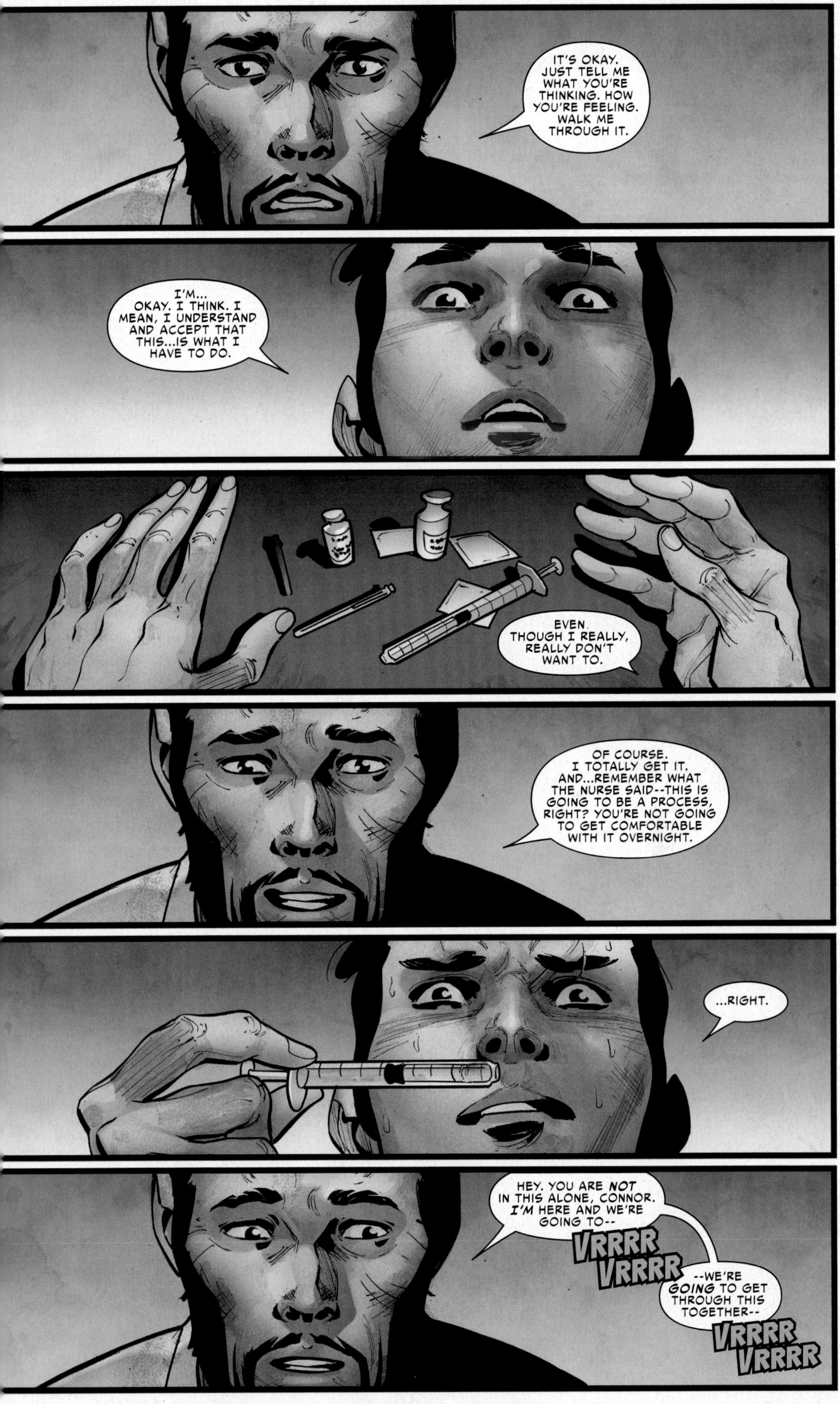
IT'S OKAY. JUST TELL ME WHAT YOU'RE THINKING. HOW YOU'RE FEELING. WALK ME THROUGH IT.
I'M... OKAY. I THINK. I MEAN, I UNDERSTAND AND ACCEPT THAT THIS...IS WHAT I HAVE TO DO.
EVEN THOUGH I REALLY, REALLY DON'T WANT TO.
OF COURSE. I TOTALLY GET IT. AND...REMEMBER WHAT THE NURSE SAID--THIS IS GOING TO BE A PROCESS, RIGHT? YOU'RE NOT GOING TO GET COMFORTABLE WITH IT OVERNIGHT.
...RIGHT.
HEY. YOU ARE NOT IN THIS ALONE, CONNOR. I'M HERE AND WE'RE GOING TO--
VRRRR VRRRR
--WE'RE GOING TO GET THROUGH THIS TOGETHER--
VRRRR VRRRR

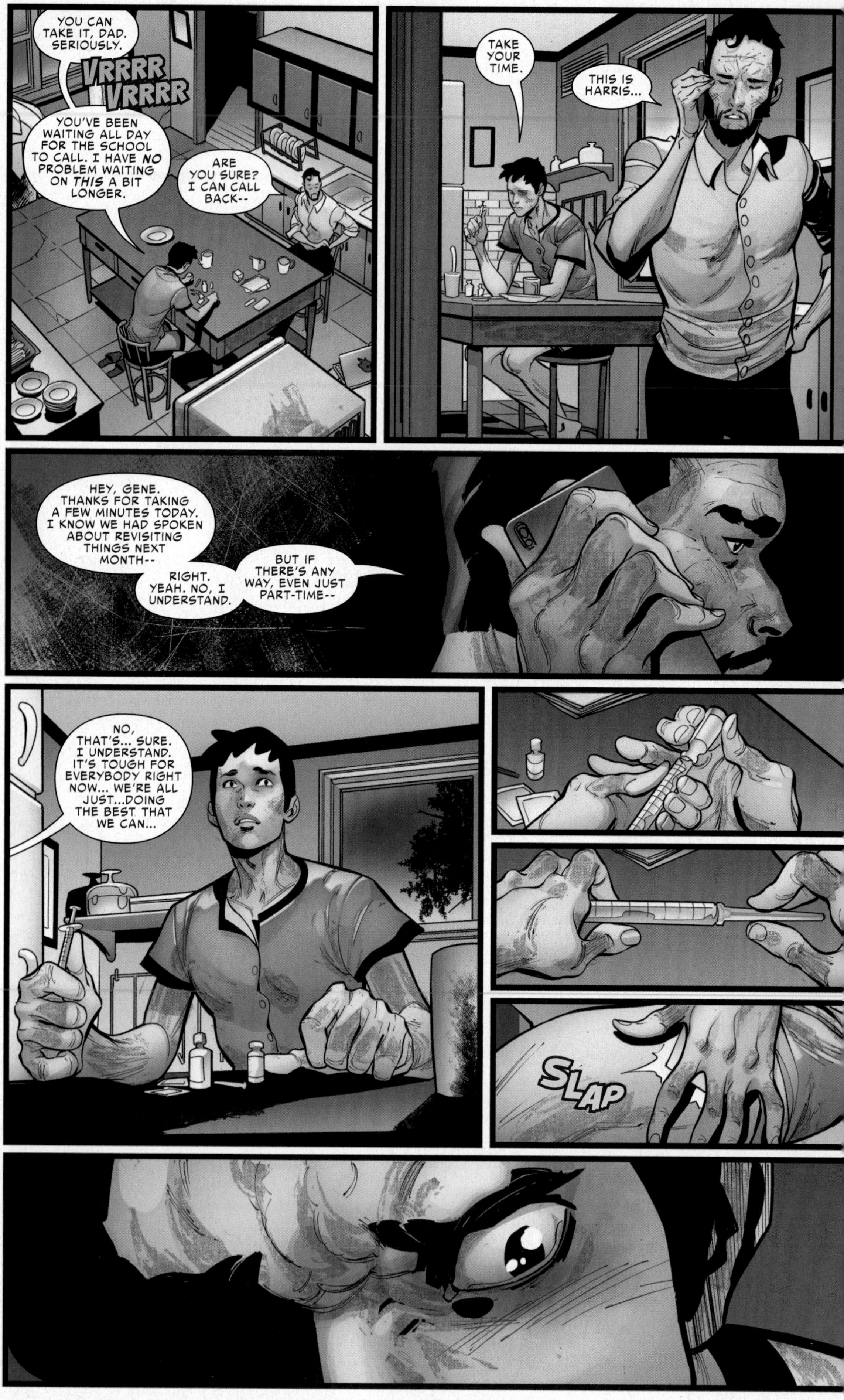
YOU CAN TAKE IT, DAD. SERIOUSLY.
VRRRR VRRRR
YOU'VE BEEN WAITING ALL DAY FOR THE SCHOOL TO CALL. I HAVE NO PROBLEM WAITING ON THIS A BIT LONGER.
ARE YOU SURE? I CAN CALL BACK--
TAKE YOUR TIME.
THIS IS HARRIS...
HEY, GENE. THANKS FOR TAKING A FEW MINUTES TODAY. I KNOW WE HAD SPOKEN ABOUT REVISITING THINGS NEXT MONTH--
RIGHT. YEAH. NO, I UNDERSTAND.
BUT IF THERE'S ANY WAY, EVEN JUST PART-TIME--
NO, THAT'S... SURE. I UNDERSTAND. IT'S TOUGH FOR EVERYBODY RIGHT NOW... WE'RE ALL JUST...DOING THE BEST THAT WE CAN...
SLAP

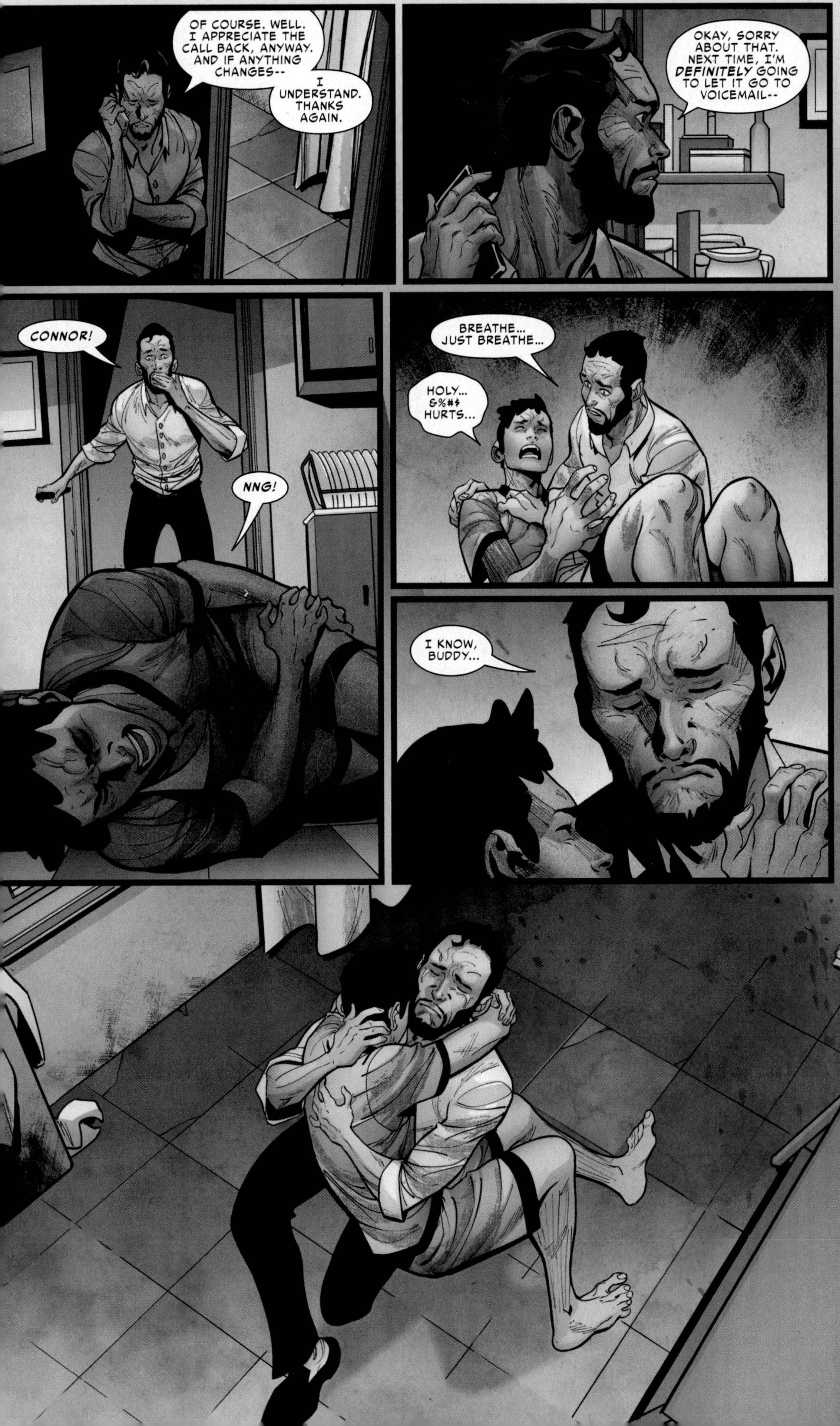
OF COURSE. WELL. I APPRECIATE THE CALL BACK, ANYWAY. AND IF ANYTHING CHANGES--
I UNDERSTAND. THANKS AGAIN.
OKAY, SORRY ABOUT THAT. NEXT TIME, I'M DEFINITELY GOING TO LET IT GO TO VOICEMAIL--
CONNOR!
NNG!
BREATHE... JUST BREATHE...
HOLY... &%#$ HURTS...
I KNOW, BUDDY...

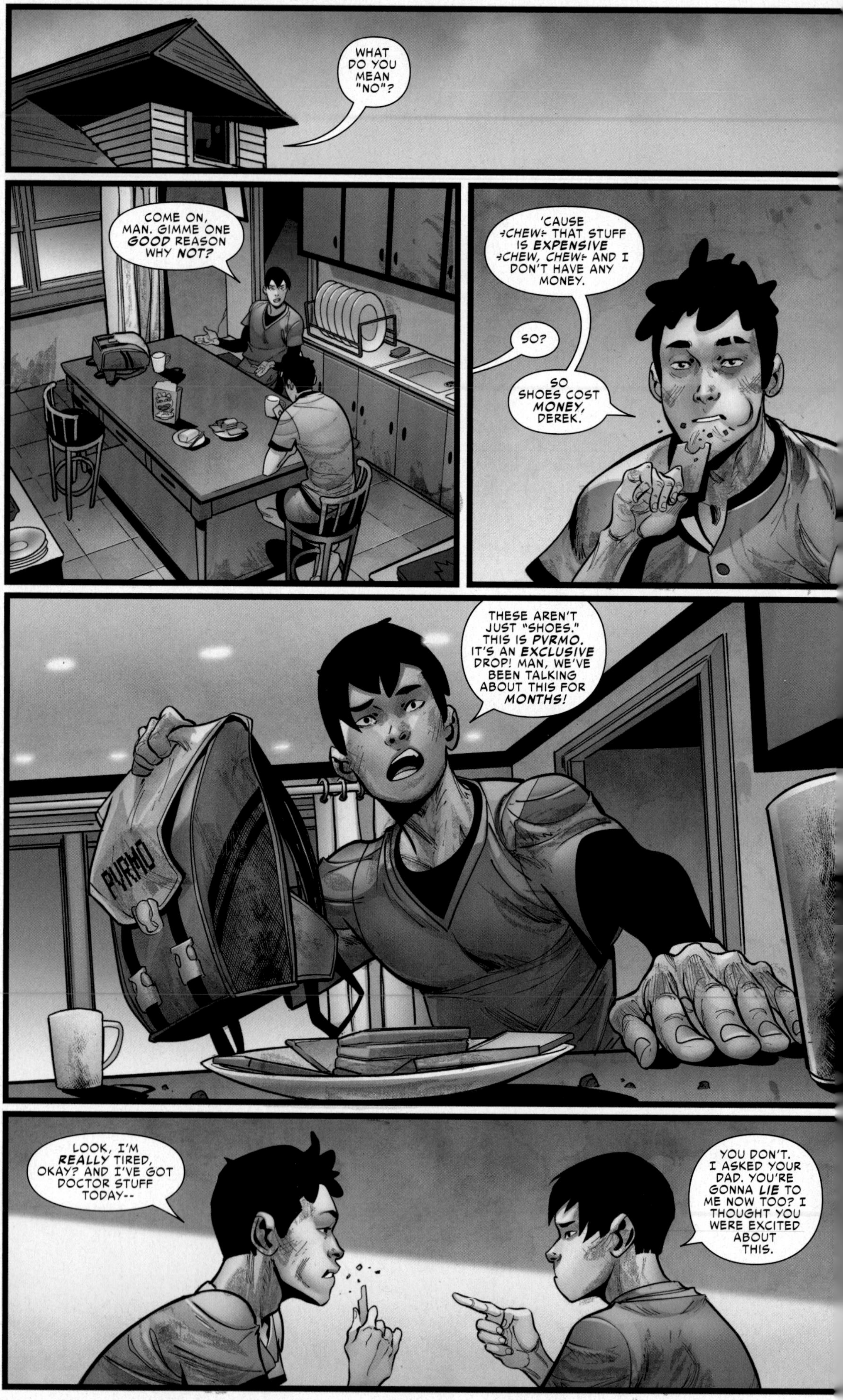
WHAT DO YOU MEAN "NO"?
COME ON, MAN. GIMME ONE GOOD REASON WHY NOT?
'CAUSE ⇉CHEW⇇ THAT STUFF IS EXPENSIVE ⇉CHEW, CHEW⇇ AND I DON'T HAVE ANY MONEY.
SO?
SO SHOES COST MONEY, DEREK.
THESE AREN'T JUST "SHOES." THIS IS PVRMO. IT'S AN EXCLUSIVE DROP! MAN, WE'VE BEEN TALKING ABOUT THIS FOR MONTHS!
PVRMO
LOOK, I'M REALLY TIRED, OKAY? AND I'VE GOT DOCTOR STUFF TODAY--
YOU DON'T. I ASKED YOUR DAD. YOU'RE GONNA LIE TO ME NOW TOO? I THOUGHT YOU WERE EXCITED ABOUT THIS.

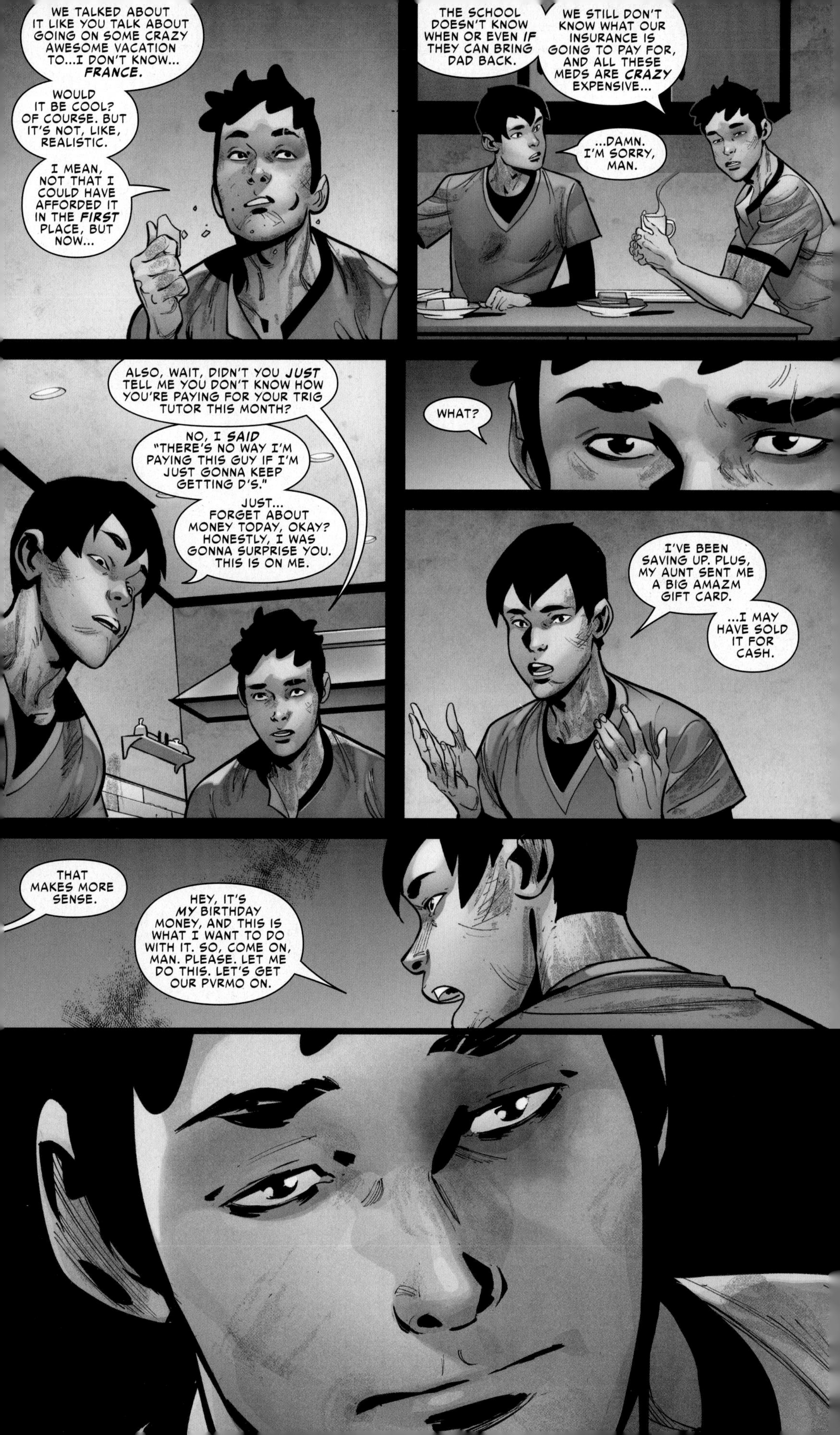
WE TALKED ABOUT IT LIKE YOU TALK ABOUT GOING ON SOME CRAZY AWESOME VACATION TO...I DON'T KNOW... FRANCE.
WOULD IT BE COOL? OF COURSE. BUT IT'S NOT, LIKE, REALISTIC.
I MEAN, NOT THAT I COULD HAVE AFFORDED IT IN THE FIRST PLACE, BUT NOW...
THE SCHOOL DOESN'T KNOW WHEN OR EVEN IF THEY CAN BRING DAD BACK.
WE STILL DON'T KNOW WHAT OUR INSURANCE IS GOING TO PAY FOR, AND ALL THESE MEDS ARE CRAZY EXPENSIVE...
...DAMN. I'M SORRY, MAN.
ALSO, WAIT, DIDN'T YOU JUST TELL ME YOU DON'T KNOW HOW YOU'RE PAYING FOR YOUR TRIG TUTOR THIS MONTH?
NO, I SAID "THERE'S NO WAY I'M PAYING THIS GUY IF I'M JUST GONNA KEEP GETTING D'S."
JUST... FORGET ABOUT MONEY TODAY, OKAY? HONESTLY, I WAS GONNA SURPRISE YOU. THIS IS ON ME.
WHAT?
I'VE BEEN SAVING UP. PLUS, MY AUNT SENT ME A BIG AMAZM GIFT CARD.
...I MAY HAVE SOLD IT FOR CASH.
THAT MAKES MORE SENSE.
HEY, IT'S MY BIRTHDAY MONEY, AND THIS IS WHAT I WANT TO DO WITH IT. SO, COME ON, MAN. PLEASE. LET ME DO THIS. LET'S GET OUR PVRMO ON.

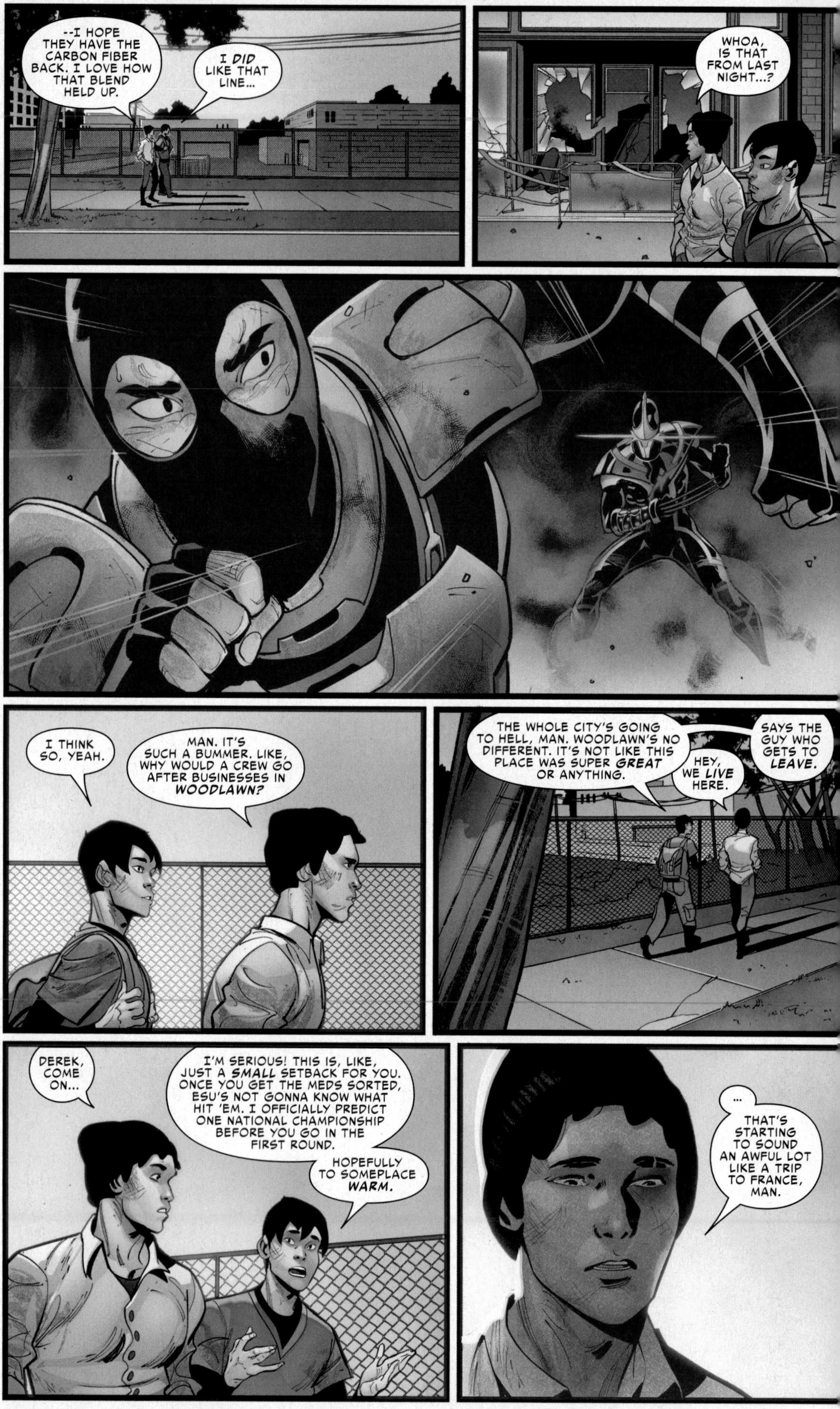
--I HOPE THEY HAVE THE CARBON FIBER BACK. I LOVE HOW THAT BLEND HELD UP.
I DID LIKE THAT LINE...
WHOA, IS THAT FROM LAST NIGHT...?
I THINK SO, YEAH.
MAN. IT'S SUCH A BUMMER. LIKE, WHY WOULD A CREW GO AFTER BUSINESSES IN WOODLAWN?
THE WHOLE CITY'S GOING TO HELL, MAN. WOODLAWN'S NO DIFFERENT. IT'S NOT LIKE THIS PLACE WAS SUPER GREAT OR ANYTHING.
SAYS THE GUY WHO GETS TO LEAVE.
HEY, WE LIVE HERE.
DEREK, COME ON...
I'M SERIOUS! THIS IS, LIKE, JUST A SMALL SETBACK FOR YOU. ONCE YOU GET THE MEDS SORTED, ESU'S NOT GONNA KNOW WHAT HIT 'EM. I OFFICIALLY PREDICT ONE NATIONAL CHAMPIONSHIP BEFORE YOU GO IN THE FIRST ROUND.
HOPEFULLY TO SOMEPLACE WARM.
...
THAT'S STARTING TO SOUND AN AWFUL LOT LIKE A TRIP TO FRANCE, MAN.

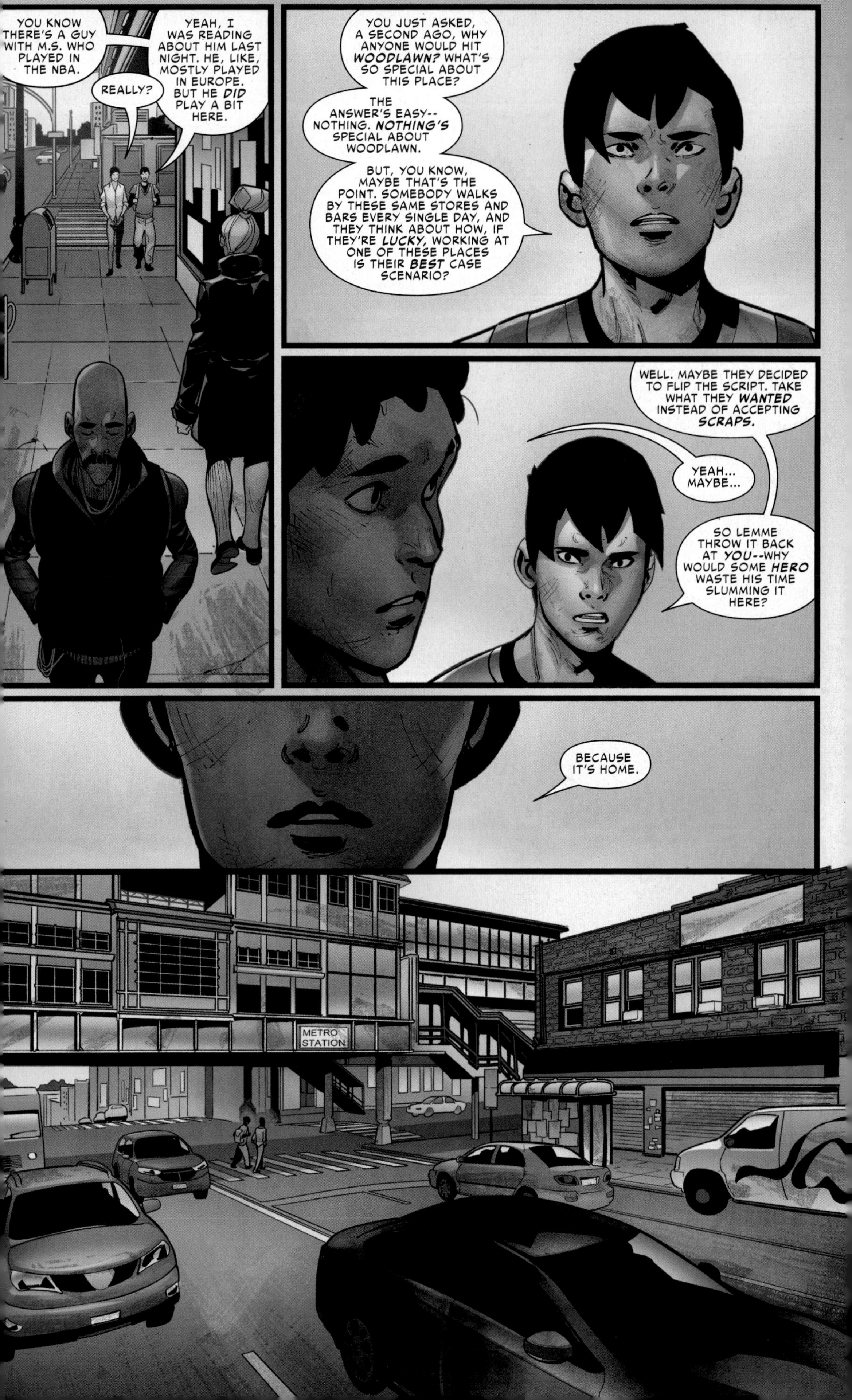

YOU KNOW THERE'S A GUY WITH M.S. WHO PLAYED IN THE NBA.
YEAH, I WAS READING ABOUT HIM LAST NIGHT. HE, LIKE, MOSTLY PLAYED IN EUROPE. BUT HE *DID* PLAY A BIT HERE.
REALLY?
YOU JUST ASKED, A SECOND AGO, WHY ANYONE WOULD HIT *WOODLAWN?* WHAT'S SO SPECIAL ABOUT THIS PLACE?
THE ANSWER'S EASY-- NOTHING. *NOTHING'S* SPECIAL ABOUT WOODLAWN.
BUT, YOU KNOW, MAYBE THAT'S THE POINT. SOMEBODY WALKS BY THESE SAME STORES AND BARS EVERY SINGLE DAY, AND THEY THINK ABOUT HOW, IF THEY'RE *LUCKY,* WORKING AT ONE OF THESE PLACES IS THEIR *BEST* CASE SCENARIO?
WELL. MAYBE THEY DECIDED TO FLIP THE SCRIPT. TAKE WHAT THEY *WANTED* INSTEAD OF ACCEPTING *SCRAPS.*
YEAH... MAYBE...
SO LEMME THROW IT BACK AT *YOU*--WHY WOULD SOME *HERO* WASTE HIS TIME SLUMMING IT HERE?
BECAUSE IT'S HOME.
METRO STATION

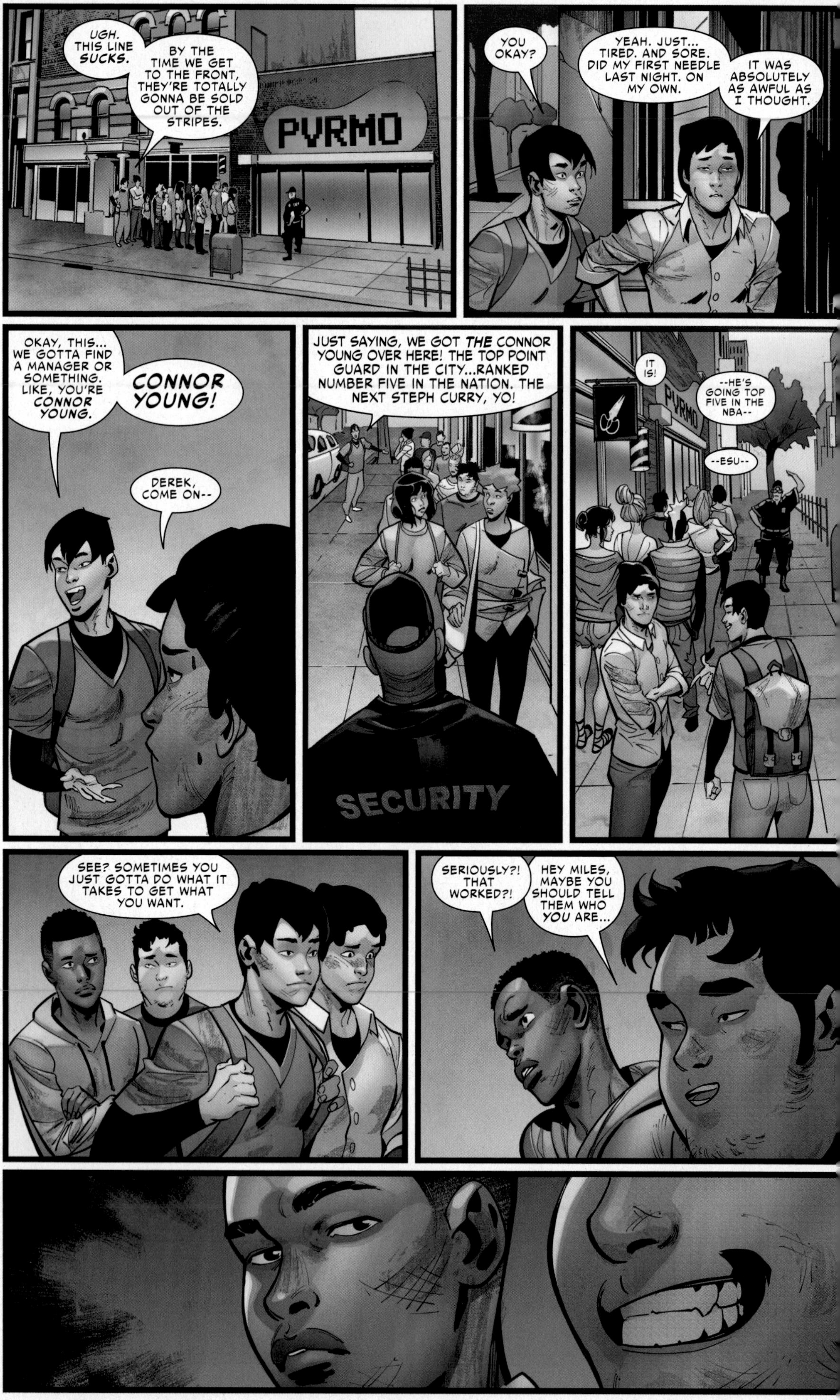
UGH. THIS LINE SUCKS.
BY THE TIME WE GET TO THE FRONT, THEY'RE TOTALLY GONNA BE SOLD OUT OF THE STRIPES.
PVRMO
YOU OKAY?
YEAH. JUST... TIRED. AND SORE. DID MY FIRST NEEDLE LAST NIGHT. ON MY OWN.
IT WAS ABSOLUTELY AS AWFUL AS I THOUGHT.
OKAY, THIS... WE GOTTA FIND A MANAGER OR SOMETHING. LIKE, YOU'RE CONNOR YOUNG.
CONNOR YOUNG!
DEREK, COME ON--
JUST SAYING, WE GOT THE CONNOR YOUNG OVER HERE! THE TOP POINT GUARD IN THE CITY...RANKED NUMBER FIVE IN THE NATION. THE NEXT STEPH CURRY, YO!
SECURITY
IT IS!
--HE'S GOING TOP FIVE IN THE NBA--
--ESU--
PVRMO
SEE? SOMETIMES YOU JUST GOTTA DO WHAT IT TAKES TO GET WHAT YOU WANT.
SERIOUSLY?! THAT WORKED?!
HEY MILES, MAYBE YOU SHOULD TELL THEM WHO YOU ARE...

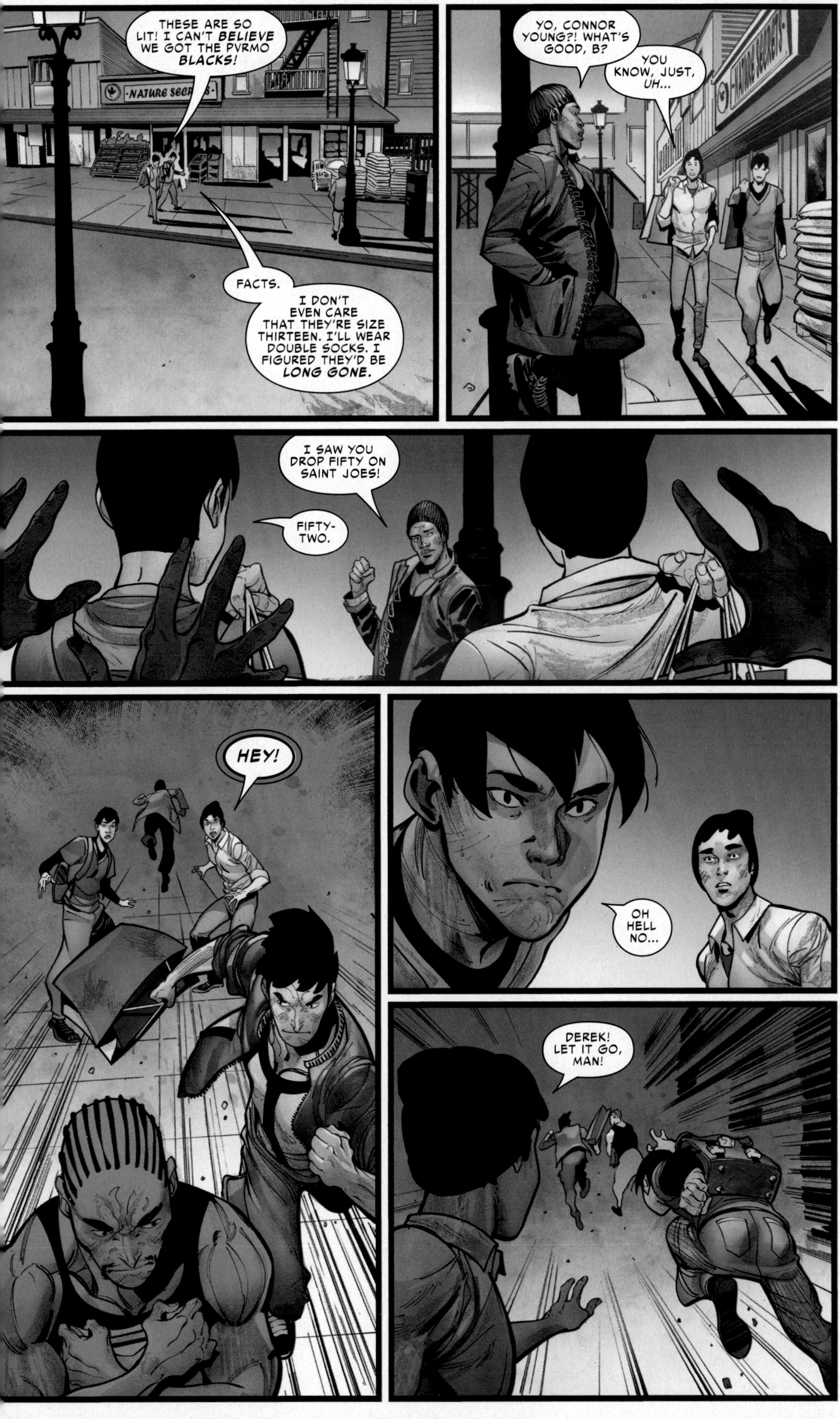
THESE ARE SO LIT! I CAN'T BELIEVE WE GOT THE PVRMO BLACKS!
FACTS.
I DON'T EVEN CARE THAT THEY'RE SIZE THIRTEEN. I'LL WEAR DOUBLE SOCKS. I FIGURED THEY'D BE LONG GONE.
YO, CONNOR YOUNG?! WHAT'S GOOD, B?
YOU KNOW, JUST, UH...
I SAW YOU DROP FIFTY ON SAINT JOES!
FIFTY-TWO.
HEY!
OH HELL NO...
DEREK! LET IT GO, MAN!

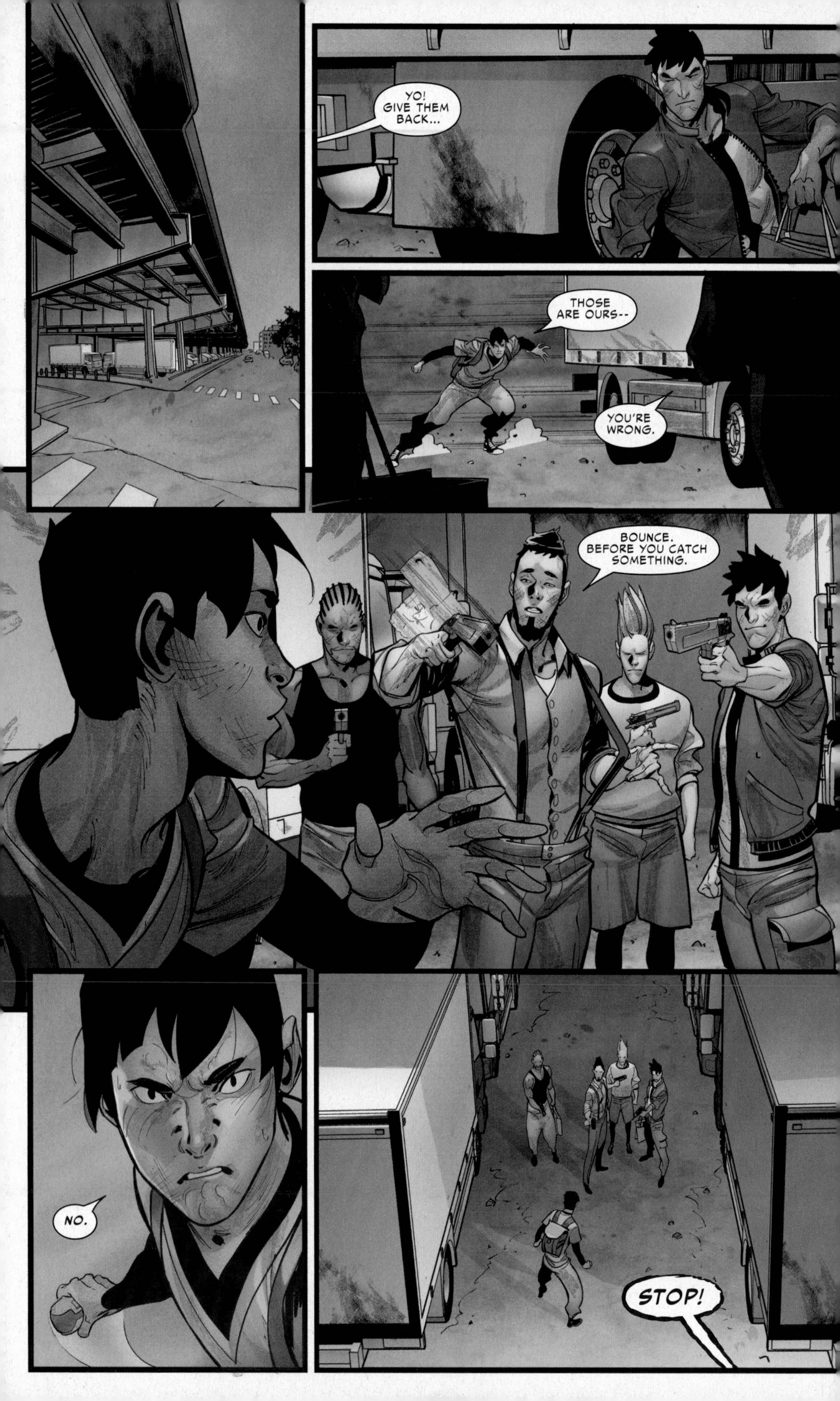

YO! GIVE THEM BACK...
THOSE ARE OURS--
YOU'RE WRONG.
BOUNCE. BEFORE YOU CATCH SOMETHING.
NO.
STOP!

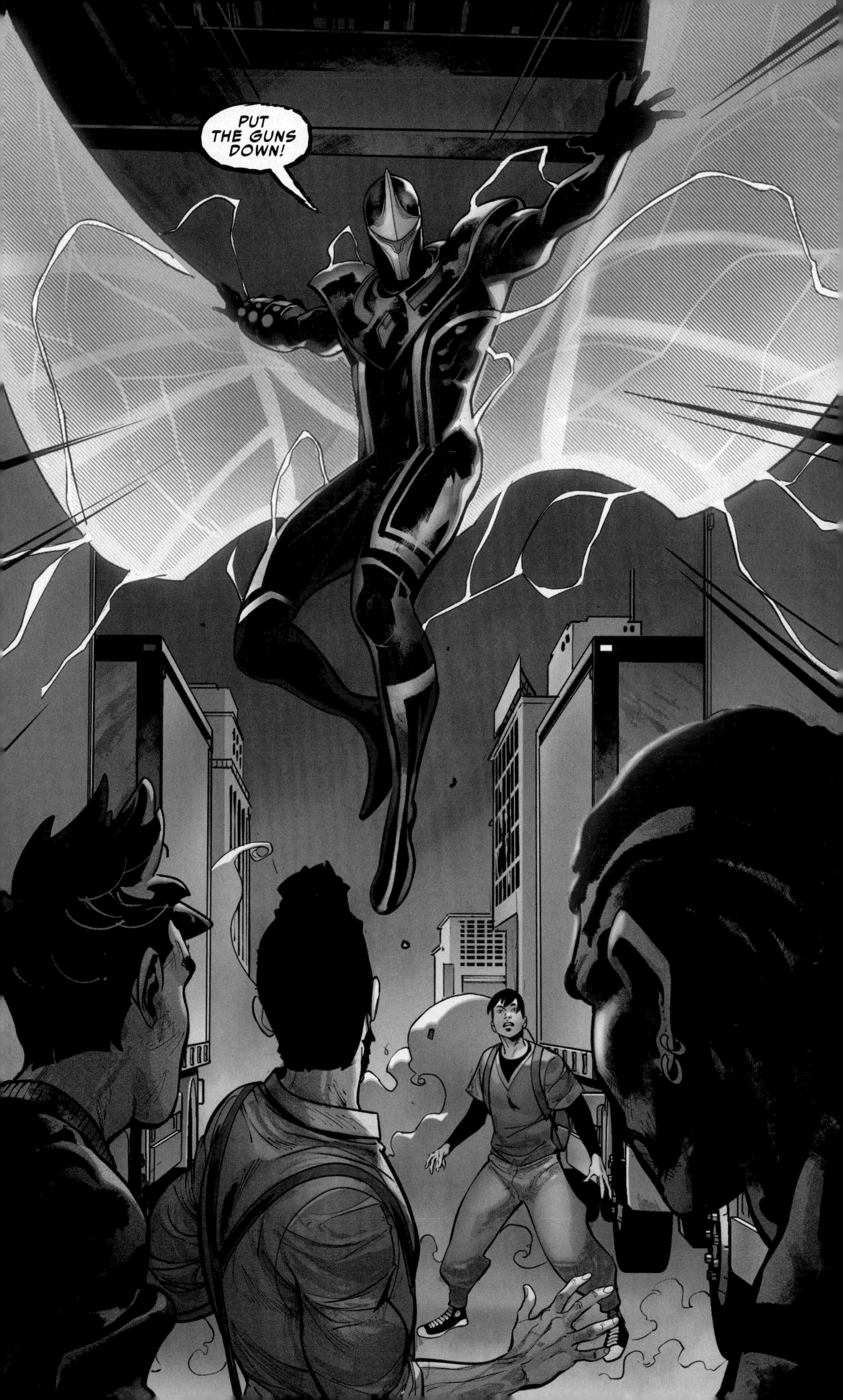
PUT THE GUNS DOWN!

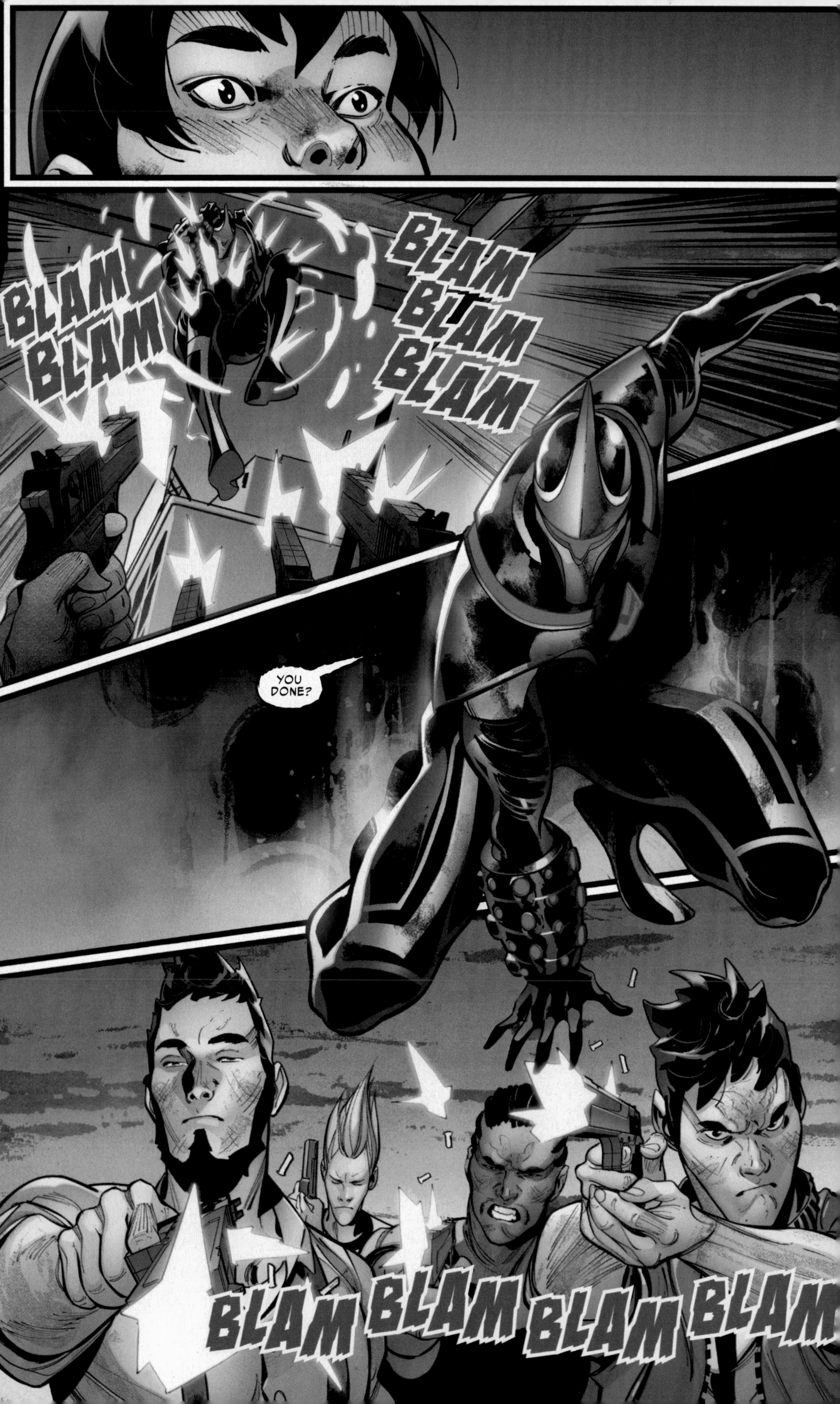
BLAM
BLAM
BLAM
BLAM
BLAM
BLAM
YOU DONE?
BLAM BLAM BLAM BLAM

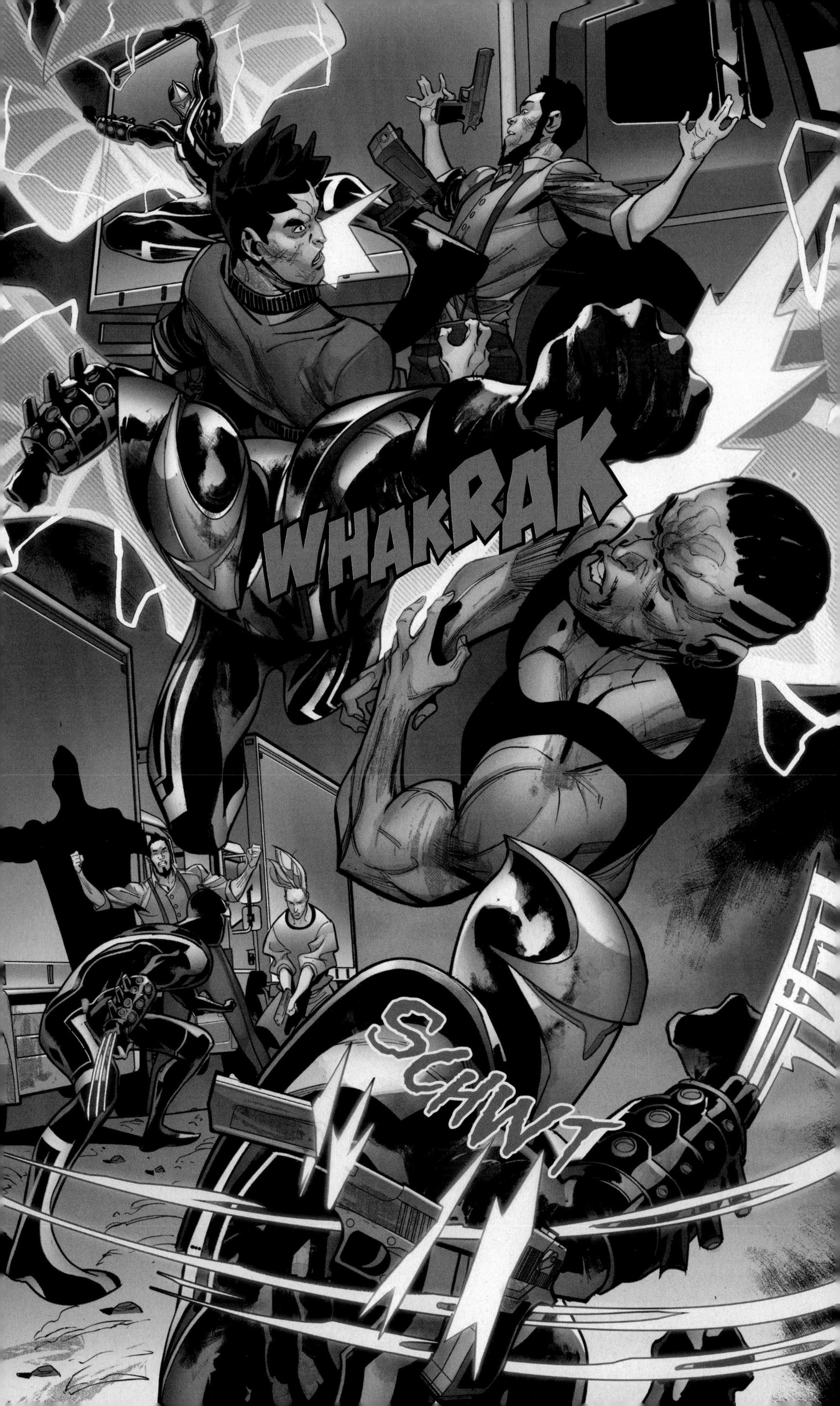
WHAKRAK
SCHWT

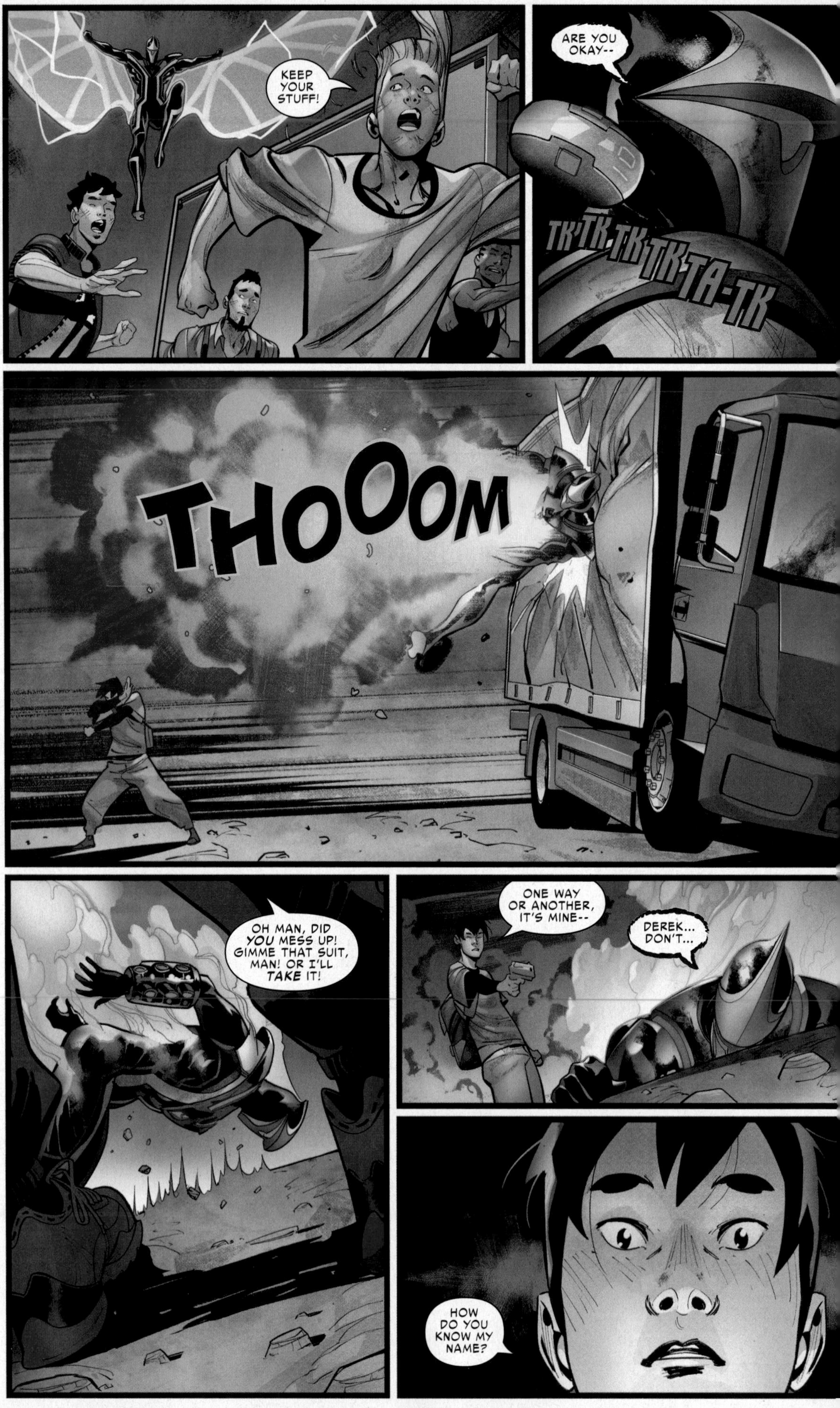
KEEP YOUR STUFF!
ARE YOU OKAY--
TK-TK TK TK TA-TK
THOOOM
OH MAN, DID YOU MESS UP! GIMME THAT SUIT, MAN! OR I'LL TAKE IT!
ONE WAY OR ANOTHER, IT'S MINE--
DEREK... DON'T...
HOW DO YOU KNOW MY NAME?

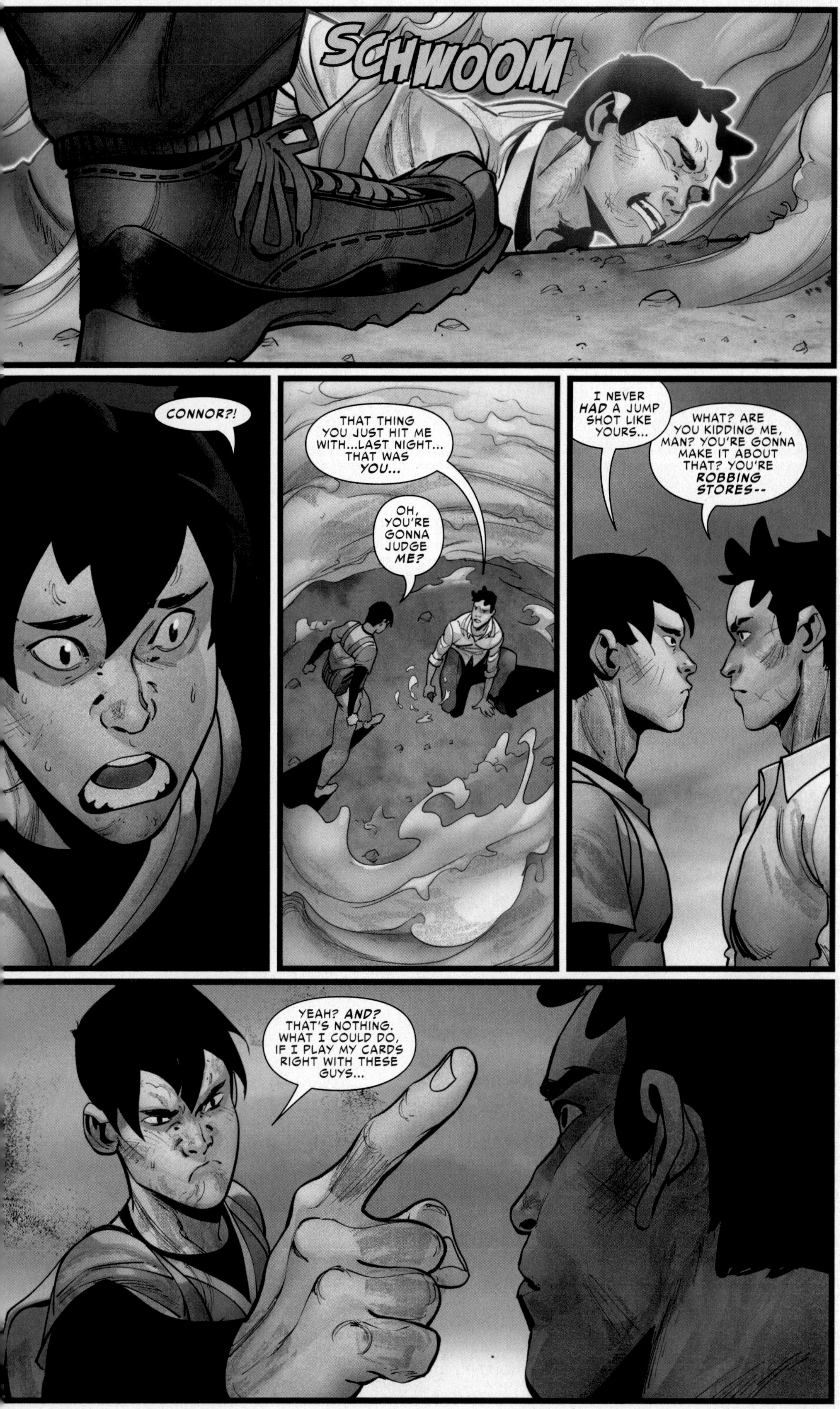
SCHWOOM
CONNOR?!
THAT THING YOU JUST HIT ME WITH...LAST NIGHT... THAT WAS YOU...
OH, YOU'RE GONNA JUDGE ME?
I NEVER HAD A JUMP SHOT LIKE YOURS...
WHAT? ARE YOU KIDDING ME, MAN? YOU'RE GONNA MAKE IT ABOUT THAT? YOU'RE ROBBING STORES--
YEAH? AND? THAT'S NOTHING. WHAT I COULD DO, IF I PLAY MY CARDS RIGHT WITH THESE GUYS...

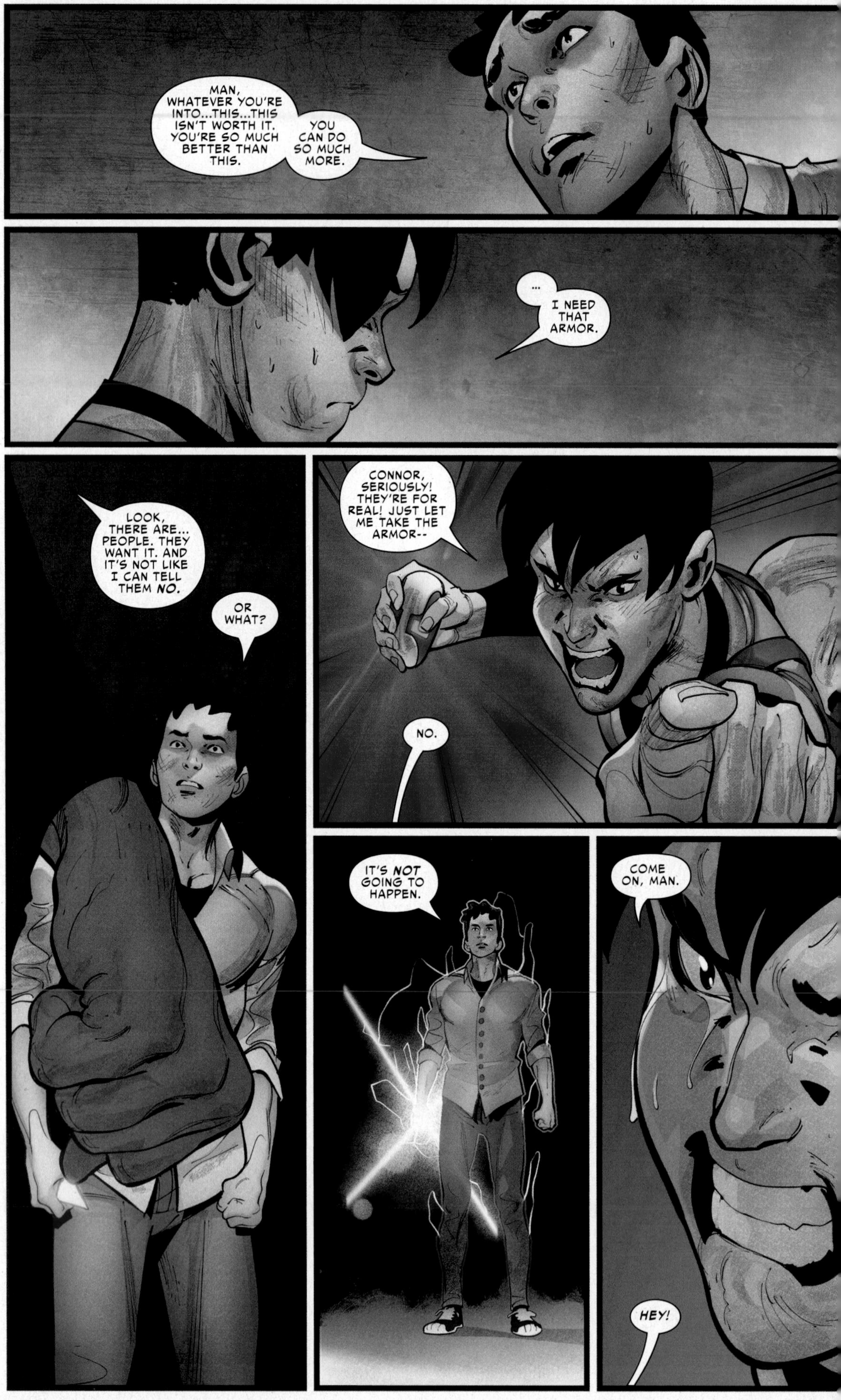

MAN, WHATEVER YOU'RE INTO...THIS...THIS ISN'T WORTH IT. YOU'RE SO MUCH BETTER THAN THIS.
YOU CAN DO SO MUCH MORE.
...
I NEED THAT ARMOR.
LOOK, THERE ARE... PEOPLE. THEY WANT IT. AND IT'S NOT LIKE I CAN TELL THEM NO.
OR WHAT?
CONNOR, SERIOUSLY! THEY'RE FOR REAL! JUST LET ME TAKE THE ARMOR--
NO.
IT'S NOT GOING TO HAPPEN.
COME ON, MAN.
HEY!

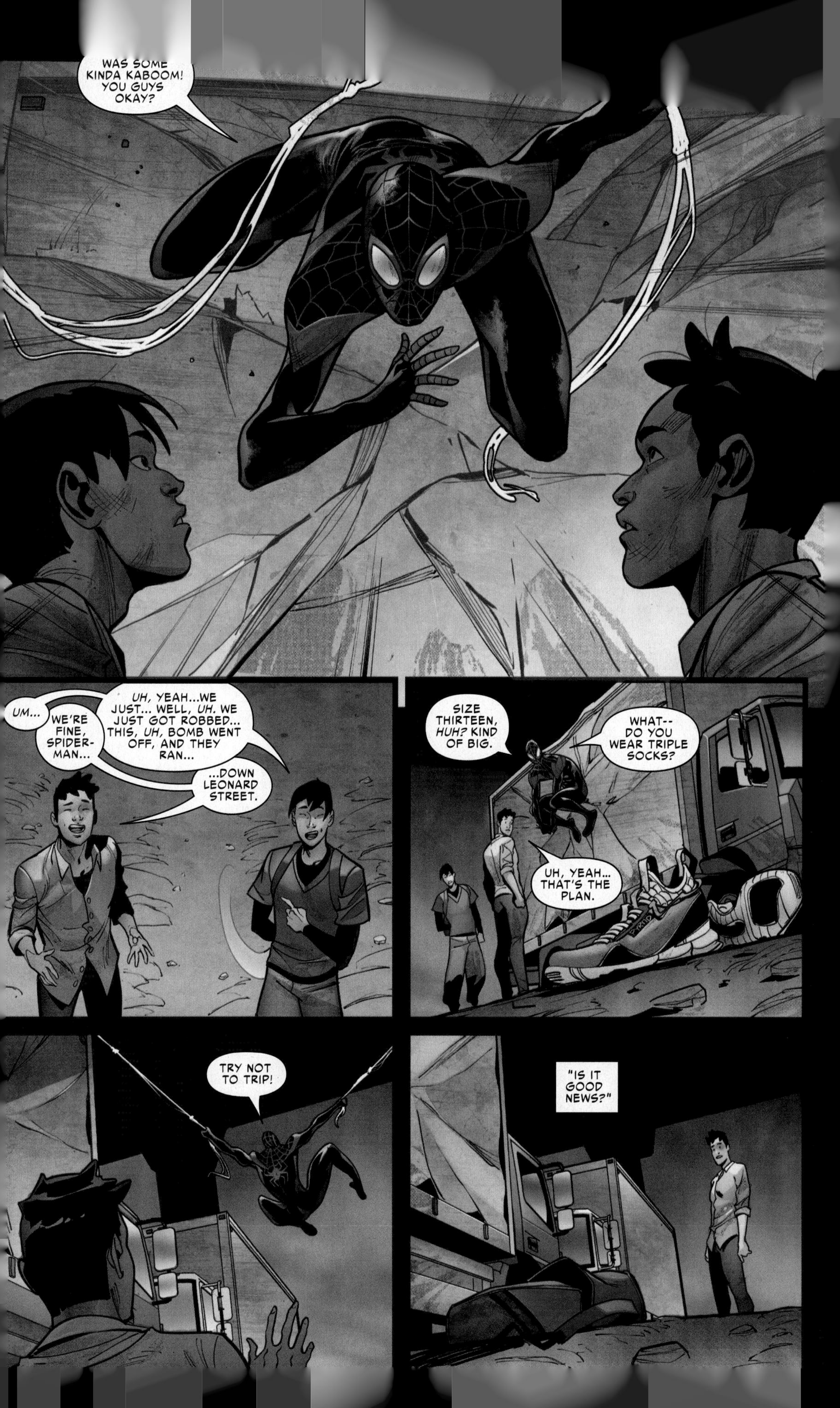
WAS SOME KINDA KABOOM! YOU GUYS OKAY?
UM...
WE'RE FINE, SPIDER-MAN...
UH, YEAH...WE JUST... WELL, UH. WE JUST GOT ROBBED... THIS, UH, BOMB WENT OFF, AND THEY RAN...
...DOWN LEONARD STREET.
SIZE THIRTEEN, HUH? KIND OF BIG.
WHAT--DO YOU WEAR TRIPLE SOCKS?
UH, YEAH... THAT'S THE PLAN.
TRY NOT TO TRIP!
"IS IT GOOD NEWS?"

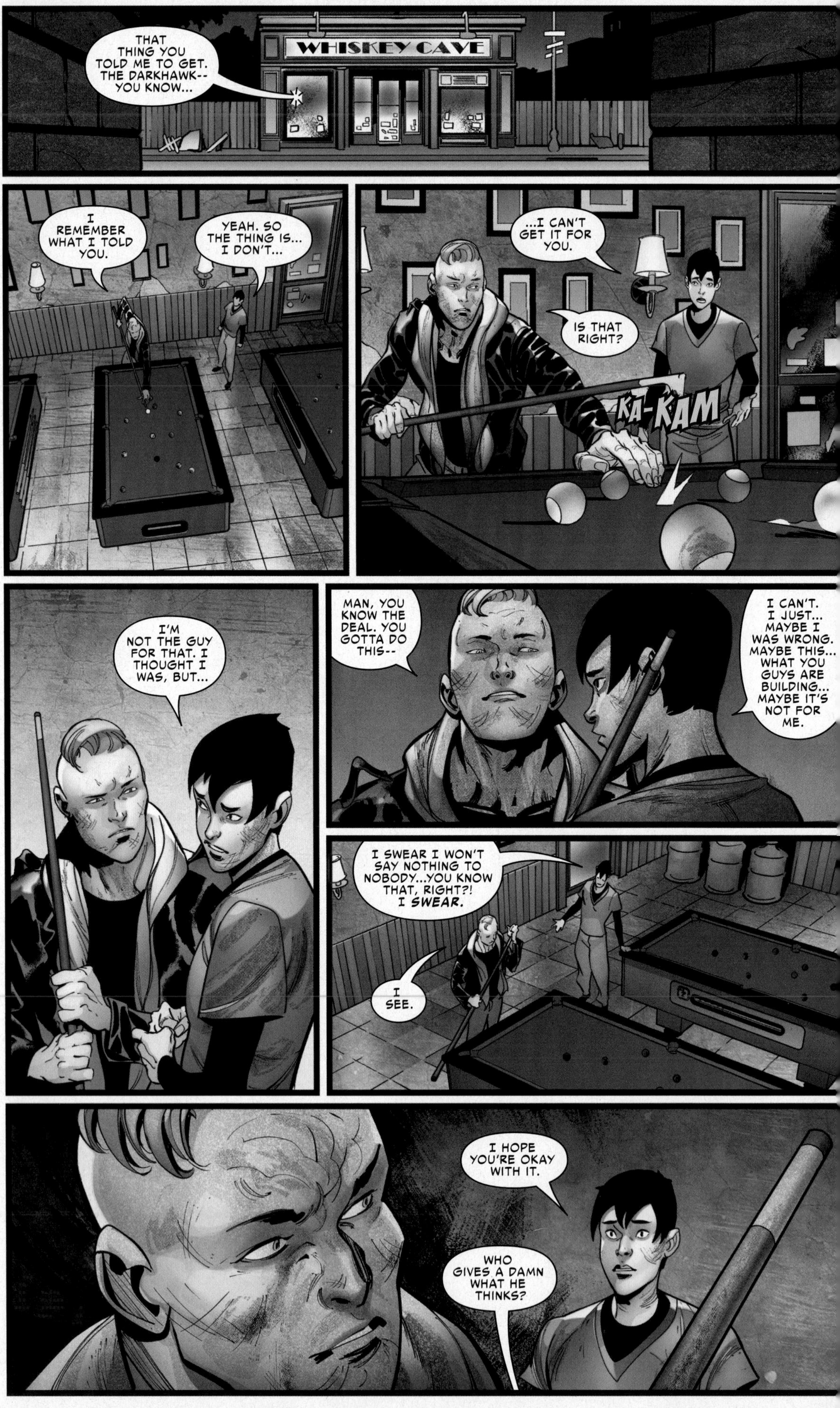

THAT THING YOU TOLD ME TO GET. THE DARKHAWK-- YOU KNOW...
WHISKEY CAVE
I REMEMBER WHAT I TOLD YOU.
YEAH. SO THE THING IS... I DON'T...
...I CAN'T GET IT FOR YOU.
IS THAT RIGHT?
KA-KAM
I'M NOT THE GUY FOR THAT. I THOUGHT I WAS, BUT...
MAN, YOU KNOW THE DEAL. YOU GOTTA DO THIS--
I CAN'T. I JUST... MAYBE I WAS WRONG. MAYBE THIS... WHAT YOU GUYS ARE BUILDING... MAYBE IT'S NOT FOR ME.
I SWEAR I WON'T SAY NOTHING TO NOBODY...YOU KNOW THAT, RIGHT?! I *SWEAR.*
I SEE.
I HOPE YOU'RE OKAY WITH IT.
WHO GIVES A DAMN WHAT HE THINKS?

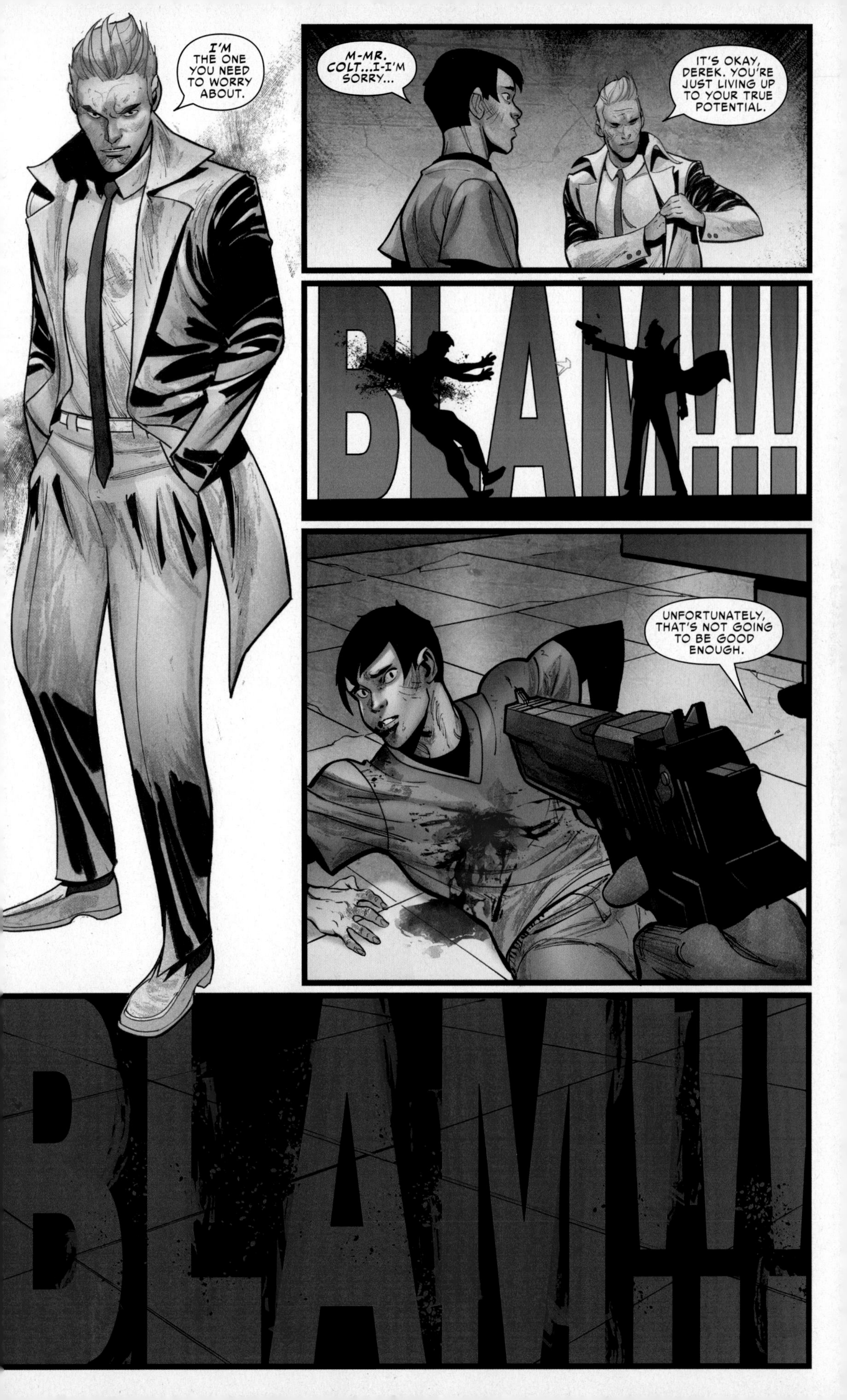
I'M THE ONE YOU NEED TO WORRY ABOUT.
M-MR. COLT...I-I'M SORRY...
IT'S OKAY, DEREK. YOU'RE JUST LIVING UP TO YOUR TRUE POTENTIAL.
BLAM!!!
UNFORTUNATELY, THAT'S NOT GOING TO BE GOOD ENOUGH.
BLAM!!!

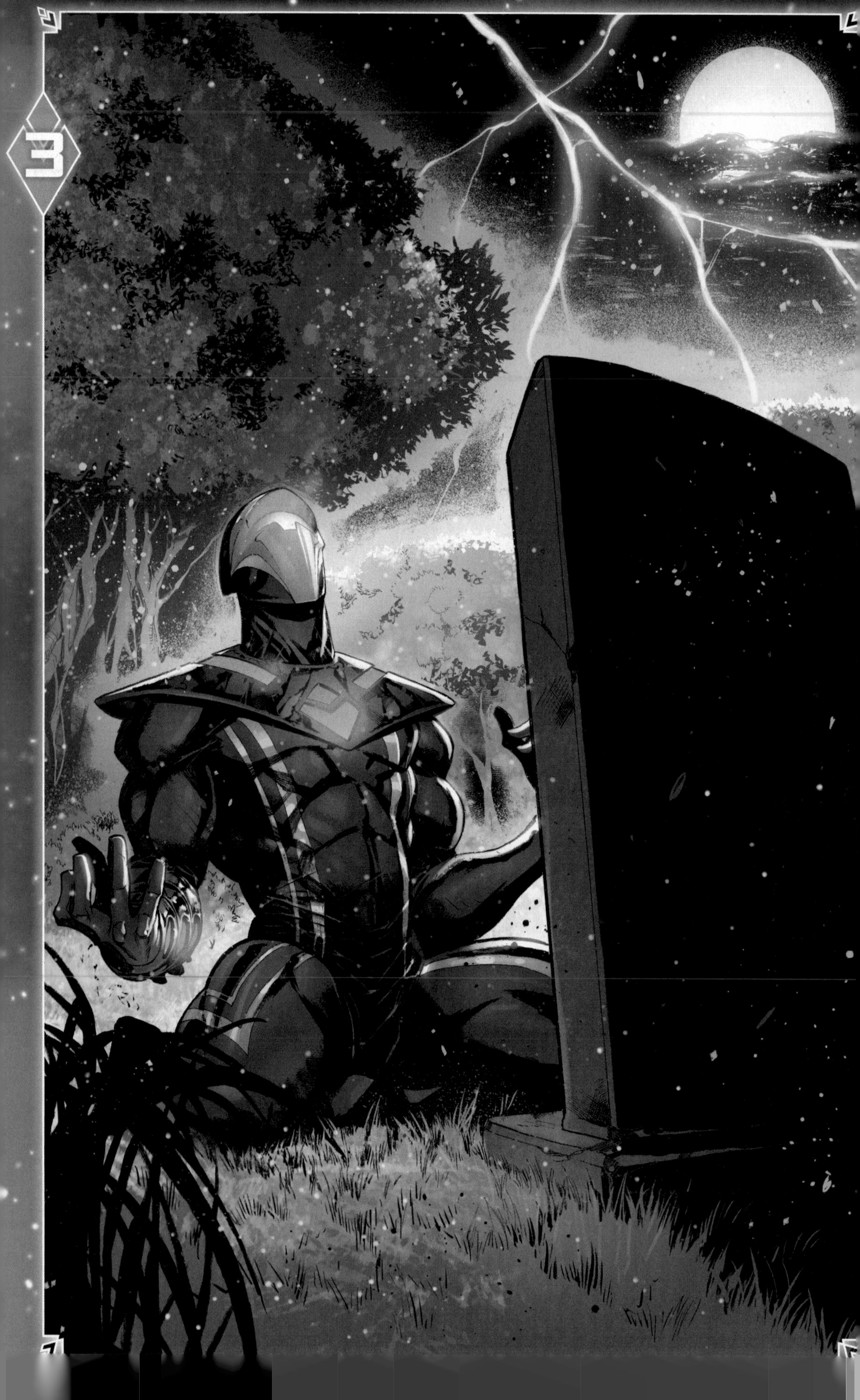
3

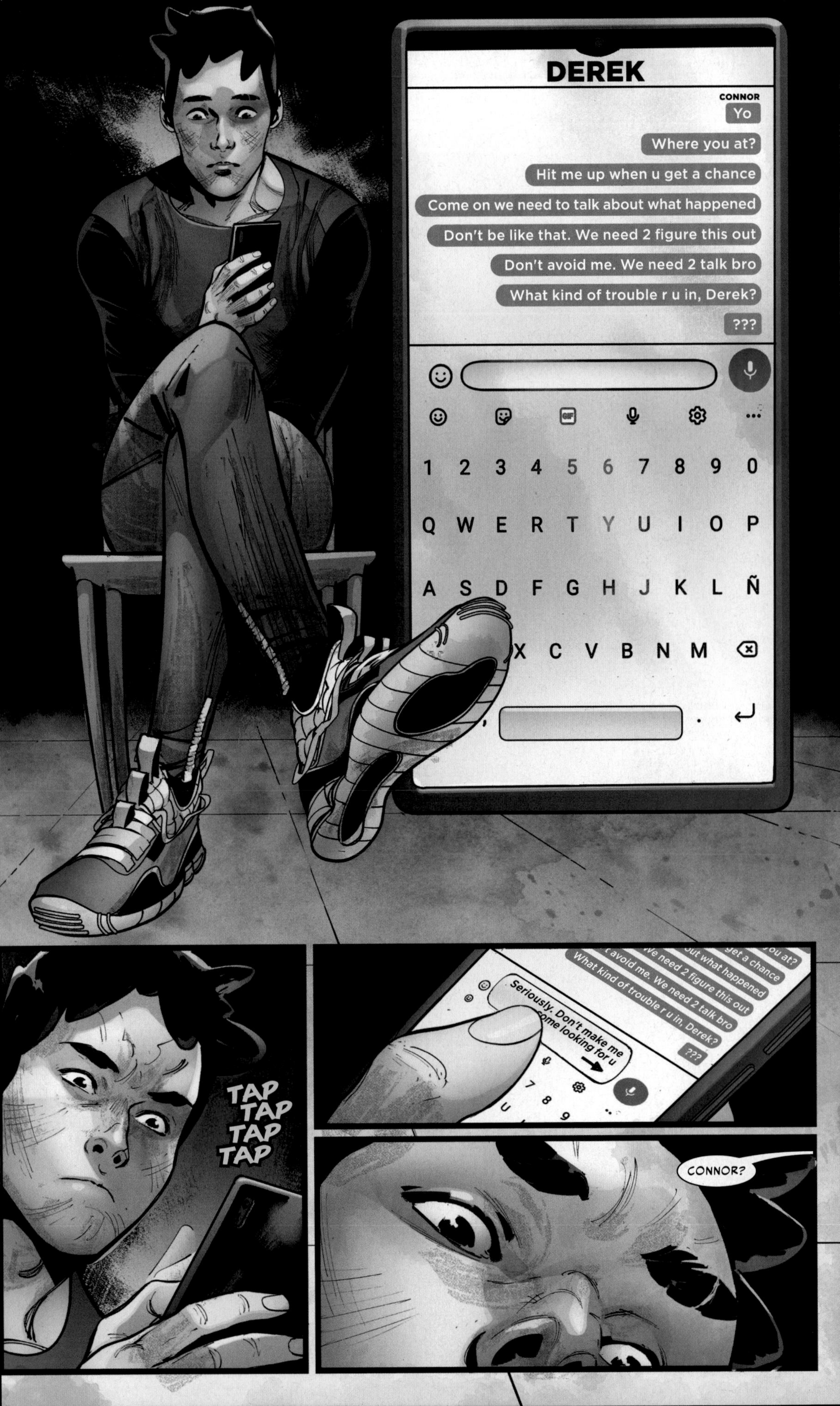
DEREK
CONNOR
Yo
Where you at?
Hit me up when u get a chance
Come on we need to talk about what happened
Don't be like that. We need 2 figure this out
Don't avoid me. We need 2 talk bro
What kind of trouble r u in, Derek?
???
TAP TAP TAP TAP
Seriously. Don't make me
ome looking for u
CONNOR?

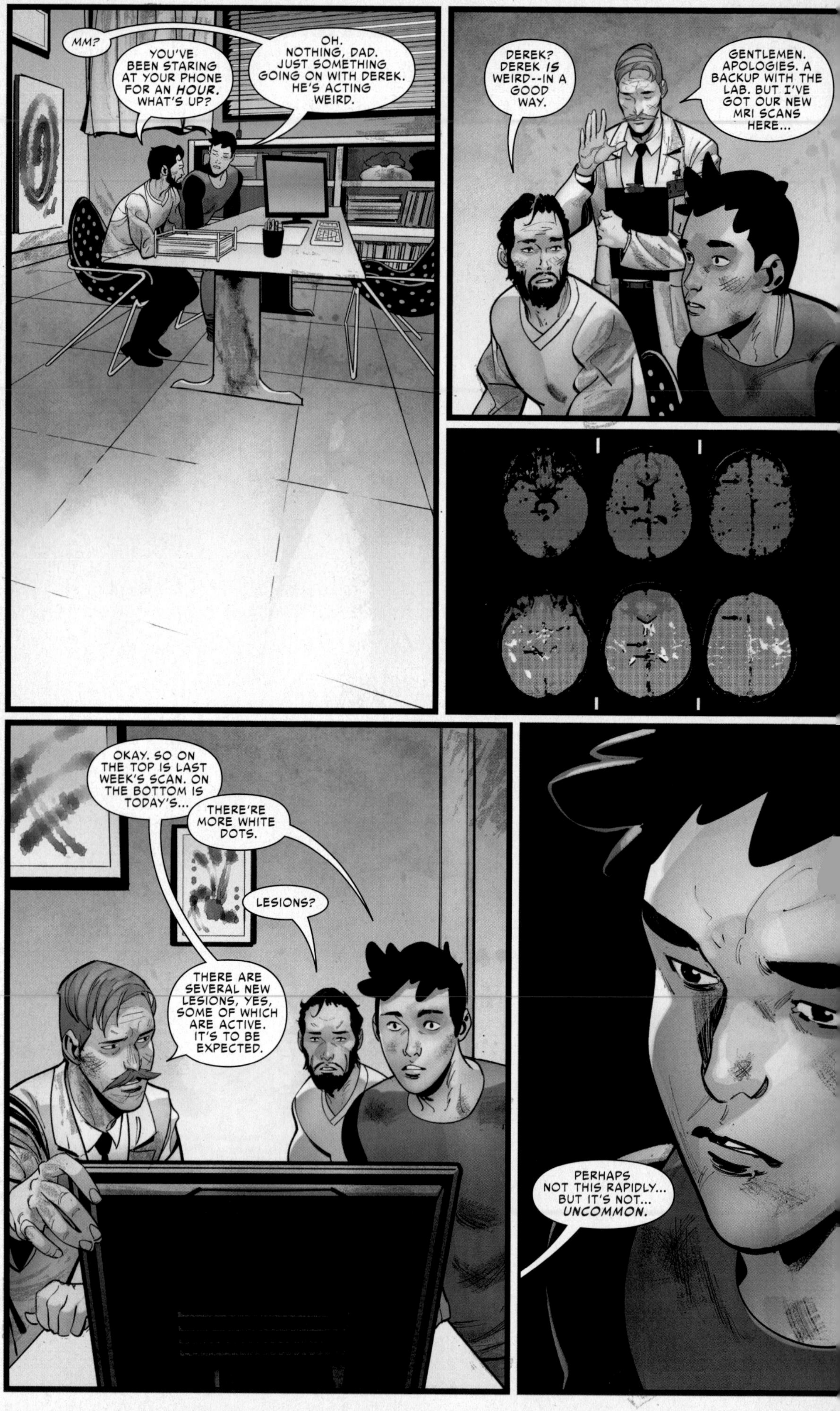
MM?
YOU'VE BEEN STARING AT YOUR PHONE FOR AN *HOUR.* WHAT'S UP?
OH. NOTHING, DAD. JUST SOMETHING GOING ON WITH DEREK. HE'S ACTING WEIRD.
DEREK? DEREK *IS* WEIRD--IN A GOOD WAY.
GENTLEMEN. APOLOGIES. A BACKUP WITH THE LAB. BUT I'VE GOT OUR NEW MRI SCANS HERE...
OKAY. SO ON THE TOP IS LAST WEEK'S SCAN. ON THE BOTTOM IS TODAY'S...
THERE'RE MORE WHITE DOTS.
LESIONS?
THERE ARE SEVERAL NEW LESIONS, YES, SOME OF WHICH ARE ACTIVE. IT'S TO BE EXPECTED.
PERHAPS NOT THIS RAPIDLY... BUT IT'S NOT... *UNCOMMON.*

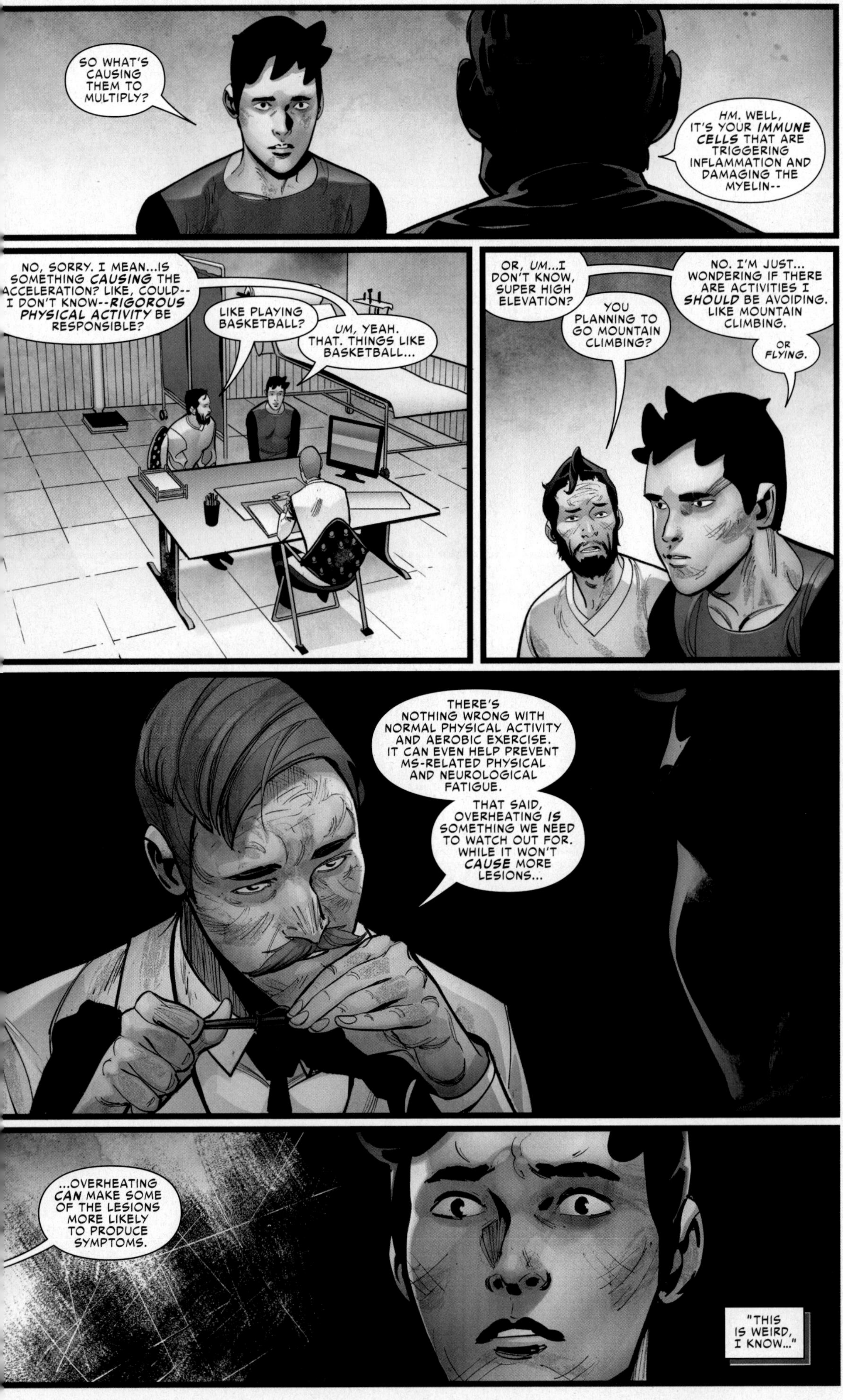

SO WHAT'S CAUSING THEM TO MULTIPLY?
HM. WELL, IT'S YOUR IMMUNE CELLS THAT ARE TRIGGERING INFLAMMATION AND DAMAGING THE MYELIN--
NO, SORRY. I MEAN...IS SOMETHING CAUSING THE ACCELERATION? LIKE, COULD-- I DON'T KNOW--RIGOROUS PHYSICAL ACTIVITY BE RESPONSIBLE?
LIKE PLAYING BASKETBALL?
UM, YEAH. THAT. THINGS LIKE BASKETBALL...
OR, UM...I DON'T KNOW, SUPER HIGH ELEVATION?
YOU PLANNING TO GO MOUNTAIN CLIMBING?
NO. I'M JUST... WONDERING IF THERE ARE ACTIVITIES I SHOULD BE AVOIDING. LIKE MOUNTAIN CLIMBING.
OR FLYING.
THERE'S NOTHING WRONG WITH NORMAL PHYSICAL ACTIVITY AND AEROBIC EXERCISE. IT CAN EVEN HELP PREVENT MS-RELATED PHYSICAL AND NEUROLOGICAL FATIGUE.
THAT SAID, OVERHEATING IS SOMETHING WE NEED TO WATCH OUT FOR. WHILE IT WON'T CAUSE MORE LESIONS...
...OVERHEATING CAN MAKE SOME OF THE LESIONS MORE LIKELY TO PRODUCE SYMPTOMS.
"THIS IS WEIRD, I KNOW..."

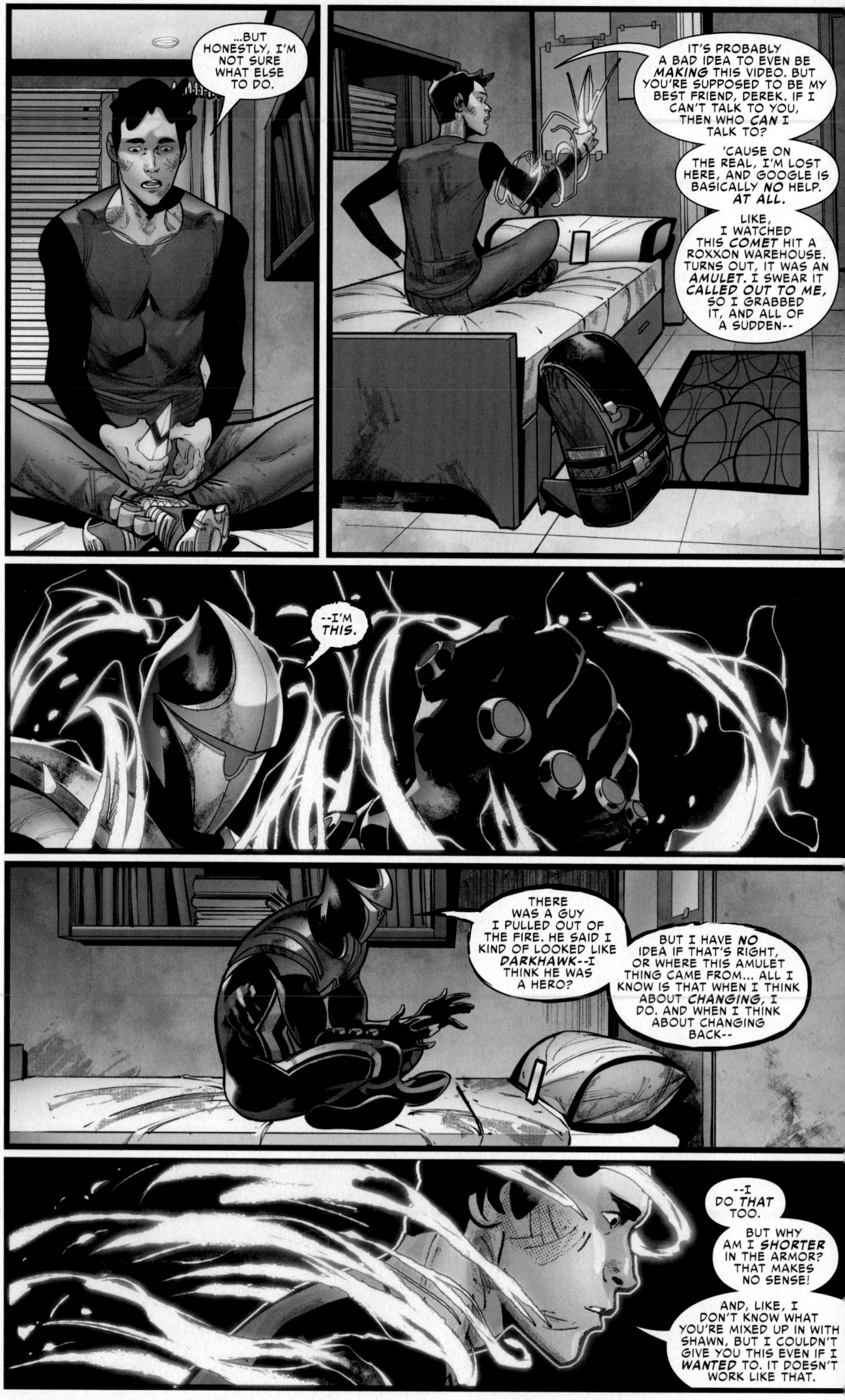
...BUT HONESTLY, I'M NOT SURE WHAT ELSE TO DO.
IT'S PROBABLY A BAD IDEA TO EVEN BE *MAKING* THIS VIDEO. BUT YOU'RE SUPPOSED TO BE MY BEST FRIEND, DEREK. IF I CAN'T TALK TO YOU, THEN WHO *CAN* I TALK TO?
'CAUSE ON THE REAL, I'M LOST HERE, AND GOOGLE IS BASICALLY *NO* HELP. *AT ALL.*
LIKE, I WATCHED THIS *COMET* HIT A ROXXON WAREHOUSE. TURNS OUT, IT WAS AN *AMULET.* I SWEAR IT *CALLED OUT TO ME,* SO I GRABBED IT, AND ALL OF A SUDDEN--
--I'M *THIS.*
THERE WAS A GUY I PULLED OUT OF THE FIRE. HE SAID I KIND OF LOOKED LIKE *DARKHAWK*--I THINK HE WAS A HERO?
BUT I HAVE *NO* IDEA IF THAT'S RIGHT, OR WHERE THIS AMULET THING CAME FROM... ALL I KNOW IS THAT WHEN I THINK ABOUT *CHANGING,* I DO. AND WHEN I THINK ABOUT CHANGING BACK--
--I DO *THAT* TOO.
BUT WHY AM I *SHORTER* IN THE ARMOR? THAT MAKES NO SENSE!
AND, LIKE, I DON'T KNOW WHAT YOU'RE MIXED UP IN WITH SHAWN, BUT I COULDN'T GIVE YOU THIS EVEN IF I *WANTED* TO. IT DOESN'T WORK LIKE THAT.

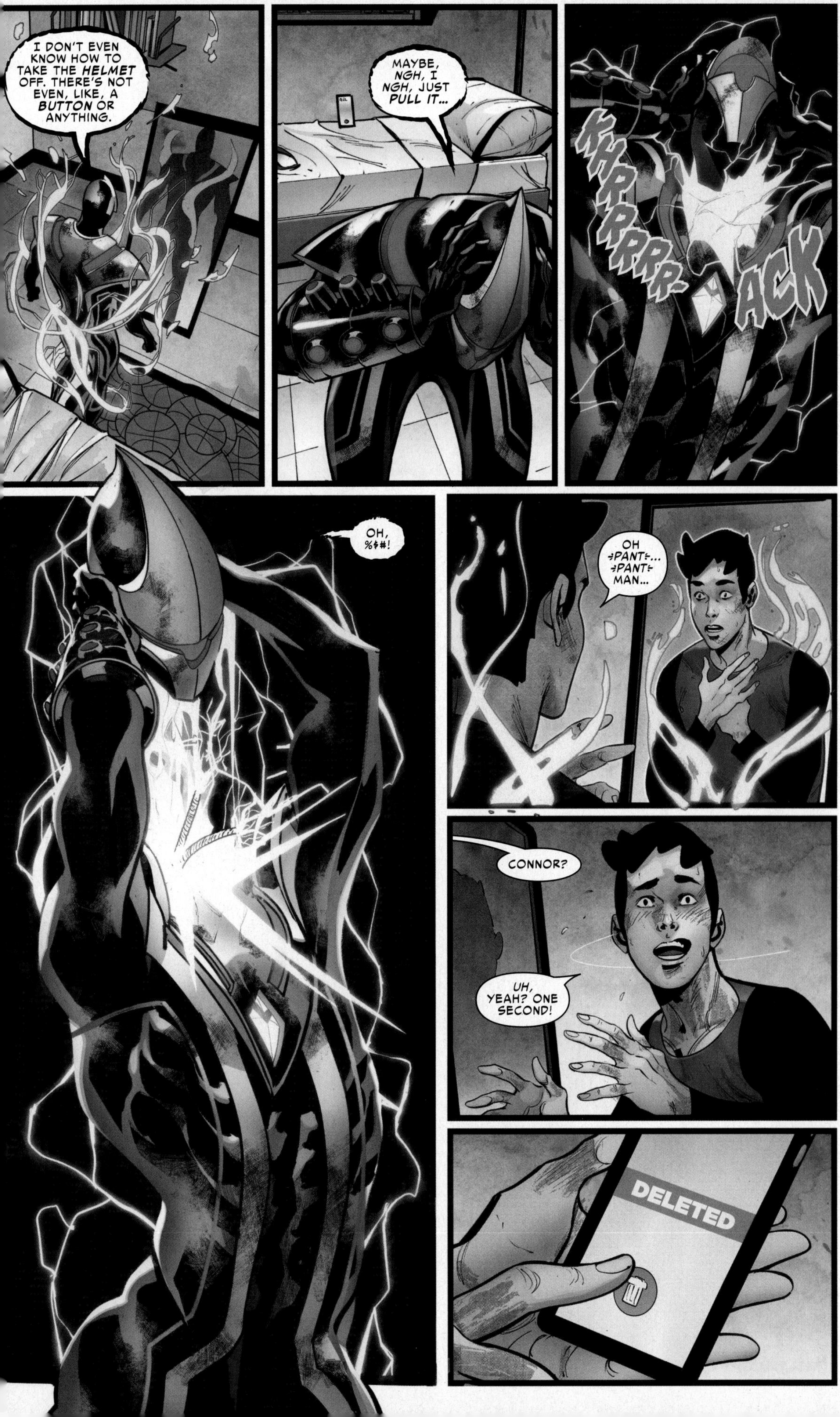
I DON'T EVEN KNOW HOW TO TAKE THE *HELMET* OFF. THERE'S NOT EVEN, LIKE, A *BUTTON* OR ANYTHING.
MAYBE, NGH, I NGH, JUST *PULL IT*...
KHRRRRR-ACK
OH, %$#!
OH =PANT=... =PANT= MAN...
CONNOR?
UH, YEAH? ONE SECOND!
DELETED

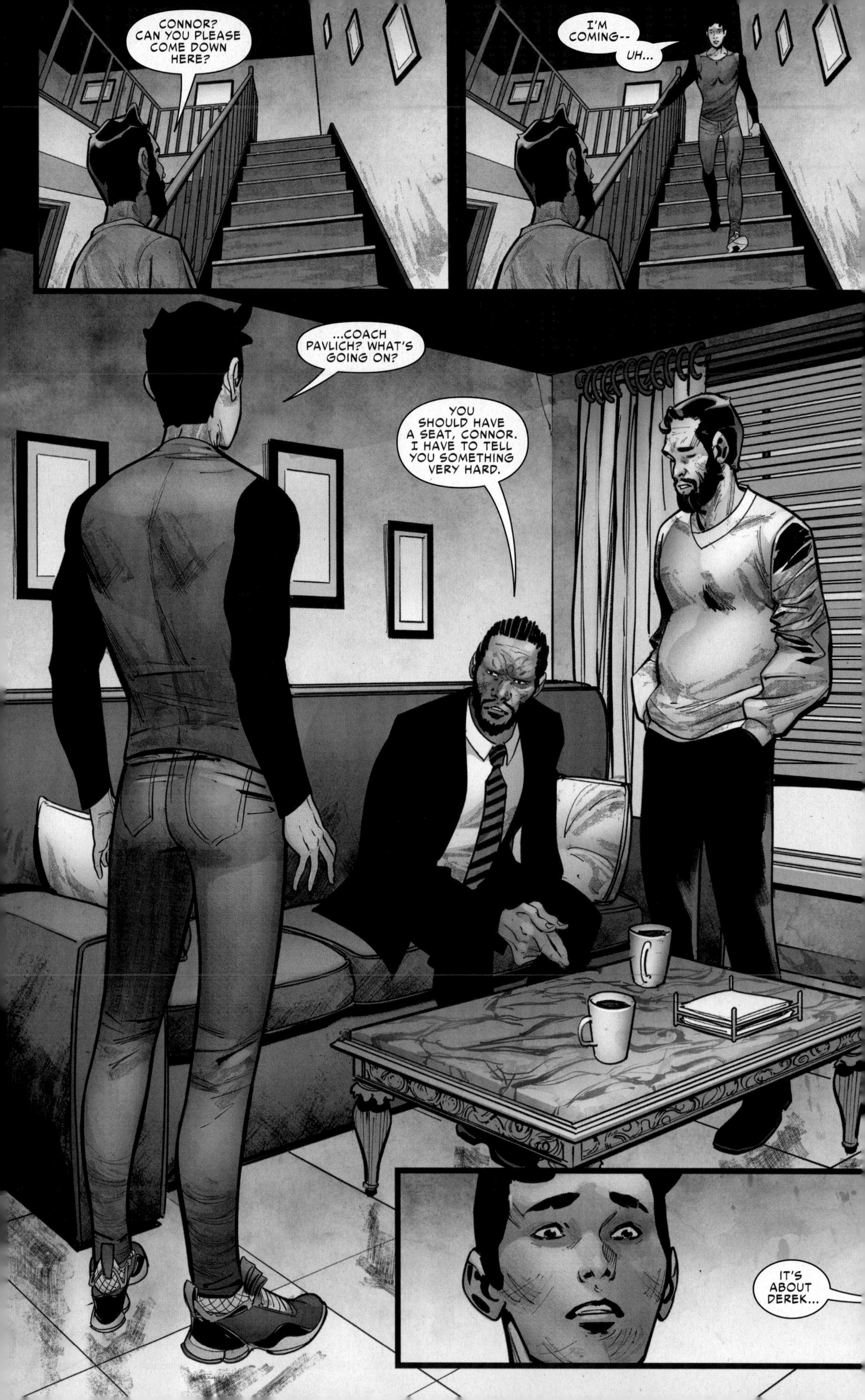
CONNOR? CAN YOU PLEASE COME DOWN HERE?
I'M COMING-- UH...
...COACH PAVLICH? WHAT'S GOING ON?
YOU SHOULD HAVE A SEAT, CONNOR. I HAVE TO TELL YOU SOMETHING VERY HARD.
IT'S ABOUT DEREK...

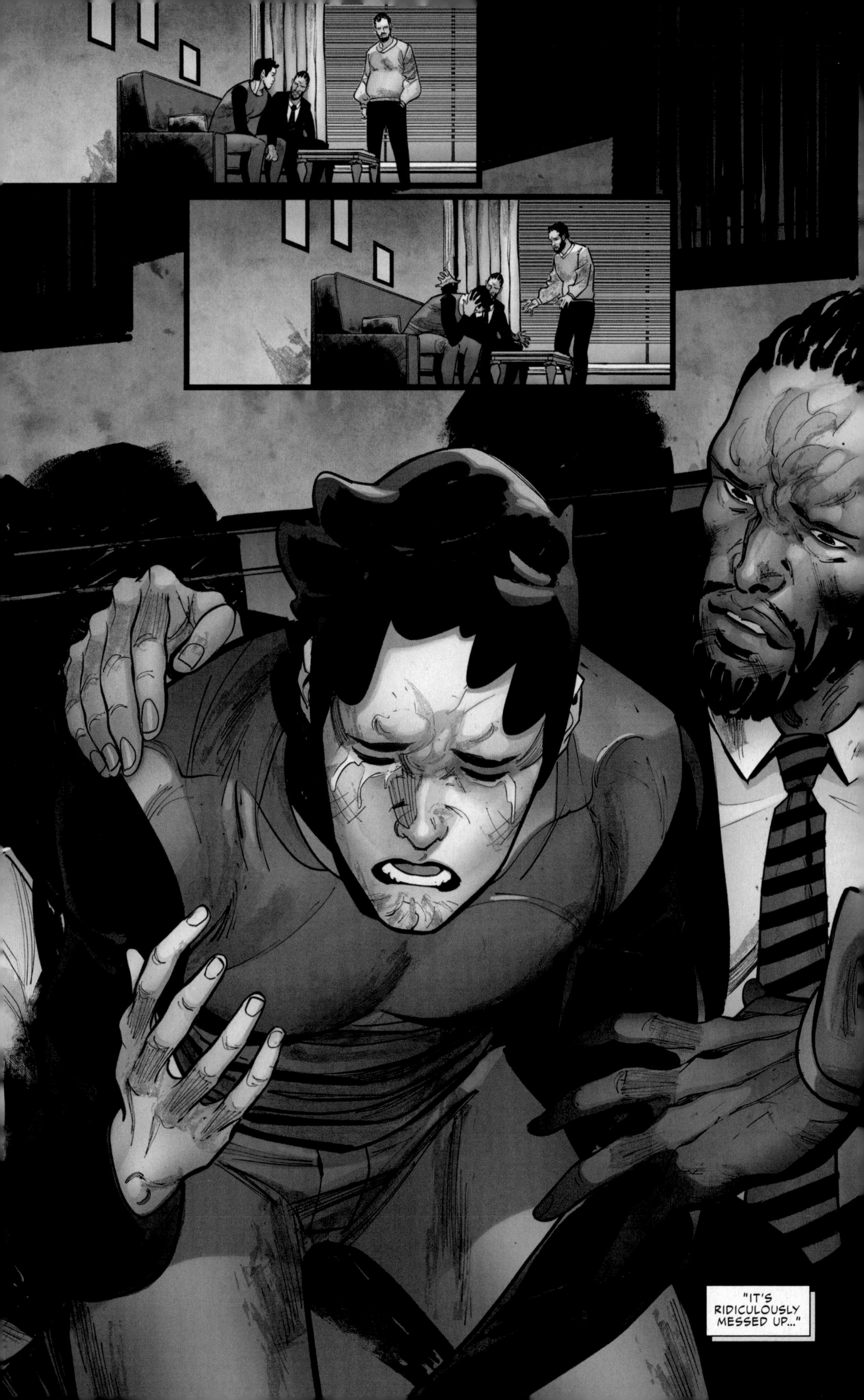
"IT'S
RIDICULOUSLY
MESSED UP..."

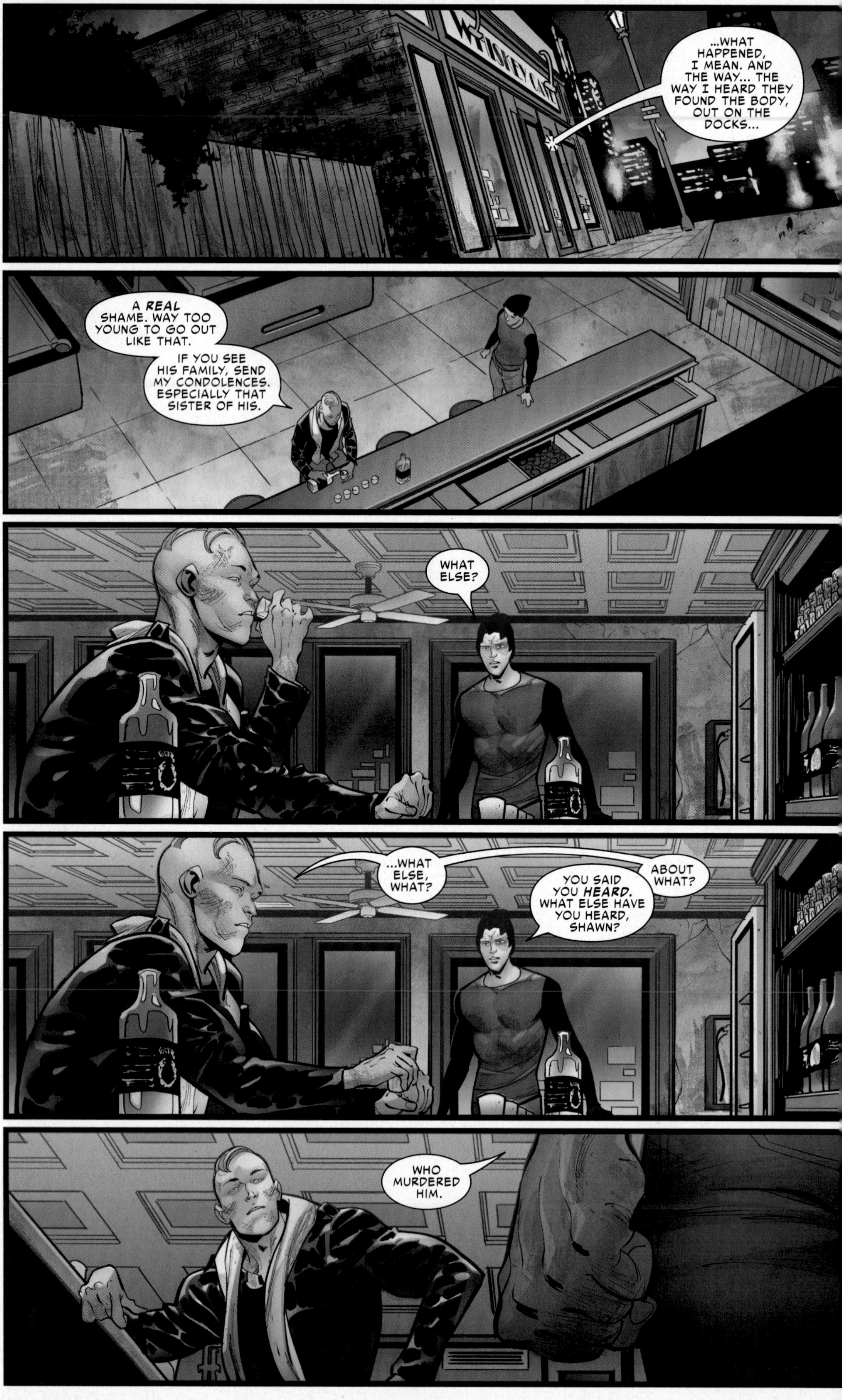

...WHAT HAPPENED, I MEAN. AND THE WAY... THE WAY I HEARD THEY FOUND THE BODY, OUT ON THE DOCKS...
A **REAL** SHAME. WAY TOO YOUNG TO GO OUT LIKE THAT.
IF YOU SEE HIS FAMILY, SEND MY CONDOLENCES. ESPECIALLY THAT SISTER OF HIS.
WHAT ELSE?
...WHAT ELSE, WHAT?
ABOUT WHAT?
YOU SAID YOU **HEARD.** WHAT ELSE HAVE YOU HEARD, SHAWN?
WHO MURDERED HIM.

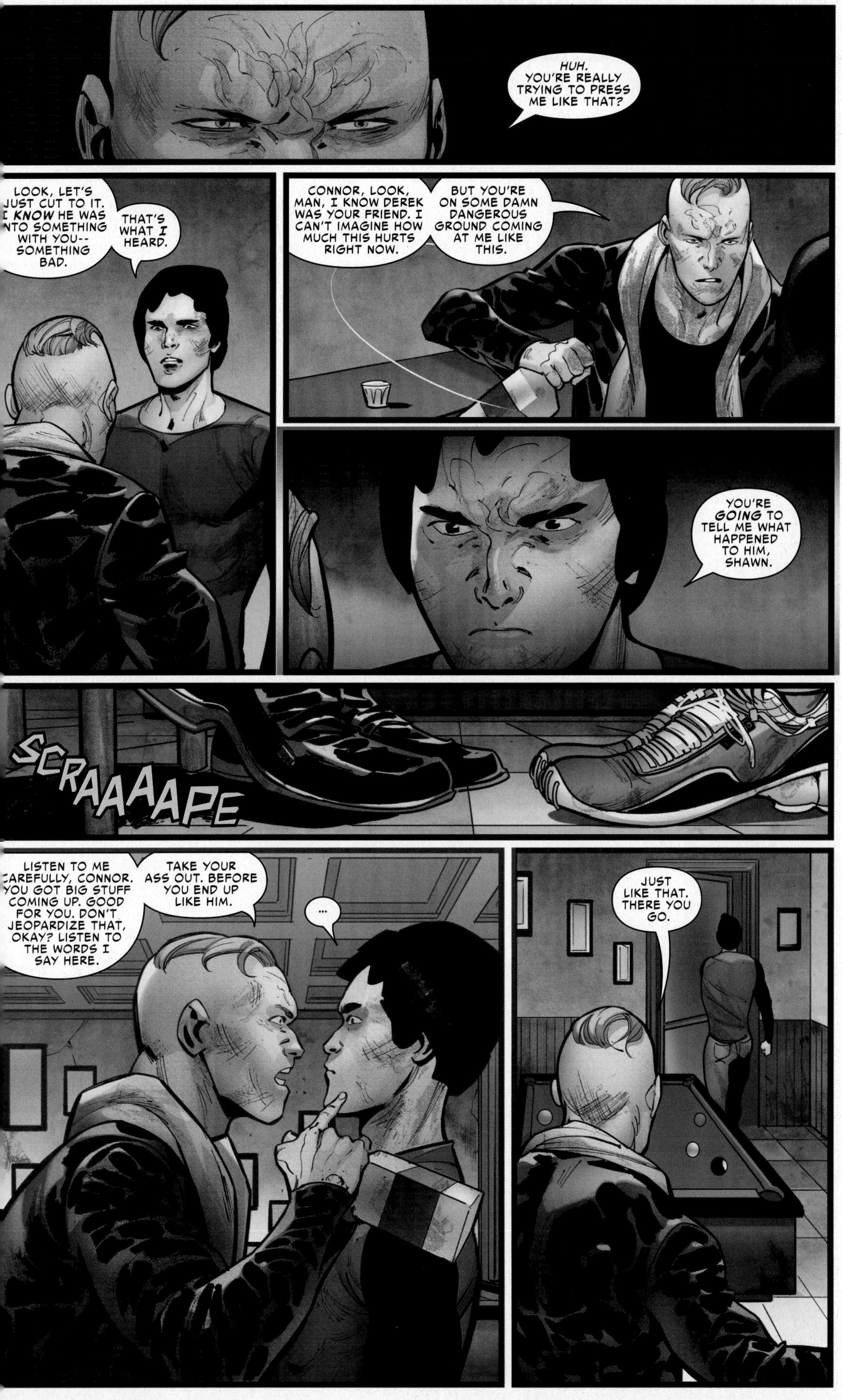
HUH. YOU'RE REALLY TRYING TO PRESS ME LIKE THAT?
LOOK, LET'S JUST CUT TO IT. I KNOW HE WAS INTO SOMETHING WITH YOU-- SOMETHING BAD.
THAT'S WHAT I HEARD.
CONNOR, LOOK, MAN, I KNOW DEREK WAS YOUR FRIEND. I CAN'T IMAGINE HOW MUCH THIS HURTS RIGHT NOW.
BUT YOU'RE ON SOME DAMN DANGEROUS GROUND COMING AT ME LIKE THIS.
YOU'RE GOING TO TELL ME WHAT HAPPENED TO HIM, SHAWN.
SCRAAAAAPE
LISTEN TO ME CAREFULLY, CONNOR. YOU GOT BIG STUFF COMING UP. GOOD FOR YOU. DON'T JEOPARDIZE THAT, OKAY? LISTEN TO THE WORDS I SAY HERE.
TAKE YOUR ASS OUT. BEFORE YOU END UP LIKE HIM.
...
JUST LIKE THAT. THERE YOU GO.

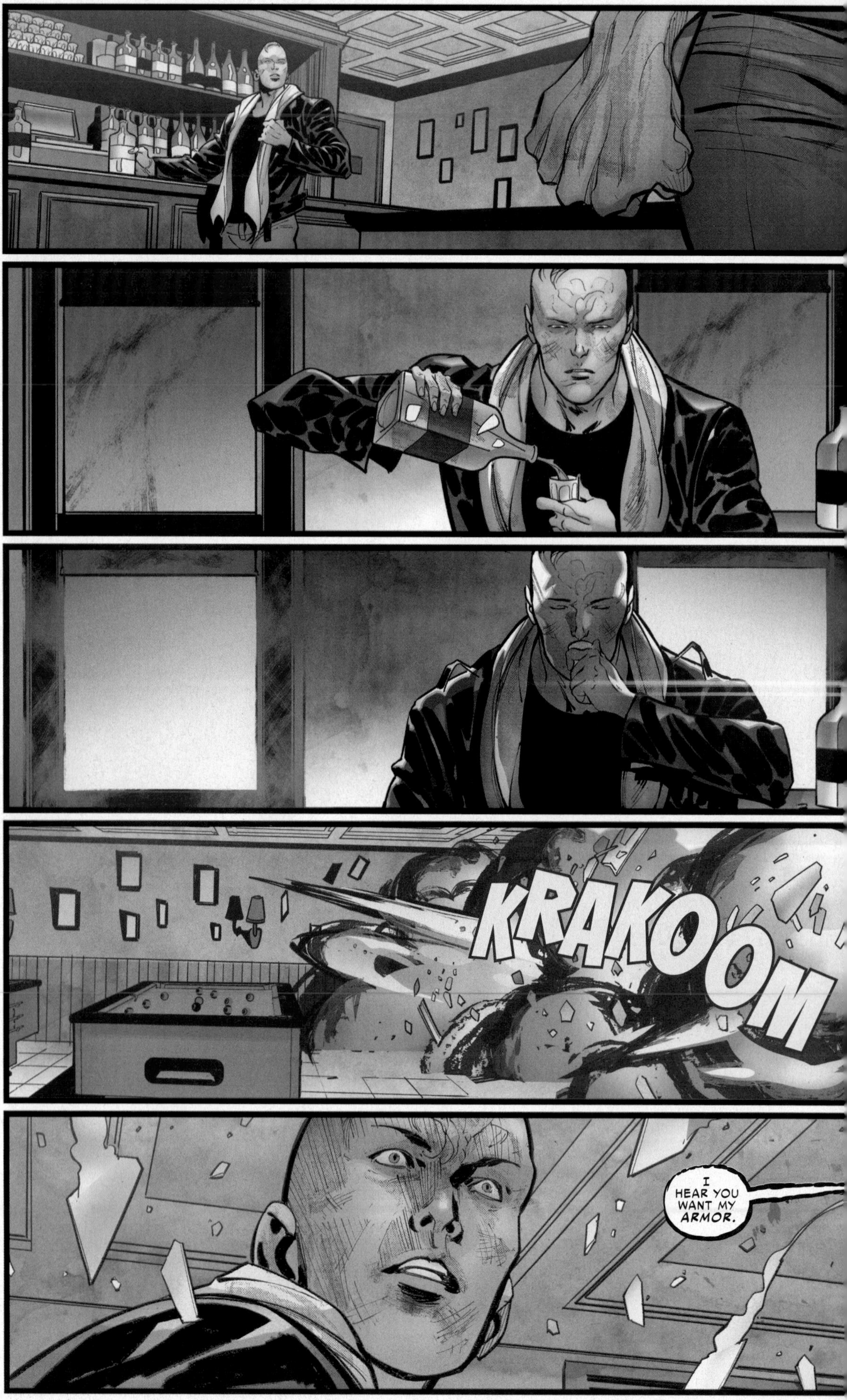
KRAKOOM
I HEAR YOU WANT MY ARMOR.

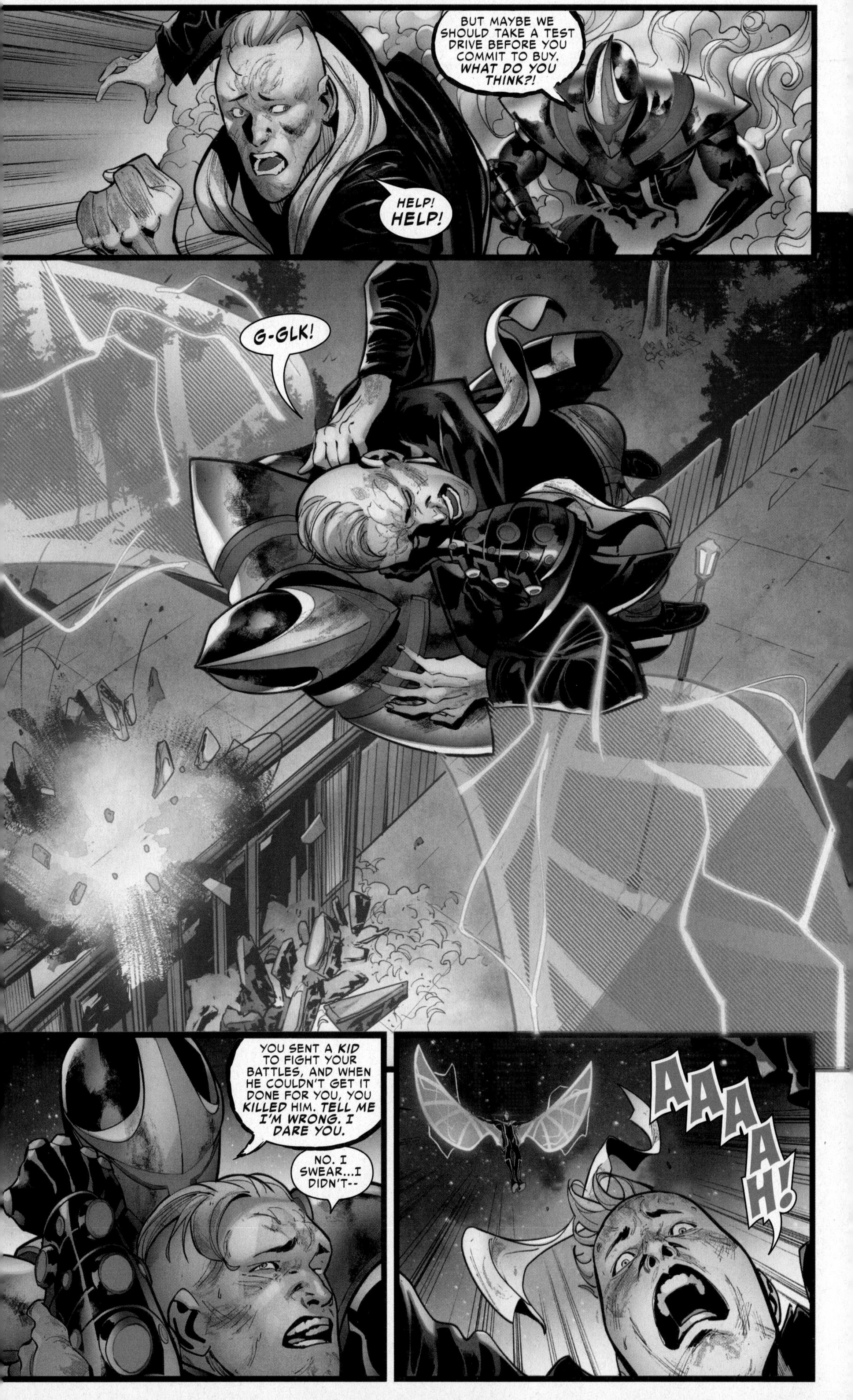
BUT MAYBE WE SHOULD TAKE A TEST DRIVE BEFORE YOU COMMIT TO BUY. WHAT DO YOU THINK?!
HELP! HELP!
G-GLK!
YOU SENT A KID TO FIGHT YOUR BATTLES, AND WHEN HE COULDN'T GET IT DONE FOR YOU, YOU KILLED HIM. TELL ME I'M WRONG. I DARE YOU.
NO. I SWEAR...I DIDN'T--
AAAAAH!

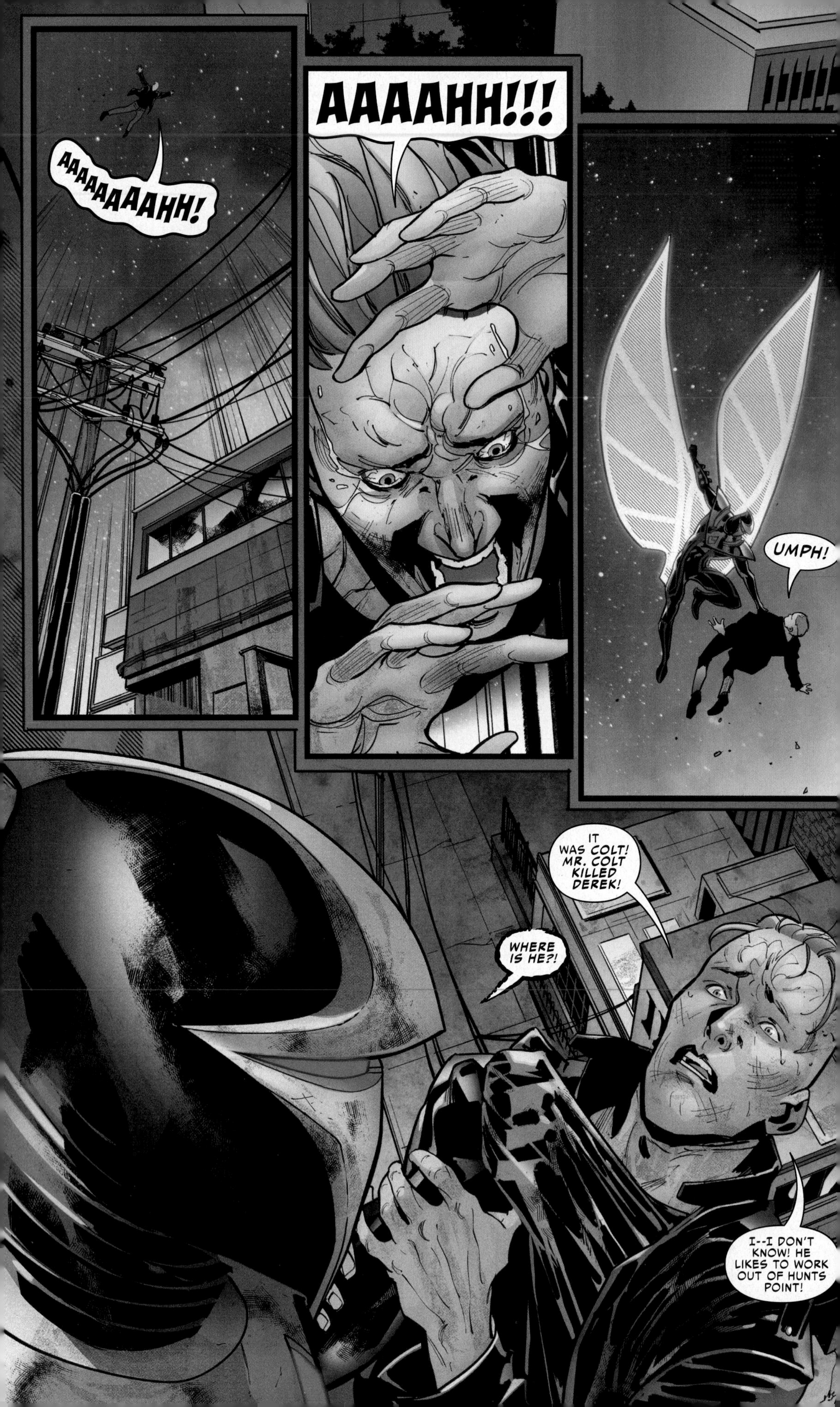
AAAAAAAAHH!
AAAAHH!!!
UMPH!
IT WAS COLT! MR. COLT KILLED DEREK!
WHERE IS HE?!
I--I DON'T KNOW! HE LIKES TO WORK OUT OF HUNTS POINT!

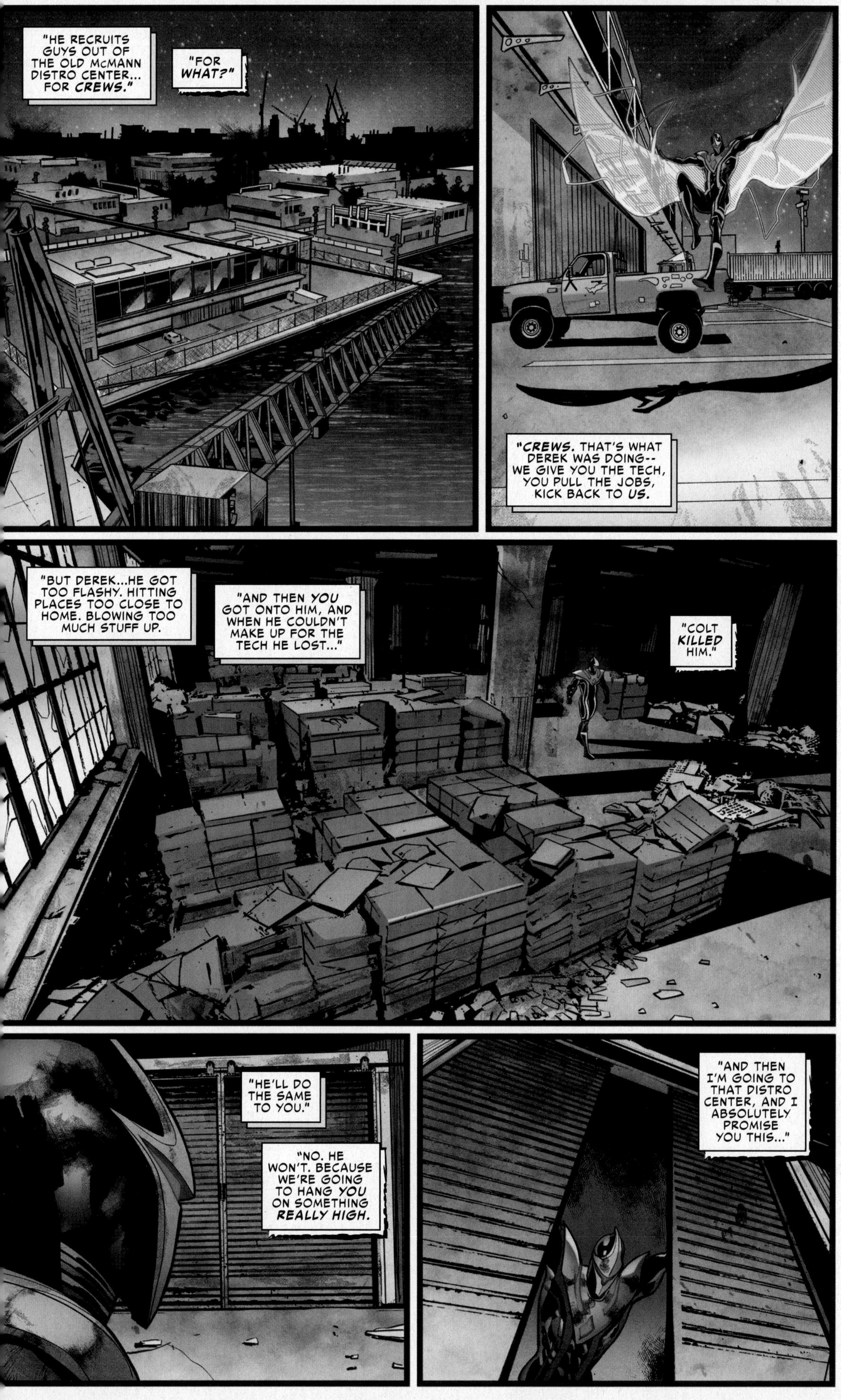
"HE RECRUITS GUYS OUT OF THE OLD McMANN DISTRO CENTER... FOR *CREWS*."
"FOR *WHAT?*"
"*CREWS*. THAT'S WHAT DEREK WAS DOING-- WE GIVE YOU THE TECH, YOU PULL THE JOBS, KICK BACK TO *US*.
"BUT DEREK...HE GOT TOO FLASHY. HITTING PLACES TOO CLOSE TO HOME. BLOWING TOO MUCH STUFF UP.
"AND THEN *YOU* GOT ONTO HIM, AND WHEN HE COULDN'T MAKE UP FOR THE TECH HE LOST..."
"COLT *KILLED* HIM."
"HE'LL DO THE SAME TO YOU."
"NO. HE WON'T. BECAUSE WE'RE GOING TO HANG *YOU* ON SOMETHING *REALLY HIGH*.
"AND THEN I'M GOING TO THAT DISTRO CENTER, AND I ABSOLUTELY PROMISE YOU THIS..."

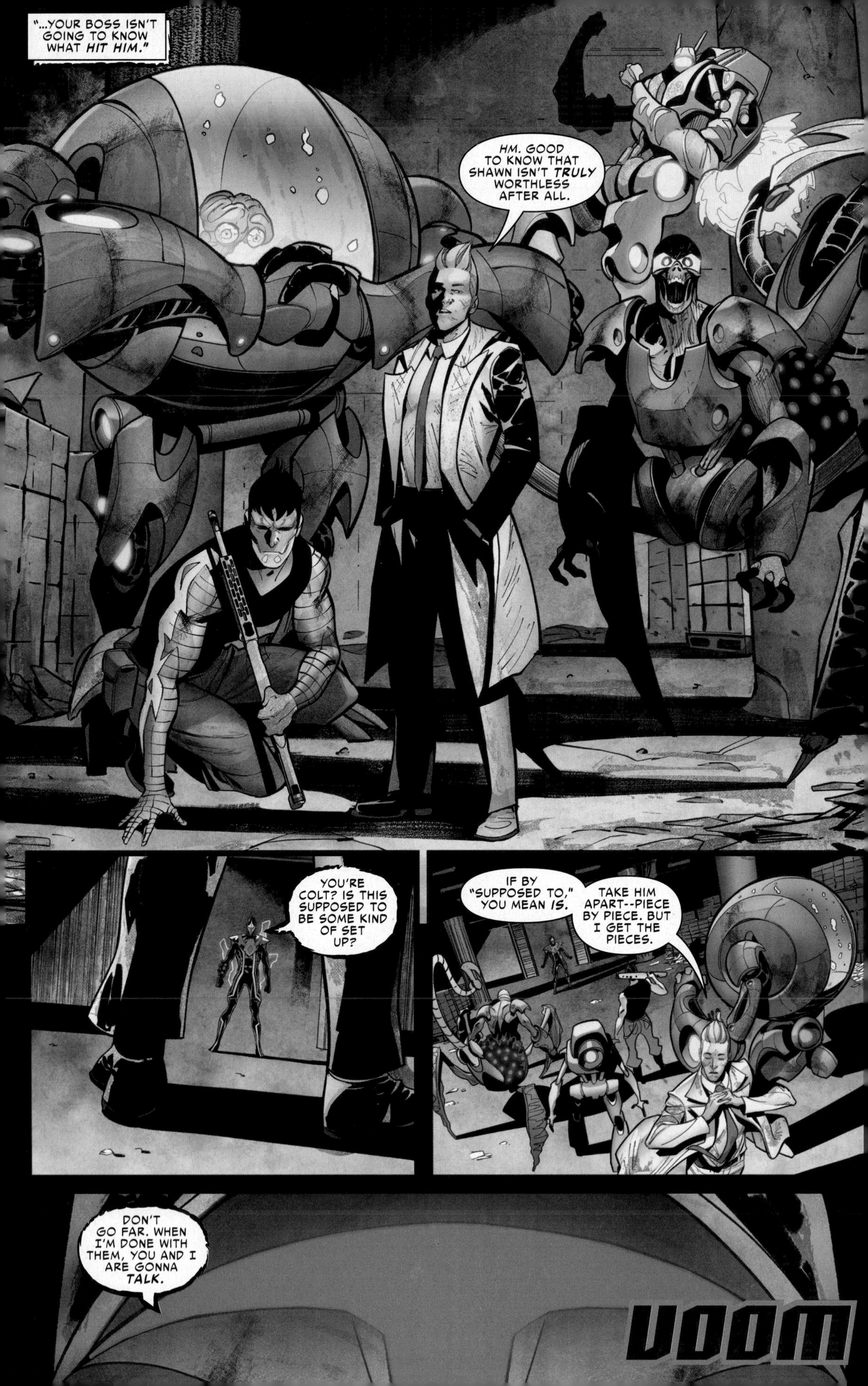
"...YOUR BOSS ISN'T GOING TO KNOW WHAT HIT HIM."
HM. GOOD TO KNOW THAT SHAWN ISN'T TRULY WORTHLESS AFTER ALL.
YOU'RE COLT? IS THIS SUPPOSED TO BE SOME KIND OF SET UP?
IF BY "SUPPOSED TO," YOU MEAN IS.
TAKE HIM APART--PIECE BY PIECE. BUT I GET THE PIECES.
DON'T GO FAR. WHEN I'M DONE WITH THEM, YOU AND I ARE GONNA TALK.
VOOM

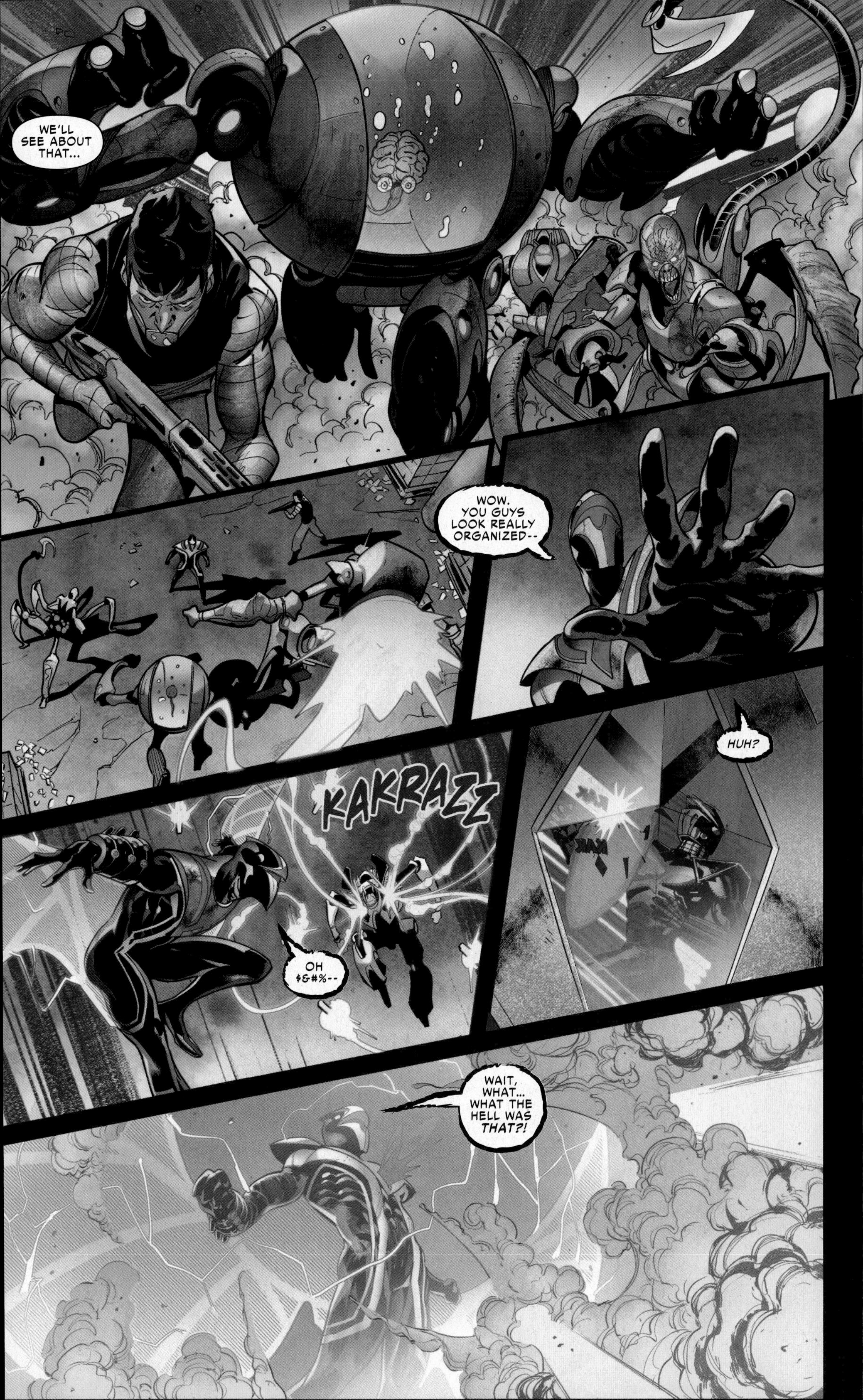
WE'LL SEE ABOUT THAT...
WOW. YOU GUYS LOOK REALLY ORGANIZED--
KAKRAZZ
OH $&#%--
HUH?
WAIT, WHAT... WHAT THE HELL WAS THAT?!

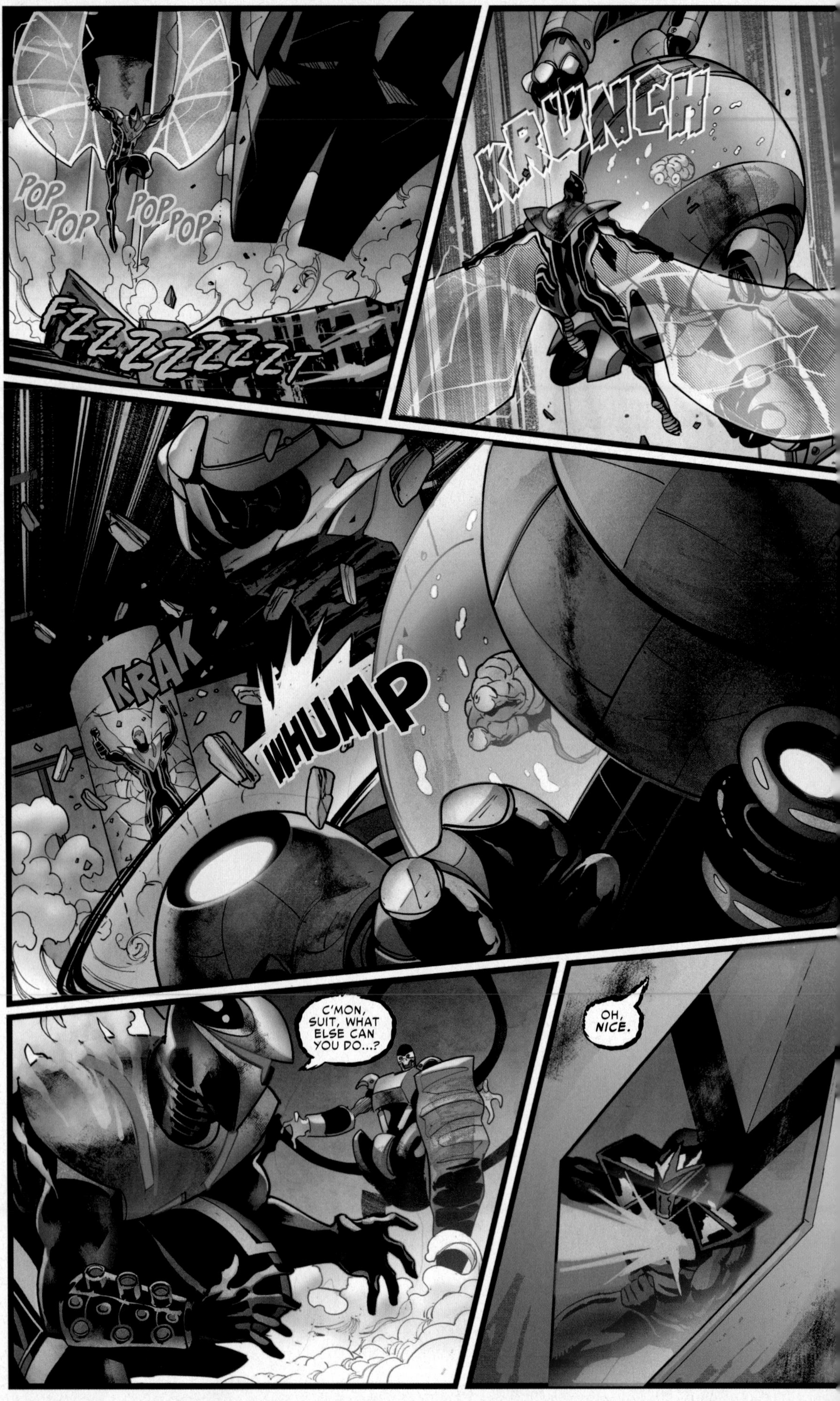
POP POP
POP POP
FZZZZZZZZZT
KRUNCH
KRAK
WHUMP
C'MON, SUIT, WHAT ELSE CAN YOU DO...?
OH, NICE.

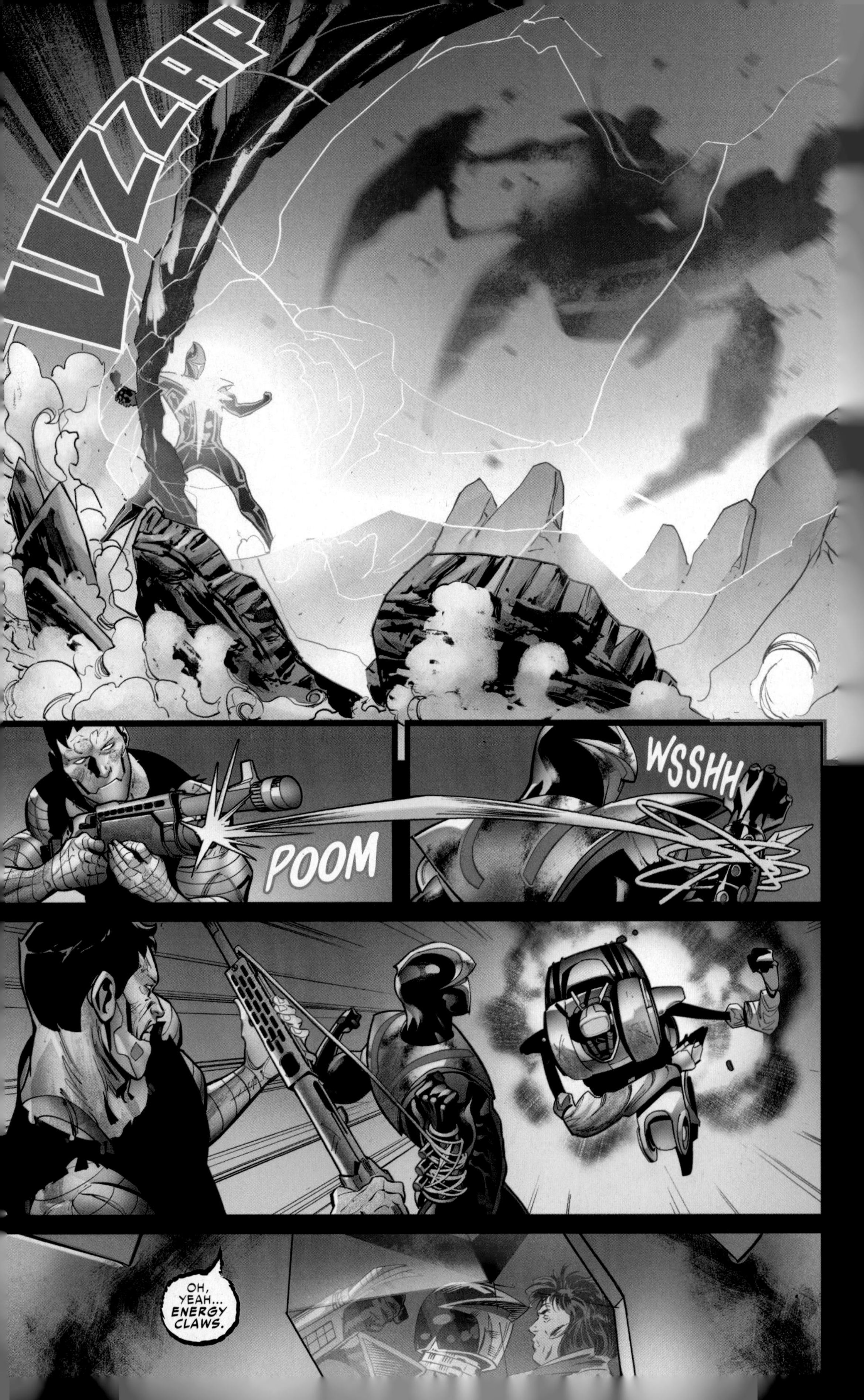
VZZAP
POOM
WSSHH
OH, YEAH... ENERGY CLAWS.

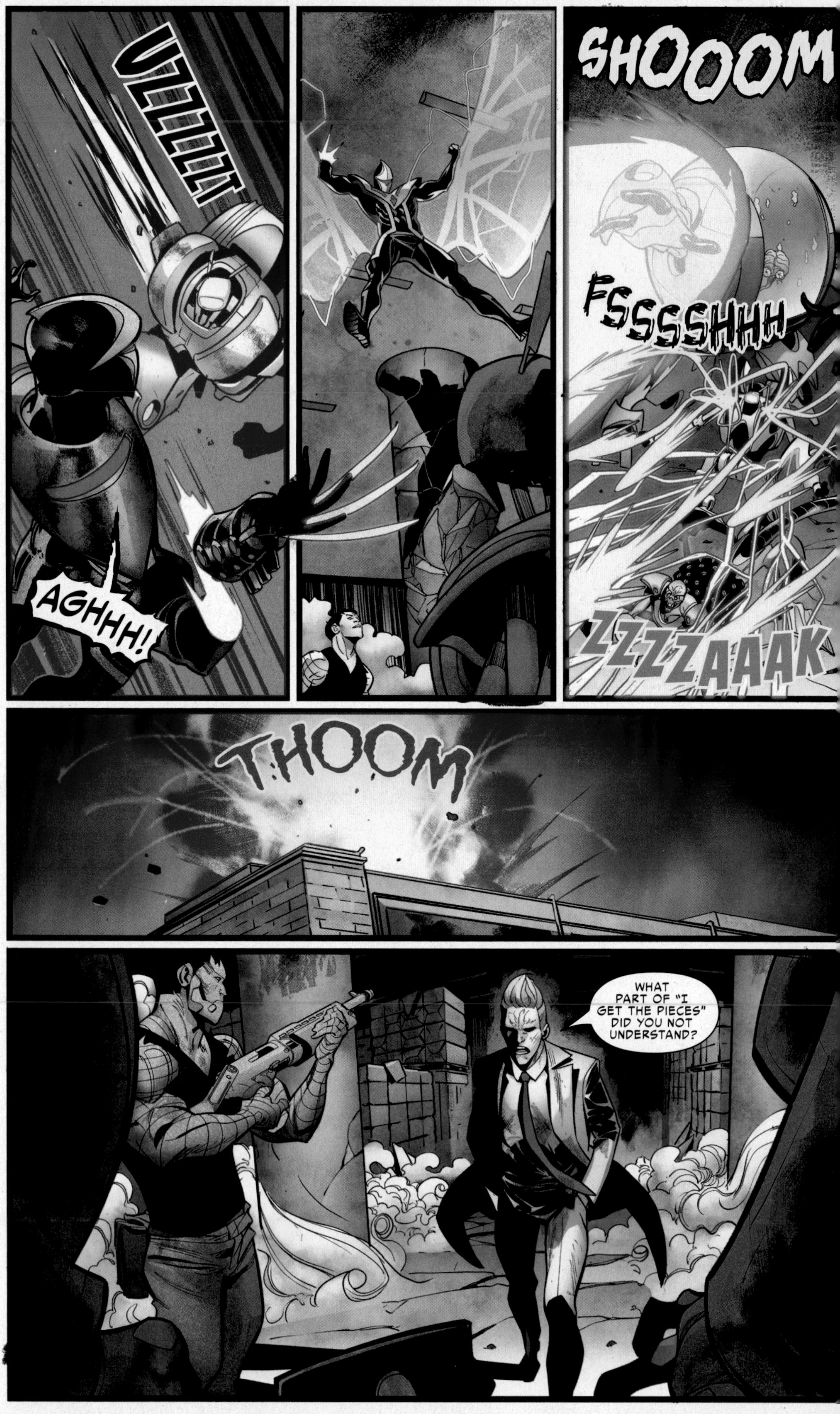
UZZZZZT
AGHHH!
SHOOOM
FSSSSHHH
ZZZZAAAK
THOOM
WHAT PART OF "I GET THE PIECES" DID YOU NOT UNDERSTAND?

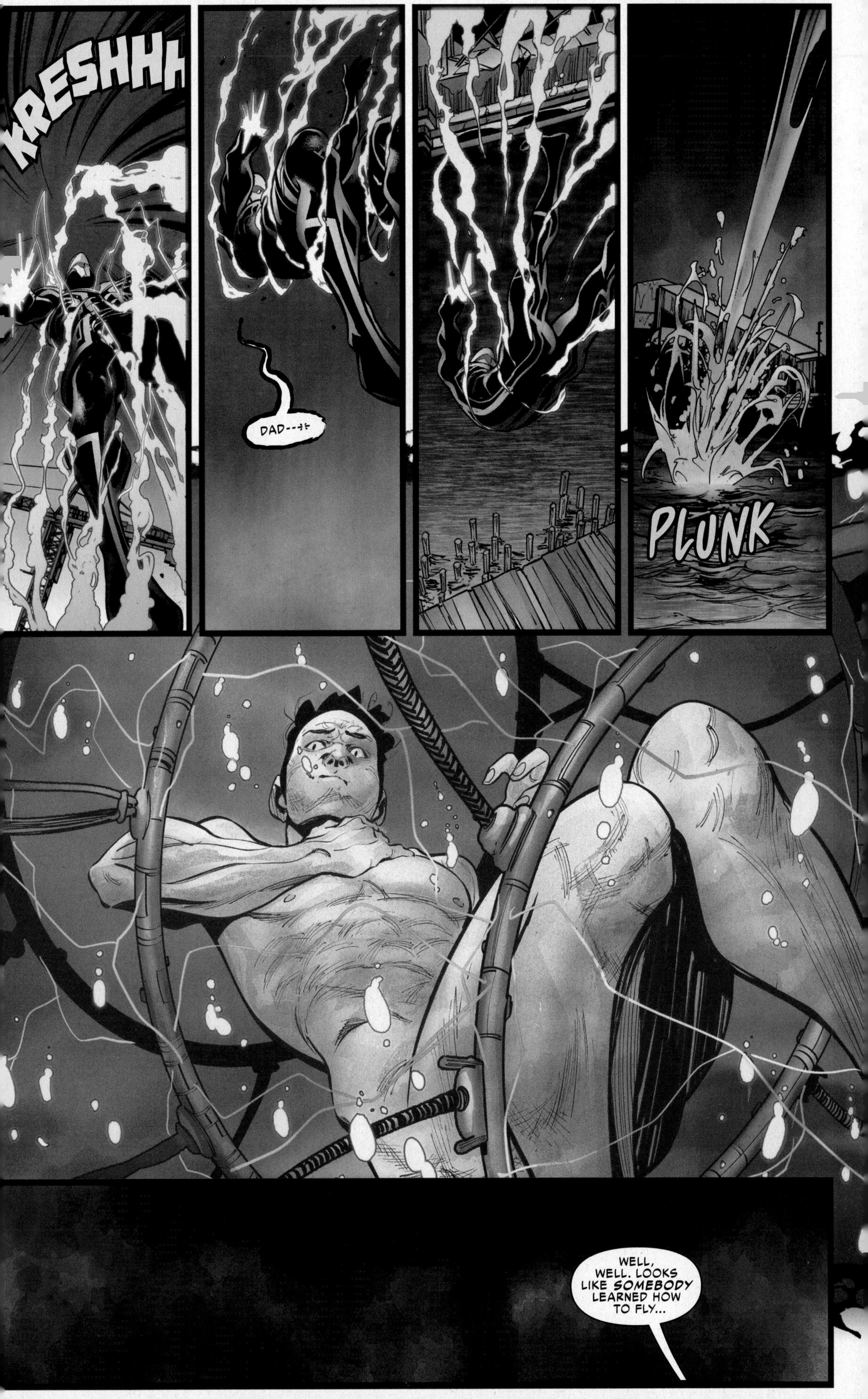
KRESHHH
DAD--
PLUNK
WELL, WELL. LOOKS LIKE SOMEBODY LEARNED HOW TO FLY...

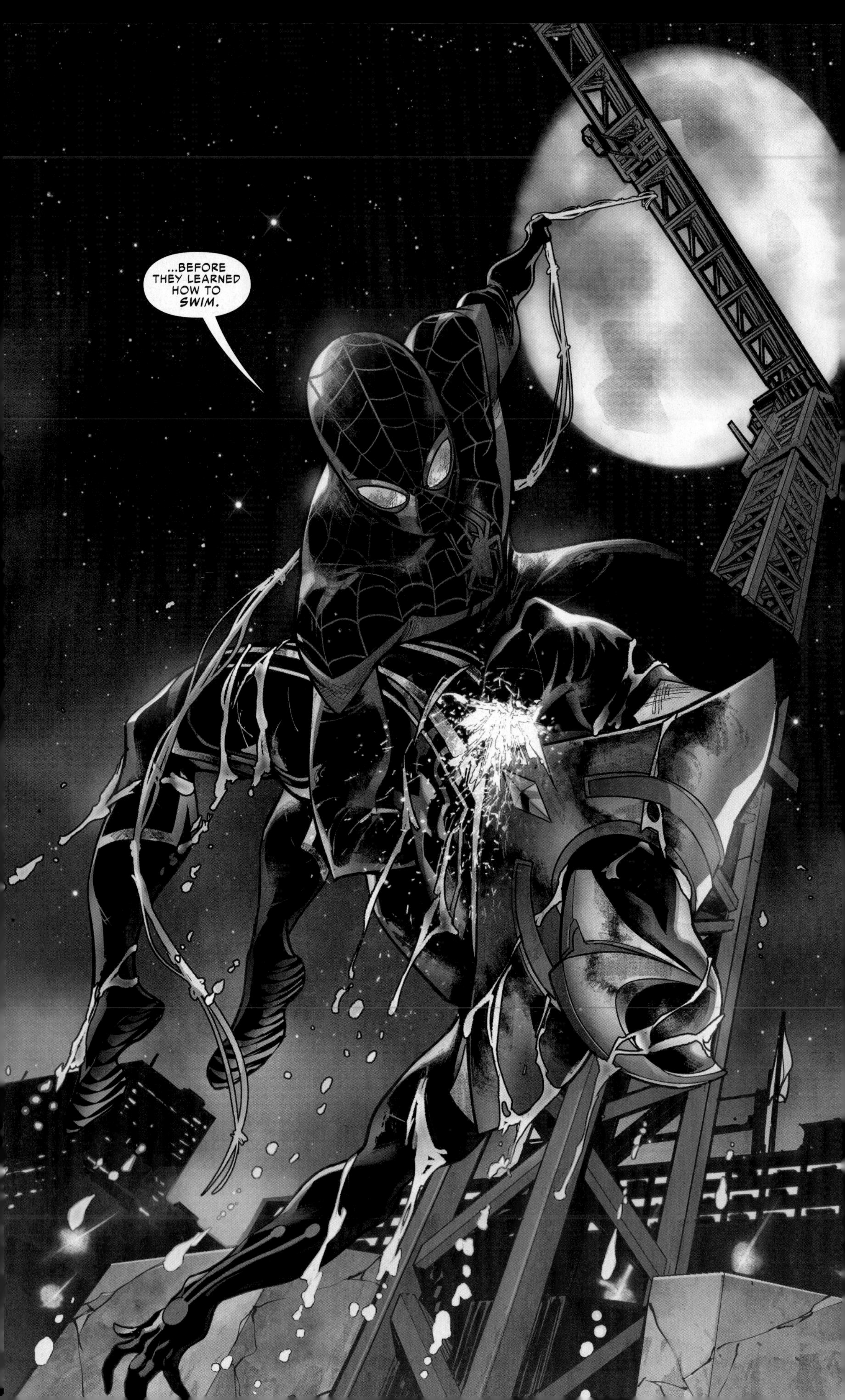
...BEFORE THEY LEARNED HOW TO SWIM.

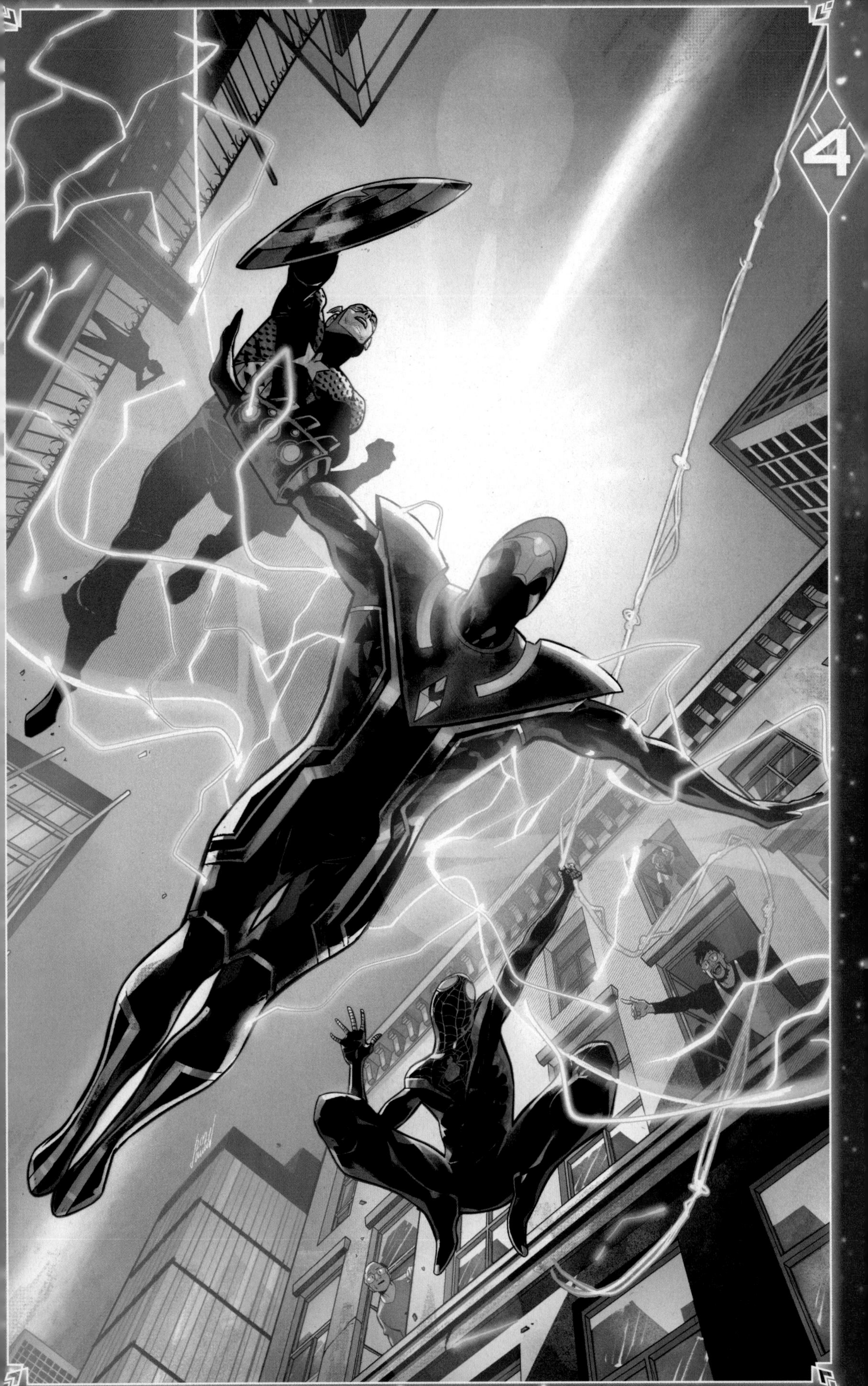
4

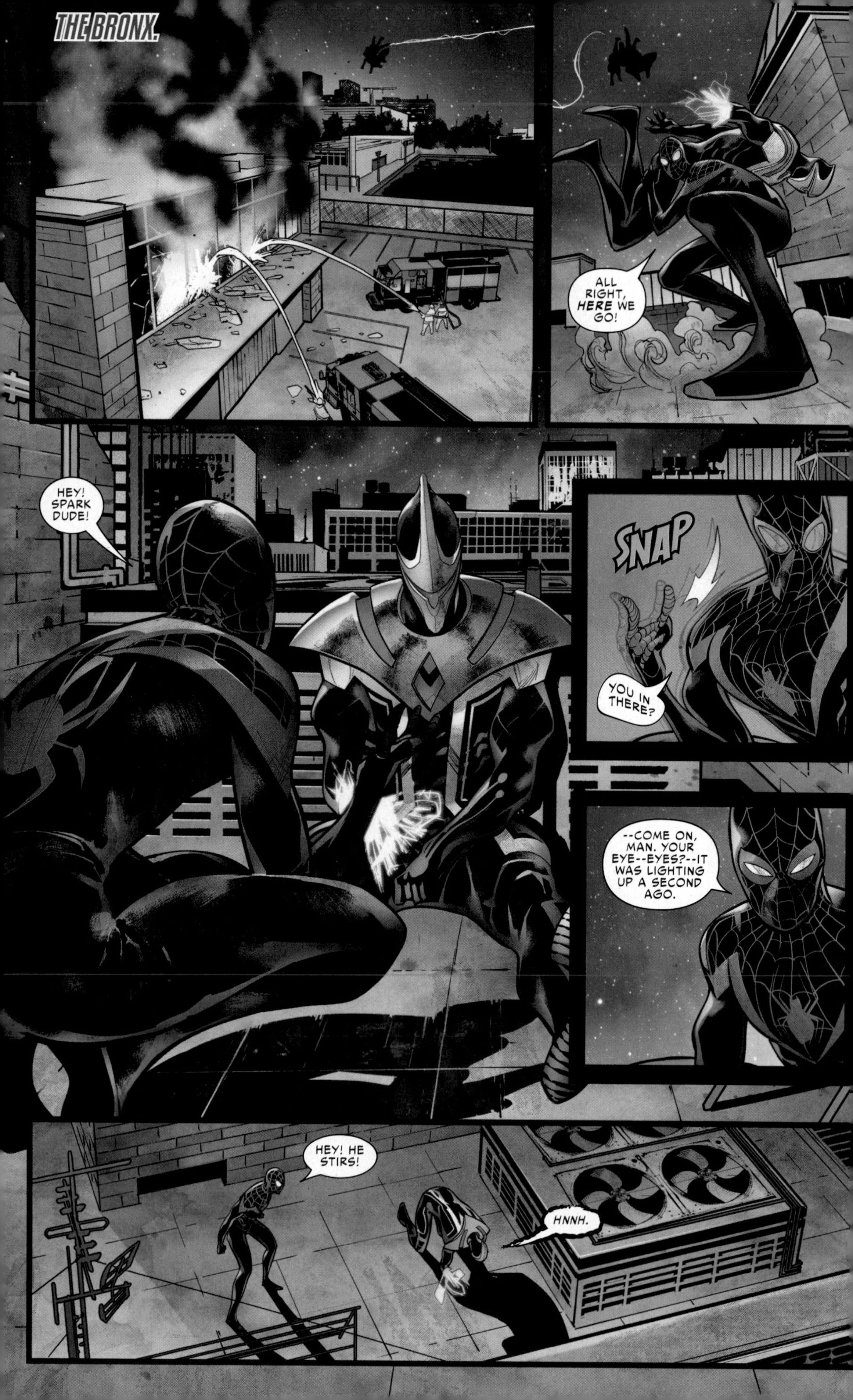
THE BRONX.
ALL RIGHT, HERE WE GO!
HEY! SPARK DUDE!
SNAP
YOU IN THERE?
--COME ON, MAN. YOUR EYE--EYES?--IT WAS LIGHTING UP A SECOND AGO.
HEY! HE STIRS!
HNNH.

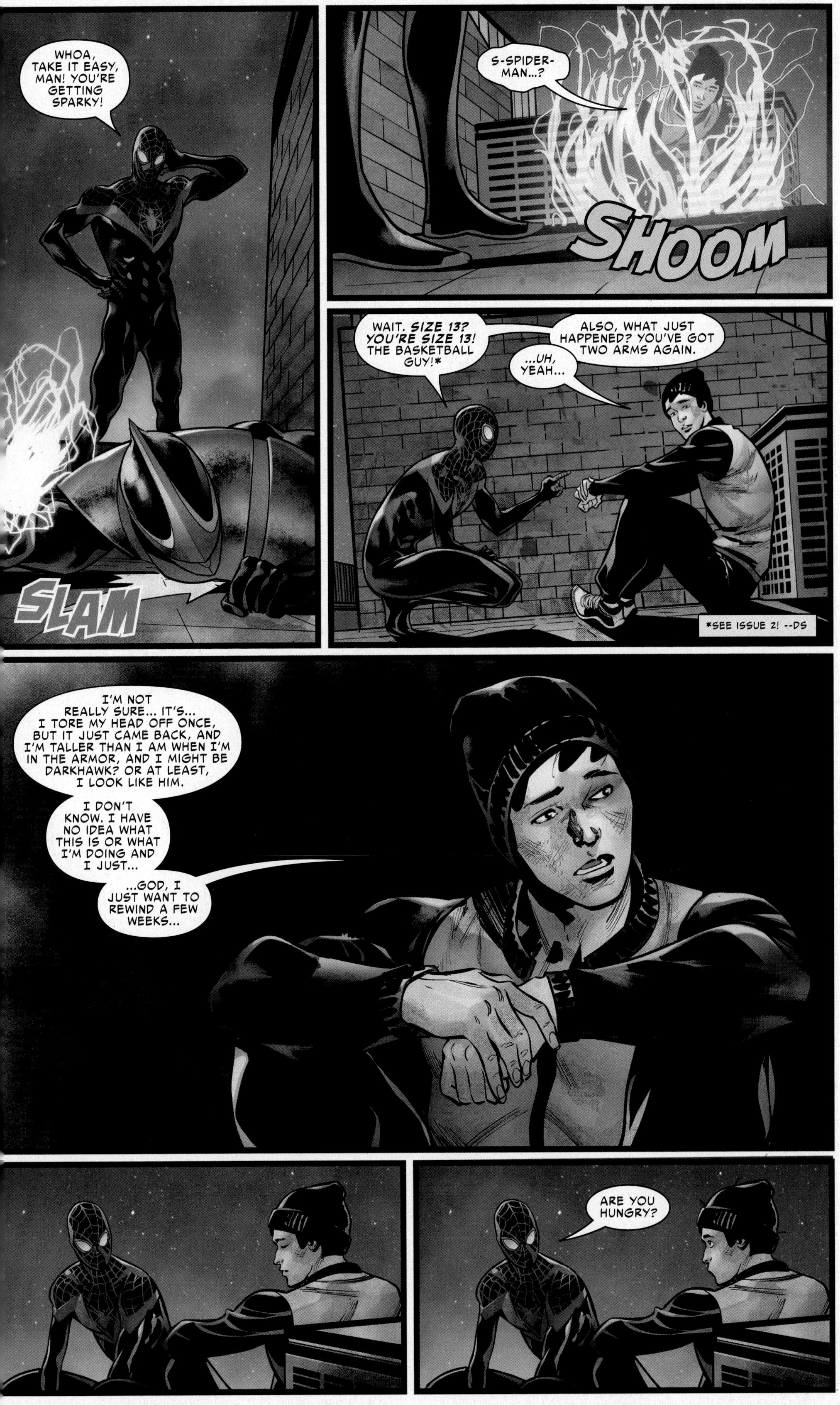
WHOA, TAKE IT EASY, MAN! YOU'RE GETTING SPARKY!
SLAM
S-SPIDER-MAN...?
SHOOM
WAIT. SIZE 13? YOU'RE SIZE 13! THE BASKETBALL GUY!*
ALSO, WHAT JUST HAPPENED? YOU'VE GOT TWO ARMS AGAIN.
...UH, YEAH...
*SEE ISSUE 2! --DS
I'M NOT REALLY SURE... IT'S... I TORE MY HEAD OFF ONCE, BUT IT JUST CAME BACK, AND I'M TALLER THAN I AM WHEN I'M IN THE ARMOR, AND I MIGHT BE DARKHAWK? OR AT LEAST, I LOOK LIKE HIM.
I DON'T KNOW. I HAVE NO IDEA WHAT THIS IS OR WHAT I'M DOING AND I JUST...
...GOD, I JUST WANT TO REWIND A FEW WEEKS...
ARE YOU HUNGRY?

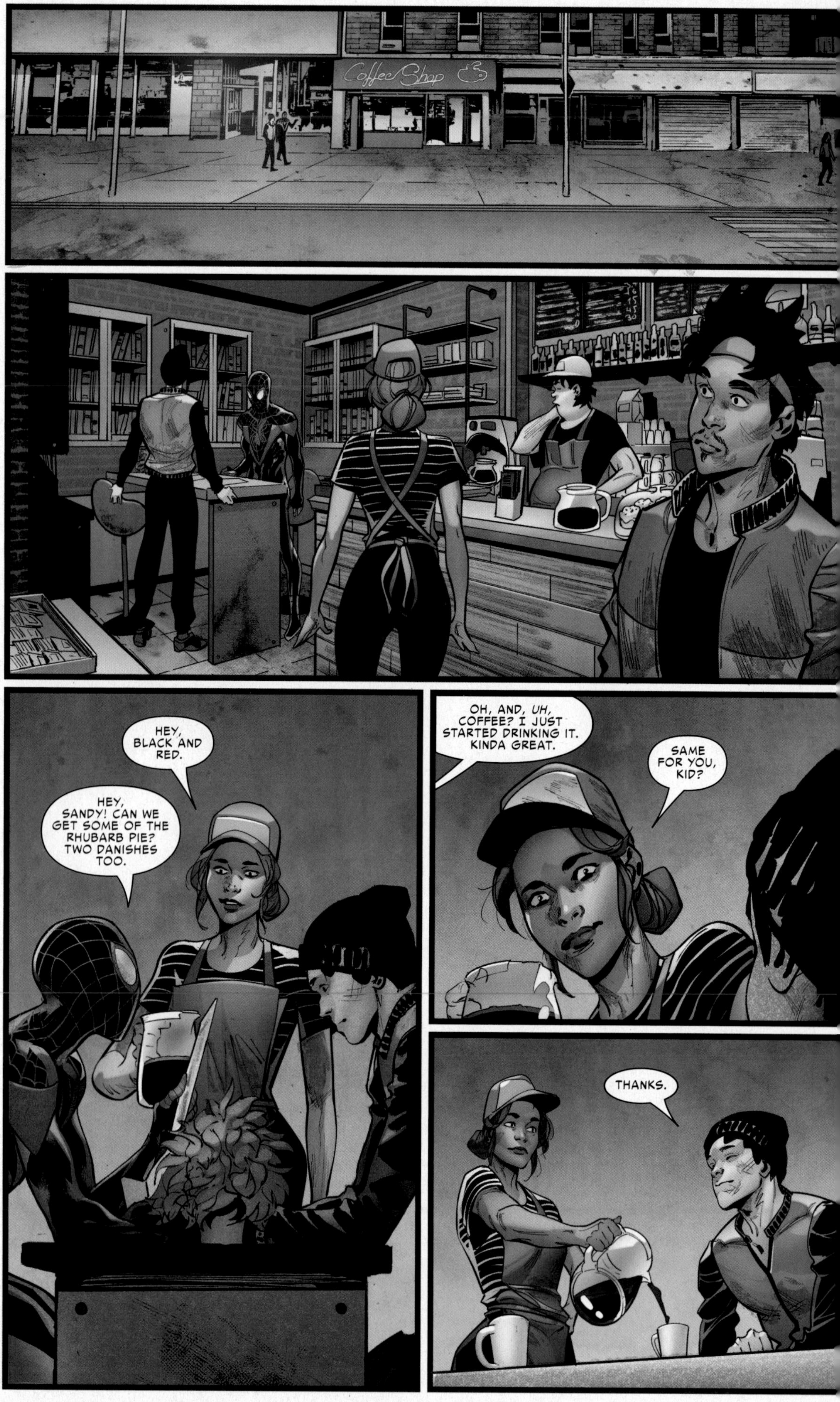
Coffee Shop
HEY, BLACK AND RED.
HEY, SANDY! CAN WE GET SOME OF THE RHUBARB PIE? TWO DANISHES TOO.
OH, AND, *UH,* COFFEE? I JUST STARTED DRINKING IT. KINDA GREAT.
SAME FOR YOU, KID?
THANKS.

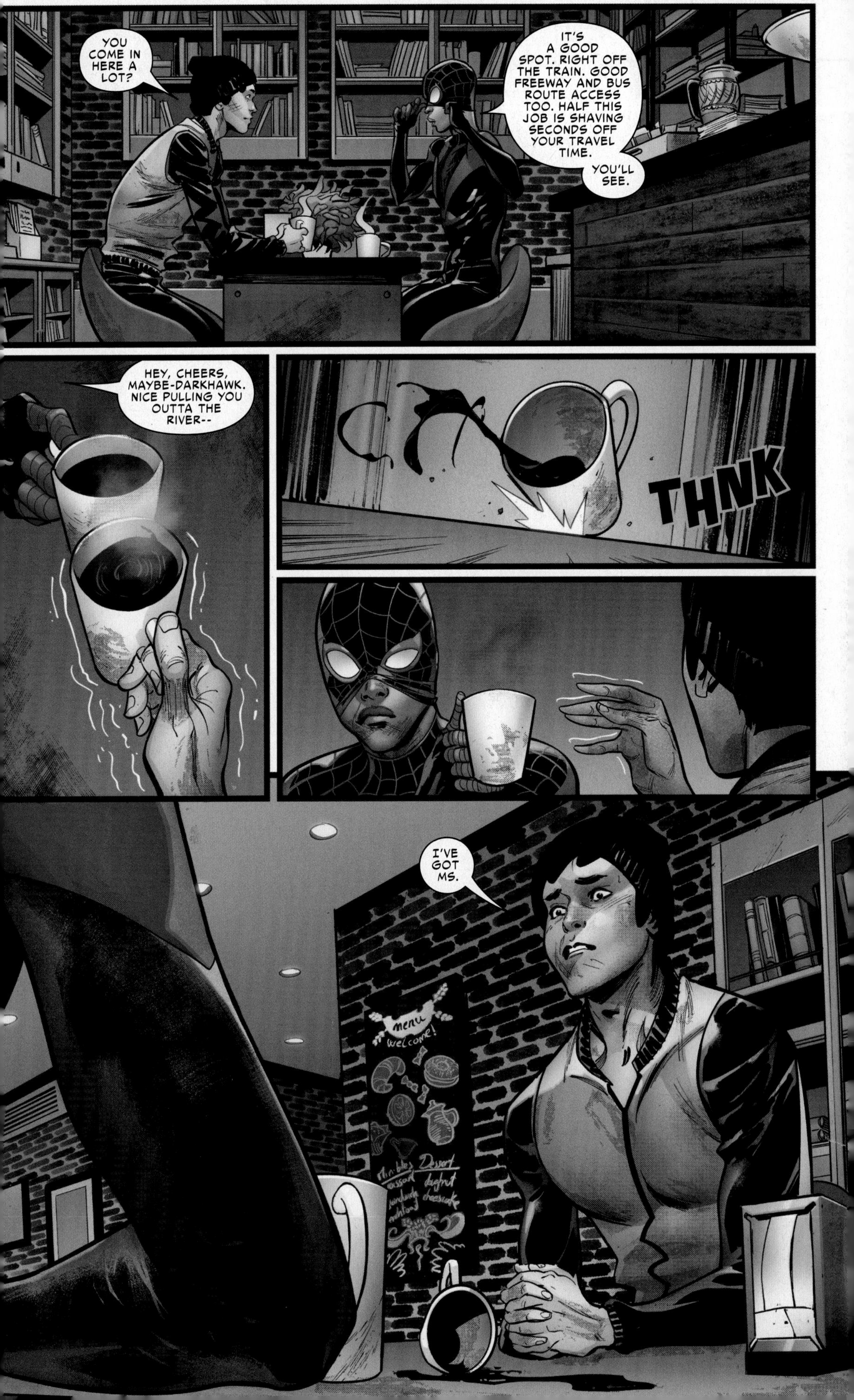
YOU COME IN HERE A LOT?
IT'S A GOOD SPOT. RIGHT OFF THE TRAIN. GOOD FREEWAY AND BUS ROUTE ACCESS TOO. HALF THIS JOB IS SHAVING SECONDS OFF YOUR TRAVEL TIME.
YOU'LL SEE.
HEY, CHEERS, MAYBE-DARKHAWK. NICE PULLING YOU OUTTA THE RIVER--
THNK
I'VE GOT MS.
menu
welcome!
Dessert

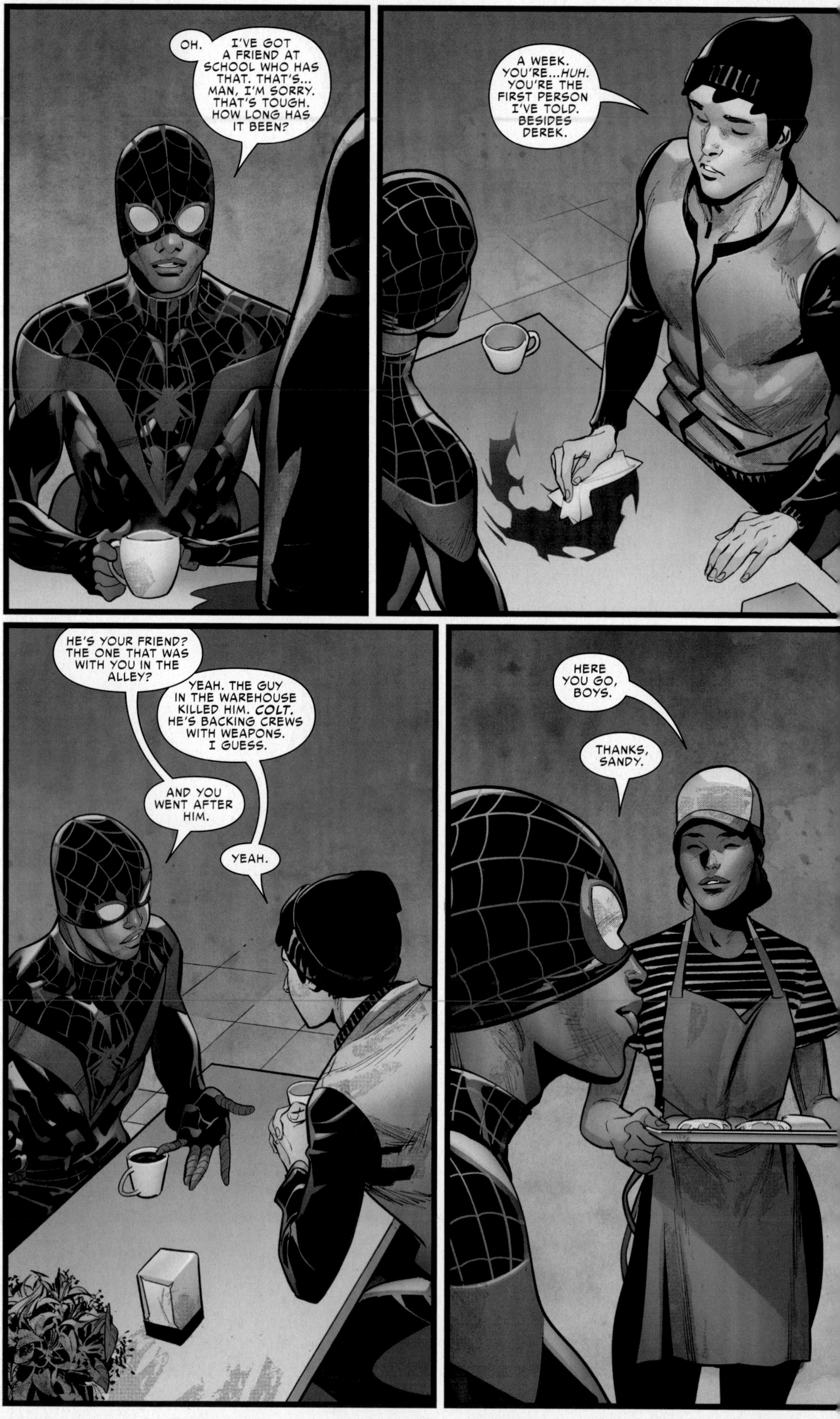
OH.
I'VE GOT A FRIEND AT SCHOOL WHO HAS THAT. THAT'S... MAN, I'M SORRY. THAT'S TOUGH. HOW LONG HAS IT BEEN?
A WEEK. YOU'RE...HUH. YOU'RE THE FIRST PERSON I'VE TOLD. BESIDES DEREK.
HE'S YOUR FRIEND? THE ONE THAT WAS WITH YOU IN THE ALLEY?
YEAH. THE GUY IN THE WAREHOUSE KILLED HIM. COLT. HE'S BACKING CREWS WITH WEAPONS. I GUESS.
AND YOU WENT AFTER HIM.
YEAH.
HERE YOU GO, BOYS.
THANKS, SANDY.

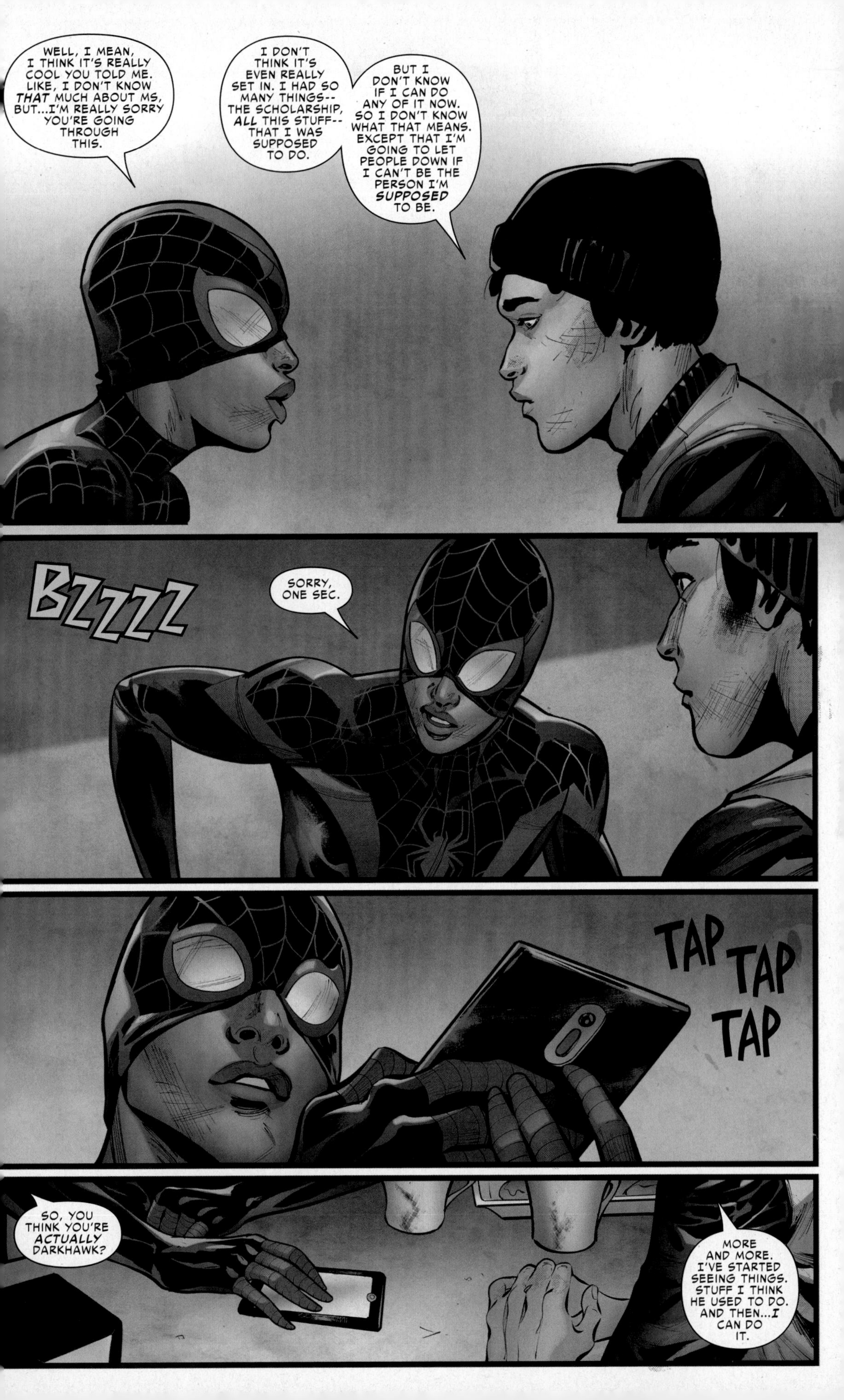
WELL, I MEAN, I THINK IT'S REALLY COOL YOU TOLD ME. LIKE, I DON'T KNOW *THAT* MUCH ABOUT MS, BUT...I'M REALLY SORRY YOU'RE GOING THROUGH THIS.
I DON'T THINK IT'S EVEN REALLY SET IN. I HAD SO MANY THINGS-- THE SCHOLARSHIP, *ALL* THIS STUFF-- THAT I WAS SUPPOSED TO DO.
BUT I DON'T KNOW IF I CAN DO ANY OF IT NOW. SO I DON'T KNOW WHAT THAT MEANS. EXCEPT THAT I'M GOING TO LET PEOPLE DOWN IF I CAN'T BE THE PERSON I'M *SUPPOSED* TO BE.
BZZZZ
SORRY, ONE SEC.
TAP TAP TAP
SO, YOU THINK YOU'RE *ACTUALLY* DARKHAWK?
MORE AND MORE. I'VE STARTED SEEING THINGS. STUFF I THINK HE USED TO DO. AND THEN...*I* CAN DO IT.

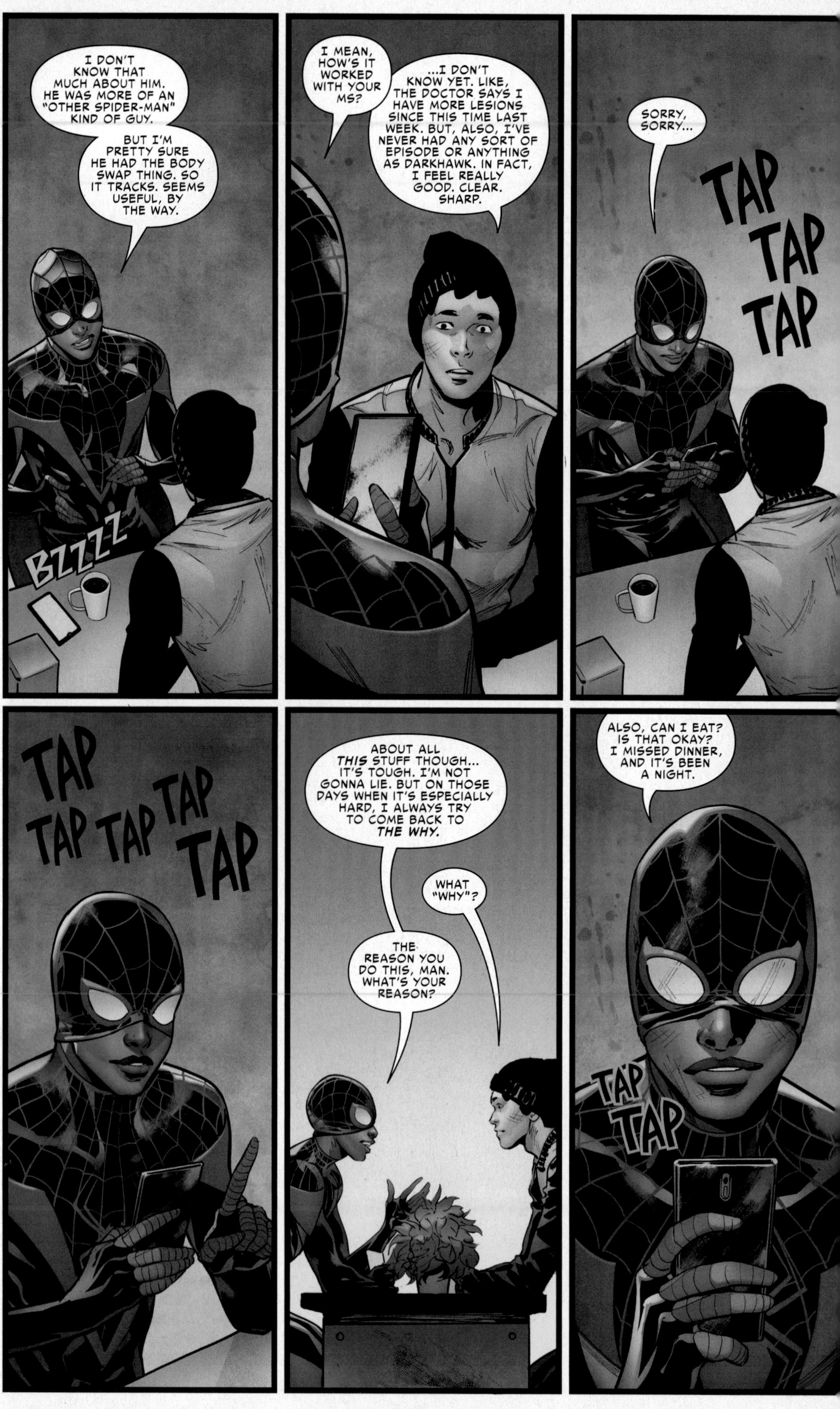
I DON'T KNOW THAT MUCH ABOUT HIM. HE WAS MORE OF AN "OTHER SPIDER-MAN" KIND OF GUY.
BUT I'M PRETTY SURE HE HAD THE BODY SWAP THING. SO IT TRACKS. SEEMS USEFUL, BY THE WAY.
BZZZZ
I MEAN, HOW'S IT WORKED WITH YOUR MS?
...I DON'T KNOW YET. LIKE, THE DOCTOR SAYS I HAVE MORE LESIONS SINCE THIS TIME LAST WEEK. BUT, ALSO, I'VE NEVER HAD ANY SORT OF EPISODE OR ANYTHING AS DARKHAWK. IN FACT, I FEEL REALLY GOOD. CLEAR. SHARP.
SORRY, SORRY...
TAP TAP TAP
TAP TAP TAP TAP TAP
ABOUT ALL *THIS* STUFF THOUGH... IT'S TOUGH. I'M NOT GONNA LIE. BUT ON THOSE DAYS WHEN IT'S ESPECIALLY HARD, I ALWAYS TRY TO COME BACK TO ***THE WHY.***
WHAT "WHY"?
THE REASON YOU DO THIS, MAN. WHAT'S YOUR REASON?
ALSO, CAN I EAT? IS THAT OKAY? I MISSED DINNER, AND IT'S BEEN A NIGHT.
TAP TAP

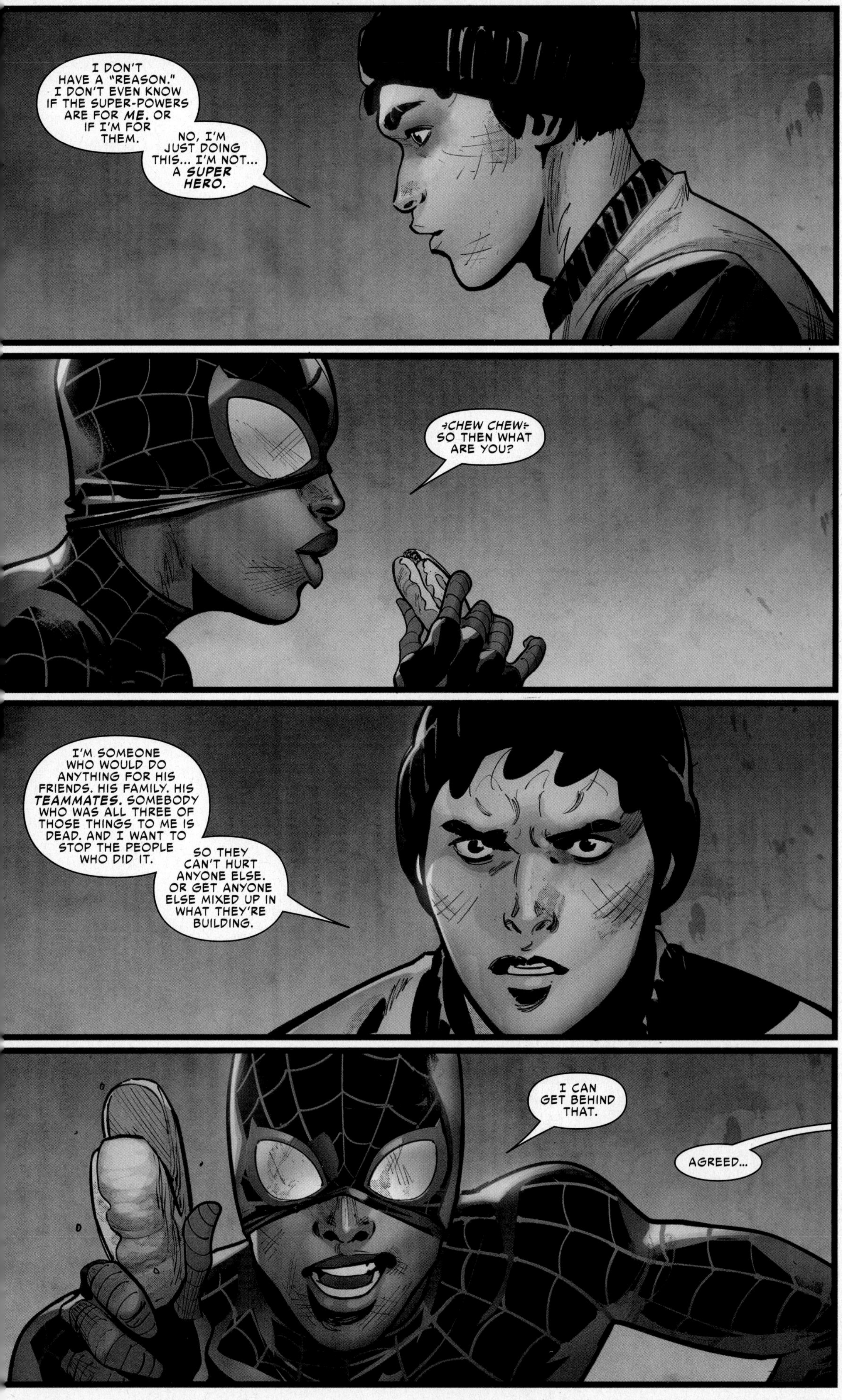
I DON'T HAVE A "REASON." I DON'T EVEN KNOW IF THE SUPER-POWERS ARE FOR *ME*. OR IF I'M FOR THEM.
NO, I'M JUST DOING THIS... I'M NOT... A *SUPER HERO*.
CHEW CHEW SO THEN WHAT ARE YOU?
I'M SOMEONE WHO WOULD DO ANYTHING FOR HIS FRIENDS. HIS FAMILY. HIS *TEAMMATES*. SOMEBODY WHO WAS ALL THREE OF THOSE THINGS TO ME IS DEAD. AND I WANT TO STOP THE PEOPLE WHO DID IT.
SO THEY CAN'T HURT ANYONE ELSE. OR GET ANYONE ELSE MIXED UP IN WHAT THEY'RE BUILDING.
I CAN GET BEHIND THAT.
AGREED...

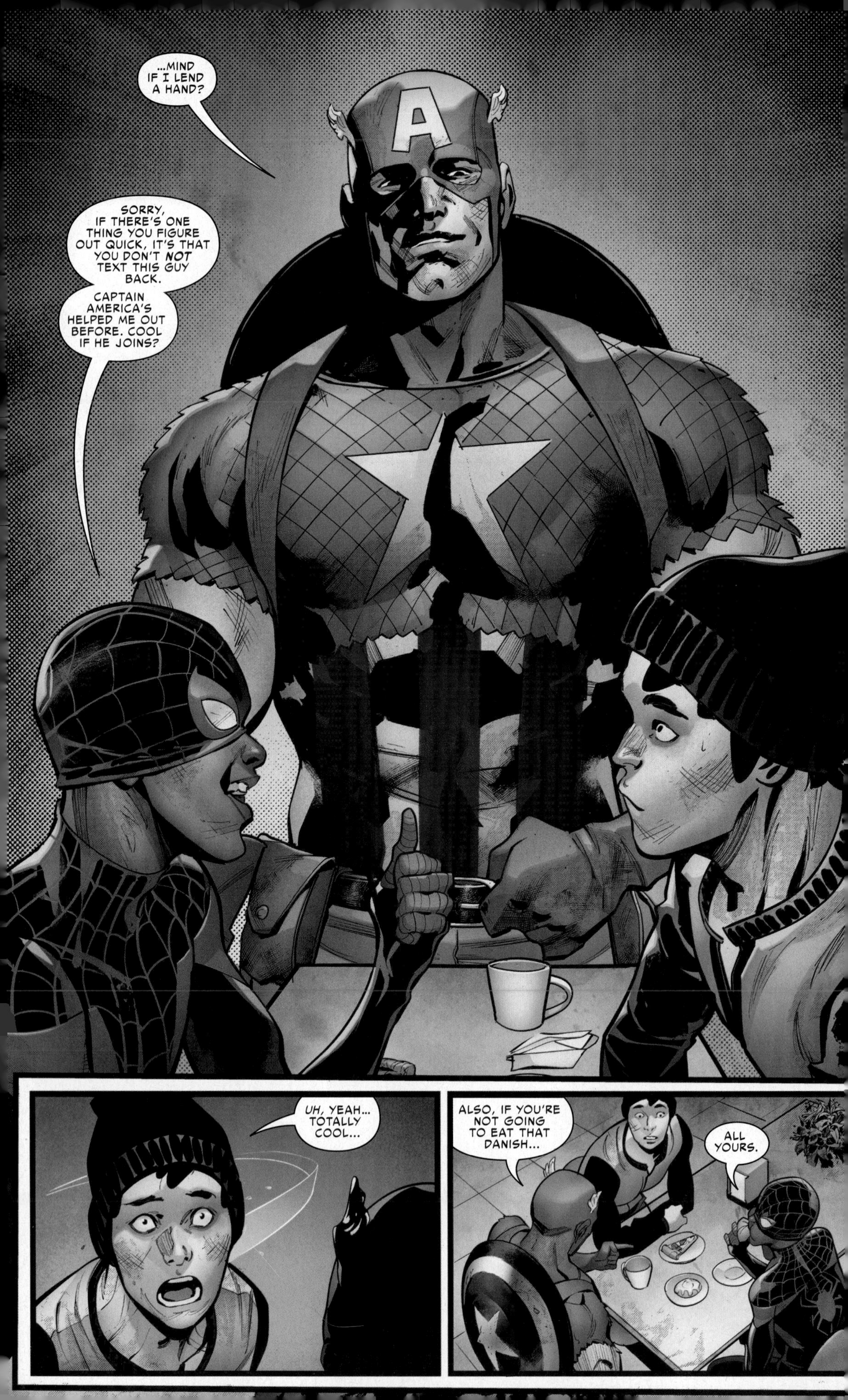
...MIND IF I LEND A HAND?
SORRY, IF THERE'S ONE THING YOU FIGURE OUT QUICK, IT'S THAT YOU DON'T *NOT* TEXT THIS GUY BACK.
CAPTAIN AMERICA'S HELPED ME OUT BEFORE. COOL IF HE JOINS?
UH, YEAH... TOTALLY COOL...
ALSO, IF YOU'RE NOT GOING TO EAT THAT DANISH...
ALL YOURS.

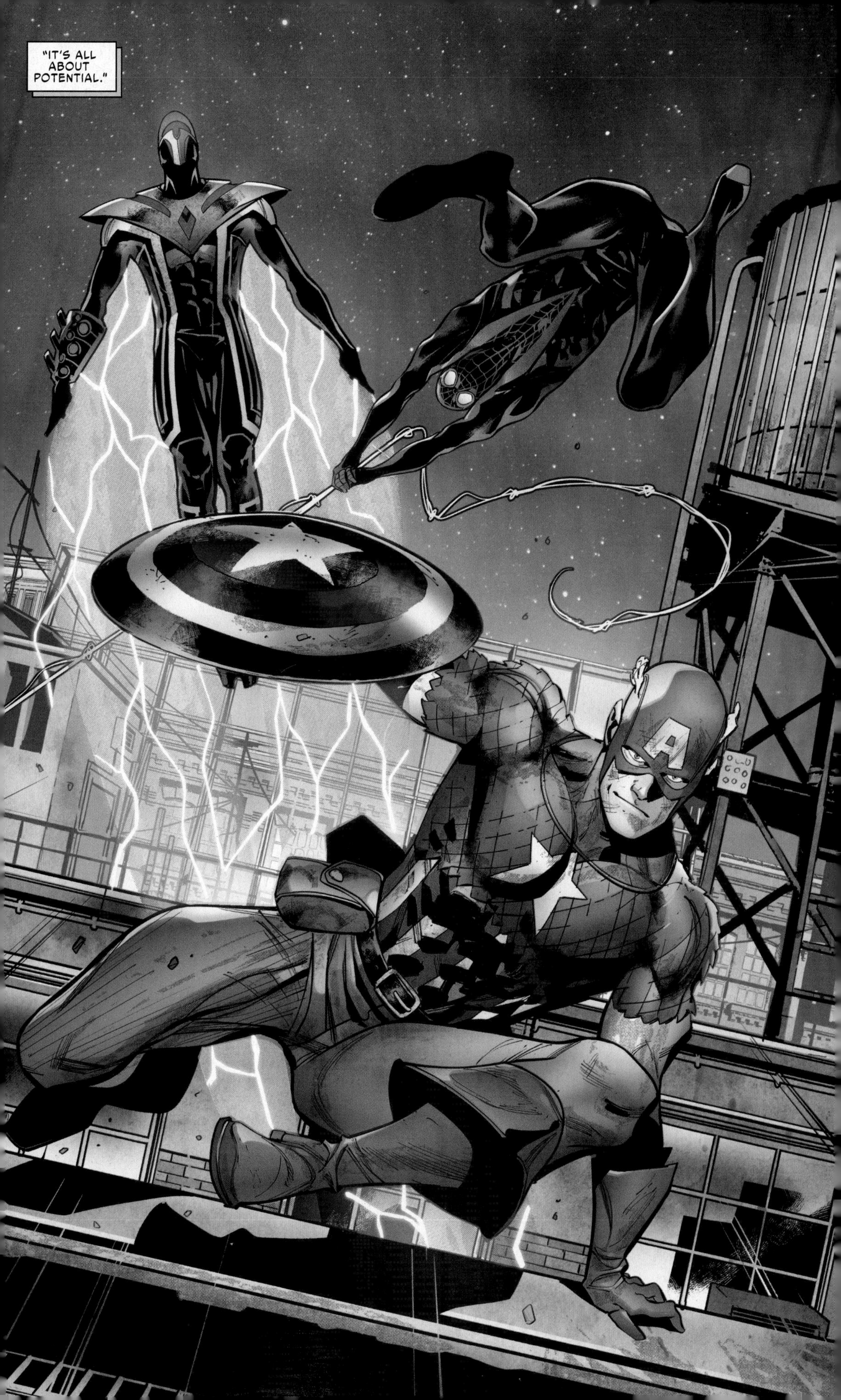
"IT'S ALL ABOUT POTENTIAL."

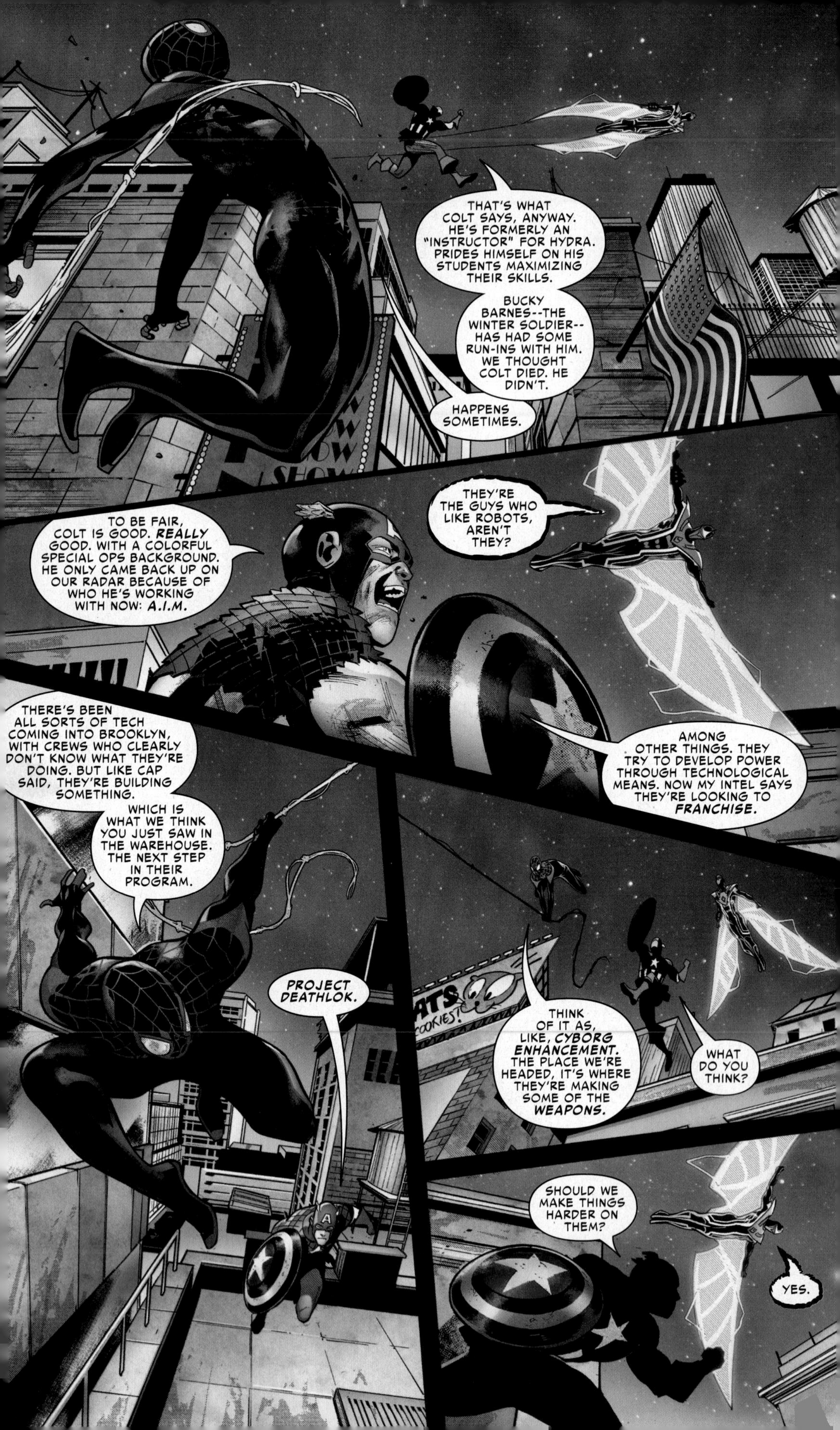

THAT'S WHAT COLT SAYS, ANYWAY. HE'S FORMERLY AN "INSTRUCTOR" FOR HYDRA. PRIDES HIMSELF ON HIS STUDENTS MAXIMIZING THEIR SKILLS.
BUCKY BARNES--THE WINTER SOLDIER--HAS HAD SOME RUN-INS WITH HIM. WE THOUGHT COLT DIED. HE DIDN'T.
HAPPENS SOMETIMES.
SHOW
TO BE FAIR, COLT IS GOOD. REALLY GOOD. WITH A COLORFUL SPECIAL OPS BACKGROUND. HE ONLY CAME BACK UP ON OUR RADAR BECAUSE OF WHO HE'S WORKING WITH NOW: A.I.M.
THEY'RE THE GUYS WHO LIKE ROBOTS, AREN'T THEY?
AMONG OTHER THINGS. THEY TRY TO DEVELOP POWER THROUGH TECHNOLOGICAL MEANS. NOW MY INTEL SAYS THEY'RE LOOKING TO FRANCHISE.
THERE'S BEEN ALL SORTS OF TECH COMING INTO BROOKLYN, WITH CREWS WHO CLEARLY DON'T KNOW WHAT THEY'RE DOING. BUT LIKE CAP SAID, THEY'RE BUILDING SOMETHING.
WHICH IS WHAT WE THINK YOU JUST SAW IN THE WAREHOUSE. THE NEXT STEP IN THEIR PROGRAM.
PROJECT DEATHLOK.
COOKIES!
THINK OF IT AS, LIKE, CYBORG ENHANCEMENT. THE PLACE WE'RE HEADED, IT'S WHERE THEY'RE MAKING SOME OF THE WEAPONS.
WHAT DO YOU THINK?
SHOULD WE MAKE THINGS HARDER ON THEM?
YES.

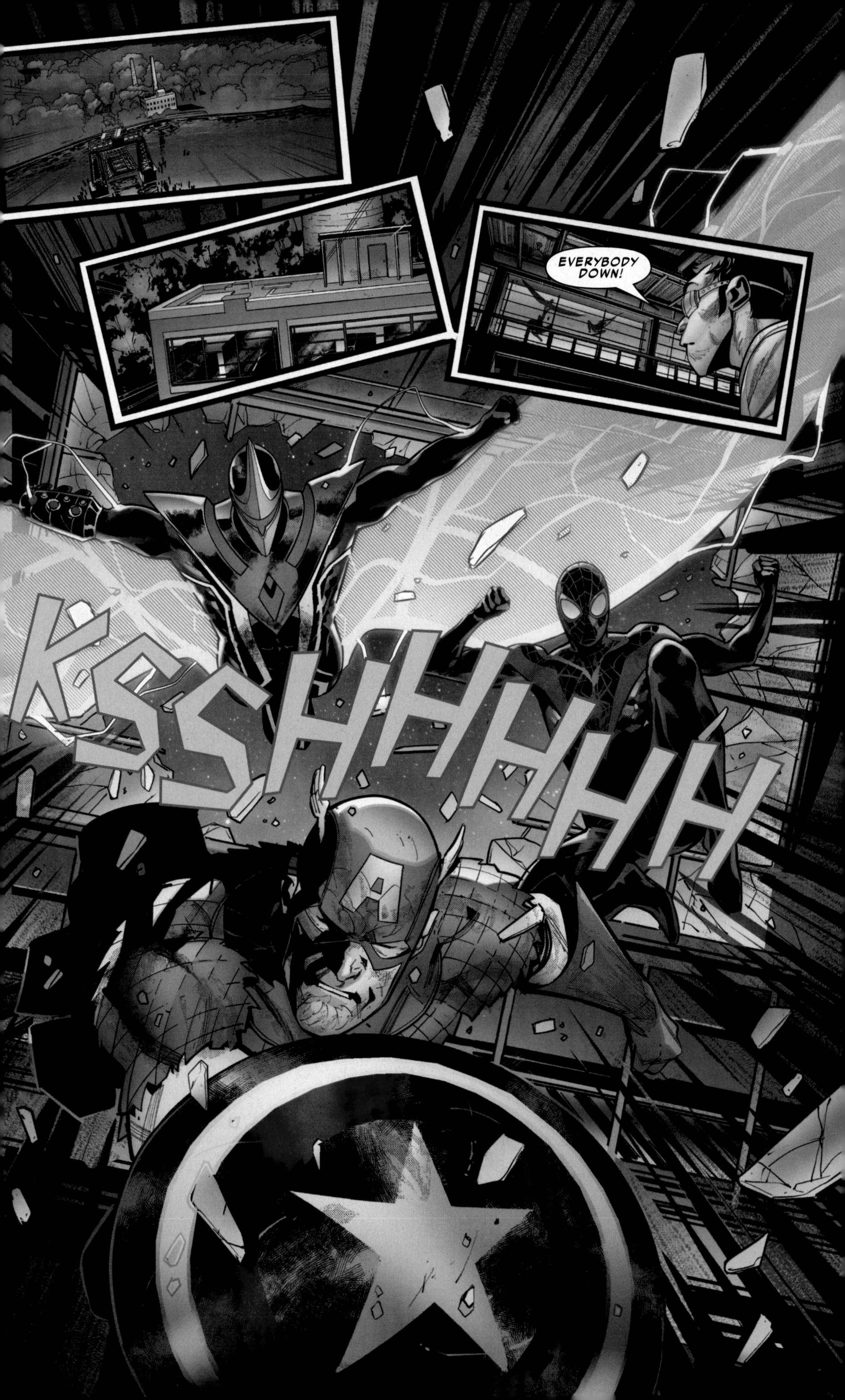
EVERYBODY DOWN!
K'SSHHHHHH

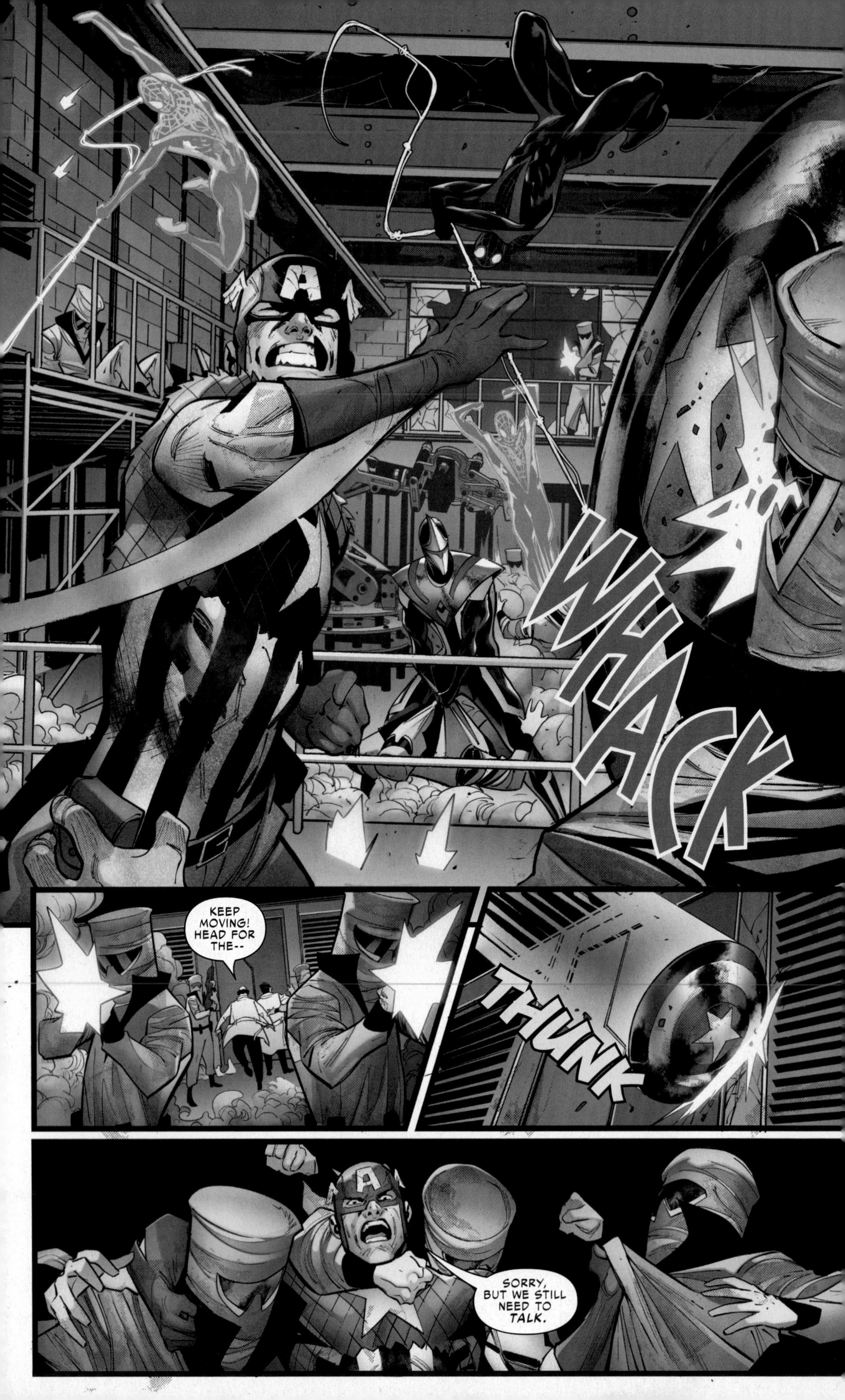
WHACK
KEEP MOVING! HEAD FOR THE--
THUNK
SORRY, BUT WE STILL NEED TO *TALK*.

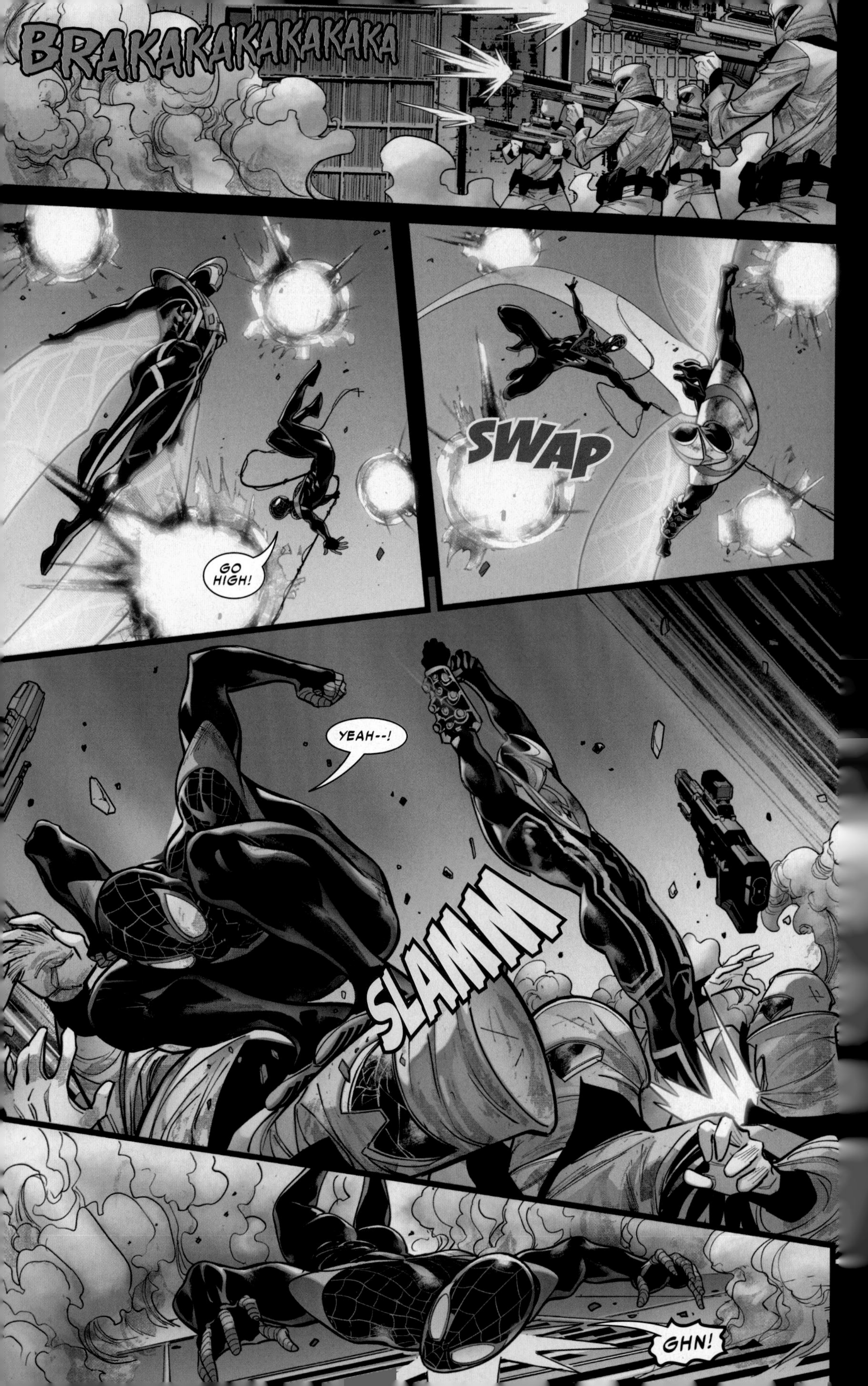
BRAKAKAKAKAKAKA
GO HIGH!
SWAP
YEAH--!
SLAMM
GHN!

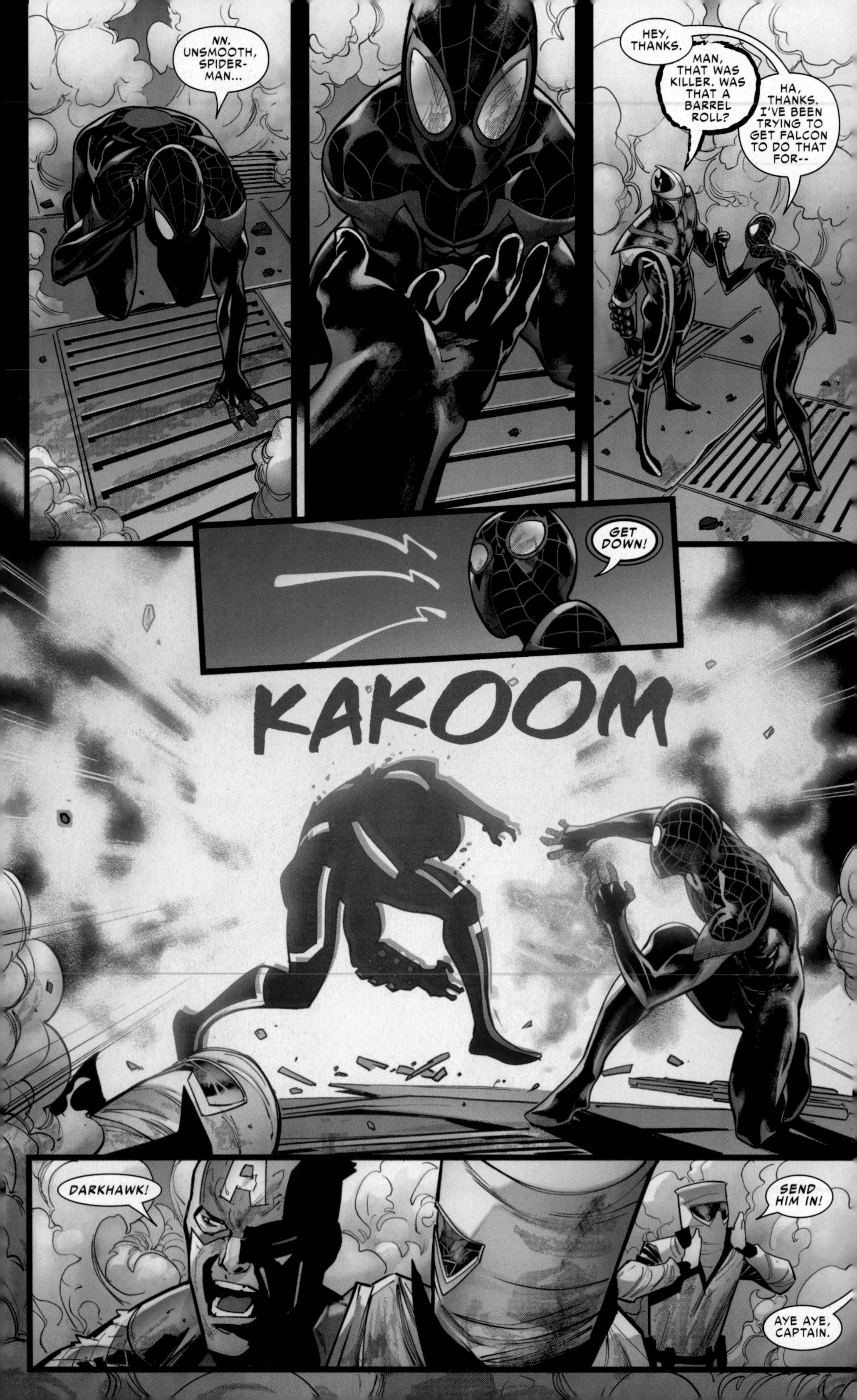
NN. UNSMOOTH, SPIDER-MAN...
HEY, THANKS.
MAN, THAT WAS KILLER. WAS THAT A BARREL ROLL?
HA, THANKS. I'VE BEEN TRYING TO GET FALCON TO DO THAT FOR--
GET DOWN!
KAKOOM
DARKHAWK!
SEND HIM IN!
AYE AYE, CAPTAIN.

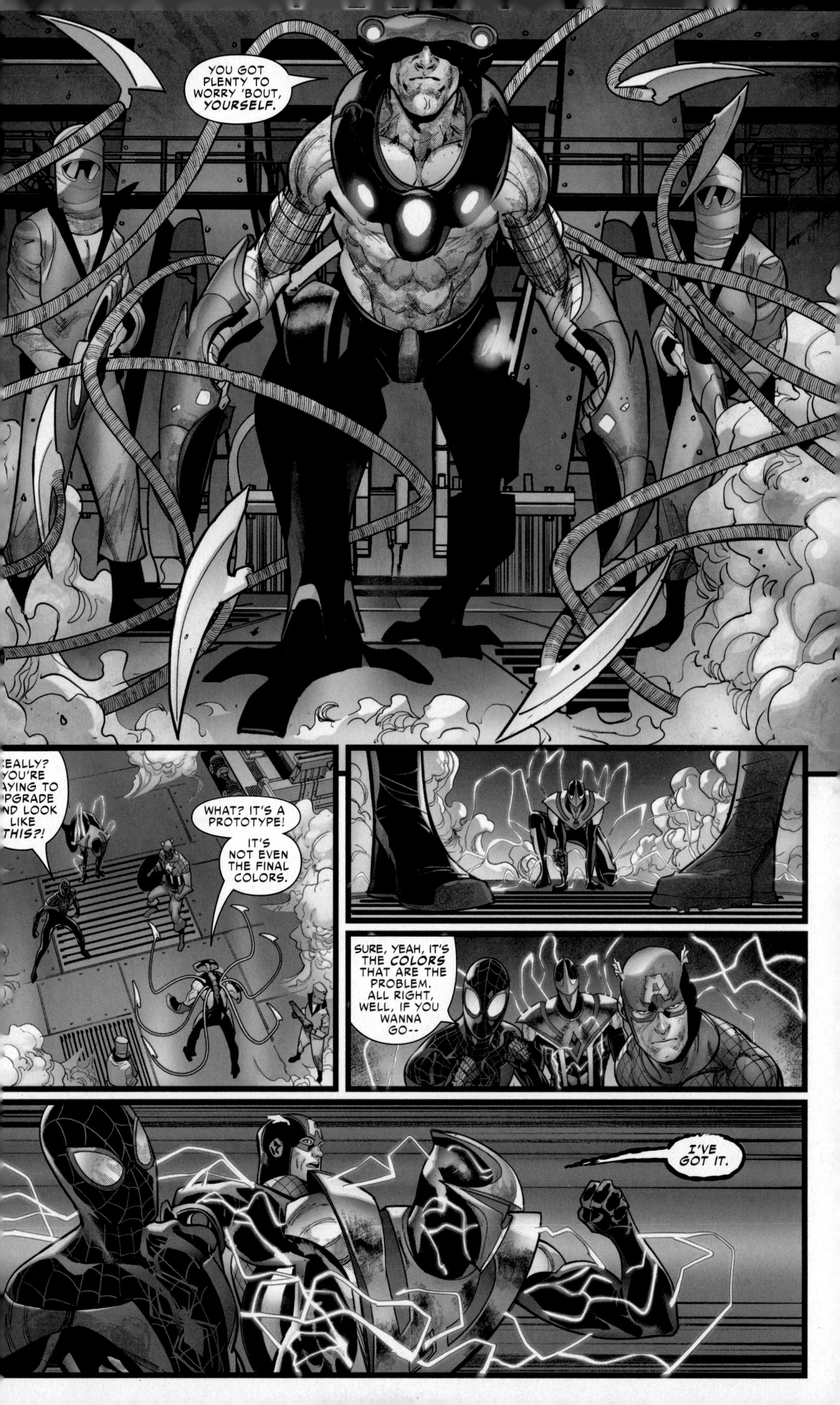
YOU GOT PLENTY TO WORRY 'BOUT, YOURSELF.
REALLY? YOU'RE AYING TO PGRADE ND LOOK LIKE THIS?!
WHAT? IT'S A PROTOTYPE!
IT'S NOT EVEN THE FINAL COLORS.
SURE, YEAH, IT'S THE COLORS THAT ARE THE PROBLEM. ALL RIGHT, WELL, IF YOU WANNA GO--
I'VE GOT IT.

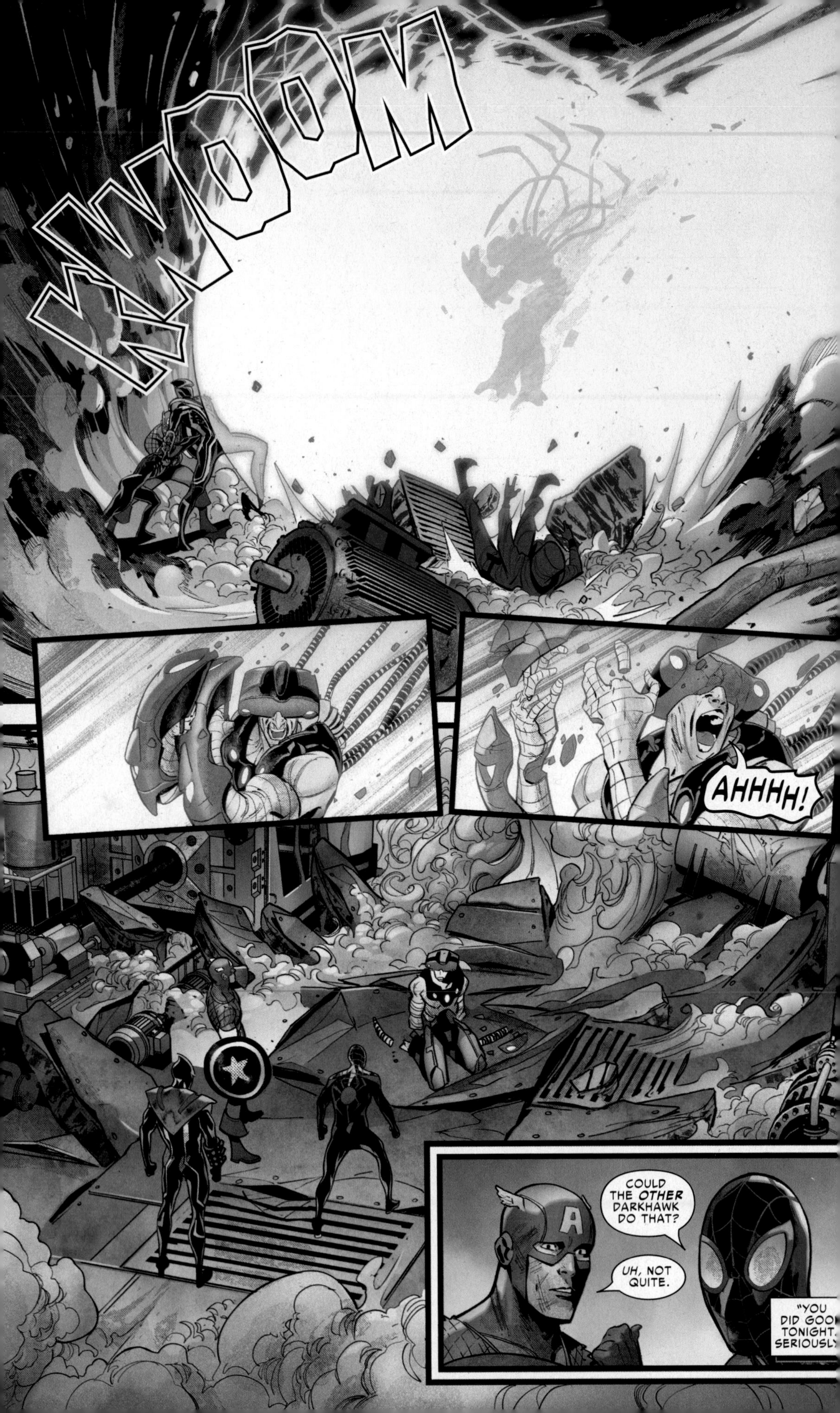
WHOOOM
AHHHH!
COULD THE OTHER DARKHAWK DO THAT?
UH, NOT QUITE.
"YOU DID GOO TONIGHT. SERIOUSL

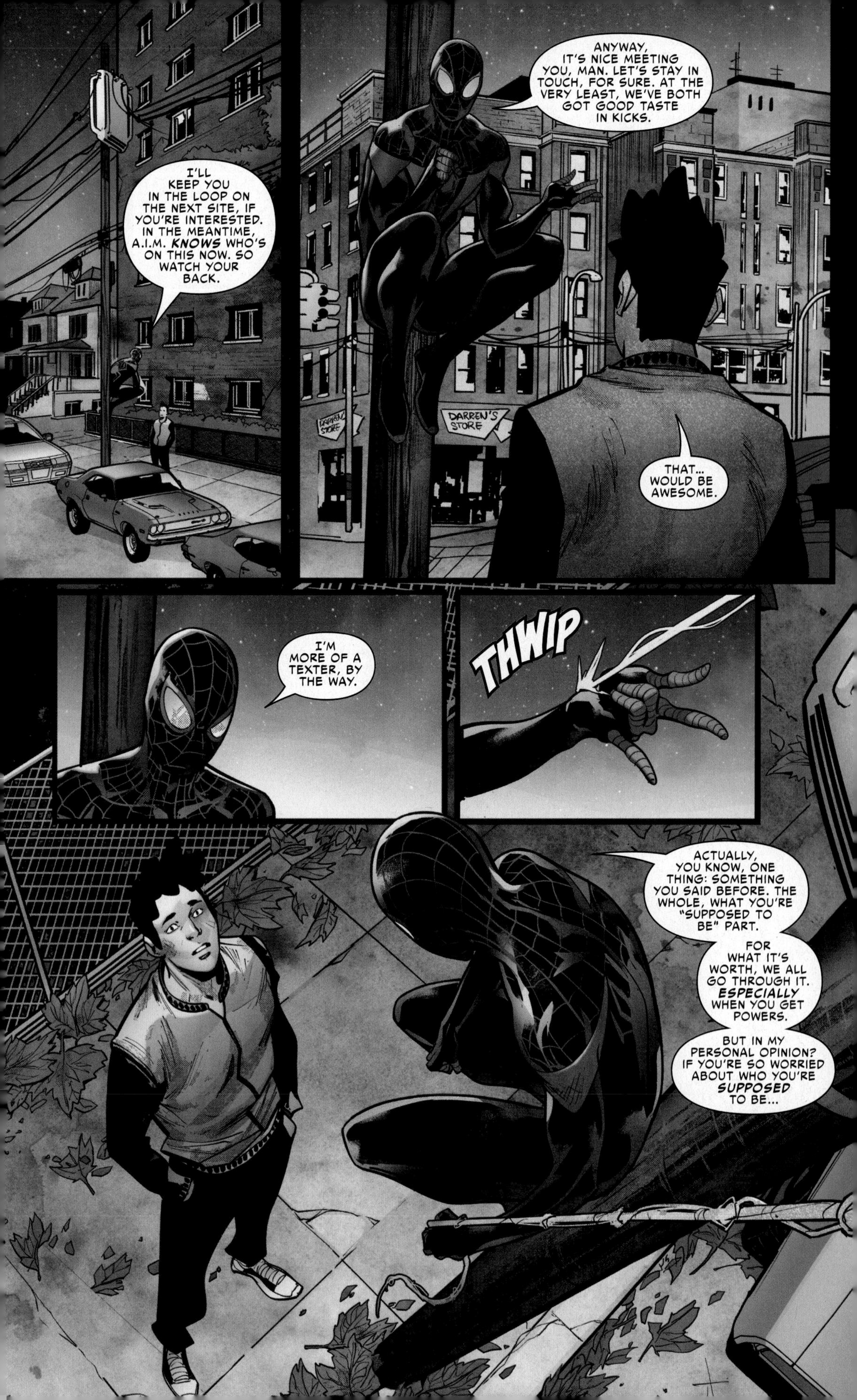
I'LL KEEP YOU IN THE LOOP ON THE NEXT SITE, IF YOU'RE INTERESTED. IN THE MEANTIME, A.I.M. KNOWS WHO'S ON THIS NOW. SO WATCH YOUR BACK.
ANYWAY, IT'S NICE MEETING YOU, MAN. LET'S STAY IN TOUCH, FOR SURE. AT THE VERY LEAST, WE'VE BOTH GOT GOOD TASTE IN KICKS.
DARREN'S STORE
THAT... WOULD BE AWESOME.
I'M MORE OF A TEXTER, BY THE WAY.
THWIP
ACTUALLY, YOU KNOW, ONE THING: SOMETHING YOU SAID BEFORE. THE WHOLE, WHAT YOU'RE "SUPPOSED TO BE" PART.
FOR WHAT IT'S WORTH, WE ALL GO THROUGH IT. ESPECIALLY WHEN YOU GET POWERS.
BUT IN MY PERSONAL OPINION? IF YOU'RE SO WORRIED ABOUT WHO YOU'RE SUPPOSED TO BE...

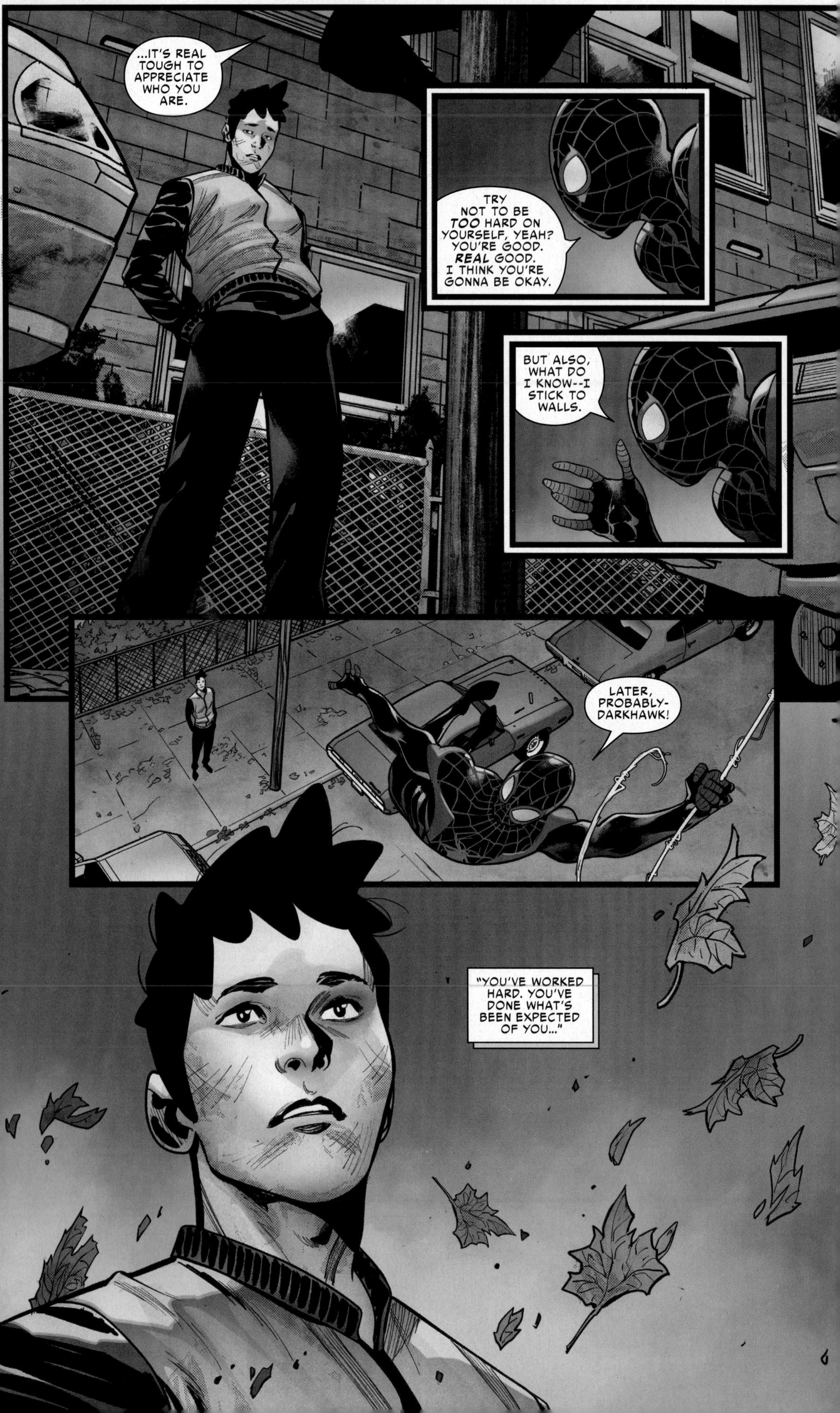

...IT'S REAL TOUGH TO APPRECIATE WHO YOU ARE.
TRY NOT TO BE TOO HARD ON YOURSELF, YEAH? YOU'RE GOOD. REAL GOOD. I THINK YOU'RE GONNA BE OKAY.
BUT ALSO, WHAT DO I KNOW--I STICK TO WALLS.
LATER, PROBABLY-DARKHAWK!
"YOU'VE WORKED HARD. YOU'VE DONE WHAT'S BEEN EXPECTED OF YOU..."

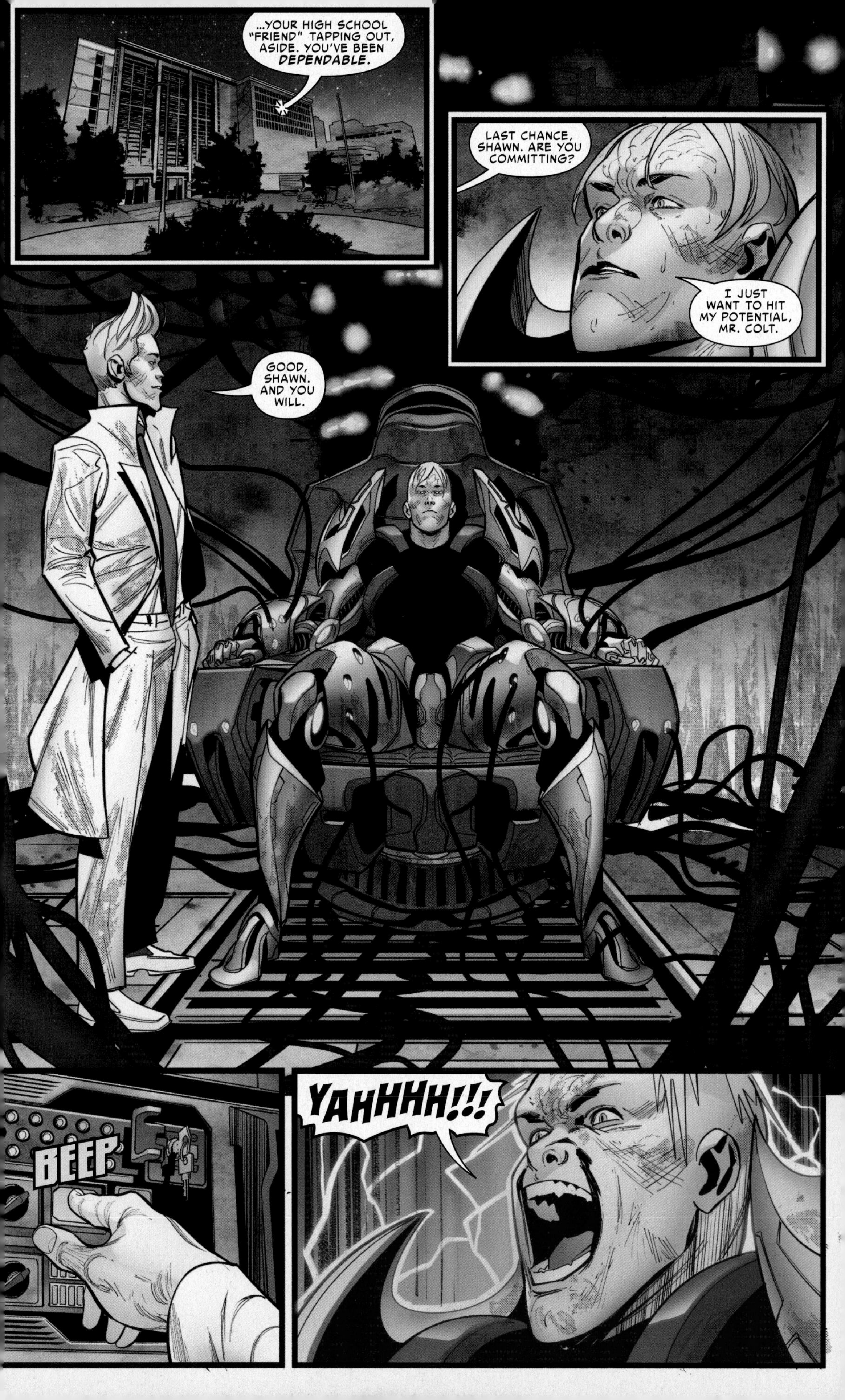
...YOUR HIGH SCHOOL "FRIEND" TAPPING OUT, ASIDE. YOU'VE BEEN DEPENDABLE.
LAST CHANCE, SHAWN. ARE YOU COMMITTING?
I JUST WANT TO HIT MY POTENTIAL, MR. COLT.
GOOD, SHAWN. AND YOU WILL.
BEEP
YAHHHH!!!

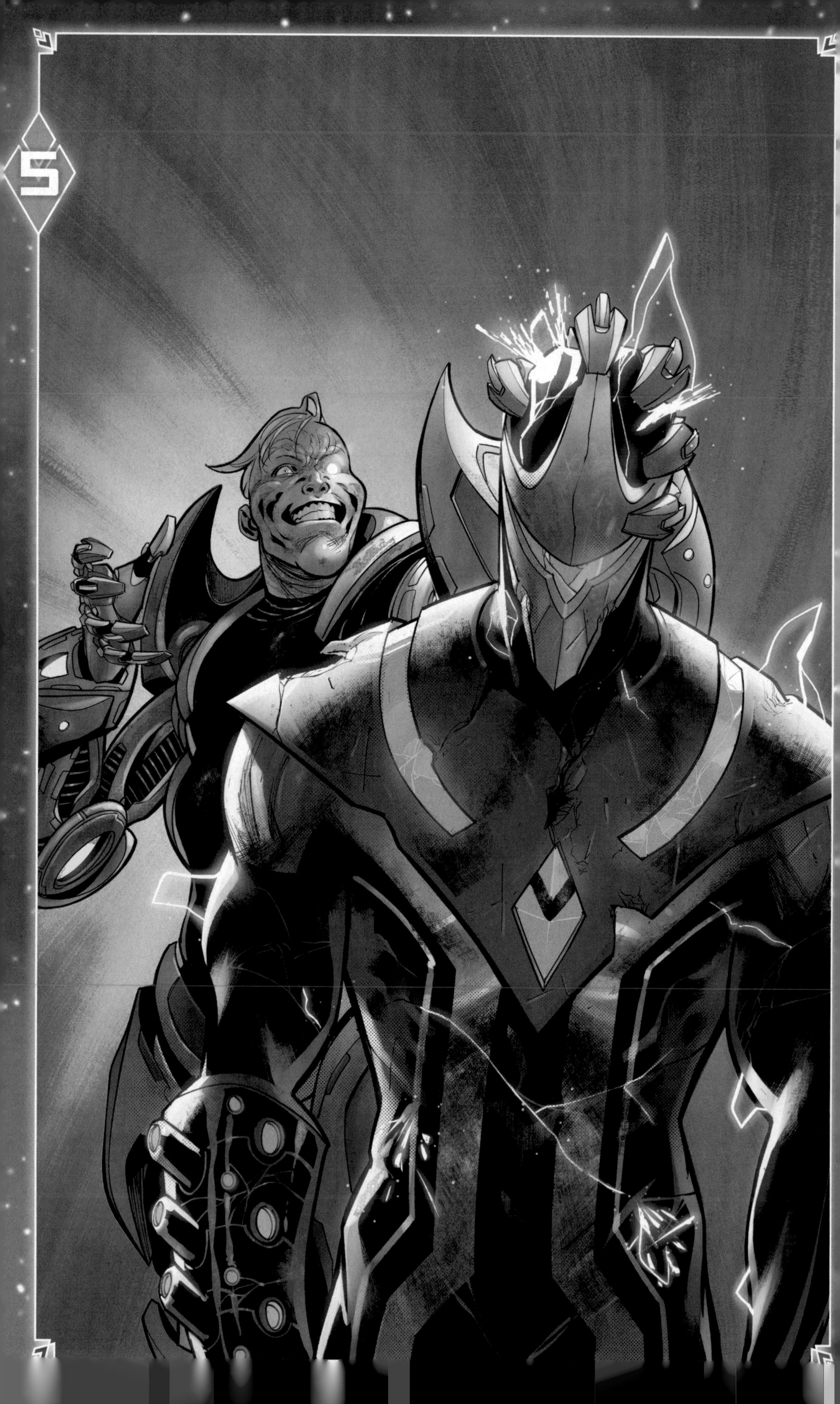
5

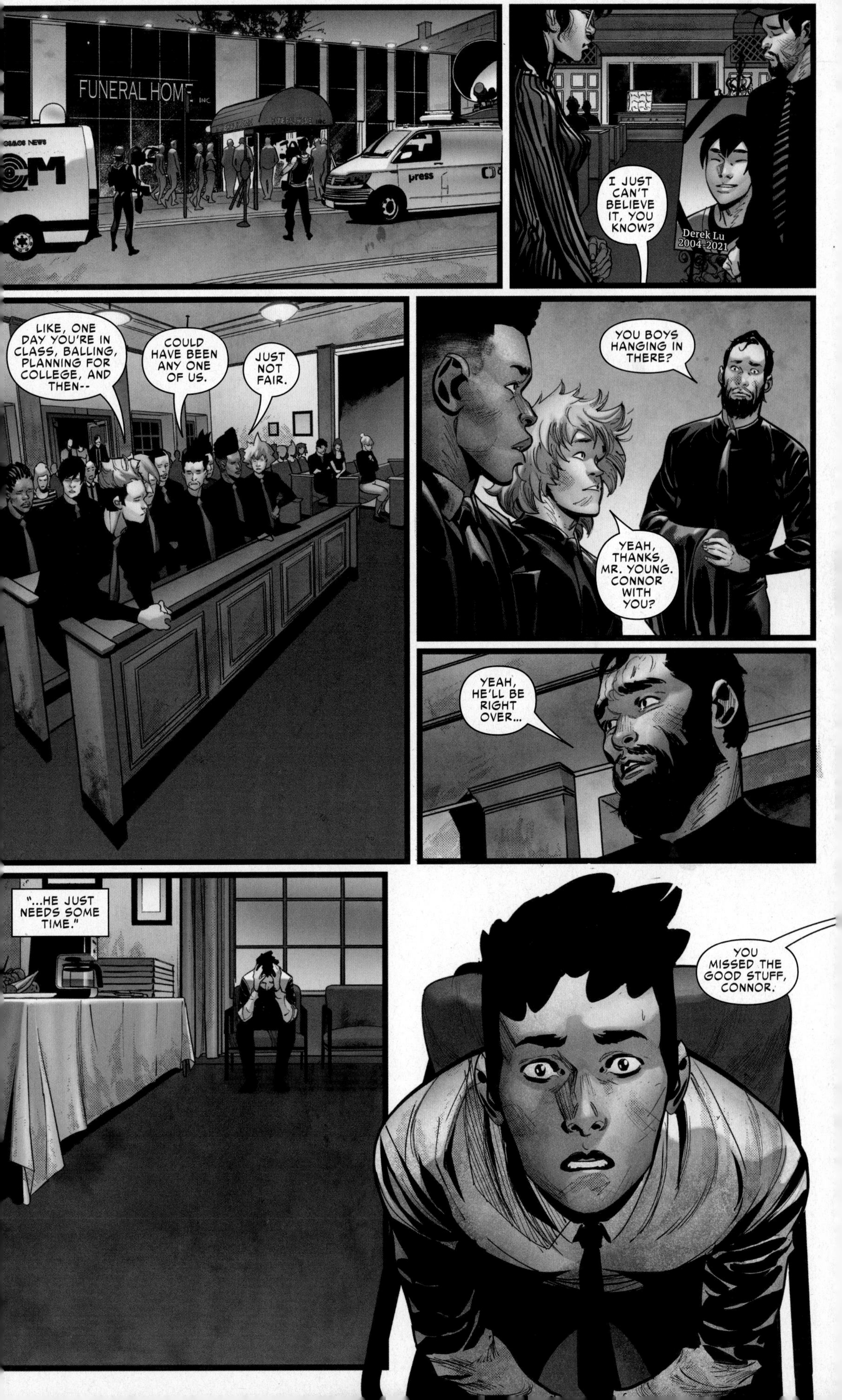
FUNERAL HOME INC
press
I JUST CAN'T BELIEVE IT, YOU KNOW?
Derek Lu 2004-2021
LIKE, ONE DAY YOU'RE IN CLASS, BALLING, PLANNING FOR COLLEGE, AND THEN--
COULD HAVE BEEN ANY ONE OF US.
JUST NOT FAIR.
YOU BOYS HANGING IN THERE?
YEAH, THANKS, MR. YOUNG. CONNOR WITH YOU?
YEAH, HE'LL BE RIGHT OVER...
"...HE JUST NEEDS SOME TIME."
YOU MISSED THE GOOD STUFF, CONNOR.

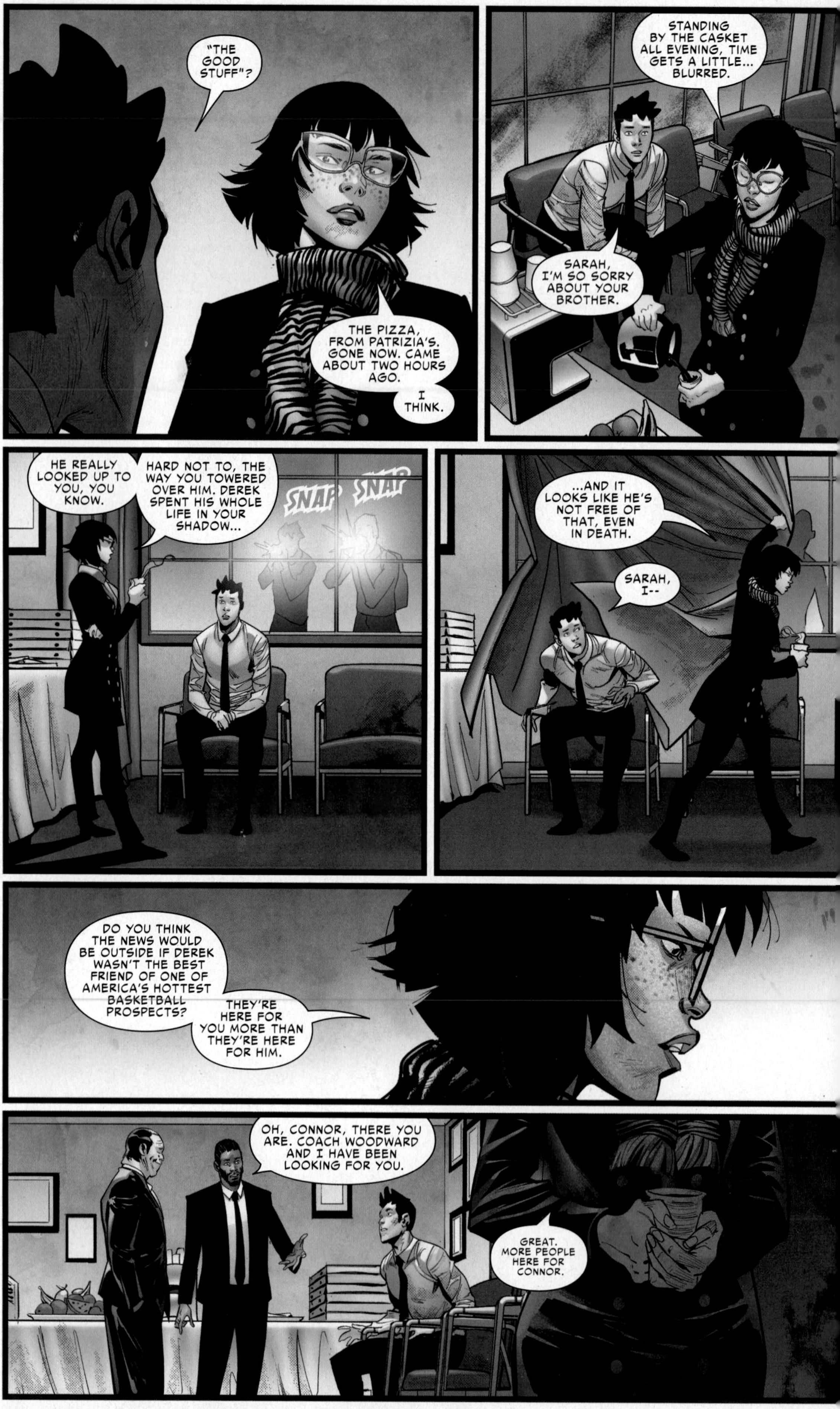
"THE GOOD STUFF"?
THE PIZZA, FROM PATRIZIA'S. GONE NOW. CAME ABOUT TWO HOURS AGO.
I THINK.
STANDING BY THE CASKET ALL EVENING, TIME GETS A LITTLE... BLURRED.
SARAH, I'M SO SORRY ABOUT YOUR BROTHER.
HE REALLY LOOKED UP TO YOU, YOU KNOW.
HARD NOT TO, THE WAY YOU TOWERED OVER HIM. DEREK SPENT HIS WHOLE LIFE IN YOUR SHADOW...
SNAP SNAP
...AND IT LOOKS LIKE HE'S NOT FREE OF THAT, EVEN IN DEATH.
SARAH, I--
DO YOU THINK THE NEWS WOULD BE OUTSIDE IF DEREK WASN'T THE BEST FRIEND OF ONE OF AMERICA'S HOTTEST BASKETBALL PROSPECTS?
THEY'RE HERE FOR YOU MORE THAN THEY'RE HERE FOR HIM.
OH, CONNOR, THERE YOU ARE. COACH WOODWARD AND I HAVE BEEN LOOKING FOR YOU.
GREAT. MORE PEOPLE HERE FOR CONNOR.

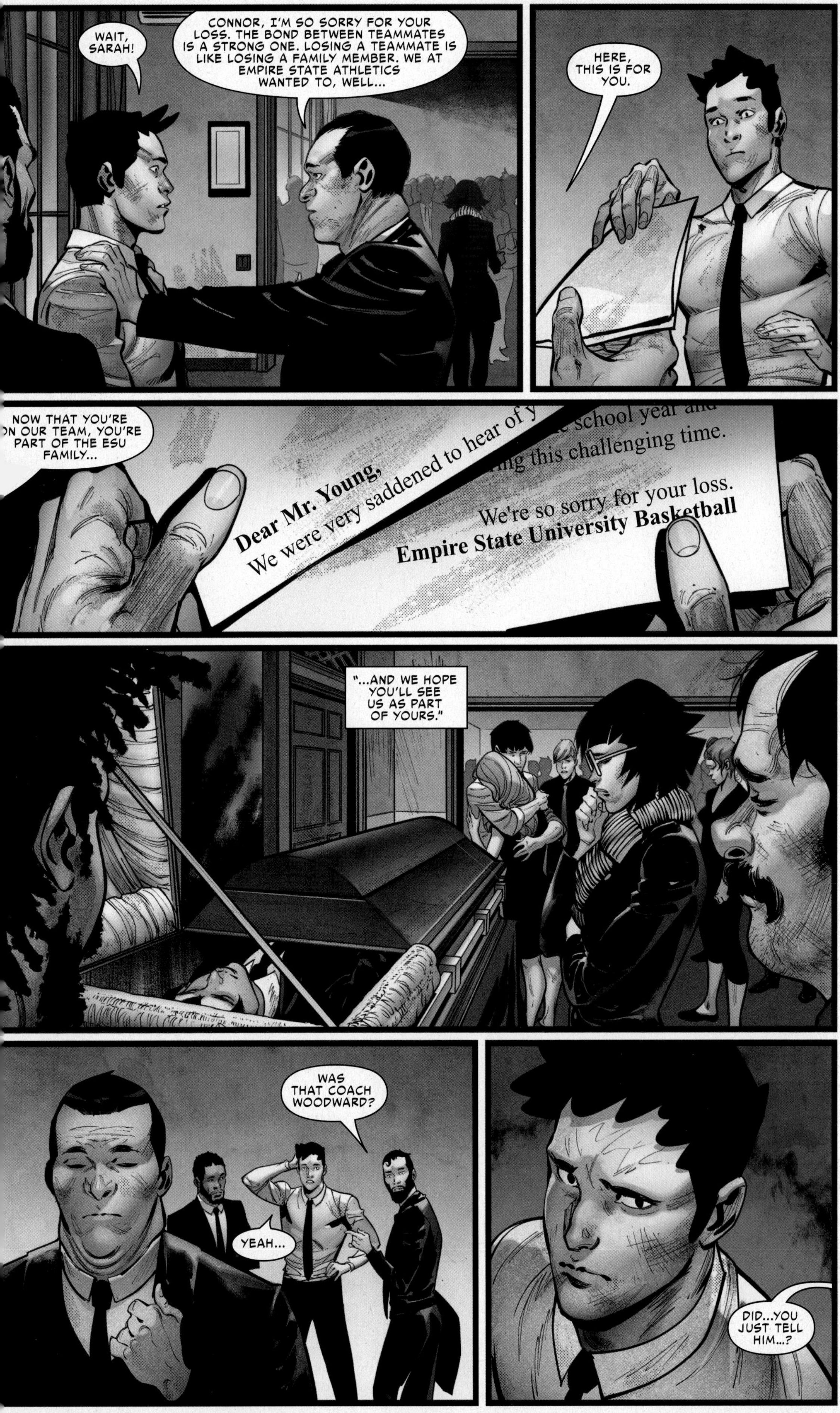
WAIT, SARAH!
CONNOR, I'M SO SORRY FOR YOUR LOSS. THE BOND BETWEEN TEAMMATES IS A STRONG ONE. LOSING A TEAMMATE IS LIKE LOSING A FAMILY MEMBER. WE AT EMPIRE STATE ATHLETICS WANTED TO, WELL...
HERE, THIS IS FOR YOU.
NOW THAT YOU'RE ON OUR TEAM, YOU'RE PART OF THE ESU FAMILY...
Dear Mr. Young,
We were very saddened to hear of y
school year and
ring this challenging time.
We're so sorry for your loss.
Empire State University Basketball
"...AND WE HOPE YOU'LL SEE US AS PART OF YOURS."
WAS THAT COACH WOODWARD?
YEAH...
DID...YOU JUST TELL HIM...?

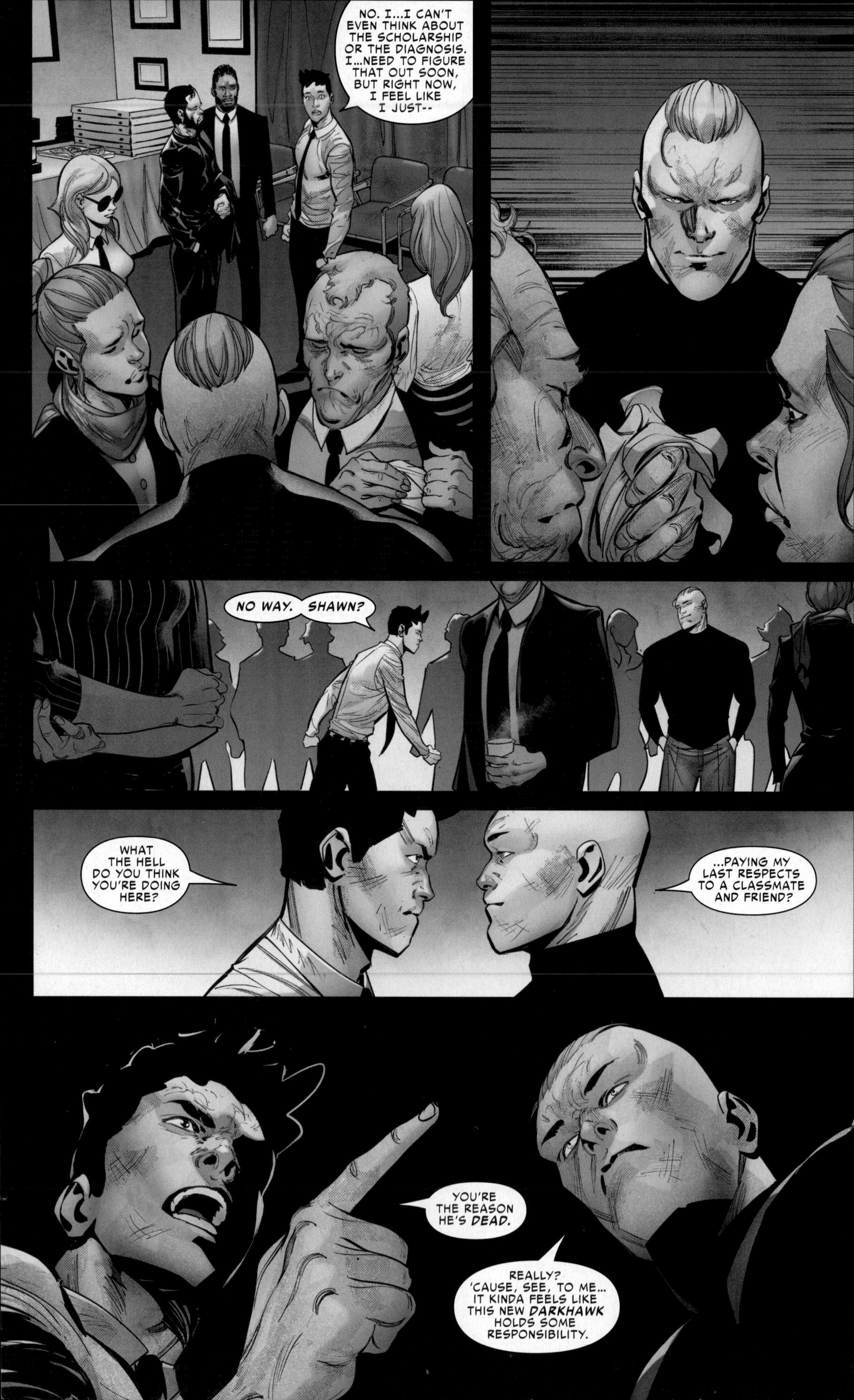

NO. I...I CAN'T EVEN THINK ABOUT THE SCHOLARSHIP OR THE DIAGNOSIS. I...NEED TO FIGURE THAT OUT SOON, BUT RIGHT NOW, I FEEL LIKE I JUST--
NO WAY.
SHAWN?
WHAT THE HELL DO YOU THINK YOU'RE DOING HERE?
...PAYING MY LAST RESPECTS TO A CLASSMATE AND FRIEND?
YOU'RE THE REASON HE'S DEAD.
REALLY? 'CAUSE, SEE, TO ME... IT KINDA FEELS LIKE THIS NEW DARKHAWK HOLDS SOME RESPONSIBILITY.

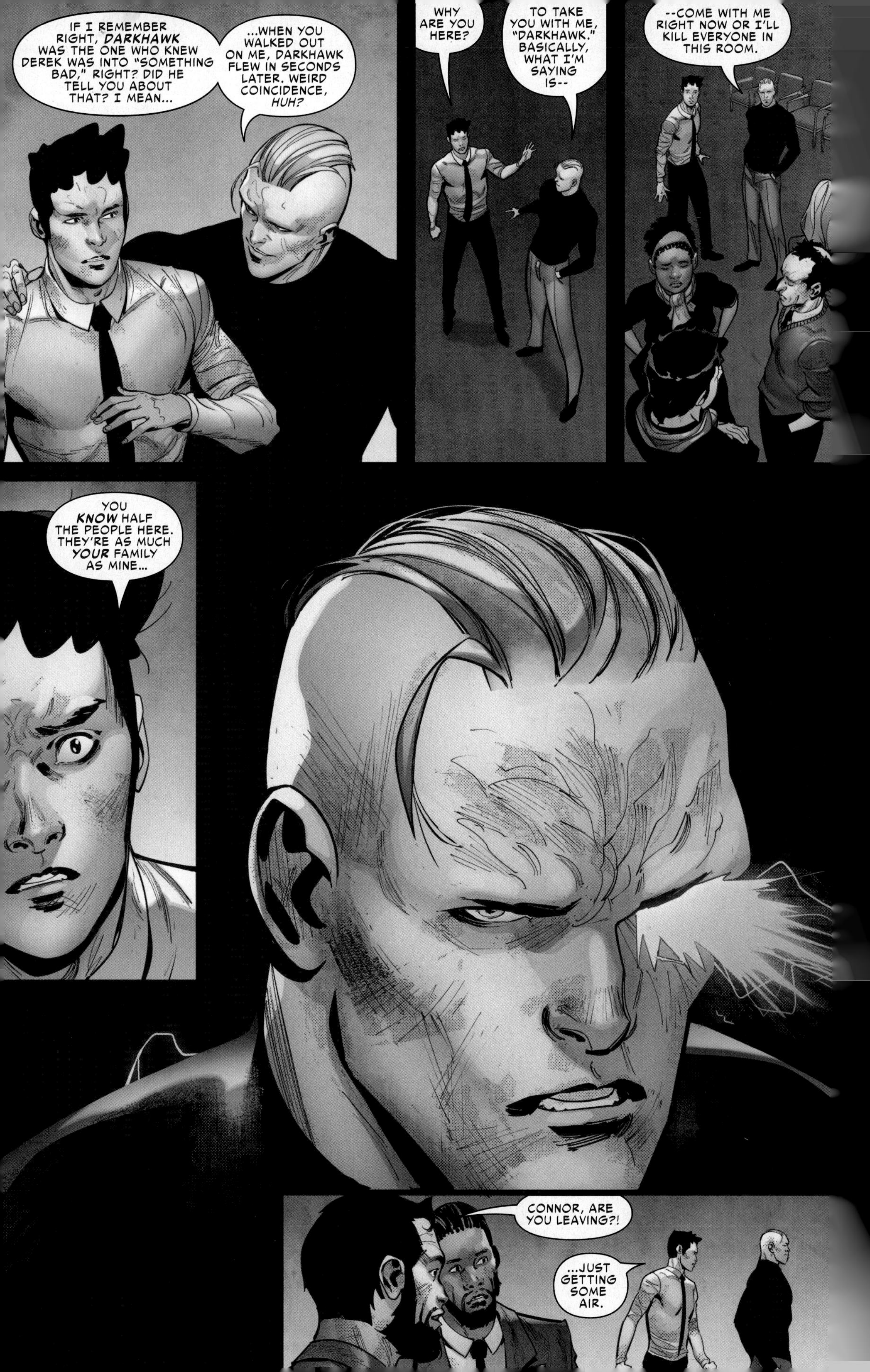
IF I REMEMBER RIGHT, DARKHAWK WAS THE ONE WHO KNEW DEREK WAS INTO "SOMETHING BAD," RIGHT? DID HE TELL YOU ABOUT THAT? I MEAN...
...WHEN YOU WALKED OUT ON ME, DARKHAWK FLEW IN SECONDS LATER. WEIRD COINCIDENCE, HUH?
WHY ARE YOU HERE?
TO TAKE YOU WITH ME, "DARKHAWK." BASICALLY, WHAT I'M SAYING IS--
--COME WITH ME RIGHT NOW OR I'LL KILL EVERYONE IN THIS ROOM.
YOU KNOW HALF THE PEOPLE HERE. THEY'RE AS MUCH YOUR FAMILY AS MINE...
CONNOR, ARE YOU LEAVING?!
...JUST GETTING SOME AIR.

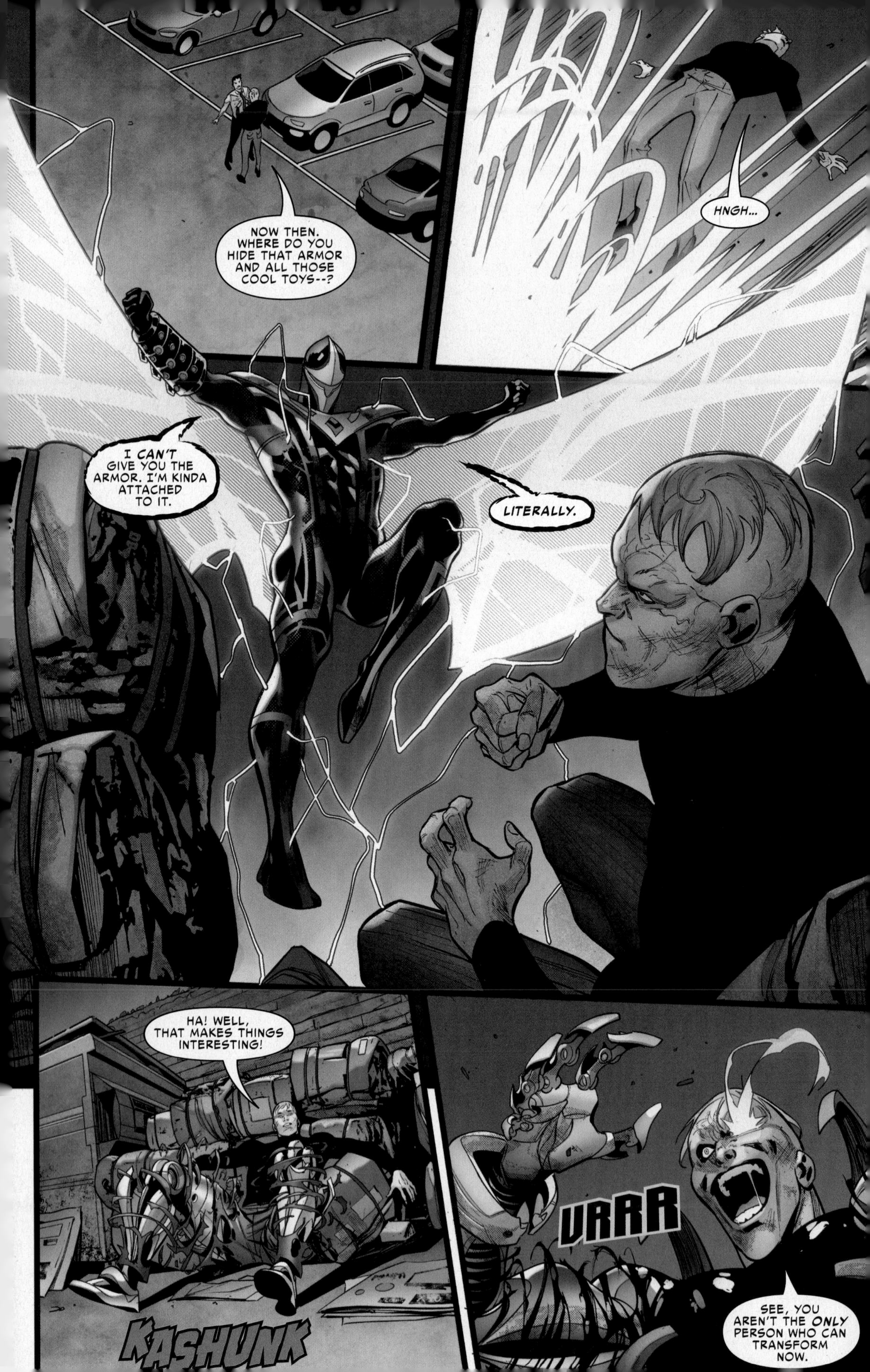

NOW THEN. WHERE DO YOU HIDE THAT ARMOR AND ALL THOSE COOL TOYS--?
HNGH...
I CAN'T GIVE YOU THE ARMOR. I'M KINDA ATTACHED TO IT.
LITERALLY.
HA! WELL, THAT MAKES THINGS INTERESTING!
KASHUNK
URRR
SEE, YOU AREN'T THE ONLY PERSON WHO CAN TRANSFORM NOW.

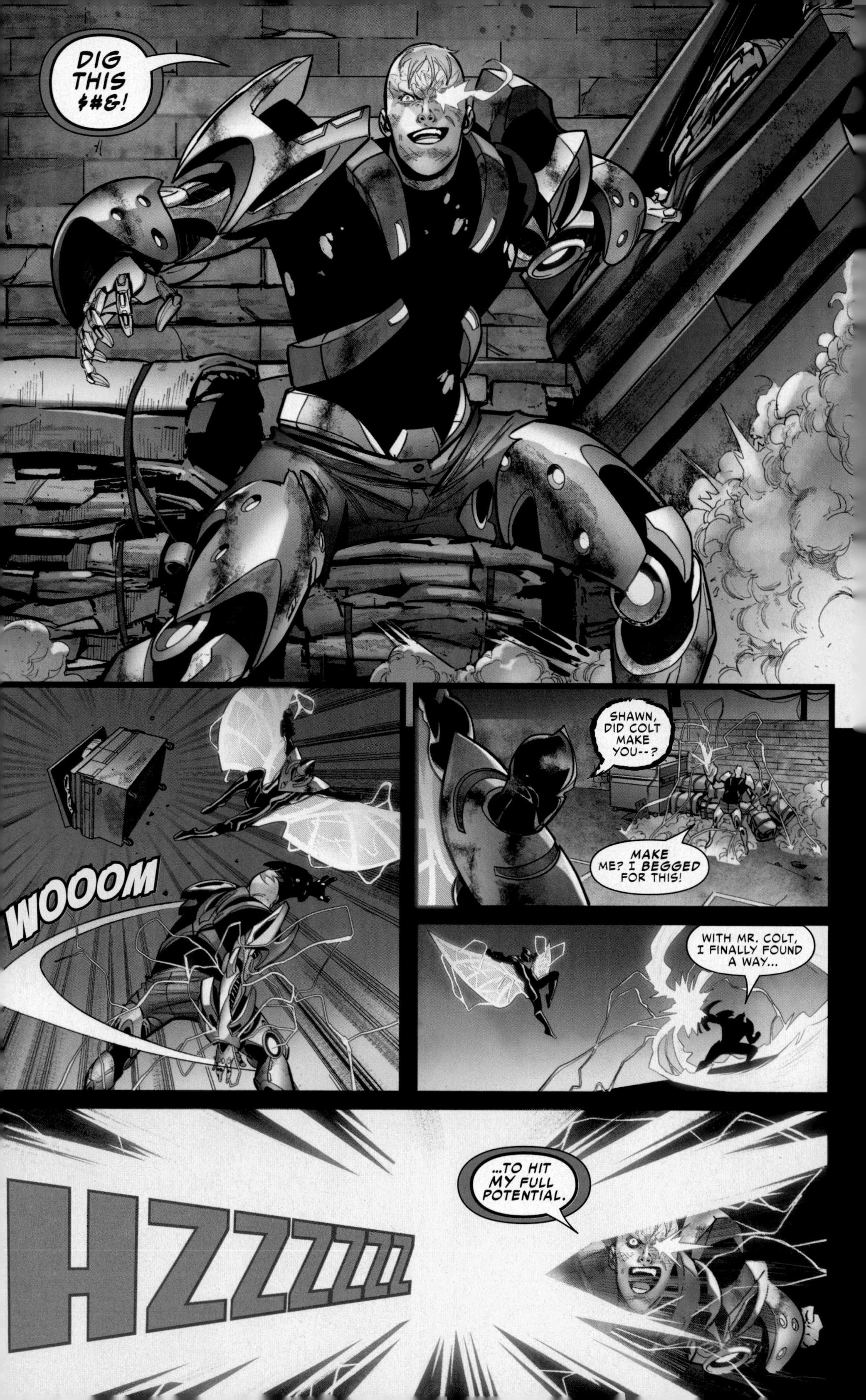
DIG THIS $#&!
WOOOM
SHAWN, DID COLT MAKE YOU--?
MAKE ME? I *BEGGED* FOR THIS!
WITH MR. COLT, I FINALLY FOUND A WAY...
HZZZZZZ
...TO HIT MY FULL POTENTIAL.

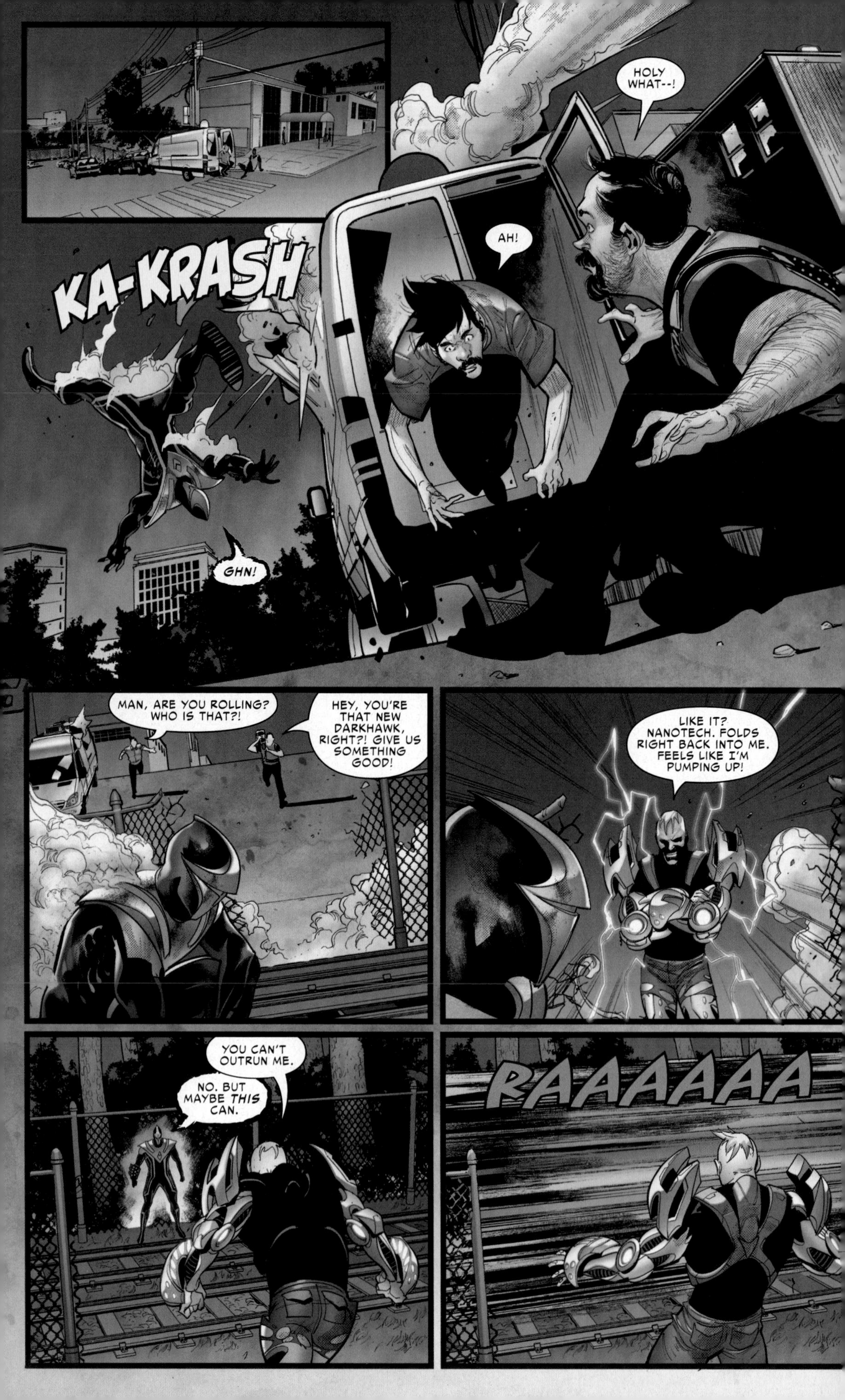
HOLY WHAT--!
AH!
KA-KRASH
GHN!
MAN, ARE YOU ROLLING? WHO IS THAT?!
HEY, YOU'RE THAT NEW DARKHAWK, RIGHT?! GIVE US SOMETHING GOOD!
LIKE IT? NANOTECH. FOLDS RIGHT BACK INTO ME. FEELS LIKE I'M PUMPING UP!
YOU CAN'T OUTRUN ME.
NO. BUT MAYBE THIS CAN.
RAAAAAA

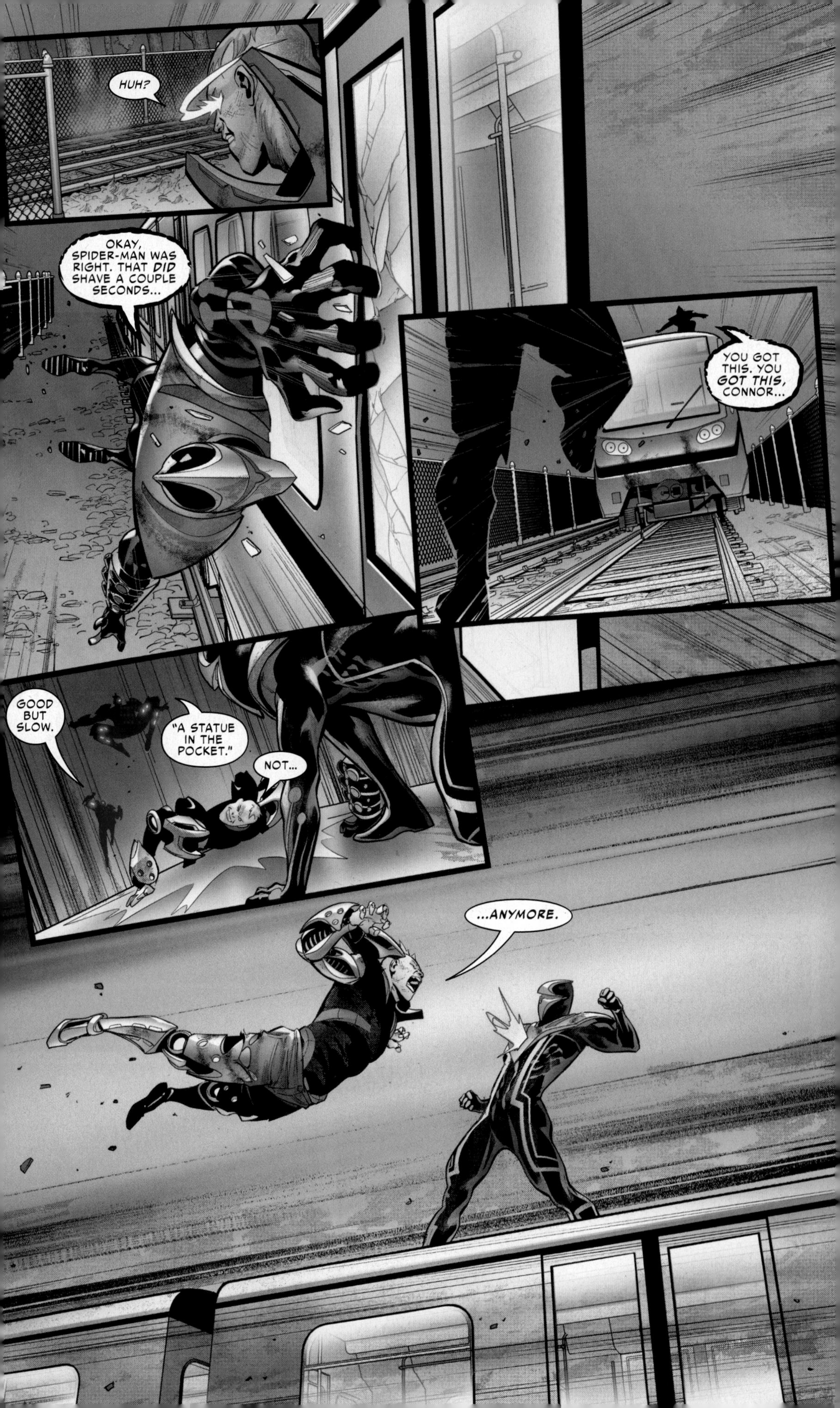

HUH?
OKAY, SPIDER-MAN WAS RIGHT. THAT DID SHAVE A COUPLE SECONDS...
YOU GOT THIS. YOU GOT THIS, CONNOR...
GOOD BUT SLOW.
"A STATUE IN THE POCKET."
NOT...
...ANYMORE.

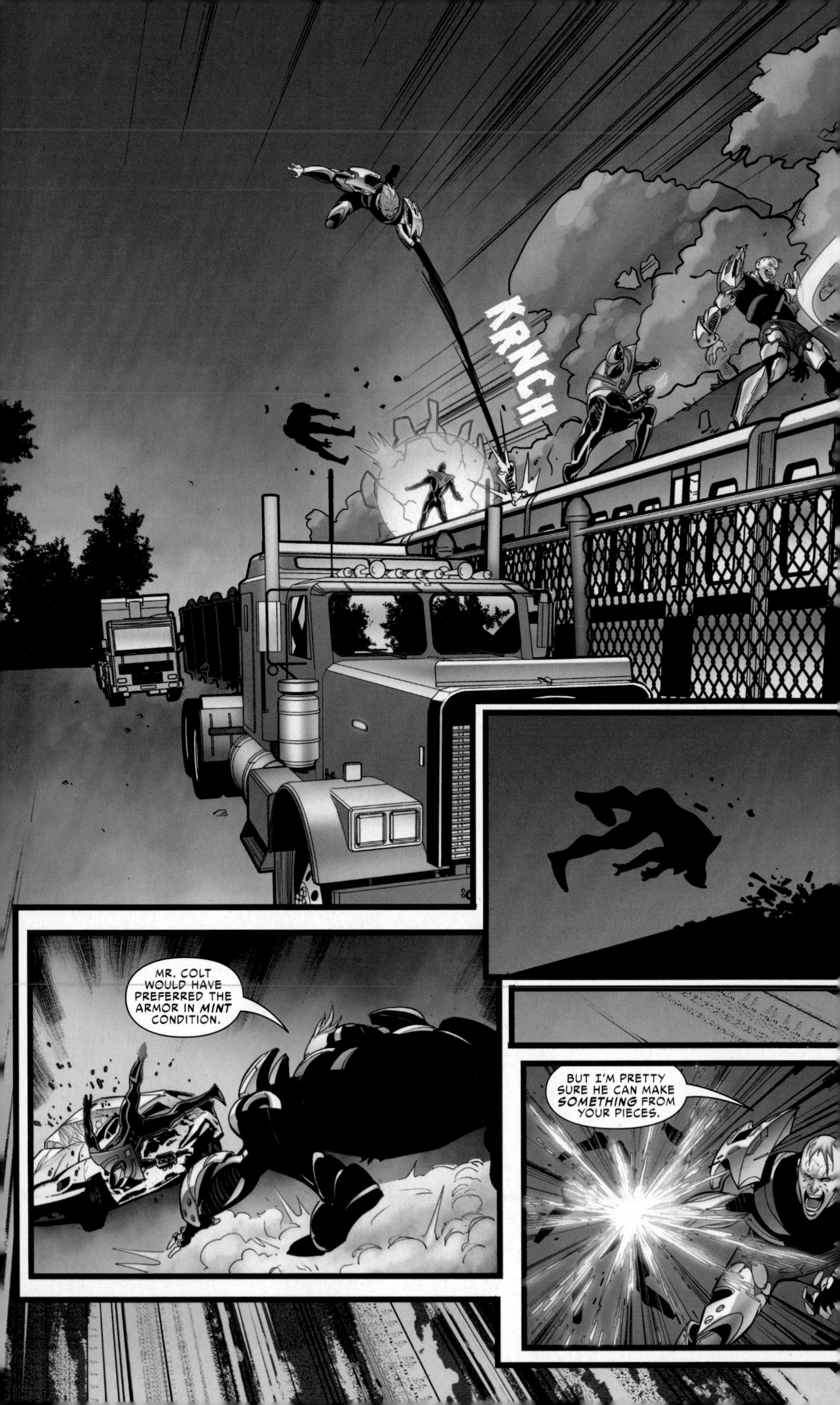
KRNCH
MR. COLT WOULD HAVE PREFERRED THE ARMOR IN MINT CONDITION.
BUT I'M PRETTY SURE HE CAN MAKE SOMETHING FROM YOUR PIECES.

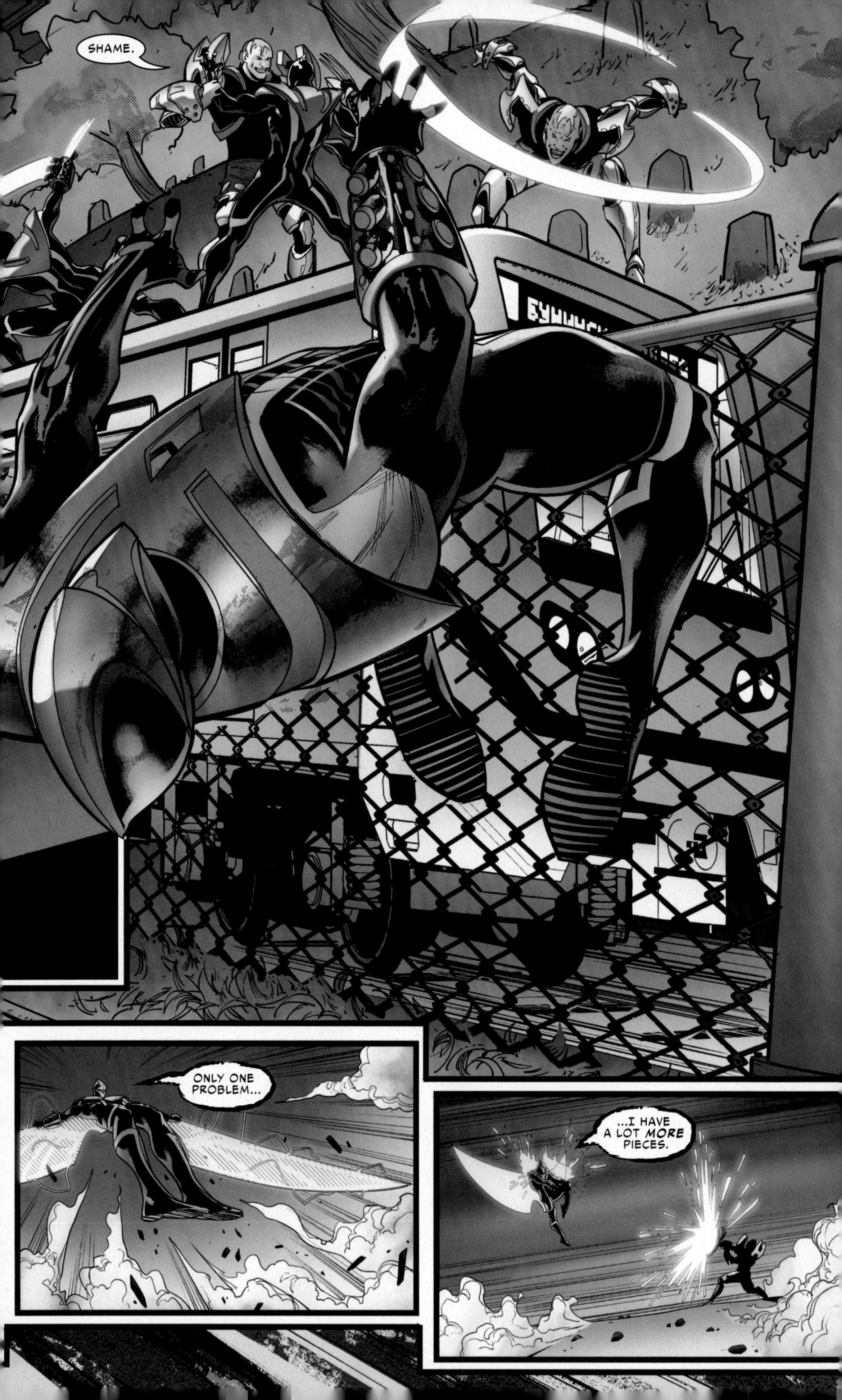
SHAME.
ONLY ONE PROBLEM...
...I HAVE A LOT MORE PIECES.

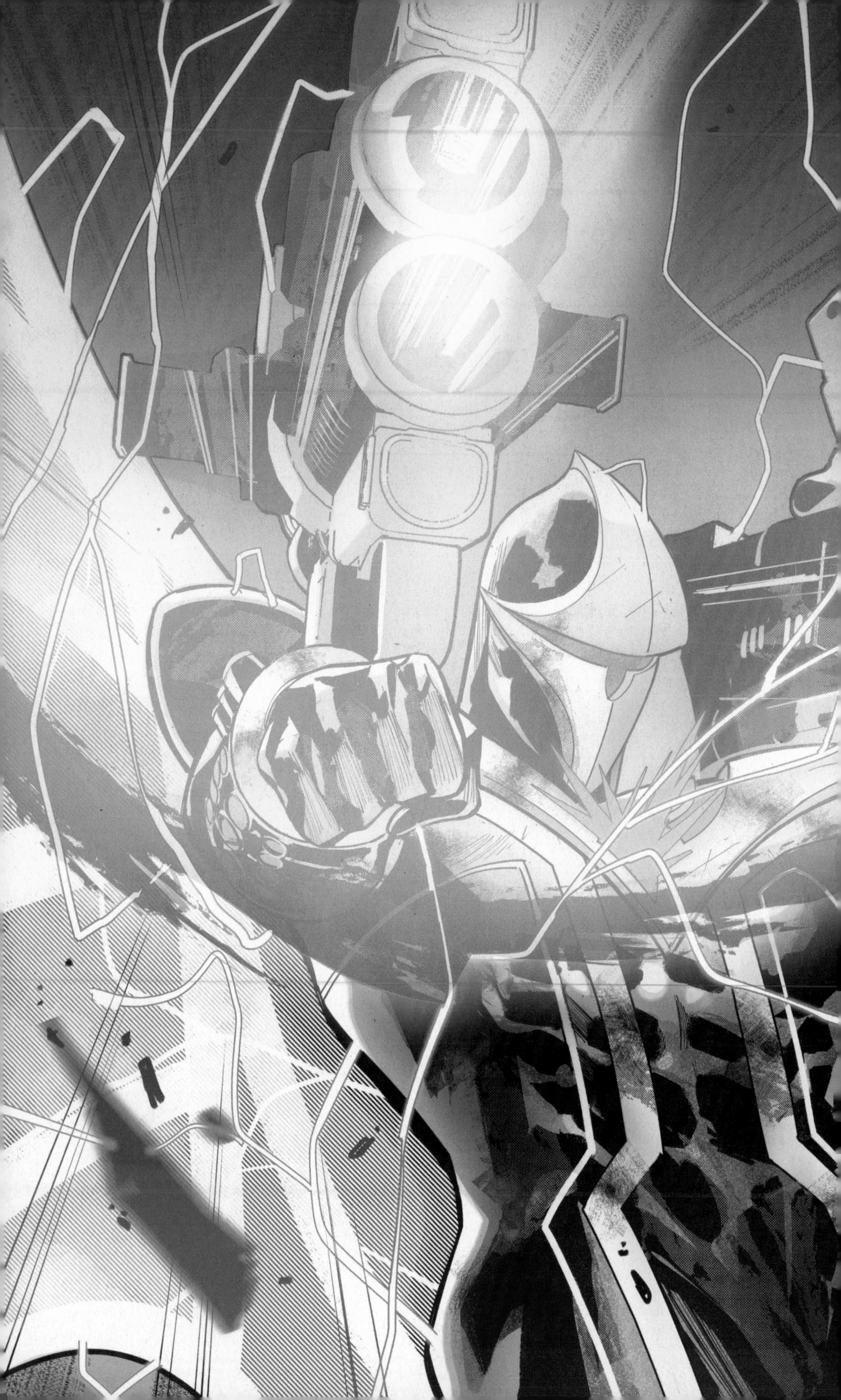

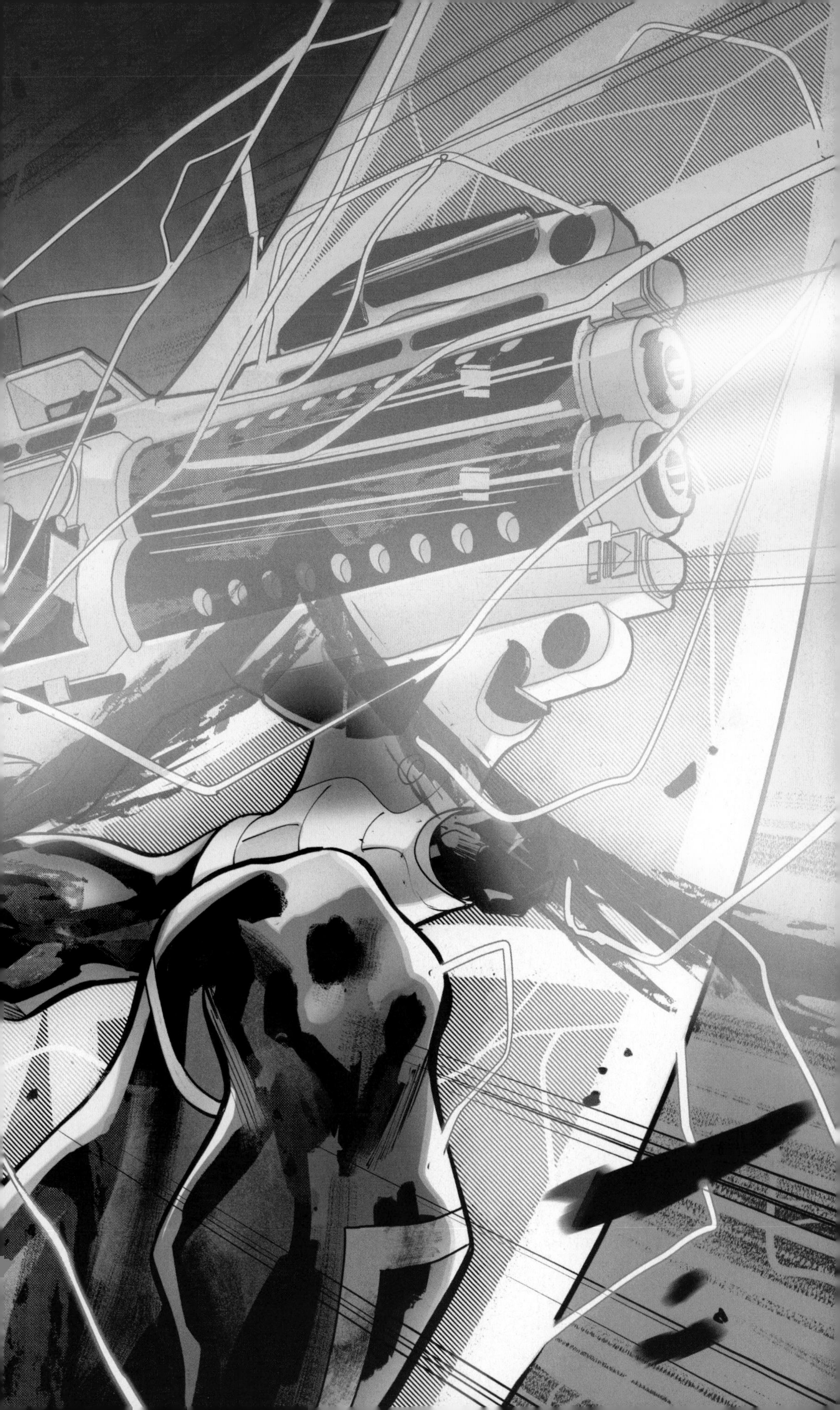

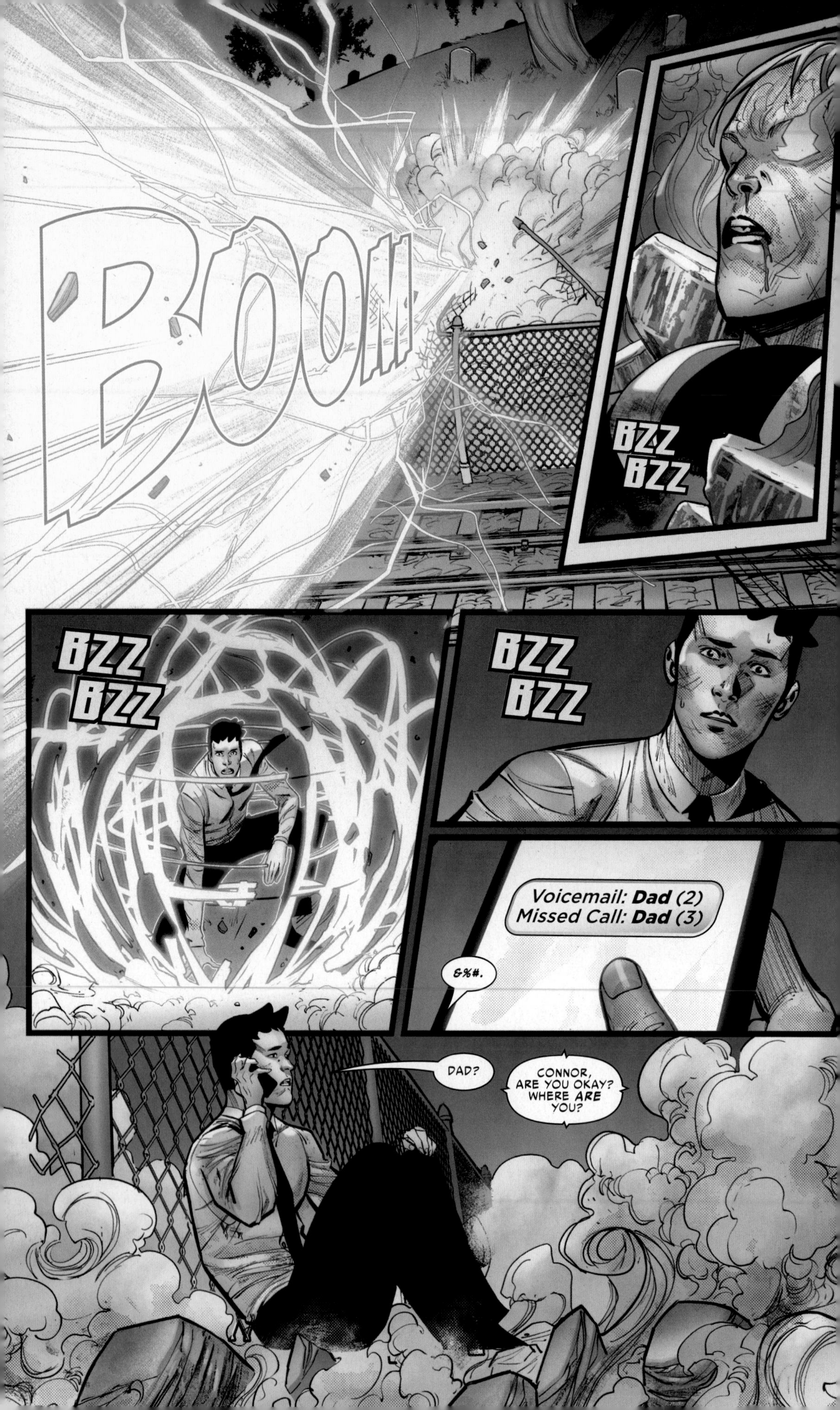
BOOM
BZZ BZZ
BZZ BZZ
BZZ BZZ
Voicemail: Dad (2)
Missed Call: Dad (3)
&%#.
DAD?
CONNOR, ARE YOU OKAY? WHERE ARE YOU?

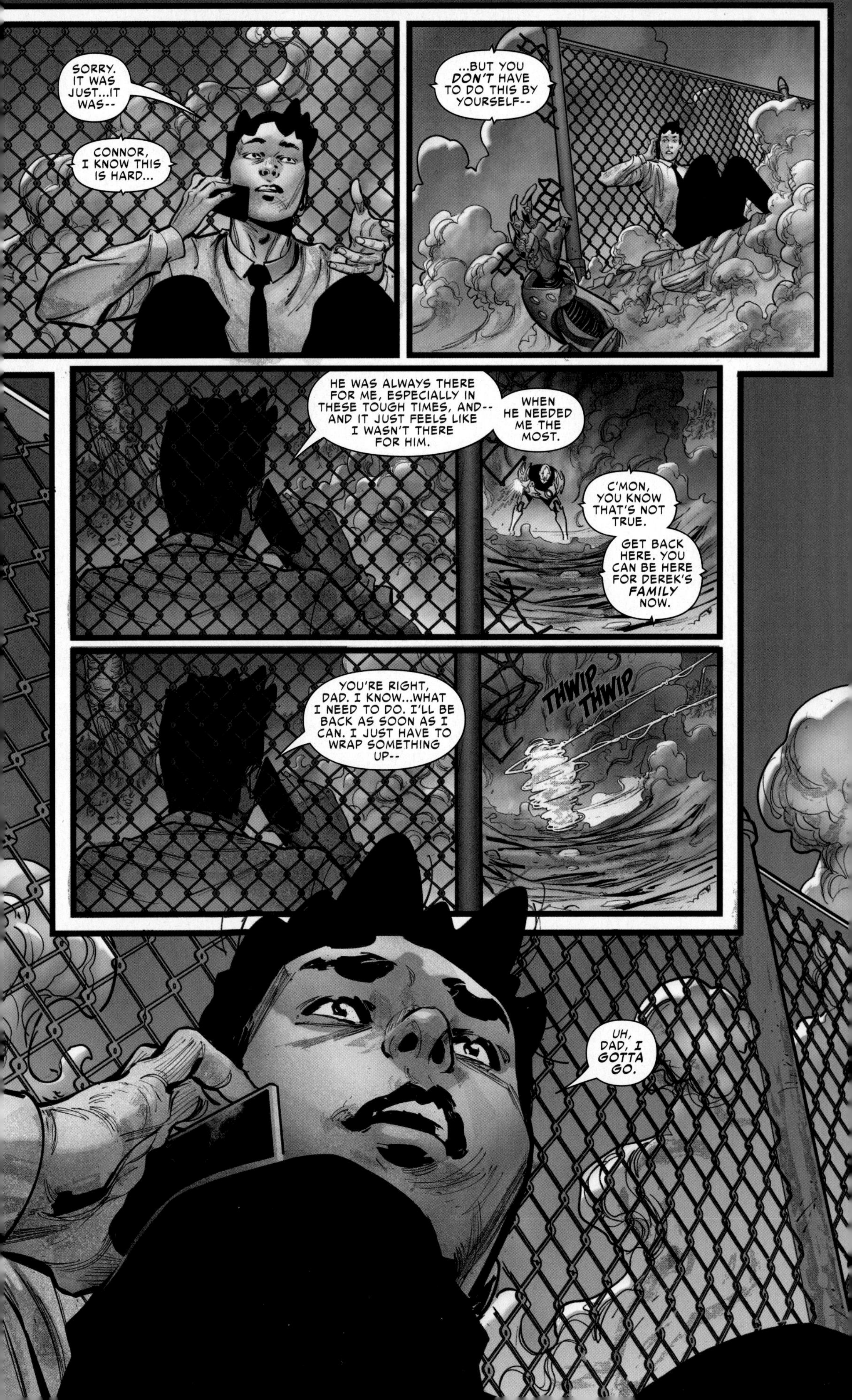

SORRY. IT WAS JUST...IT WAS--
CONNOR, I KNOW THIS IS HARD...
...BUT YOU *DON'T* HAVE TO DO THIS BY YOURSELF--
HE WAS ALWAYS THERE FOR ME, ESPECIALLY IN THESE TOUGH TIMES, AND-- AND IT JUST FEELS LIKE I WASN'T THERE FOR HIM.
WHEN HE NEEDED ME THE MOST.
C'MON, YOU KNOW THAT'S NOT TRUE.
GET BACK HERE. YOU CAN BE HERE FOR DEREK'S *FAMILY* NOW.
YOU'RE RIGHT, DAD. I KNOW...WHAT I NEED TO DO. I'LL BE BACK AS SOON AS I CAN. I JUST HAVE TO WRAP SOMETHING UP--
THWIP THWIP
UH, DAD, I GOTTA GO.

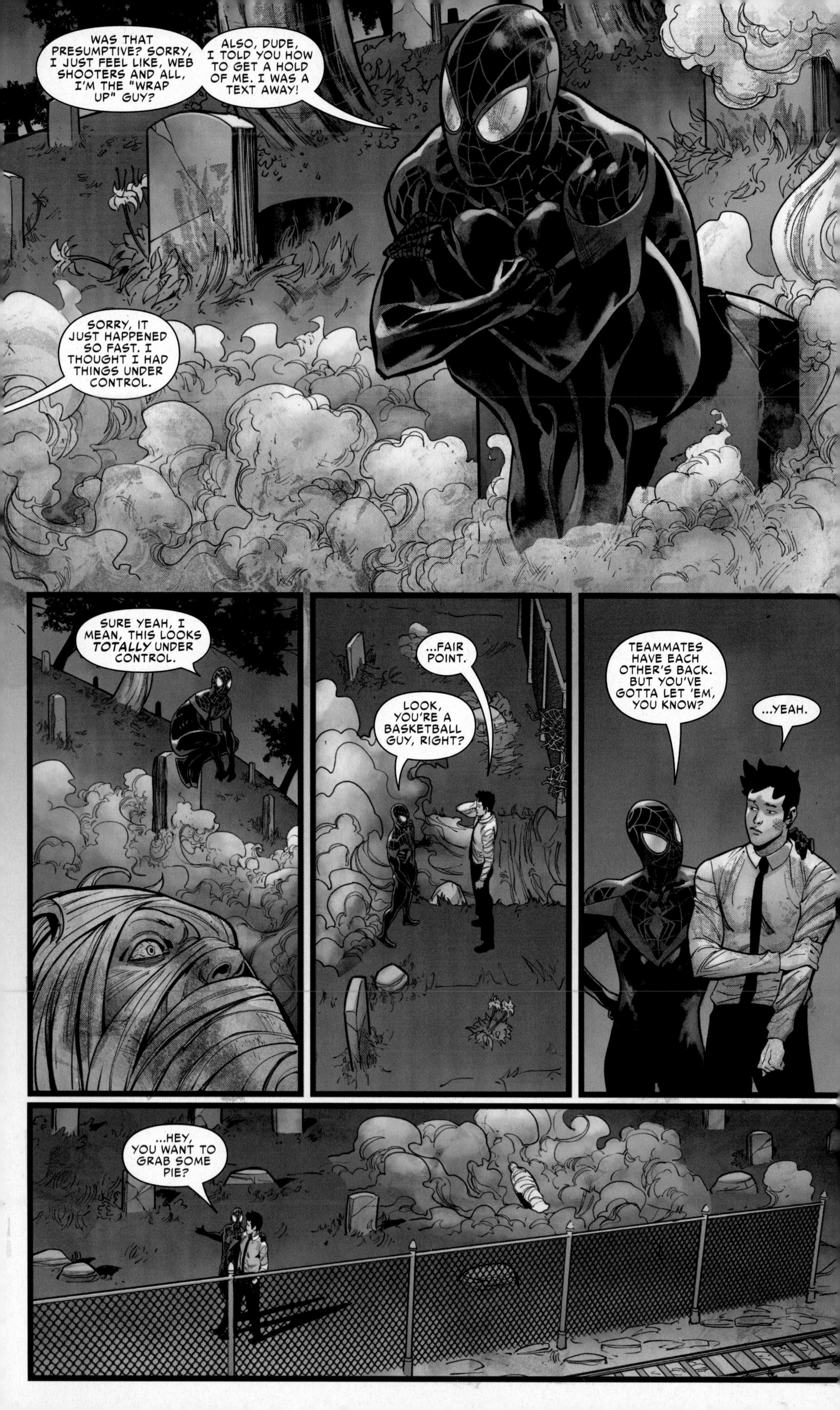
WAS THAT PRESUMPTIVE? SORRY, I JUST FEEL LIKE, WEB SHOOTERS AND ALL, I'M THE "WRAP UP" GUY?
ALSO, DUDE, I TOLD YOU HOW TO GET A HOLD OF ME. I WAS A TEXT AWAY!
SORRY, IT JUST HAPPENED SO FAST. I THOUGHT I HAD THINGS UNDER CONTROL.
SURE YEAH, I MEAN, THIS LOOKS *TOTALLY* UNDER CONTROL.
...FAIR POINT.
LOOK, YOU'RE A BASKETBALL GUY, RIGHT?
TEAMMATES HAVE EACH OTHER'S BACK. BUT YOU'VE GOTTA LET 'EM, YOU KNOW?
...YEAH.
...HEY, YOU WANT TO GRAB SOME PIE?

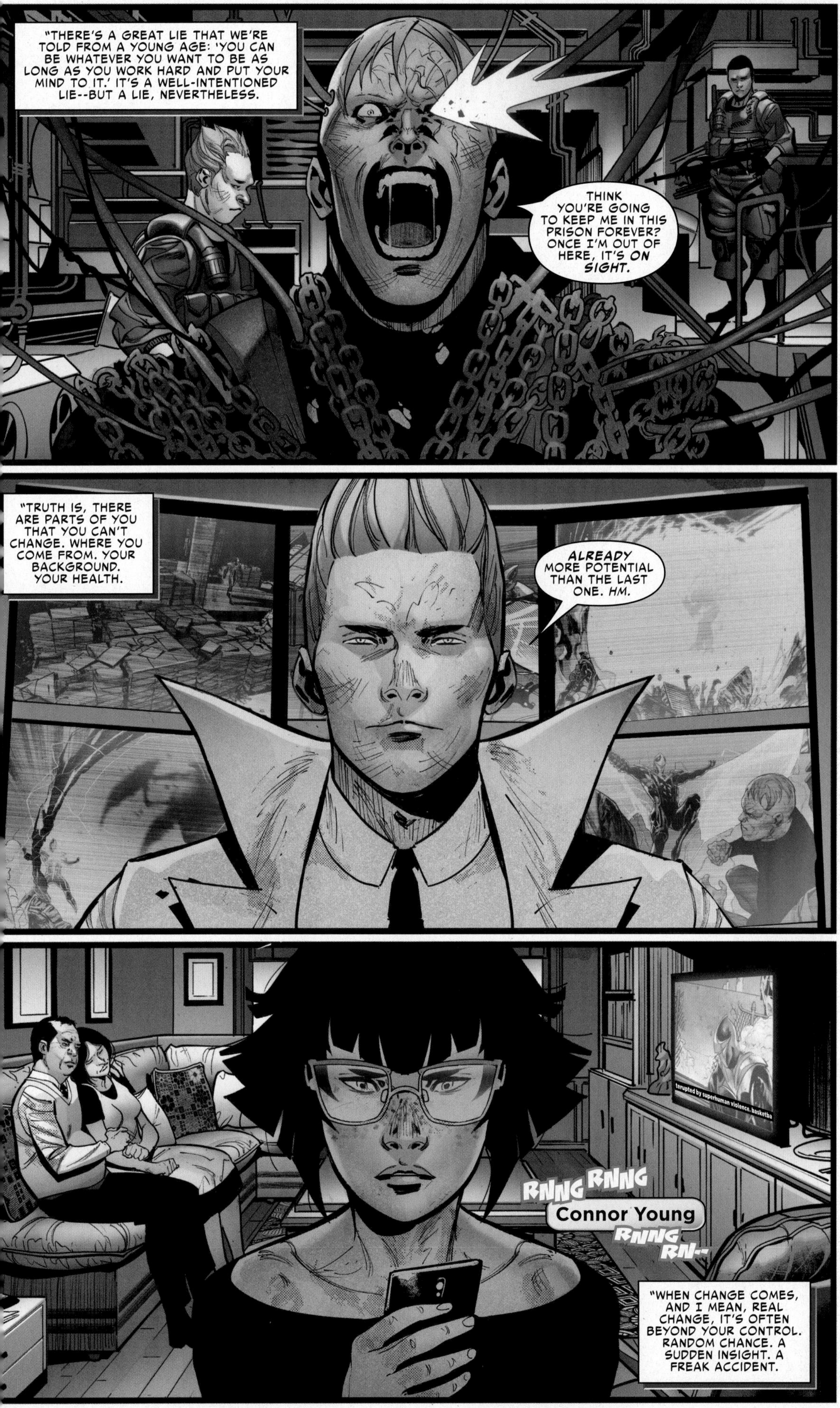
"THERE'S A GREAT LIE THAT WE'RE TOLD FROM A YOUNG AGE: 'YOU CAN BE WHATEVER YOU WANT TO BE AS LONG AS YOU WORK HARD AND PUT YOUR MIND TO IT.' IT'S A WELL-INTENTIONED LIE--BUT A LIE, NEVERTHELESS.
THINK YOU'RE GOING TO KEEP ME IN THIS PRISON FOREVER? ONCE I'M OUT OF HERE, IT'S ON SIGHT.
"TRUTH IS, THERE ARE PARTS OF YOU THAT YOU CAN'T CHANGE. WHERE YOU COME FROM. YOUR BACKGROUND. YOUR HEALTH.
ALREADY MORE POTENTIAL THAN THE LAST ONE. HM.
terupted by superhuman violence. basketba
RNNG RNNG
Connor Young
RNNG RN--
"WHEN CHANGE COMES, AND I MEAN, REAL CHANGE, IT'S OFTEN BEYOND YOUR CONTROL. RANDOM CHANCE. A SUDDEN INSIGHT. A FREAK ACCIDENT.

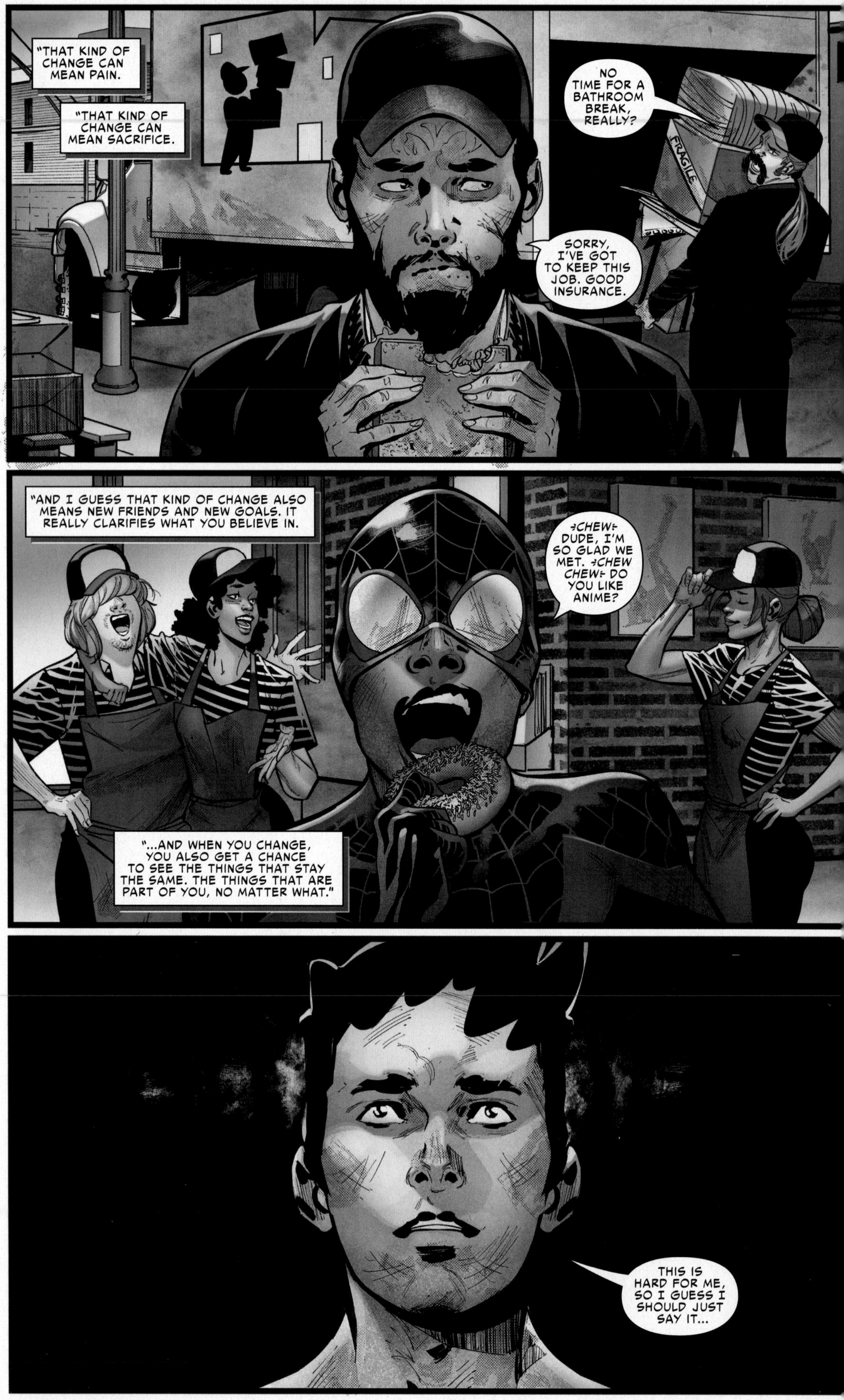
"THAT KIND OF CHANGE CAN MEAN PAIN.
"THAT KIND OF CHANGE CAN MEAN SACRIFICE.
NO TIME FOR A BATHROOM BREAK, REALLY?
FRAGILE
SORRY, I'VE GOT TO KEEP THIS JOB. GOOD INSURANCE.
"AND I GUESS THAT KIND OF CHANGE ALSO MEANS NEW FRIENDS AND NEW GOALS. IT REALLY CLARIFIES WHAT YOU BELIEVE IN.
⇛CHEW⇚ DUDE, I'M SO GLAD WE MET. ⇛CHEW CHEW⇚ DO YOU LIKE ANIME?
"...AND WHEN YOU CHANGE, YOU ALSO GET A CHANCE TO SEE THE THINGS THAT STAY THE SAME. THE THINGS THAT ARE PART OF YOU, NO MATTER WHAT."
THIS IS HARD FOR ME, SO I GUESS I SHOULD JUST SAY IT...

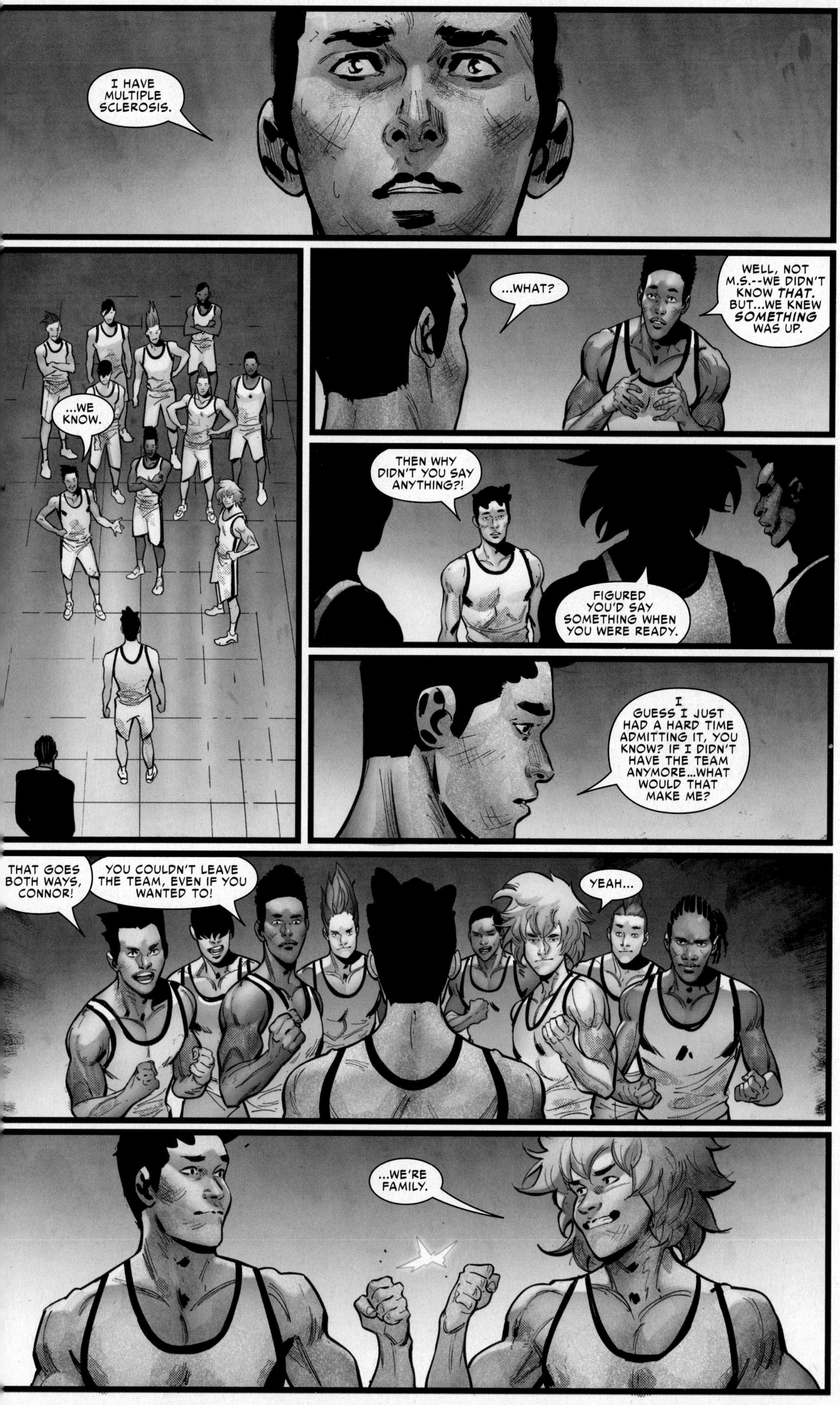
I HAVE MULTIPLE SCLEROSIS.
...WE KNOW.
...WHAT?
WELL, NOT M.S.--WE DIDN'T KNOW THAT. BUT...WE KNEW SOMETHING WAS UP.
THEN WHY DIDN'T YOU SAY ANYTHING?!
FIGURED YOU'D SAY SOMETHING WHEN YOU WERE READY.
I GUESS I JUST HAD A HARD TIME ADMITTING IT, YOU KNOW? IF I DIDN'T HAVE THE TEAM ANYMORE...WHAT WOULD THAT MAKE ME?
THAT GOES BOTH WAYS, CONNOR!
YOU COULDN'T LEAVE THE TEAM, EVEN IF YOU WANTED TO!
YEAH...
...WE'RE FAMILY.

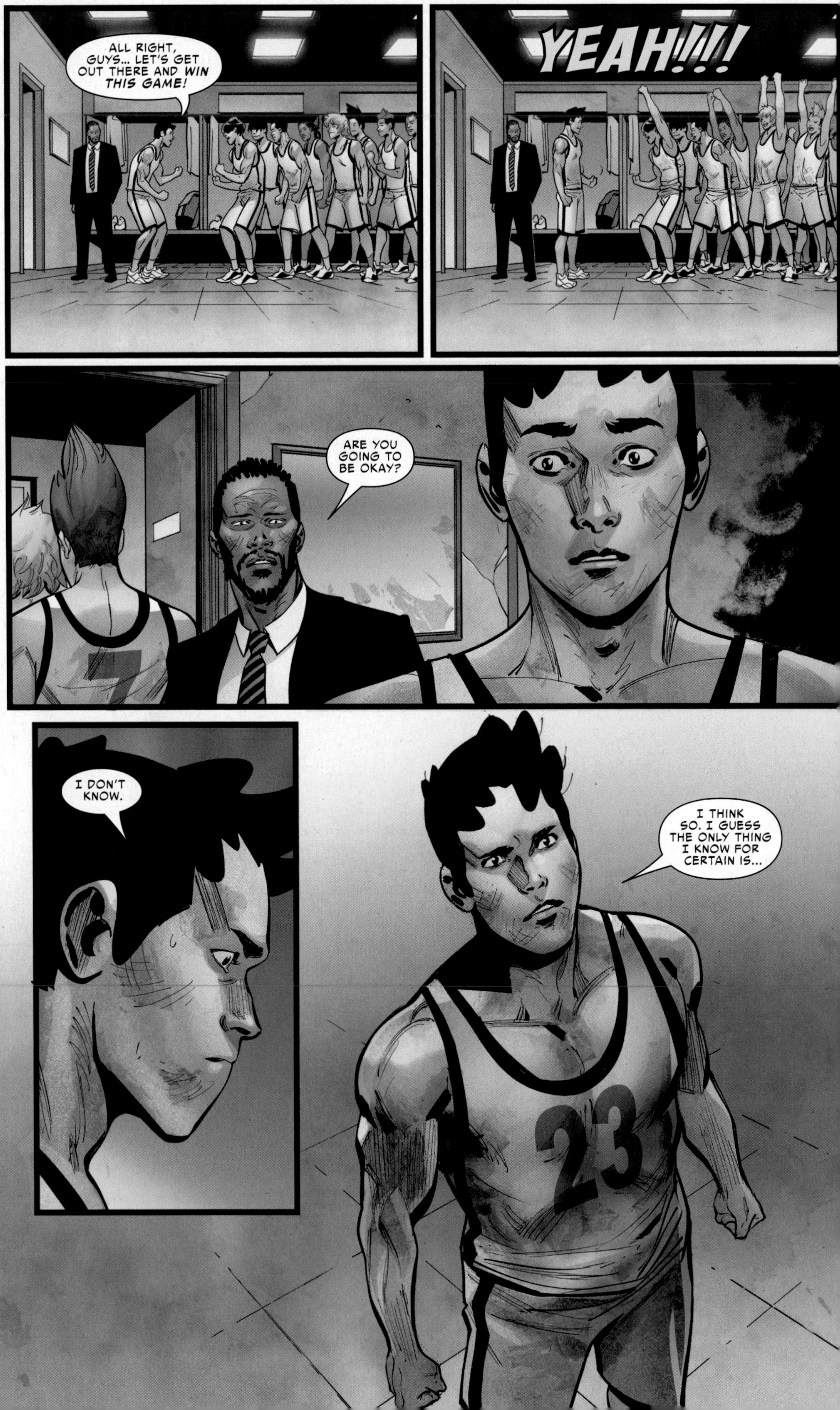

ALL RIGHT, GUYS... LET'S GET OUT THERE AND WIN THIS GAME!
YEAH!!!!
ARE YOU GOING TO BE OKAY?
I DON'T KNOW.
I THINK SO. I GUESS THE ONLY THING I KNOW FOR CERTAIN IS...

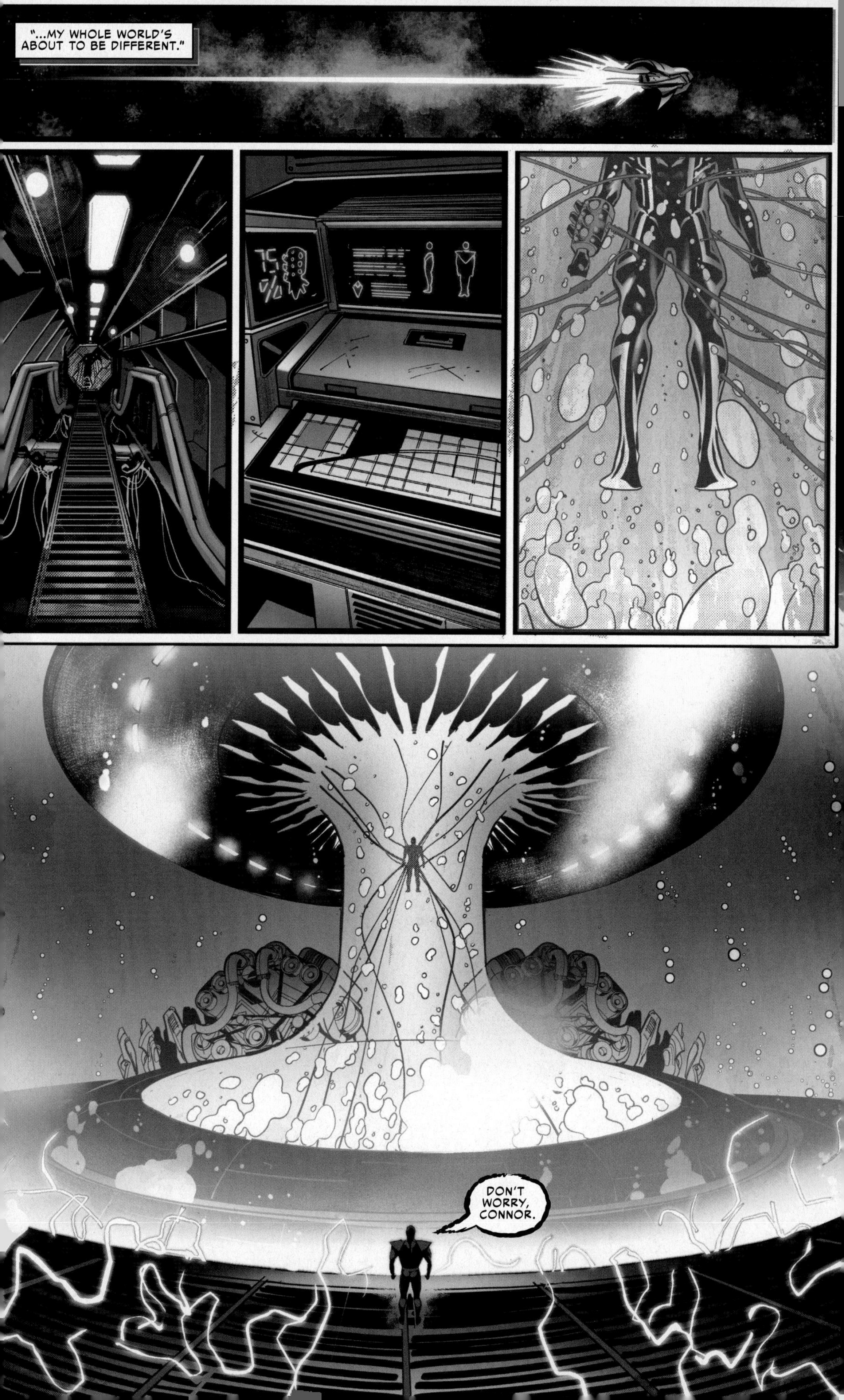
"...MY WHOLE WORLD'S ABOUT TO BE DIFFERENT."
75%
DON'T WORRY, CONNOR.

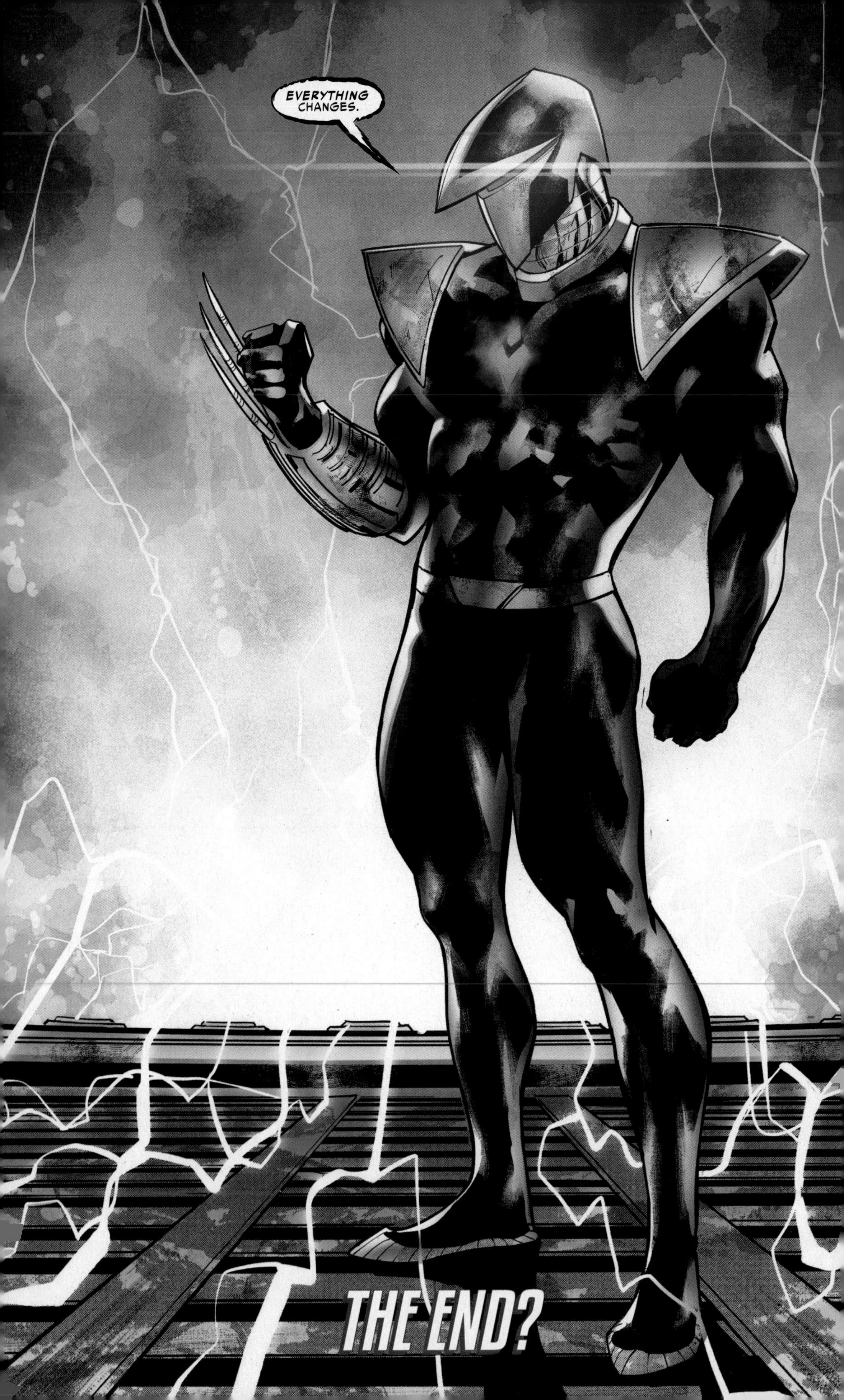
EVERYTHING CHANGES.
THE END?

AIR SPACE

A CONVERSATION WITH **KYLE HIGGINS** AND **BROOKE PELCZYNSKI**

"Stan Lee proudly presents the premiere adventure of the greatest hero of the nineties…" That was the opening line of DARKHAWK Vol. 1 #1 in 1991. A pretty bold statement for an era that also introduced Marvel heroes like Deadpool, Cable, Gambit, Bishop, Spider-Man 2099, Scarlet Spider (hmm…I'm seeing a trend here…) and so many more (New Warriors!). But 30 years later, the name Darkhawk still makes '90s fans perk up. Well, if you read our recent DARKHAWK: HEART OF THE HAWK one-shot, you saw us celebrate the hero's past and present. Now get ready for the future! If you were too young to remember the OG Darkhawk, we hope you get to experience how everyone felt 30 years ago. And if you're a fan from that era, we hope this new iteration will remind you of what made you fall in love with the guy in the first place. (And yes, we know exactly what's happened to Chris Powell. And no, we're not telling you just yet!)*

Every issue, our writer, Kyle Higgins, will interview somebody from the multiple sclerosis community. Our first guest is Brooke Pelczynski! Brooke is an artist, illustrator and comic-creating multiple sclerosis fighter based in Brooklyn, NY. She uses her art to express the challenges of MS and has spoken openly about the struggles that come with it. Brooke has also been our sounding board in the creation of Connor Young, to make sure our portrayal is as authentic as can be. We at Team Darkhawk owe everything to Brooke.

Okay, enough gabbing from me—take it away, Kyle!

What is your relationship with comics and art?

It's actually quite funny as I didn't start reading comics until maybe three or four years ago. My partner really likes comics. And I always liked graphic novels a lot, but I had always been given them as gifts. I never bought them on my own.

But over the course of our relationship, I started to pick them up more, like, "Oh, this is really cool!" And I started to realize that I was drawn more to the art and less to the story—I'll read it and maybe sometimes not even like the story. I'm just like, "Ahh, that art was really cool!"

Throughout my MS history and my art history, in the beginning, I wanted my work to be something akin to my favorite comic book artists—very stylized. I wanted to be that. And then I got my diagnosis, and it was really falling apart right in front of me.

I was like, "I can't hold pencils like this. I cannot do this." So I leaned into watercolors, and I was like, "Oh, this is great." It can be abstract, and everything with watercolors is a happy accident. I just make it work.

And as my illness is progressing and I am progressing as an artist, I've learned to balance the two, where I can mix these worlds together. And it seems to be working, and I'm thrilled by that. My lines are never going to be perfect because of my life. And I think that's okay. And I think it makes it a more interesting piece in my life. But who knows what the viewers say.

When did you first get diagnosed with MS?

I was still in college, just finishing up my junior year. I had to do my senior thesis still, and I remember after my diagnosis, I didn't even know if I wanted to draw anymore.

It's such an inconsistent disease. Some days are really great. Some days are really not great. And I needed to impress my professor, so I was just like, I'm going to scrap all these illustrations and I'm going to move to photo collages.

And although I loved it, I'm not great at it. And my professors were like, this is something you needed to start out of the gate with—you can't just pick this up and become very good at it.

So I went back to watercolor, and it seems to be working for me. And now I have an iPad. It's great.

I'd like to take a step back because I feel like a lot of people have heard the abbreviation MS and even the word multiple sclerosis, but if they were forced to describe it, they wouldn't know how.

They always think, like, you have scoliosis. And I'm like, no, it's not scoliosis—my back is fine. And you have to explain it to them. It's quite difficult to explain to somebody from your point of view and then to have them go Google it, because if you Google it, it's terrifying. It's really overwhelming. And it sounds like you have 30 years to live.

When you meet someone who's never heard of MS, how do you describe it to them?

I always tell people I have a neurological degenerative disease. And I'm usually okay, but I will have days where I'm really not okay and I will stay home. And they're like, "What does that mean?"

And I'm like, well, it kind of means I fumble a lot. I drop a lot of things.

And I'll be out with my friends at the bar or just having a casual dinner and I'll drop a cup. In the beginning, it was really embarrassing for me. And now I'm just like, "Well, sorry. I don't have a sticker that says I'm ill, but this is from an illness. This is not from my being overly intoxicated." Not to say that hasn't happened before. [*Laughs*]

I am sick. I drop things. I'm sorry. And it's funny because in the very beginning, I was out with a group of friends and I dropped a big cup. And it was really embarrassing. And it was so overwhelming because [the diagnosis] was brand new.

Then my best friend just took her cup and dropped it. Like, well, we **both** dropped a cup. Let's go home. And it was great to have that camaraderie. It's necessary, I think. I think in the beginning of having an illness, you need to find your circles that know you feel sick. You have these people who you can complain to—but who also will not let you become a recluse.

There's nothing wrong with people that want to spend their time with their illness, but it's definitely not how I am doing it. I enjoy being around the people I care about and who care about me.

You touched on this a little bit a few minutes ago, but with regard to art—not necessarily in the creation of it, but from an appreciation standpoint—have the last seven or eight years changed your appreciation of art? Or the way you view it?

For sure. I definitely like things that are more…I think "impressionistic" is a great word. Where I'm just like, this is someone's emotions on a piece of paper or on a screen. And I like that because I often find it very difficult to express myself.

As an artist, I go from creative thing to creative thing to creative thing because, depending on my illness, it depends on what I'm capable of doing that week or that day. So I dabble in so many things. And I like artists that are like that. I think it's made me more accepting of being an artist—you don't just have to have one great talent. You can be a jack-of-all-trades, master of none.

So, pivoting slightly, what did you think when I first reached out about our Darkhawk plans?

It's very, very cool to see MS in the mainstream where it's not portrayed as some super-debilitating disease. Because I watch television, and a character will come in with MS

and they'll have a wheelchair. And they'll have a caregiver. And they'll be very ill looking. And that is okay, because I do understand that down the line with MS, people do become very ill looking. And I do understand that with some people that's just the hand they're dealt. But that's not everybody with MS—that's not everybody with a disease. Some of these illnesses are completely invisible.

And it's nice to see a character go through the diagnosis process—which is the worst part—and then see them do something with it, which I like. I think it's very cool, the way it's been portrayed. And I like that he has a dad that's like, right there. Dad cares a lot. I think that's cool to see too. Yeah, it was exciting.

I can't wait to tell my friends and family, like, "Look at this. I helped with this a little bit." It's going to be great. And I think that it's something people need to see—that your friends or family might have a disability, but you shouldn't write them off.

A special thanks again to Brooke for her time and contribution to this book. We couldn't have done this without you! For more of Kyle and Brooke's conversation, check out Marvel.com!

—Darren Shan

AIR SPACE

A CONVERSATION WITH **KYLE HIGGINS** AND **DR. TIM COETZEE**

Welcome back, everyone, for another segment of AIR SPACE! This month, Kyle spoke with Dr. Tim Coetzee. Dr. Coetzee serves as the National MS Society's Chief Advocacy, Services and Science Officer. In this capacity, he leads the Society's work in the areas of state and federal advocacy, delivery of services and connection programs for people with MS, healthcare professional engagement and training, as well as the Society's global research programs. Dr. Coetzee received his PhD in molecular biology from Albany Medical College in 1993 and has since been involved in the field of multiple sclerosis research. He has been with the National MS Society since the fall of 2000.

I was wondering if you could explain what exactly the National MS Society is and then how you got involved.

So the National MS Society is a nonprofit organization founded by Sylvia Lawry, whose brother was diagnosed with MS in 1945. She was told there was nothing that could be done for her brother, and she said, "Well, we've cured polio--let's figure out how we can cure MS." And to this day we exist to fund the research to try to find a cure. At the same time, for the nearly one million people who live with MS in the United States, the Society helps them discover how they can live powerfully of whatever their journey is. Everybody has a unique journey, and we want to be there to walk alongside them, whether they're a teenager or somebody in their 70s with MS.

I got connected to the society in 1995. I did my PhD in Albany. I was studying mRNA before anybody knew or cared about what that was. I was interested in mRNA and how it gets transported around in the brain and nerve cells. After I got my PhD, I worked in a lab that was focused on MS and the research which was funded by the MS Society. At the time I was an all-out science nerd. Multiple sclerosis was this disease that you heard about, but I wasn't really oriented around it. But it was because of the funding of the MS Society and being around people who actually lived with the disease that

I then got connected. I did MS research for a few years and then joined the MS Society to lead my research programs and do a variety of other things within the organization.

What is happening in the brain with regard to MS that's unique to this specific neurodegenerative condition?

So if you imagine, as I'm talking to you, I talk with my hands and all of that. The ability of my brain to tell my hands to move is all influenced by the signal that comes out of my brain, telling my hand to move forward. The nerves in my hand go back and forth. And what's happening in MS is that these nerves, which are a network, that are connected and really guide everything about our lives are basically being broken apart in various parts like you get your wires crossed.

And what's happening in a person living with MS is that their immune system basically has decided that it's going to attack this network of nerves in your brain and your spinal cord and very specifically attack the insulation that wraps around all of these nerve cells. And it really is like the electrical insulation in your house, your network, whatever devices. And when that insulation gets destroyed, you start getting short circuits.

But in effect, what's happening is that those immune cells are leaving your bloodstream, where they're normally supposed to be fighting viruses, and instead going into your brain, basically chewing away at that insulation. Your nerve cells basically short circuit. So let's say the MS affects the nerves that connect your eye…you start having trouble seeing or you could wake up one morning and your leg's not working right. You could have pain and different symptoms because of MS.

And what we're focused on with our research and the kind of treatments we have is what's the trigger. Why would your body decide to start chewing away at the insulation around your nerve cells? What are the immune cells that are involved? What tells them to go to the brain and start chewing away at them? And

...en also what are the differences between men and women? Between different groups of people? Why is it that sometimes we don't have MS in some parts of the world? And then specifically what treatments can you come up with that can really turn that down?

The good news is that back in 1994, we had one disease-modifying treatment approved. Today, we've got more than 20. So there's a lot of progress in the disease, but still a lot more places to go. As a biologist, I'd say there're so many more questions to answer about what develops into MS.

Is there something about a person's genetics that contributes to it? Are there factors of diet, lifestyle, exercise? All of those things that, as a biologist, I want to try to get my hands on. And then the other part is--our immune system is amazing. It has this incredible ability to fight off so many things, and I want to understand, why do some of those cells decide that the brain is the enemy. And that uncertainty is what we're trying to get at.

Have you had any experience with or seen firsthand over the years, an athlete diagnosed with MS?

I haven't seen it firsthand myself, but I'll tell you that there are people who are quite athletic, and the main thing that people will pay attention to when they're an athlete and living with MS is the challenge of getting overheated. Heat in particular comes from a lot of exhaustion or even just living with MS in a hot climate. One of the challenges about the way our nervous systems work is that when our body core gets hot, our nervous system starts acting really crazy because the nerve cells actually work faster when they're hotter. If you've got the kind of disruption in your nerves that MS has, it just makes things even worse. So staying cool is really, really critical. As an athlete, there's nothing that would stop that person. Just make sure you stay hydrated and cool and make adjustments for any mobility issues that might appear.

There's a young man that the Society knows who was a high school football player. And he continued to play football living with MS as a 17-year-old and grappling with the fatigue. As a parent, I would be worrying about him or her. But at the same time it's that embracing of life that really matters, and that's so important.

Is there anything that you might speak to as far as where we're at and where we're going for someone whose life may have just recently been changed by MS?

I would say to someone like Connor Young, who was just diagnosed with MS: Focus on living well. Focus on continuing to live life and not letting MS become this weight around you and really say "I can live powerfully...

I can take action. I have the ability to shape the journey that I'm on."

The other thing I would say is start shaping your journey as early as you can. There's a lot of stuff to process and think about when you live with MS. But you're going to live a full life and you're going to walk a journey. You don't need to walk MS alone. You've got health systems--you've got people. We're going to get more and better treatments. We're figuring out how we're going to get those treatments to repair the brain from ever being damaged.

We know the things that people should be doing in terms of diet and exercise to live well. I believe that we are on the cusp of being able to figure out what it is that causes MS and start tackling it so we can prevent it from ever happening and prevent someone from hearing those words at some point in the future.

Thank you so much to Dr. Coetzee for his time and contribution to this book! I highly encourage everyone to check out Kyle and Dr. Coetzee's full interview on Marvel.com. Their conversation was fascinating and educational! Who said comics can't teach ya a thing or two!

—*Darren Sha...*

AIR SPACE

A CONVERSATION WITH **KYLE HIGGINS** AND **DEVIN GARLIT**

What up, Hawklings! How do you guys like my new name for Darkhawk fans? ...I'll keep working on it. For this month's AIR SPACE, Kyle interviewed writer, Devin Garlit. Devin has been around multiple sclerosis his entire life--growing up with a grandfather who had the disease and then being diagnosed himself just after starting college. Devin now uses his experience to write about the disease and to advocate for others that have it. MultipleSclerosis.net has called him one of their "superstar advocates." Take it away, Kyle!

How would you describe your relationship with multiplesclerosis.net, the focus of your writing and the disease?

I've been writing for and working with multiplesclerosis. net a little over five years. It's funny. I never set out to be an advocate or whatever. I just had the disease for a while and saw that you could submit some stories to them. So I did that a few times. And after a while, they asked me to be a full-time contributor.

I enjoy doing the writing thing. I enjoy talking to people about the disease. I've always been someone who doesn't really have a problem saying what's on his mind. So that's finally been a positive for me with this kind of activity.

As far as the disease goes, I grew up with a grandfather who had MS. He moved in with my family and we took care of him. He actually became completely disabled.

They didn't really have any kind of medication back in the day, so we took care of him. He ended up on a ventilator and eventually passed due to complications with the disease.

You know it's funny--I had a chance to read the first issue and there were a lot of similarities that I saw that really hit home. I was young, I had barely started college, ice hockey was my sport--I was really, really into it. I was maybe not the star, but I was definitely playing in college and it was a big deal.

And then I suddenly started falling a lot. I ended up in a doctor's office with my father just like in that first issue. I had some MRIs, got the diagnosis, and the world changed. So yeah, that issue hit home because it really echoed a lot of my exact experience.

How did it change your relationship with hockey?

I wasn't as good. I developed a lot of balance problems. A lot of weakness in my legs. I eventually

was able to continue playing a few years later, just on some club teams and men's teams, but I was never the player that I once was.

I just started coaching more, which was pretty neat. So I still stayed involved with the game as long as I could, even though I wasn't the player that I was.

I want to talk about writing for a second, because as a writer, I feel quite qualified to say that most of us have an incredibly challenging, complicated, oftentimes frustrating relationship with writing, even on our best days. What is your relationship with writing like? And as it pertains to the topics that you're specifically covering, is it an outlet for you? Or do you have the same challenges that we all have?

Well, I definitely do have some challenges now and again. I have some cognitive issues because of MS that sometimes I just can't operate. It's funny--I never sought out to be a writer. My degree is in physics. I was a software engineer.

I haven't done a tremendous amount of writing since I was in college. It's something that I don't want to say comes easy to me, but when I'm in the right frame of mind and my body is feeling well, I basically just try to talk to people like they're talking directly to me. My writing is very much, in my mind, a conversation, or at least, a conversation starter. I like to tell my story and talk about my problems. And I feel like it's a little--I don't want to say it's easy for me to open up, but I feel like it's helpful to people.

So that makes it a bit easier. And I know that there was a long time, early in my diagnosis, where I read a lot about MS and a lot of stories from people that had MS. And they were usually very positive stories about people who would say, "oh, I have MS, but I just finished my first 5K." There's a lot of positive stories out there.

So from the get-go, I said, "You know, it'd be helpful if I read something more realistic." Something that I'm actually going through. And I found out through the years that by writing about that and writing about even the most embarrassing things, it's actually been able to help people.

Writing has definitely been an outlet and a way to put myself out there. But it's also been my way to be able to help people. I may not be able to have the career that I once had, but I can do this and actually make more of a difference. And that makes my life feel a lot more worthwhile.

Considering your history having grown up around MS, I'm curious how that affected you during your diagnosis. Was having prior knowledge beneficial? Did it make things scarier or less scary?

Well, as I said, my grandfather, at the time I was diagnosed, was completely nonverbal. Completely bedridden. Pretty much one of the worst situations you could have with MS. So when I was diagnosed, it was really, really scary.

But at the same time, my family who were also around my grandfather and helped take care of him, they were really devastated. And because of that and my being so young, I was able to spend more time trying to convince them that I would be okay. As I had seen the very worst of what the disease could do.

I was still a young punk athlete who just thought that I would get through this too. I get through everything, you know? But it's not going to happen to me. Even though I've seen what it can do, that won't be me. I'll be fine.

I spent a lot of time trying to comfort my friends, comfort my parents—especially my mother. When I told them the diagnosis, I think it was the first time I had seen my father cry, which was crazy. So seeing my family so devastated, I almost didn't really have a chance to be devastated myself if that makes any sense.

I tried to console them. I tried to put on a brave face. I broke down by myself now and again, but for the most part, early on I was pretty strong. I think it would have been better if I had not seen my grandfather. It would have been less scary had I not been witness to it all.

Are there any common misconceptions that drive you crazy when it comes to multiple sclerosis?

Yeah, I think probably one of the biggest things is that everybody may know somebody who has MS. So when they do, they tend to think we're all the same. And I think that that's a misconception. MS is such a variable disease. It can really affect everybody so differently that you can't lump us all in one group.

In addition to that, they may say they've seen their aunt, uncle, grandfather, or whoever with MS, and they say, oh, they look pretty good. They look fine. But you don't really know that because so much of it is invisible. There's so much you can't see.

People with MS are trying to put on a brave face and not show our disease. So we're always acting a little bit. To assume that people are okay is a problem.

What have you seen in the last 23 years since you were diagnosed as far as developments we've made in science and medicine as it relates to where we are now?

Yeah, well, again, even before my experience, my wife and my grandfather. I've seen so much reason for hope. Even right now, there are medications that just weren't available when I was diagnosed. If I had had the medications that I'm on now when I was diagnosed, I would still be working. My life would be complete. I have no doubt about that.

One of the biggest things I've noticed is that science is making some headway and they're coming up with new treatments all the time.

I used to do the MS walk every year when I was younger, and MS read-a-thon, and all these charities and stuff. And I think it's easy to become cynical about those types of things. But when you're someone like me with my disease, you can see how that kind of fundraising has helped. It has made a difference. They have made breakthroughs in MS. They're not cures but they're pretty major breakthroughs.

Through charity and science together, we've started to make some real headway with the disease. Also, a lot more people are aware of the disease. And that's just something I hope continues over the years.

I think the more people who can learn about the disease, even just the very basics, that helps everything. That's the kind of thing that gets people to say, "Okay well, then I'll donate $5 to this MS fund." And then that trickles down. The more people do that, the more breakthroughs we end up making.

From the bottom of our hearts at Team Darkhawk, thank you for being so open in sharing your journey with us, Devin! Check out Kyle and Devin's full interview on Marvel.com! And come back here next month to see Connor's heart-to-heart with Spider-Man, Miles Morales! Oh, and some punching with Captain America too.

—Darren Shan

AIR SPACE

A CONVERSATION WITH **DR. LAUREN KRUPP**

Welcome back, Hawklings! Yup, I'm sticking with that name till someone suggests something better! This month, Kyle interviewed neurologist, Dr. Lauren Krupp, MD. Dr. Krupp leads the Pediatric Multiple Sclerosis Center, part of Hassenfeld Children's Hospital at NYU Langone, as well as their Multiple Sclerosis Comprehensive Care Center. She's a pediatric neuropsychiatrist who opened the first dedicated center for children with MS in the United States. She was also a huge help in consulting on issue 3! But mostly, I'm just excited to have another New Yorker grace these pages (yeah, yeaaaah!).

How would you describe your specialty and how it relates to multiple sclerosis?

I'm a neurologist and I deal with the nervous system. I am involved in the care of people with multiple sclerosis, which affects the brain and the spinal cord, or also known as the central nervous system. Multiple sclerosis is one of these conditions that usually affects people from young adults to middle-aged adults typically between ages 20 and 50. It can be a somewhat unpredictable disorder where things like losing your vision can happen, but then it can get better, or you can suddenly have problems with numbness and tingling that lasts for a while and then typically gets better, or you can have problems with walking or your balance. One of the things that caught my attention, some years ago, was the fact that there were some young people, teenagers, and even younger kids who would come down with some symptoms, and everybody would get confused because there was this notion that multiple sclerosis did not happen to kids. But it turns out it can. It's just rare.

Fortunately, probably only 5% of all people with MS are under 18 years of age. But still, when it happens, it's a big deal to the families and to the persons involved. And sometimes the process of getting to the diagnosis is challenging because unless you're in a place where there's a lot of familiarity both with multiple sclerosis and with the fact that it can occur in the pediatric age range, families can go through more than one provider looking for answers to their questions. I've also seen situations where kids are sent out of the emergency room and told, you're stressed or you're anxious, when in fact there's a neurologic process that's going on that explains the symptoms they're experiencing.

Today, we can make the diagnosis with MRIs, a careful history and a careful examination. And as a neurologist, we examine people's vision, their strength, their balance, their coordination, and we can prescribe medications that are very effective in preventing the episodes of neurologic dysfunction which we call clinical events, attacks or relapses that are associated with the type of MS that occurs in the pediatric age-group.

My family and I are neurodivergent. And growing up, I've had quite a bit of firsthand experience with diagnosis and the process of diagnosing during adolescent ages or an adolescent age range. And one of the things that has always struck me is how complicated the diagnosis process is for an adult but how extra complicated it is for children of any sort of nontraditional condition.

When you're talking about the diagnosis process in 2021 compared with perhaps even in the 90s, what are people looking for now, and what are parents hopefully attuned to as far as behavior or things that you typically see that lead them on the diagnosis journey? And how has it gotten better looking for this very rare, but very real percentage of those affected in a younger age range?

All right, so the big challenge is that during adolescence years 12-17, which is the typical age range, most young people who have pediatric MS, experience symptoms about 85% to 90% of the time. But adolescents are really experiencing other sorts of things too. They're going through growth spurts, they're struggling to fit in with their peers in school, sports, or other groups. And the notion of being different is extremely stressful. So they're usually not very pleased to have to go to the doctor. And so sometimes, it's very hard to get a history. And sometimes, there's a lot of discomfort about the whole notion of having to sit in a doctor's office, get examined and undergo testing. And that can make it very difficult, not only for the patient, but the family.

And that was true in the '90s and it's still true today. However, one of the things that's changed for the better is that in some cases, parents are much better equipped to be engaged as equal partners in the health care process, and they have higher expectations today to play that kind of role. The other thing that's improved is that our fund for knowledge in medicine and neurology is really growing at an astronomical rate, so whereas in the '90s there was no center and there was no group of people who were talking about pediatric MS at all.

Now, there are centers all over the United States and all over the world, and there are websites. The National MS Society has a lot of information about pediatric MS, we at NYU have a pediatric MS center and there's a network of centers that work together. There's also a tremendous amount of collaboration that's been facilitated by the use of videoconferencing and the internet that has led to the expansion of knowledge that we have. So we now know that there are highly effective treatments that work for pediatric MS patients, and there are also mechanisms for people to share their story, which there were less so before.

And MRI has made a huge difference in terms of just facilitating the diagnosis. It also sometimes leads to misdiagnosis because there are situations where kids have migraines, headaches, and other conditions that can cause some spots on the MRI, and suddenly, a family member gets panicked that their kid has a condition that they don't have. It's due to something else. So I would say the big changes are growth of knowledge, the empowerment of families and patients, the integration of physicians and other health care providers, and workers across the world really trying to make things better and move their knowledge further.

Does pediatric MS manifest any differently than adult-onset multiple sclerosis?

So, as you are talking about different age groups, there are some ways in which MS manifests somewhat differently between them. So teenagers and children have a more inflammatory type of MS, which on the one hand is good because it's much more easily treatable.

Whereas older adults have, as a generalization, a more aggressive type of MS that is more challenging to treat. So if untreated, kids can have a lot of what we call relapses, or MS flare-ups and miss school, have physical ailments and require treatment acutely with steroids which can cause all sorts of issues, but will in general lower the symptoms. Increased inflammation is one difference. Another difference is that kids are in this learning environment—school. And it's a time when social skills, cognitive skills, emotional skills, are developing. And to have a chronic illness of any sort occur during that developmental period is very disruptive.

So I would say that that destruction and the effects of that on the family and on the patient are somewhat unique. And there's a lot of discussion about the effects of MS on cognition because, of course, cognition is such an important element to do well in our society. While early on when we were first describing the effects of MS in children, we were seeing a lot of cognitive problems and we still sometimes do. But I think that as our recognition and treatment of MS has gotten better, the cognitive aspects are, I think, better also.

On the other hand, there's a lot of nonspecific but significant psychosocial stressors that are associated with a chronic illness during adolescence. MS in particular is where it's unpredictable and hard to quite understand, and you don't know anybody else your age with this sort of problem. And a lot of kids have challenges dealing with it and deciding whether or not to share the diagnosis with a friend or not. I've seen situations where parents are incredibly upset about the whole thing and don't want their kids to let anybody else know, and that just makes everything worse.

So often, the family needs help and are not always willing to think in those terms. So as a clinician, I think it's very important to be sensitive to all the medical and non-medical factors that are going on. And it helps to have a team with you, so a social worker, nurse or psychologist could help with the dynamics that are facing the family literally.

Thank you so much to Dr. Krupp for her time and providing her valuable insight! As always, check out the full interview on Marvel.com! Next month, the finale!

–Darren Shan

LOGAN LUBERA &
RACHELLE ROSENBERG
HEART OF THE HAWK VARIANT

RUSSELL DAUTERMAN
& MATTHEW WILSON
HEART OF THE HAWK VARIANT

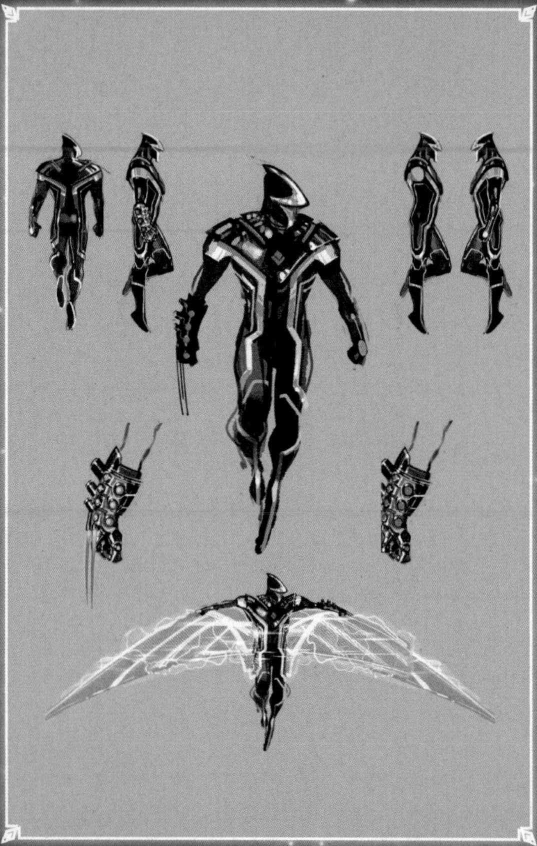

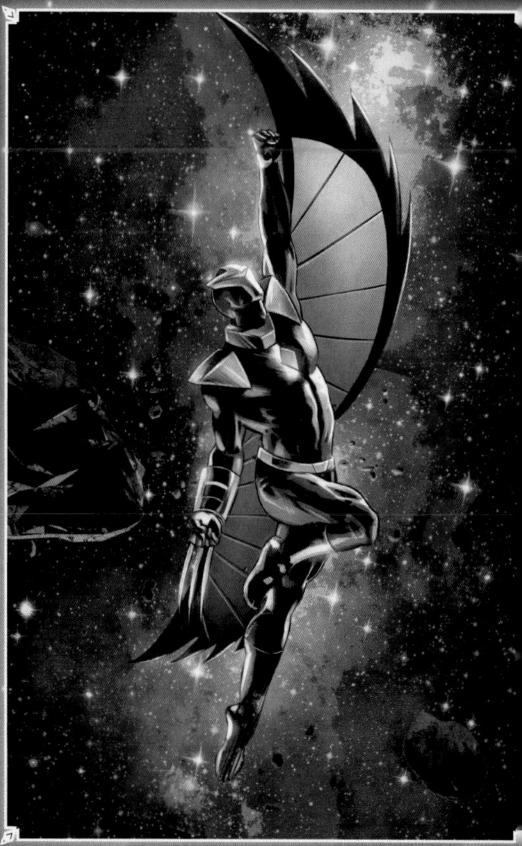

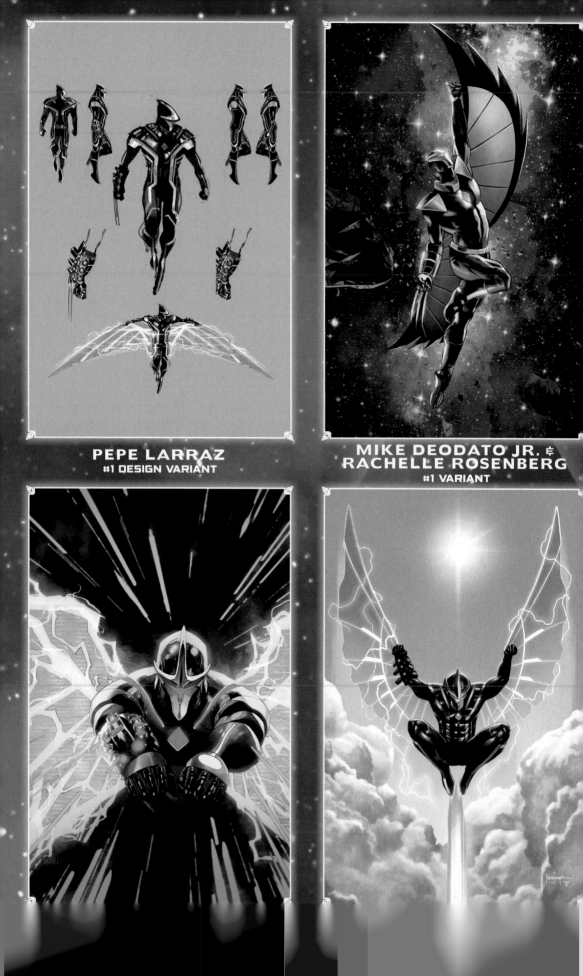

PEPE LARRAZ
#1 DESIGN VARIANT

MIKE DEODATO JR. &
RACHELLE ROSENBERG
#1 VARIANT

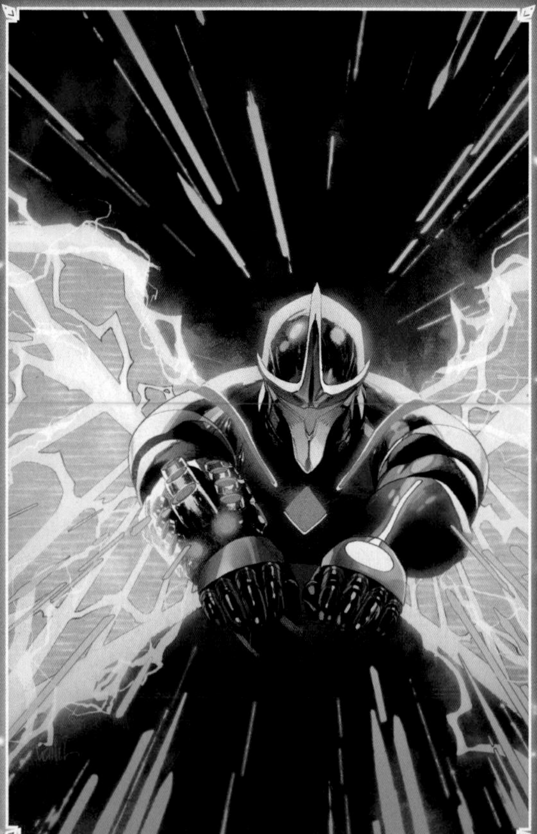

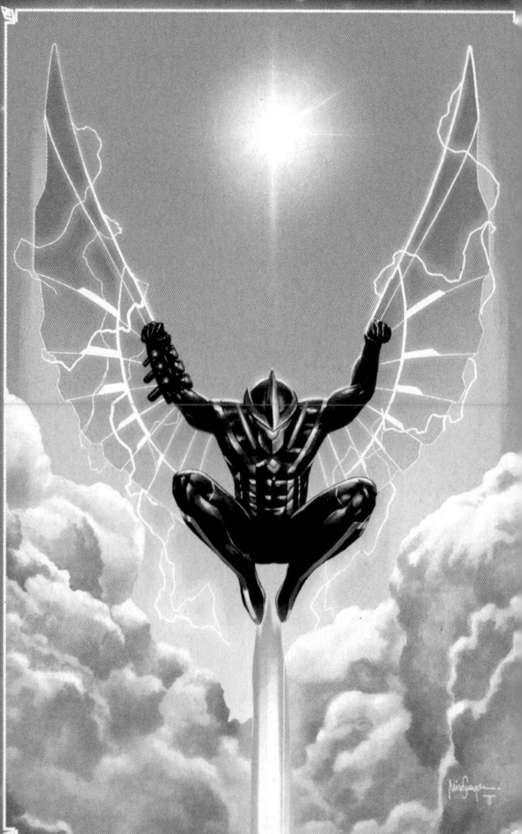

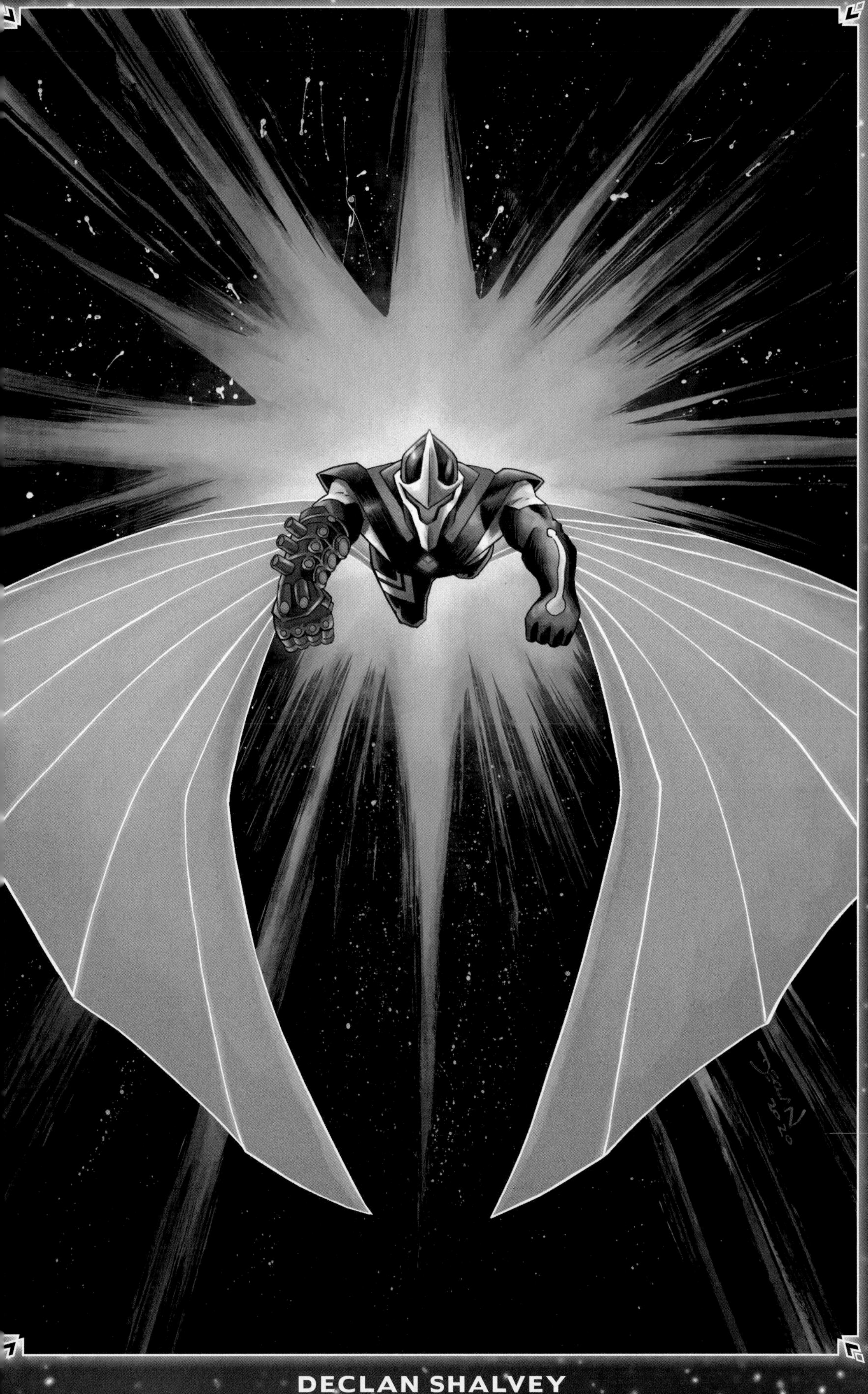

DECLAN SHALVEY
#Z VARIANT

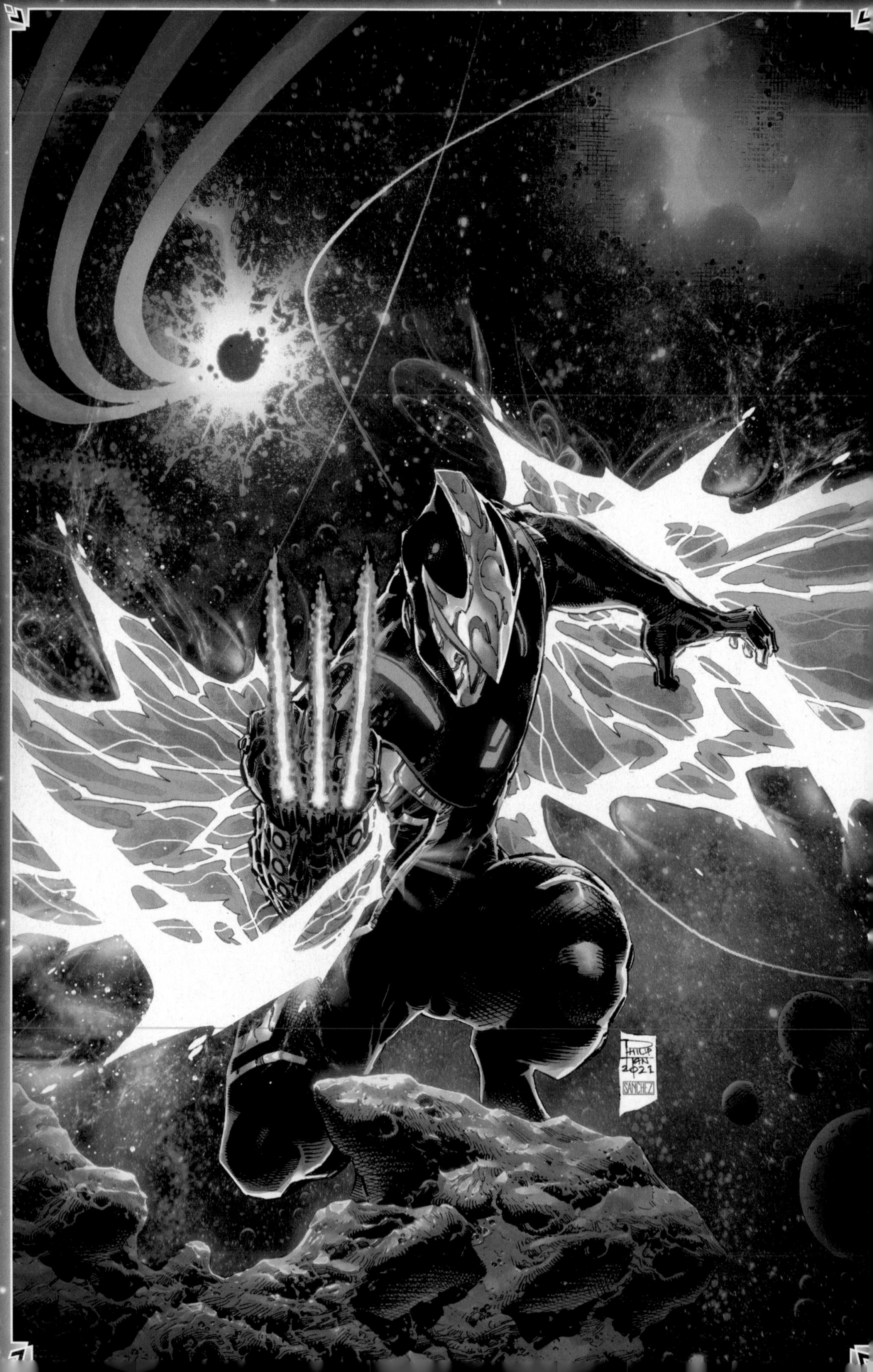
PHILIP TAN 2021
SANCHEZ

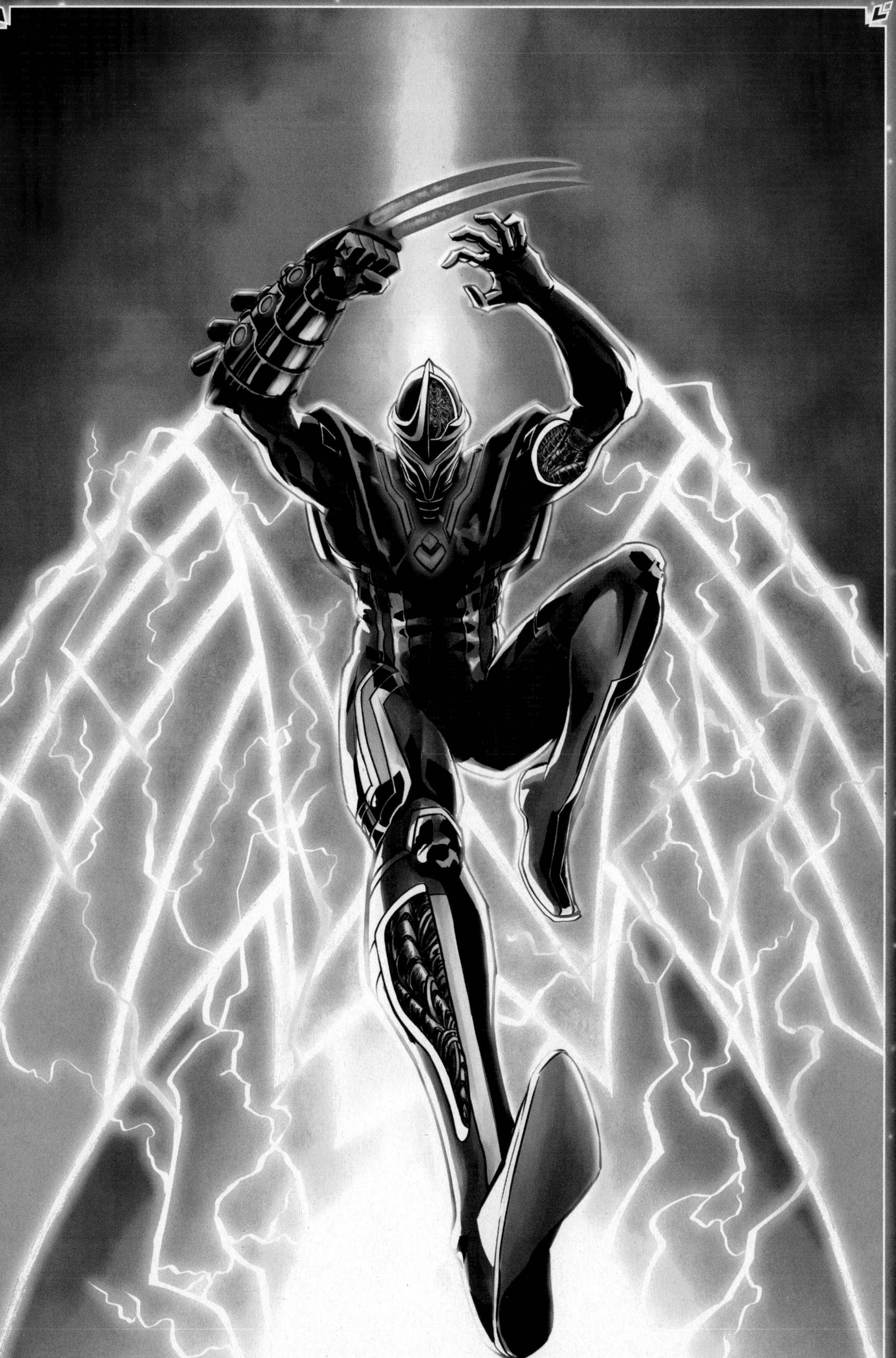

PHILIP TAN & ALEJANDRO SÁNCHEZ
#4 VARIANT

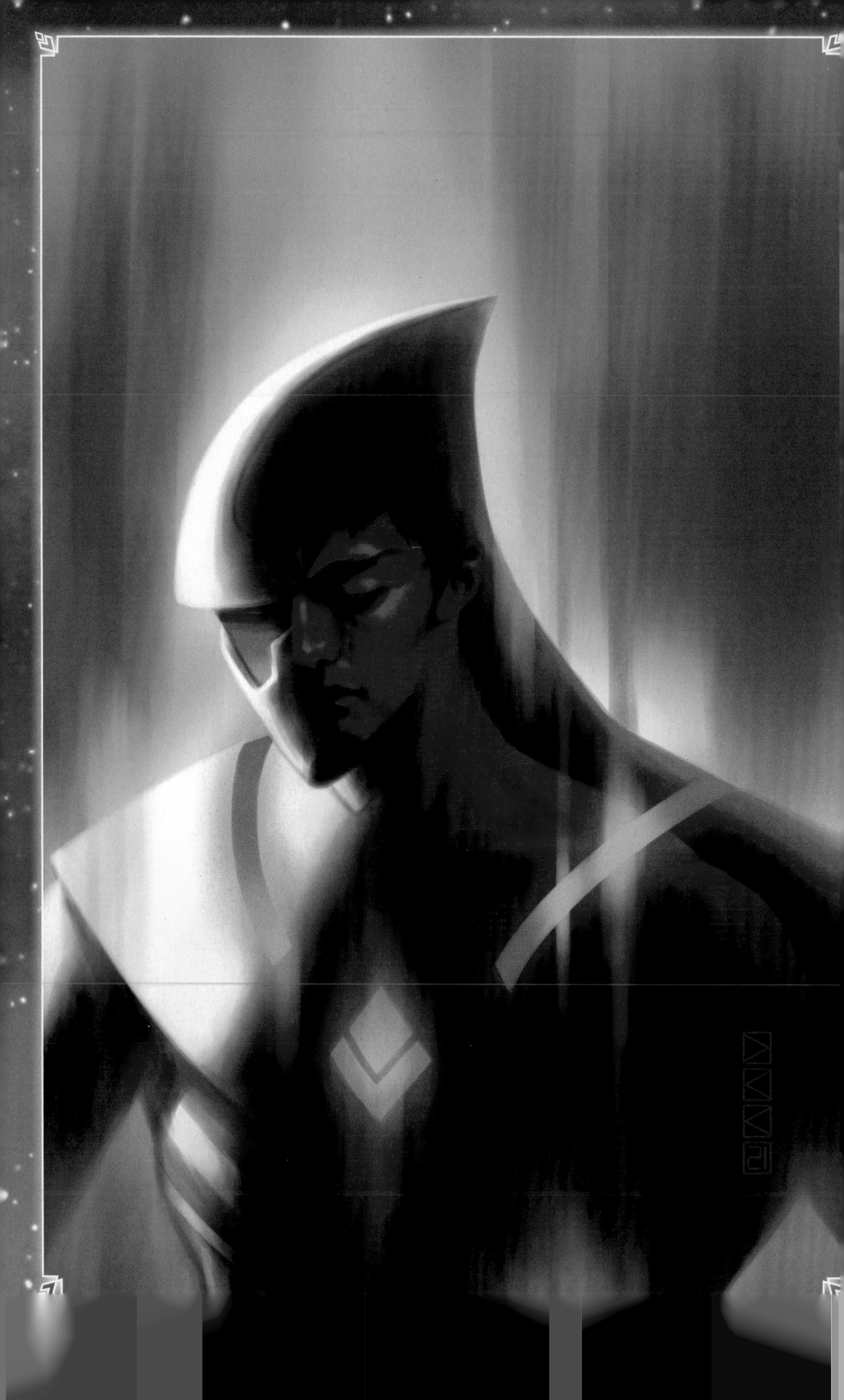

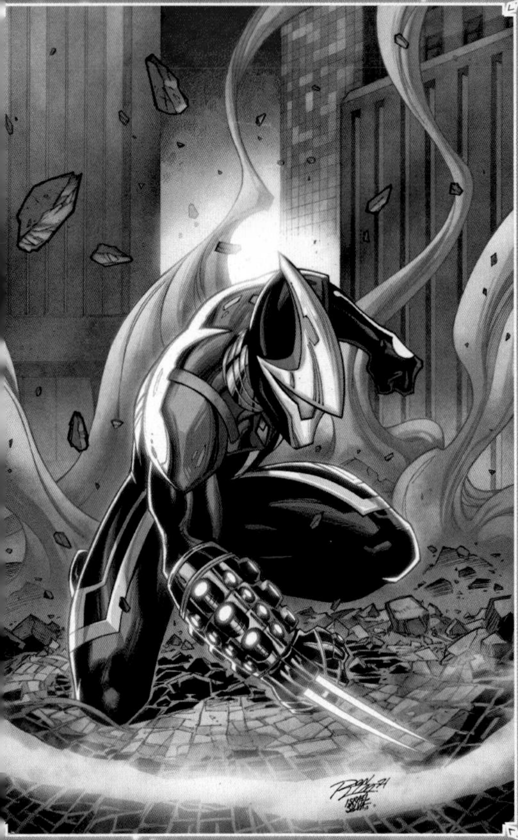

RON LIM & ISRAEL SILVA
#1 VARIANT

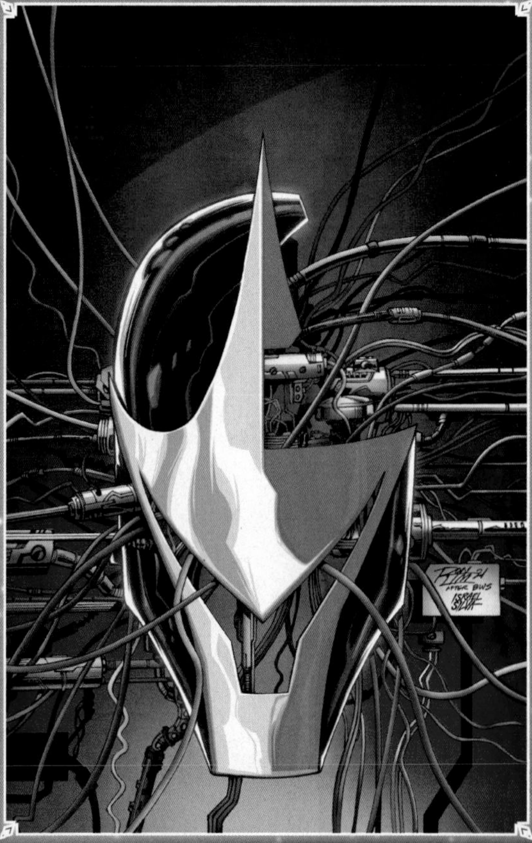

RON LIM & ISRAEL SILVA
#2 VARIANT

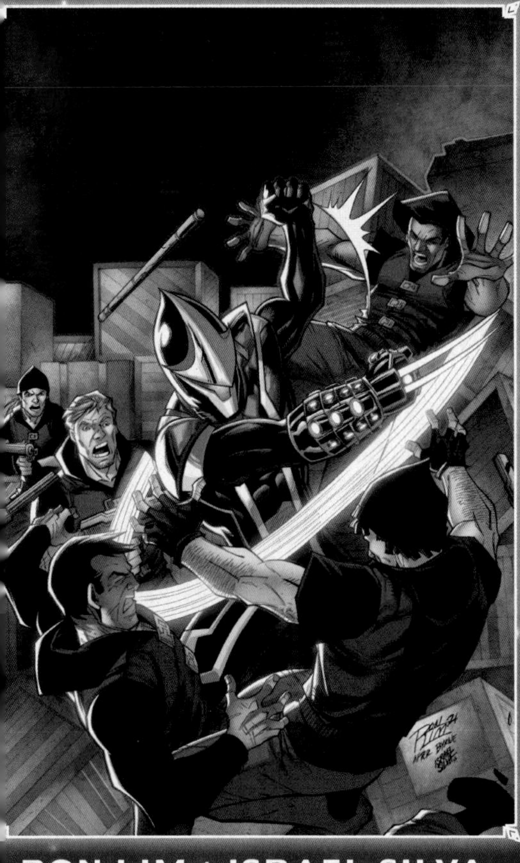

RON LIM & ISRAEL SILVA
#3 VARIANT

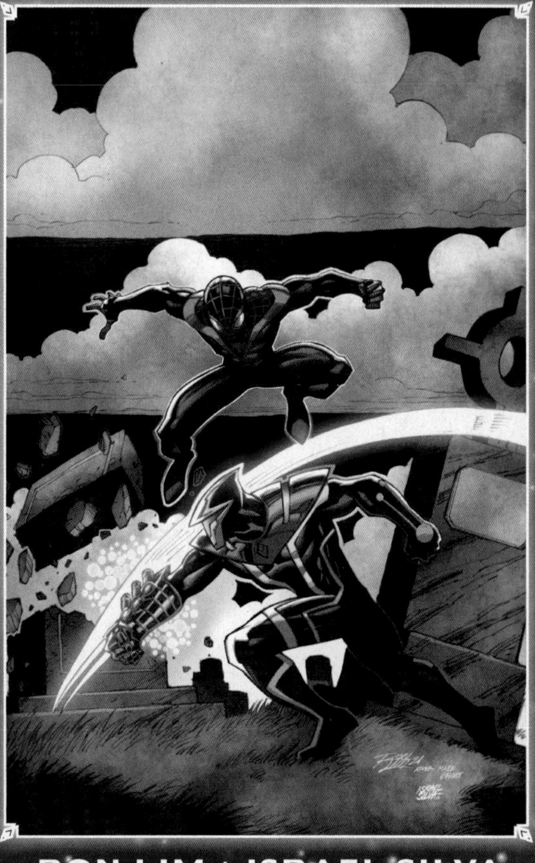

RON LIM & ISRAEL SILVA
#4 VARIANT

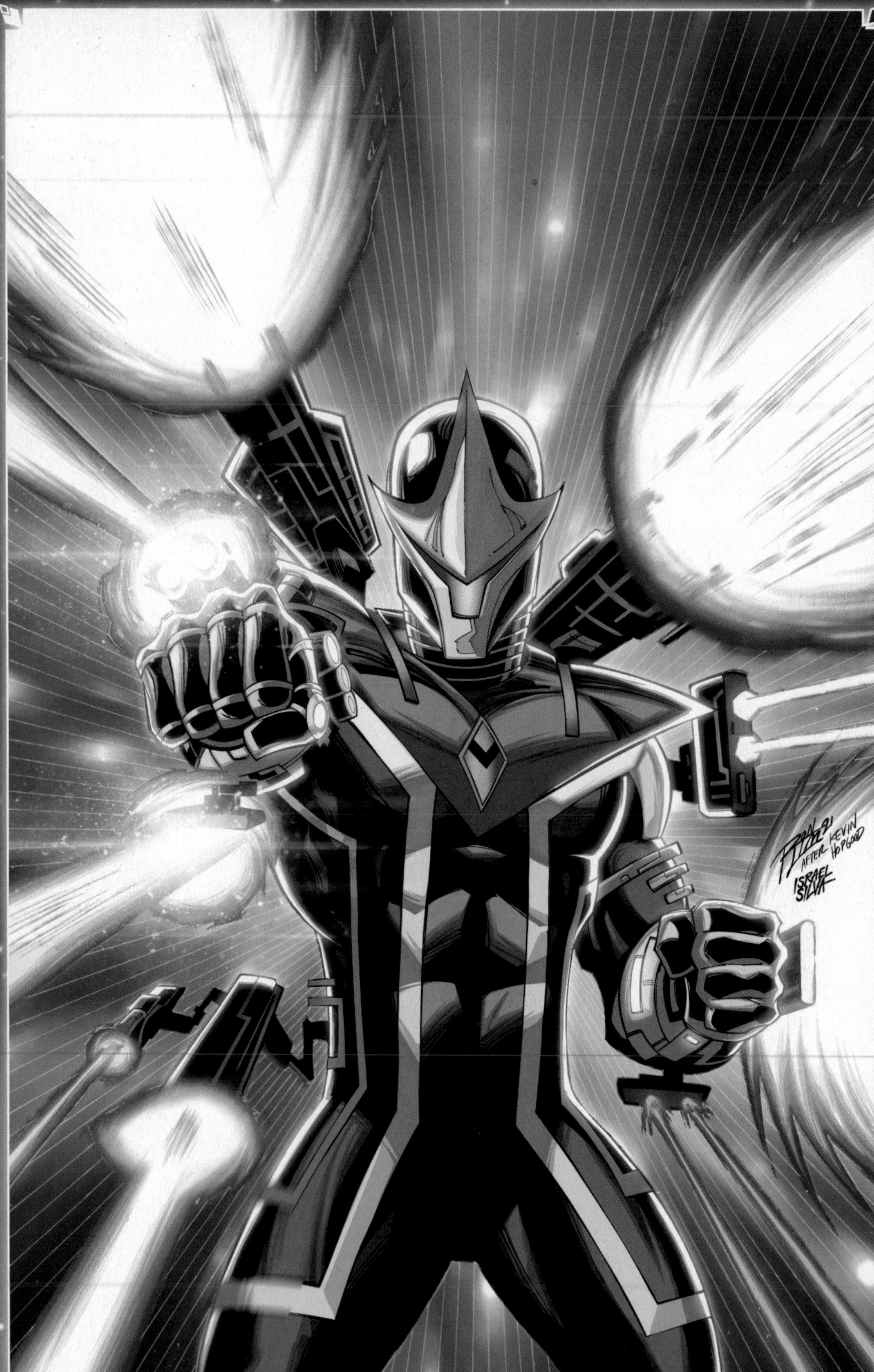
AFTER KEVIN HOPGOOD
ISRAEL SILVA